THE NATURE OF CHINESE POLITICS

Contemporary China Books

Australian National University

Series Editor: Jonathan Unger
Australian National University

Titles in this series published by M. E. Sharpe are:

NO. 20: THE PRO-DEMOCRACY PROTESTS IN CHINA
Reports from the Provinces
Edited by Jonathan Unger

NO. 21: USING THE PAST TO SERVE THE PRESENT
Historiography and Politics in Contemporary China
Edited by Jonathan Unger

NO. 22: DIRECTORY OF OFFICIALS AND
ORGANIZATIONS IN CHINA
A Quarter-Century Guide
Malcolm Lamb

NO. 23: CHINESE NATIONALISM
Edited by Jonathan Unger

NO. 24: CHINA'S ROAD TO DISASTER
Mao, Central Politicians, and Provincial Leaders in the Unfolding of
the Great Leap Forward, 1955–1959
Frederick C. Teiwes
with Warren Sun

NO. 25: DIRECTORY OF OFFICIALS AND
ORGANIZATIONS IN CHINA
Third Edition
Malcolm Lamb

THE NATURE OF CHINESE POLITICS

From Mao to Jiang

Jonathan Unger
Editor

LOWELL DITTMER	SUSAN L. SHIRK
JOSEPH FEWSMITH	FREDERICK C. TEIWES
ANDREW J. NATHAN	KELLEE S. TSAI
MICHEL OKSENBERG	TANG TSOU
LUCIAN W. PYE	YOU JI

AN EAST GATE BOOK

M.E.Sharpe
Armonk, New York
London, England

An East Gate Book

Copyright © 2002 by M. E. Sharpe, Inc.

Library of Congress Cataloging-in-Publication Data

The nature of Chinese politics : from Mao to Jiang / [edited by] Jonathan Unger.
    p. cm. — (Contemporary China books)
  "An east gate book."
  Includes bibliographical references and index.
  ISBN 0-07656-0847-2 (alk. paper); ISBN 0-7656-0848-0 (pbk. : alk. paper)
    1. China—Politics and government—1976– I. Unger, Jonathan. II. Series.

  JQ1510.N376 2002
  320.951′09′045—dc21   2002066510

Printed in the United States of America

The paper used in this publication meets the minimum requirements of
American National Standard for Information Sciences
Permanence of Paper for Printed Library Materials,
ANSI Z 39.48-1984.

BM (c)   10   9   8   7   6   5   4   3   2   1
BM (p)   10   9   8   7   6   5   4   3   2   1

This book is warmly dedicated to

Tang Tsou (1918-1999)

and

Michel Oksenberg (1938-2001)

CONTENTS

PART I: The Nature of Politics Under Mao and Deng

PART II: The Nature of Politics Under Jiang

Acknowledgements

In 1995, close to the end of the period in which Deng Xiaoping exerted a dominant influence in Chinese political life, *The China Journal* solicited a set of major papers by leading scholars, analysing the changing nature of Chinese politics under Mao and Deng. Five and a half years later, in 2001, as the tenure of Deng's successor, Jiang Zemin, drew to a close, *The China Journal* published a further set of papers by leading analysts, focusing on both the continuities and the significant shifts that had occurred during the period of Jiang's rule. This book draws upon selected papers from those two journal issues. To help create a well-rounded, cohesive, up-to-date volume, the authors have revised and, in some cases, substantially expanded and reshaped their contributions. A debt of gratitude is due to them for the thought and care they have put into this work.

The book contains the last major writings of two of the most eminent scholars in modern China studies—Professors Tang Tsou and Michel Oksenberg—who passed away before the book's publication. Thanks are owed to Joseph Fewsmith for helping to prepare Tang Tsou's chapter for publication and to Kenneth Lieberthal and Andrew Mertha for providing the footnote citations for Michel Oksenberg's chapter.

Anita Chan helped in the content editing. The book was copy-edited by Sarah Leeming and Gary Anson, and the index was prepared by Sarah Leeming. Heli Brecht almost single-handedly took charge of the book's production. Their contributions are gratefully acknowledged.

CONTRIBUTORS

THE NATURE OF CHINESE POLITICS

Lowell Dittmer is Professor of Political Science at the University of California at Berkeley and Editor of *Asian Survey*. His most recent books include *Informal Politics in East Asia* (with Haru Fukui and Peter Lee, 2000), *Liu Shaoqi and the Chinese Cultural Revolution* (2nd ed. 1997) and *China's Quest for National Identity* (with Samuel S. Kim, 1993).

Joseph Fewsmith is Professor of International Relations at Boston University. He is the author, most recently, of *Elite Politics in Contemporary China* (2001) and *China Since Tiananmen: The Politics of Transition* (2001).

Andrew J. Nathan is Class of 1919 Professor of Political Science at Columbia University. His recent books include *The Great Wall and the Empty Fortress* (co-authored with Robert S. Ross, 1997), *China's Transition* (1997) and *The Tiananmen Papers* (co-edited with Perry Link, 2001).

Michel Oksenberg passed away in 2001. He served as a Senior Fellow at the Institute for International Studies at Stanford University, where he was also a Professor of Political Science. His most recent books include *China Joins the World: Progress and Prospects* (with Elizabeth Economy, 1999) and, as co-editor, *Making China Policy: Lessons from the Bush and Clinton Administrations* (2001).

Lucian W. Pye is Ford Professor of Political Science (Emeritus) at MIT. He is the author of numerous books, including *The Spirit of Chinese Politics: A Psychocultural Study of the Authority Crisis in Political Development* (1968), *Asian Power and Politics: The Cultural Dimensions of Authority* (1985) and *The Mandarin and the Cadre: China's Political Cultures* (1988).

Susan L. Shirk is Professor in the Graduate School of International Relations and Pacific Studies at the University of California, San Diego, and is Research Director of the University of California's system-wide Institute on Global Conflict and Cooperation. From 1997 to 2000, she served as Deputy Assistant Secretary of State, with responsibility for China, Taiwan, Hong Kong and Mongolia. Her books include *The Political Logic of Economic Reform in China* (1993), *Competitive Comrades: Career Incentives and Student Strategies in China* (1982) and *How China Opened Its Door: The Political Success of the PRC's Foreign Trade and Investment Reforms* (1994).

Frederick C. Teiwes holds a Personal Chair in Chinese Politics at the University of Sydney, and is also an Australian Research Council Special Investigator for the Social Sciences. He has written widely on Chinese elite politics, including *Politics at Mao's Court* (1990), *Politics and Purges in China* (2nd ed. 1993) and, jointly with Warren Sun, *The Tragedy of Lin Biao* (1996) and *China's Road to Disaster* (1999).

Kellee S. Tsai is Assistant Professor of Political Science at Johns Hopkins University. She is the author of *Back-Alley Banking: Private Entrepreneurs in China* (2002) and has published articles in *The China Journal*, *The China Quarterly* and *The Journal of International Affairs*.

Tang Tsou, who passed away in 1999, was the Homer J. Livingston Professor in Political Science at the University of Chicago. He was the author of numerous books and papers, including *America's Failure in China, 1941–1950* (1963) and *The Cultural Revolution and Post-Mao Reforms: A Historical Perspective* (1986).

Jonathan Unger is Director of the Contemporary China Centre at the Australian National University and Co-Editor of *The China Journal*. He has published more than a dozen books, the most recent of which is *The Transformation of Rural China* (2002).

You Ji is Senior Lecturer in Political Science at the University of New South Wales in Sydney. He has published widely on China's political, economic, military and foreign affairs. He is the author of three books: *In Quest of High Tech Power: The Modernization of China's Military in the 1990s* (1996), *China's Enterprise Reform: Changing State–Society Relations after Mao* (1997) and *The Armed Forces of China* (1999).

FOREWORD

Jonathan Unger

How can we best depict the nature of elite Chinese politics under Mao Zedong? What have been the essential changes in the political system under Deng Xiaoping and subsequently under Jiang Zemin, and what are the continuities in political life?

To answer these questions, it is important to examine the sinews of the Chinese political system—the informal dimensions of how power is structured and how leaders in Beijing interact. Analyses before the Cultural Revolution had often posited a consensual, collegial Politburo and Central Committee under Mao's leadership, with loose "opinion groups" that formed temporarily over particular issues.[1] But the Cultural Revolution turmoil of 1966–69, which dramatically exposed the inner tensions and divisions of Chinese politics, altered the views of some China specialists. In 1973, to cite a prime example, Andrew Nathan presented a model of factionalism based upon clientalist ties. The system of persisting factions that he depicted anchored informal politics within the Party and thus had to be tolerated by the top leader.[2]

Nathan's conceptualization of Party politics elicited a response in 1976 by Tang Tsou, who argued that rather than featuring ongoing or recurrent factions, the Chinese leadership system exhibits a contest for supremacy in which rival opponents and groups were denied legitimacy and instead were subdued: "Chinese Communist leaders have always assumed, explicitly in some periods and implicitly in other periods, that 'anti-Party factions' will arise and must be defeated and eliminated".[3]

Two other senior analysts, Lucian Pye and Frederick Teiwes, provided different frameworks for comprehending Party politics. Pye, in a book-length

---

[1]   On this, particularly see Franz Schurmann, *Ideology and Organization in Communist China* (Berkeley: University of California Press, 1996), esp. pp. 55–7.

[2]   Andrew J. Nathan, "A Factionalism Model for CCP Politics", *The China Quarterly*, No. 53 (January 1973), pp. 34–66.

[3]   Tang Tsou, "Prolegomenon to the Study of Informal Groups in CCP Politics", *The China Quarterly*, No. 65 (March 1976), p. 103; the article is also published in Tang Tsou (ed.), *The Cultural Revolution and Post-Mao Reforms: A Historical Perspective* (Chicago: University of Chicago Press, 1986).

analysis of Chinese political behaviour, depicted an underlying political culture and shared socio-psychological patterns that go far back into imperial times. The crux of his argument was "that the fundamental dynamic of Chinese politics is a continuous tension between the imperative of consensus and conformity, on the one hand, and the belief, on the other hand, that one can find security only in special, particularistic relationships, which by their very nature tend to threaten the principle of consensus".[4] Factions exist and persist, in Pye's view, as a means to find security by way of a powerful patron, but these groupings are somewhat precarious.

In some respects, Pye's and Nathan's portrayals of the salience of patron–client and factional proclivities in the Chinese political system seem similar. But Nathan perceived this factionalism very much in institutional rather than cultural terms, and in fact saw direct parallels with the factionalism found in political systems elsewhere in the world. Pye, in sharp contrast, stressed the uniquely Chinese impetus for particularistic political allegiances.

Frederick Teiwes, in a series of books on Communist Chinese politics under Mao, repudiated the premise shared by Nathan and Pye that factionalism was part of the equation in Mao-era politics. Teiwes instead emphasized the importance of the prestige of leaders—and above all others, Mao. There was no balance-among-factions or conflict-between-factions scenario here, but rather a court in which Mao reigned supreme and in which any constraints on his behaviour in the form of "rules of the game" receded over time.[5] In Teiwes's more recent writings, as more evidence has come to light, this theme of Mao's unchallenged supremacy and the near-irrelevance of factions has become even firmer.[6]

These four authors' arguments have provided the most influential frameworks for analysing elite politics in China. In the opening chapter of this book, Lowell Dittmer reappraises these four theses and, on the basis of an examination of leadership behaviour during the Party's history, develops a fifth conceptualization of the nature of Chinese politics. He does so from the vantage point of taking into consideration the changes that occurred in China after Mao's

---

[4]   See, e.g., Lucian W. Pye, *The Dynamics of Chinese Politics* (Cambridge, Mass.: Oelgeschlager, Gunn and Hain, 1981), p. 4.

[5]   See, e.g., Frederick C. Teiwes, "'Rules of the Game' in Chinese Politics", *Problems of Communism* (September-December 1979); *Politics and Purges in China: Rectification and the Decline of Party Norms, 1950–1965* (Armonk: M. E. Sharpe, 1979); and *Politics at Mao's Court: Gao Gang and Party Factionalism in the Early 1950s* (Armonk: M. E. Sharpe, 1990). In most respects, Michel Oksenberg's portrait of the elite political system was congruent with Teiwes's; see Oksenberg's "Policy Making Under Mao, 1949–68: An Overview", in John M. H. Lindbeck (ed.), *China: Management of a Revolutionary Society* (Seattle: University of Washington Press, 1971).

[6]   See the Bibliography at the rear of this book for a listing of Teiwes's recent writings.

death. Dittmer's ambit is wide. His chapter grapples not only with the question of factionalism and informal relationships among the leadership, but also a range of other major factors influencing the Chinese political system. Among these is the role of the supreme or "core" leader, and Dittmer provides insightful comparisons of the roles played by Mao and Deng.

In the chapters that follow, the four scholars who had put forward the earlier influential analyses—Andrew Nathan (with Kellee Tsai), Tang Tsou, Lucian Pye and Frederick Teiwes—present updated perspectives on elite politics that range across both the Mao and Deng periods. Their chapters do more than just describe Chinese politics at the top; they conceptualize the underpinnings of politics in China, measuring empirical evidence against political science theory, recent Chinese history and Chinese political culture. Unlike many edited books that are essentially collections of discrete papers, the chapters here engage each other explicitly, in what is tantamount to a debate over how best to comprehend Chinese politics. To further flesh out this debate, Lowell Dittmer was invited to contribute a second essay, Chapter Six, as a response to these four chapters. Here, Dittmer highlights not only the underlying assumptions and differences in the positions taken by his fellow authors and himself, but also the areas of emerging consensus among them.

This book is divided into two sections. Part One, containing the above six chapters, focuses on the Chinese political system up until the end of Deng's rule, while the seven chapters in Part Two focus directly on the period of Jiang Zemin's tenure. To open the second half of the book, Michel Oksenberg discusses the overall structural features of the political system today. Within the context of this new political environment, the chapters that follow Oksenberg's focus on the major themes regarding leadership politics that were discussed in Part One. The contributors examine how the nature of elite Chinese politics has changed now that the first generation of leaders—Deng and the other Party elders who had won the revolutionary civil war—have passed from the scene. Do "factional" politics, coalitions, and informal groupings exist today, and if so, have these changed in nature? Have the "rules of the game" of Party politics changed? To what extent, and in what ways, are institutional constraints manifested? At the very top of the system, have the bases of power and legitimacy of the paramount leader changed—and is the style of leadership different? Is a system of collective leadership or dominance by one man more the norm in Chinese politics today?

Three of the scholars who contributed to Part One—Lowell Dittmer, Lucian Pye and Frederick Teiwes—bring their conceptualizations of Chinese politics to bear on these questions. Tang Tsou died before this book came to fruition, but his conceptual framework is carried forward in Chapter Eleven by Joseph Fewsmith, a former student of Tsou who is himself one of the major analysts today of elite Chinese politics. You Ji, a political scientist who specializes in both Chinese leadership politics and the armed forces, fills an important gap in Chapter Twelve by describing how Jiang Zemin's leadership of the military has affected his political power. A final overview chapter, engaging the positions taken by these authors and analysing the politics of leadership succession, is provided by Susan Shirk, a political scientist who dealt directly with China's leadership when she served in the Clinton administration as Deputy Assistant Secretary of State for East Asia and the Pacific.

The book demonstrates the conceptual sophistication that has been reached today in the analysis of China's political arena. This level of analytical insight into elite Party politics will be appreciated not only by students of China but also by readers interested more generally in comparative political systems.

I

The Nature of Politics

Under Mao and Deng

ONE

Modernizing Chinese Informal Politics[*]

Lowell Dittmer

In the study of modern Chinese politics, the informal dimension has always played an unusually vital part.[1] This is due in part to the unsettled nature of the Chinese political scene throughout the twentieth century, making it difficult for any political arrangement to become securely institutionalized. It is also due in part to the traditional aversion to law and a cultural preference for more moralistic and personalized authority relations. And finally, it is due in part to the revolutionary ethos that formerly prevailed in China, according to which any commitment to the *status quo* was apt to be considered "reactionary". Though not typically part of an explicit analytical framework, the informal dimension was tacitly taken into account in biographical analyses of prominent leaders and in the attempt by analysts to explain shifting leadership coalitions and cleavages. Informal politics *per se* did not, however, become the basis of social science theory on China until the 1970s—specifically, with the publication of a pioneering article by Andrew Nathan and an influential rebuttal by Tang Tsou.[2]

While their contributions have taken us a long way toward a consensually acceptable analytical framework, there are many contradictions in the canonical

[*]   I am grateful to Haruhiro Fukui, Jonathan Unger and Peter N. S. Lee for offering valuable suggestions on an earlier draft of this chapter. I am grateful, too, to the "Informal Politics, Democracy, and Patterns of Economic Development in East Asia" project, funded by the University of California Pacific Rim Research Program, for financial support of this research. In addition, I am deeply indebted to the work and insights of Tang Tsou on this topic.

[1]   A relatively comprehensive bibliography of writings on Chinese informal politics may be found in Lucian Pye, *The Dynamics of Chinese Politics* (Cambridge, Mass.: Oelgeschlager, Gunn & Hain, 1981), pp. 267–76.

[2]   Andrew Nathan, "A Factionalism Model for CCP Politics", *The China Quarterly*, No. 53 (1973), pp. 33–66; Tang Tsou, "Prolegomenon to the Study of Informal Groups in CCP Politics", *The China Quarterly*, No. 65 (1976), pp. 98–114; "Andrew Nathan Replies", *The China Quarterly*, No. 65, pp. 114–17.

theoretical literature that need to be reconciled, and many once secure empirical findings that will require updating to take political changes into account. The present analysis contains three parts: it begins with a review of previous efforts to condeptualize the underpinnings of Chinese politics, introduces a schema that attempts conceptual synthesis, and concludes with an application of that schema to the informal politics of the reform era.

Notions of Informal Politics

The central variable in Andrew Nathan's model is the faction, which he uses to explain patterns of conflict and coalition among the elite leadership in the Chinese Communist Party (CCP). His analysis is informed by Franz Schurmann's distinction between elite "opinion groups" and "factions". The "opinion groups" are coalitions that contain their disagreements within a demarcated decision-making arena (without mobilizing outside constituencies) and resolve their differences through reasoned "discussion" (*taolun*), whereafter they promptly disband, whereas a "faction" conspires for power over a longer time span and may endeavour to mobilize outside organizational forces to overthrow the consensus.[3] Focusing on this distinction, Nathan launches a wide-ranging tour through the comparative social science literature in search of a universally valid model of factional behaviour. He then applies this construct to China—and finds that it fits. Recent CCP elite political history is then reconstrued in the light of the model.

Nathan defines a faction as a vertically organized patron-client network linked by personal face-to-face "connections" (*guanxi*). It is external to but dependent upon the formal structure along which it extends, like a "trellis" (in Nathan's now-famous metaphor). Altogether a faction has no fewer than fifteen "structural characteristics": including a "code of civility" governing normal intra-elite relations (as factions discover that they can never really eliminate one another they learn mutual toleration), an overarching ideological consensus that subsumes hair-splitting wrangles over policy or "line" differences, and so forth. Nathan deems the Cultural Revolution to have been an exception to this conceptualization. The Cultural Revolution's wholesale purges represented Mao's determination to overcome and destroy the hated factional system as Nathan describes it. This attempt, however, ultimately failed, according to Nathan, permitting Chinese elite politics to revert to the factional *status quo ante*.

Tang Tsou first subjects Nathan's model to a thorough critique and then erects his rival conceptualization upon its debris. Tsou begins by substituting "informal group" for "faction". The main reason given is that the former term is more inclusive, with a tradition of social science scholarship behind it. Moreover, the term "informal groups" eschews any pejorative taint (which in the case of "factionalism" is even more pronounced in the Chinese terms *paibie*, *paixing*).

---

[3]   See Franz Schurmann, *Organization and Ideology in Communist China* (Berkeley: University of California Press, 1966), pp. 54–7, 196 ff.

The new term has the added advantage of highlighting the relationship between formal and informal organization, avoiding cultural exceptionalism and facilitating cross-fertilization with the rich post-Weberian literature on informal organizations. Agreeing with Nathan's "trellis" analogy, Tsou emphasizes that a formal structure is assumed to be the "precondition rather than the product" for the development of informal groups—the informal grows from the formal. But although his conceptualization makes it possible for him to differentiate among types of informal groups, in his empirical discussions Tsou tends to use "faction" and "informal group" interchangeably.

Tsou makes three important criticisms of Nathan. First, whereas Nathan argues for "rampant" factionalism (namely, factions operating independently of formal structures), Tsou argues that structures place various constraints upon factions. For example, factions share the ideology of the "host" organization, including many of its goals, norms and interests (not to mention personnel). If the formal organization is the trellis, informal organizations normally follow the trellis. There may of course be more than one informal group within a given formal organization. Though the factions within an organization may differ stridently, their differences are couched in the same (or only minutely differentiated) language.

Second, in contrast to Nathan's assumption of an overarching ideological consensus, Tsou contends that ideology is up for grabs, with the victor claiming a monopoly on legitimacy and roundly denouncing the loser in both ideological and moral terms. (This claim stands in some tension to the first point, which assumes that all factions accept the legitimacy of the host organization.)

Third, and most fundamentally, Tsou denies the hypothesized "live-and-let-live", "no win" pattern of factional contests. Factional fights typically end in a clear-cut victory of one faction over the other, whereupon the former seizes control of the formal organization, breaks the decision-making logjam and rams its own policy preferences through. Without altogether denying the existence of a "code of civility" that governs intra-elite relationships during certain periods, Tsou reconstrues its meaning: this is not a "live-and-let-live" compromise that stems from the fact that no faction is able to defeat its rivals; it is merely the somewhat more tolerant form of domination exercised by a now confident victor over subordinates who in any case are most likely clients in the same informal network. To be sure, Tsou concedes that a "balance-of-power" type of arrangement obtained when the leadership split into first and second "fronts" in the early 1960s, but he tacitly dismisses this as a tactical truce pending later opportunities to renew the struggle and finally prevail decisively.

In addition to the points addressed by Tsou, Nathan's seminal construct raises a number of other important unresolved issues for further empirical investigation. First, are factions always vertically organized on a patron-client basis? This does seem to have been true in the case of the initial targets of the Cultural Revolution—Peng Zhen, Luo Ruiqing, Lu Dingyi and Yang Shangkun (who, whatever their previous connections, seem to have colluded to restrain public criticism of their colleague Wu Han)—or of the Gang of Four, in which Jiang Qing was the patron to Zhang Chunqiao, Yao Wenyuan and Wang

Hongwen by dint of seniority as well as her own empowering "apron-string relationship" (*chundai guanxi*) with Mao,[4] or in the case of Hua Guofeng's "small gang of four" (always written in strict hierarchical order: Wang Dongxing, Ji Dengkui, Wu De, and Chen Xilian). But vertical linkages are less clear-cut in the cases of the Gao Gang-Rao Shushi coalition in the early 1950s, the Liu Shaoqi-Deng Xiaoping alliance up through the early 1960s,[5] or the factional collaboration (in fact, conspiracy) between Hua Guofeng and Ye Jianying that led to the sudden arrest of the Gang of Four in September 1976.[6]

Second, Nathan's fifteen characteristics are too numerous to serve as a practical checklist. In an attempt to define the essence of factionalism these would have to be carefully winnowed and reduced to a few critical points. As is, some of the characteristics are not specific to factionalism but were normative features of CCP intra-elite relations in general (such as the "climate of civility").

Third, the point that factions are based on "connections" (*guanxi*) generated through face-to-face interaction is a valid and percipient insight that may go far to explain both the persistent elitist bias in PRC politics and the key role of convening meetings to mobilize support and flush out opposition. Yet two factors qualify this point. Albeit perhaps primarily based upon face-to-face contacts, connections are to some extent fungible: a factional contact may be transferred to a third party. Thus entire factional networks may be transmitted intact from one patron to another. The remnants of Liu Shaoqi's political base seem to have shifted allegiance successively to Zhou Enlai and to Chen Yun and Deng Xiaoping during the 1970s, just as Hu Yaobang's faction migrated first to Zhao Ziyang upon Hu's demotion in early 1987, and then to Zhu Rongji after Zhao's fall at Tiananmen. The other factor is that despite the *guanxi*-limited, elitist bias of Chinese politics there have been occasions when elite factions have been augmented by mass constituencies, and it is impossible to account for such coordination based purely on face-to-face contacts. Face-to-face contacts

---

[4]   During their active careers, the Gang of Four were listed in the hierarchical order of their formal positions: Wang Hongwen, Zhang Chunqiao, Jiang Qing and Yao Wenyuan. When legal proceedings were initiated against them in 1980, they were listed in the order of their informal power bases: Jiang, Zhang, Yao and Wang.

[5]   The Liu-Deng alliance, based upon a compatible ideological outlook and work style rather than any anti-Maoist conspiracy, was reinforced by such acts as Liu's suggestion that Deng be appointed Secretary-General when Mao complained of an excessive workload in December 1953, and Deng's nomination of Liu as Chief-of-State in 1959. See Frederick Teiwes, *Politics at Mao's Court: Gao Gang and Party Factionalism in the Early 1950s* (Armonk: M. E. Sharpe, 1990), p. 26 ff.; Hei Yannan, *Shi nian dongluan* [Ten Years of Chaos] (Hong Kong: Xingzhen, 1988), p. 50.

[6]   On the Hua-Deng-Ye connection, see Lin Qingshan, *Fengyun shi nian yu Deng Xiaoping* [A Decade of Turmoil and Deng Xiaoping] (Beijing: Liberation Army Daily Press, 1989), p. 440.

between, say, central and local leaders may still play a certain role in coordinating large-group movements, as when Zhou Enlai and members of the Cultural Revolution Small Group (*wenhua geming xiaozu*) toured the countryside and met with Red Guard faction leaders during 1967–68, or when Mao went on tour in the summer of 1971 seeking support for his move against Lin Biao, or when Deng Xiaoping convened intensive meetings with PLA leaders in May 1989 preparatory to the mobilization of troops for the crackdown at Tiananmen. In other cases the link may be initiated from below, as when Democracy Wall activists mobilized in support of Deng Xiaoping in the autumn of 1978, or when democracy protesters in the spring of 1989 gravitated to support Zhao Ziyang after Hu Yaobang's death—in both cases without evident coordination from above. In any case factional theory will need to be supplemented by a principal-agent model (including political-economic variables and leadership acknowledgement of public opinion) to account for such coordinated large-scale movements, even when the latter seem to mimic factionalism on a larger scale.[7]

Lucian Pye's contribution in the early 1980s to the analysis of factionalism (he reverts to Nathan's original term) also merits our attention. Rejecting the premise that factions are defined by "primordial" ties such as shared generation, class or geographical origins, Pye likewise discards relations "achieved" in previous bonding experiences, such as old school ties, organizational associations, or even ideological affinity, pointing out exceptions to each presumptive link.[8] Factionalism, he argues, constitutes a central, even modal, pattern of Chinese political behaviour that is deeply rooted in cultural and psychological security drives. The faction-centred reality of Chinese politics is obscured by a "veil of consensus", which stems from an equally powerful cultural imperative that identifies political authority with unchallenged moral and doctrinal correctness. China's political culture is averse to conflict, and norms of consensus predominate, but meanwhile the search for personal security generates a ceaseless counter-mobilization of informal loyalty networks. It is the intimate and indissoluble linkage between these contradictory imperatives that is the key to the political process; the failure of Western analysts to grasp this, Pye suggests, is what accounts for the alternating adoption and rejection of conflict and consensus models of Chinese leadership politics. Because factions are power-maximizing entities constrained only by the moral imperative to affirm a nominal leadership solidarity, factional struggle does not serve as a vehicle for rational policy debate, organizational interest articulation, or aggregation of political demands and support. China emerges as a "bureaucratic polity" without "bureaucratic politics", a system in which policy conflict is perpetual, but policy issues become essentially symbolic of unstated personal rivalries. The Alice in Wonderland quality of

---

[7]   D. Roderick Kiewiet and Matthew D. McCubbin, *The Logic of Delegation* (Chicago: University of Chicago Press, 1991), Ch. 1.

[8]   Pye, *The Dynamics of Chinese Politics*, pp. 7, 77–126.

Chinese politics is typified for Pye in the 1970s paradoxes of a technology-intensive air force exalting "men over machines", and an industrially advanced Shanghai lobbying on behalf of China's rural poor. Such symbolic transpositions suppress policy debate and obscure accountability on behalf of a purely nominal consensus.[9]

Whereas Pye deftly illustrates the paradoxical or illogical relationships between formal and informal power in Chinese politics, these contradictions also provide useful starting points for the positive analysis he tends to neglect. There are several distinctions implicit in Pye's critique which might fruitfully be sifted out and linked to specific hypotheses. To wit:

(a) Some informal ties are relatively self-sufficient—that is, they can stand on their own in an institutional vacuum. Examples include the Cultural Revolution coalitions between radical Red Guard faction leaders and the Cultural Revolution Small Group, or between moderate faction leaders and the Central work teams and later regional PLA commanders. The hunger strike grouping that wrested leadership of the Tiananmen protests in early May 1989 seems to have been autonomous of any central leadership. Such factions may be expected to function independently of the formal structure, as demonstrated by the tenacious power of Deng Xiaoping and certain other leaders after they were divested of formal power bases in 1976–77.

(b) Informal ties as the independent variable, with formal organization as the dependent variable: for instance, the gerontocratic networks that led to the formation of the Central Advisory Committee and the Central Disciplinary Inspection Commission, and that led to the reconstitution of the Party Politburo in 1982–86. In such cases the formal structure can be artificially (but only temporarily) inflated by the appointment of a powerful leadership personality, such as Liu Shaoqi's appointment as chief of state in 1959, or Peng Zhen's appointment as chair of the National People's Congress Standing Committee in 1982.

(c) Formal organization as the independent variable, with informal ties as the dependent variable: for example, clientage or the aggregation of informal power on the basis of the personal use (or abuse) of the perquisites of office, as in the studies of rural and urban patronage networks in Jean Oi's and Andrew Walder's studies, respectively.[10]

The central focus of Frederick Teiwes's magisterial historical analyses has not been factions or informal groups *per se* but the normative framework or "rules of the game" he perceives to be regulating the process of intra-elite conflict and

---

[9]   Ibid., passim.

[10]   See Jean Oi, *State and Peasant in Contemporary China: The Political Economy of Village Government* (Berkeley: University of California Press, 1989), Chs 7 and 9; and Andrew Walder, *Communist Neo-Traditionalism: Work and Authority in Chinese Industry* (Berkeley: University of California Press, 1986), Chs 4 and 5.

"rectification".[11] This normative framework, permitting open discussion and vigorous debate of conflicting proposals before a decision is made, followed by maintenance of iron discipline during its subsequent implementation, was allegedly introduced during the Rectification Campaign in the 1940s to replace the "ruthless struggles and merciless blows" type of rectification associated with the Returned Students' leadership, and lasted (with momentary lapses, such as the Gao-Rao purge) from the late 1940s through the mid-1950s.[12] "Mistaken" viewpoints were tolerated and even allowed to persist so long as organizational discipline was maintained—that is, no conspiratorial activity and no mobilization of outside organizational resources. So long as conflict was conducted according to the norms, elite solidarity behind a decisive and apparently monolithic leadership could be maintained while permitting a full airing of views. Teiwes credited this new pattern of rectification primarily to Mao Zedong, with whose rise to power it coincided, at the same time blaming Mao for its lapse at the Lushan plenum in 1959 and, more explosively, during the Cultural Revolution. Whereas in his earlier studies Teiwes attributed considerable independent efficacy to the "rules of the game", his more recent work has tended to subordinate this code to the historical prestige attained by the players by dint of their achievements in the revolutionary period. Status considerations, according to this perspective, tend to eclipse policy orientation or a bureaucratic base as a source of power, becoming more significant than formal "rules of the game" in sustaining a climate of civility.

It goes without saying that any attempt to review and assess these varied formulations is still tentative. Nathan's model was clearly seminal and remains a primary reference point, though it operates with a set of definitions that perversely preclude its application to the very period to which it might have been considered most relevant (the Cultural Revolution). Tsou's central criticism of Nathan, that his "code of civility" is based on an intra-factional balance of power that is empirically exceptional, and that a hierarchical intra-elite relationship is more typical than pluralistic power balancing, seems to be largely correct. This is

---

[11]   See Teiwes's *Politics and Purges in China: Rectification and the Decline of Party Norms, 1950–1965* (White Plains, NY: M. E. Sharpe, 1979), and *Politics at Mao's Court*; also see Teiwes and Warren Sun (eds), *The Politics of Agricultural Cooperativization in China: Mao, Deng Zihui, and the "High Tide" of 1955* (Armonk: M. E. Sharpe, 1993).

[12]   This generalization is qualified in Teiwes' *Politics at Mao's Court*, which finds that the confrontation with Gao Gang-Rao Shushi took place in a considerably more rough-and-tumble fashion than previously assumed. Based on new documentary evidence plus interviews with Chinese scholars and bureaucrats, Teiwes finds that "Such phenomena as attacks by proxy, vague and politically loaded accusations, exaggerating past 'errors' without regard for historical circumstances, and collecting material on political enemies, which would become such a feature of the Cultural Revolution, were already present in the Gao-Rao affair" (p. 151).

borne out in Teiwes's more recent research, which likens high-level politics during the early Maoist period to "court politics": that is,

> a process dominated by an unchallenged Chairman surrounded by other leaders attempting to divine his often obscure intentions, adjusting their preferences to his desires and trying to exploit his ambiguities to advance their bureaucratic and political interests, and squabbling among themselves when Mao's actions exacerbated old tensions or created new ones among them.[13]

Yet does this necessarily imply that intra-elite conflict inevitably culminates in a showdown resulting in the clear-cut victory of one group and its establishment in a position of hegemony, in a "game to win all"? Such a generalization, it seems to me, requires two qualifications.

First, there do seem to be periods, sometimes fairly extended, when a certain level of elite pluralism or balance-of-power politics does obtain. One of these was the post-Leap recovery period preceding the Cultural Revolution, and a second includes the first several years of the post-Mao period, during which Deng was obliged to share power with a series of strong rivals, including Hua Guofeng, Ye Jianying, Li Xiannian, Bo Yibo, Peng Zhen and Chen Yun. Even after Deng consolidated his supremacy at the Third Plenum of the 11th Central Committee in late 1978, his relationship to Chen Yun was less than authoritative. Collective leadership is after all a norm among the Party elite, as Teiwes has emphasized, and the exercise of domineering leadership is frequently derogated as a "personality cult", "hegemonism", and so on. (Mao himself, upset by Deng Xiaoping's failure to consult, once stormed: "What emperor decided this?"). This norm is strongly sanctioned in the canonical literature and is accorded lip service in the public rituals of leadership politics. To assume that norms are always adhered to would be naive, but norms are an important component of organizational culture. One may of course dismiss periods of apparent calm and balance as concealing periods of frenzied subterranean factional maneuver that anticipate later opportunities for renewed struggle, but how can we justify privileging the latter with a higher level of "reality" than the former? If periods of compromise are preparatory to renewed conflict, are not bouts of struggle also followed by efforts to establish periods of stability and balance? Clearly, both phases are part of the Chinese political reality.

Second, even in those cases in which factional struggle culminates in the victory of one faction and the destruction of its rival, this is typically followed by the recurrence (often quite promptly) of a new factional balance in which new actors step into the position of the eliminated faction, leading not to hierarchical consolidation but to a new rivalry. One is tempted to infer that opposition is a "functional requisite" of the system. Thus no sooner was the alleged Liu-Deng "bourgeois reactionary line" destroyed during the Cultural Revolution, than first

---

[13]   Personal communication from Teiwes.

Zhou Enlai and then a renascent Deng Xiaoping re-emerged to assume ideological and organizational leadership of a moderate "line" that many of the leading radicals deemed analogous to the earlier alleged Liu-Deng line.[14] Nor has the purge of Zhao Ziyang at the Fourth Plenum of the 13th Party Congress in June 1989 resulted in the destruction of his line, which seems to have survived with the help of Li Ruihuan, Zhu Rongji and Tian Jiyun. Deng Xiaoping himself, frustrated by the consolidation of resistance to further economic reform, found it useful to resuscitate this group in the spring of 1992, after having brought it to the brink of ruin. So if Nathan is wrong to assume that a factional balance of power is a normal state of affairs, it would also be a mistake to assume that just because one faction decisively destroys a rival faction, this will result in an enduring leadership consensus. We may perhaps make the weaker inference that a destructive factional outbreak is likely to be followed by a period of what one might call "contained factionalism".

Lucian Pye has made an important contribution in pointing to the psychological insecurity at the root of factional affiliation and maneuver, and to the environmental conditions tending to exacerbate or alleviate that insecurity. But to conclude by dismissing all objective bases for such affiliations is, I think, going too far. Just because no one node (such as generation, territory or old school tie) can function as an invariably reliable indicator of factional linkage does not mean that all of them may be dispensed with. These may function as interchangeable options, at least one being necessary but not sufficient, with the specific selection likely to be based upon situational factors and mutual needs.

Toward a Conceptual Synthesis

Any new conceptualization should avoid the two opposing problems—excessive modesty and overweening ambition—that have plagued earlier definitional efforts. In the case of the former, we are given a purely negative definition of the central term, defining informal politics not in terms of what it is but in terms of what it is not: formal politics. Clearly, it is important to note the interdependency between formal and informal politics, but informal politics should not be derogated to the status of a residual variable, dependent upon the definition of its positive counterpart. The opposite problem is the tendency to strive for prematurely

---

[14] This telescopes events slightly: in 1969–71, Zhou aligned with Lin Biao to shut out the radicals, thus earning Jiang Qing's ire and precipitating the purge of Chen Boda in 1970 and Lin Biao in 1971. Chen Boda and Lin Biao could not, however, be considered functional replacements of Liu and Deng because their policy preferences were diametrically opposite to Liu and Deng. The elimination of the military radicals, however, allowed Zhou Enlai to consolidate his position on the right, and he proceeded to revive economic policies previously associated with Liu and Deng. This in turn brought him into confrontation with the radicals, in a factional power balance redolent of the 1966–69 "line struggle".

ambitious conceptualizations—to aim at a model of factionalism that is valid throughout the Third World, for example, or applicable to organizations throughout the Chinese cultural oecumene—and then to interpolate from these general models to the political situation within the Chinese Party Politburo during the last two or four decades. This sort of abstract model-building is tempting, in view of the paucity of hard empirical evidence about the inner workings of the Politburo and other powerful leadership organs. Yet a definition that is valid for a universal or even comparatively broad range of factional behaviour cannot be expected to capture the *differentia specifica* of the Party leadership. A more prudent strategy, it seems to me, would be to set a middle-range boundary for inquiry—say, the arena enclosing the 20 to 35 top members of the Party and governmental elite—and then see to what extent the theories and explanations derived from this limited sample can be more broadly generalized. With limited time and resources, this is a good place to start even if our findings turn out not to be easily generalizable, given the pivotal role assigned to the "Centre" in Chinese politics and the tendency of subordinate political institutions to emulate this "model".

The central term in our conceptualization of informal politics is relationships. As Liang Shuming noted long ago, Chinese culture is neither individualistic (*geren benwei*, or individually based) nor group-oriented (*shehui benwei*), but rather relationship-based (*guanxi benwei*).[15] Ambrose King has postulated that in contradistinction to Japanese relationships, which are based on fixed frames or *ba* (the family, workplace or village) that set a clear unit boundary and give a common identity to a set of individuals, Chinese relationships are formed on the basis of attributes (such as kinship, classmate, school ties) that are infinitely extendable.[16] Attributes provide a pluralistic basis for identification depending on the specific attribute shared; thus the more attributes one has, the more relationships one is able to establish.[17] While it is certainly true that Chinese attributes sometimes articulate into vast networks, some Chinese attributes are also defined by fixed frames, such as those within the same family, parochial village, or "basic work unit" (*jiben danwei*). Perhaps Chinese political culture includes both types of connections.

Analytically we may usefully distinguish between two types of relationships: those in which the relationship with the other is valued as an end in itself, to use the Kantian language, and those in which the other is merely a means to other ends. We may term the former "value-rational" relationships and the latter

---

[15]   Liang Shuming, *Zhongguo wenhua yaoyi* [An Outline of Chinese Culture] (Hong Kong: Jizheng Tushu Gongsi, 1974), p. 94.

[16]   Cf. Chie Nakane's brilliant *Japanese Society* (Berkeley: University of California Press, 1970).

[17]   Ambrose Yeo-chi King, "*Kuan-hsi* and Network Building: A Sociological Interpretation", *Daedelus*, Vol. 120, No. 2 (Spring 1991), pp. 63–85.

"purpose-rational" relationships.[18] Both may be useful in high-level elite politics, but they have different uses. A purpose-rational relationship is typically formed with colleagues, subordinates and superiors with whom one has routine work-related or functional contacts. These relationships may be mobilized in support of career objectives so long as they are in the collective interests of the organization of which all are a part. We may refer to this ensemble of occupational relationships as one's formal base. By mobilizing one's formal base one is able to exert official power, which Chinese refer to as *quanli*. Some high-level leaders seem to have relied exclusively on official power, either out of principle, as seems to have been the case for Liu Shaoqi or Deng Xiaoping,[19] or because they lacked sufficient opportunities to build a mobilizable informal base, as seems to have been true in the cases of Hua Guofeng or Zhao Ziyang.

Yet there are two important limitations to what one can do with official power. First, in most cases it is a relatively simple matter to be divested of one's formal base: a job rotation or demotion and it is gone. Chinese cadres have not, historically, had "tenure" or legally stipulated terms of office, and their positions hence have been far more tenuous from a strictly formal perspective than those of a civil servant in the West (either elective or appointed). Thus, when Hu Yaobang failed to crack down energetically enough on young protesters in December 1986, he was promptly relieved of his position as General Secretary. Although he remained a full Politburo member, he was in effect in internal exile, for without a hierarchical organization beneath him that he could convene at meetings and thus mobilize in support of his interests, his ability to exert official power was sharply curtailed. When the official responsible for one's official demotion is also one's informal patron (as in the Deng-Hu and Deng-Zhao clashes, though not in the Mao-Deng or Hua-Deng confrontations), dismissal is normally a career-ending event. Kang Sheng is an interesting variant: in the course of over-zealously "rectifying" suspected ideological deviants during the Rectification Campaign of the early 1940s in his capacity as head of the six-man campaign committee, Kang became so unpopular within the Party that after Liberation he was divested of control of the security apparatus and (like his contemporary, Beria) rendered politically impotent. Relegated to the governorship of Shandong province, Kang

---

[18]   Though I have obviously borrowed these terms from Max Weber, Weber employed them differently, using value-rationality or *Wertrationalitaet* to refer to actions oriented to ultimate ends, and purpose-rationality or *Zweckrationalitaet* to refer to actions oriented to more immediate payoffs. In adapting this terminology to refer to "*relationships*", we shall see that it has a quite different connotation.

[19]   Liu did nothing to protect Peng Zhen when the latter came under fire during the Cultural Revolution, for example, and Deng did little on the same occasion to support Wu Han, his bridge partner, or Li Jingchuan. Nor is there much evidence that the informal groups below the Party centre rallied to the support of their putative patrons—they were too busy defending themselves. Although Deng rehabilitated Liu posthumously, he did not support his own presumptive clients and designated heirs, Hu Yaobang and Zhao Ziyang.

took "sick leave" throughout the early 1950s. He continued to lose power at the 8th Party Congress in 1956, falling to a mere candidate membership within the Politburo. Yet though he may have lost Mao's favour he retained an alternative "connection" to the Chairman through Mao's wife Jiang Qing. He used this conduit to regain favour at "court" when the Mao-Liu rift began to emerge in the early 1960s, by involving himself in the Sino-Soviet dispute and by editing, with Chen Boda, the "little red book" of Mao quotations. By dint of such services he succeeded in being named again to various *ad hoc* committees, including the Cultural Revolution Small Group, culminating in his comeback as *de facto* secret police chief during the Cultural Revolution. Kang's experience conforms to the pattern that a formal position is normally a prerequisite to informal influence. There are, however, important exceptions to this generalization, which will merit consideration later when the issue of the relationship between formal and informal politics is more closely examined.

The second limitation is that one cannot rely on one's formal base to defend one's personal career interests, insofar as these are detachable from the interests of the host organization. For example, if I were to come under attack for some serious ideological transgression not based on my performance in office but characterizing my entire career, it would not be in the interests of my professional associates to jeopardize their careers and the interests of our organization to come to my defense, for to do so would be to risk becoming implicated in my crime. Under such circumstances the prudent course for my professional associates would be to repudiate and ostracize me—especially in view of the presumption that an authoritative accusation is tantamount to conviction. If my career is jeopardized by an assault on my character, I have but two recourses: allay the accuser's attacks through a persuasive self-criticism (by definition well-nigh impossible in the case of an "antagonistic contradiction") or mobilize my personal base to resist.

Thus most members of the Party elite find it useful to cultivate value-rational as well as purpose-rational relationships, which typically have more long-term utility and can be mobilized if their life-chances or career is at stake. Such relationships comprise an informal "political base" (*zhengzhi jichu*), on the basis of which one can exercise informal power, or *shili*. A political base may be measured in terms of its depth and breadth: a "broad" base consists of a network of cronies located throughout the Party, military, diplomatic, and governmental apparatus, whereas a "deep" base consists of supporters going all the way back to the early generations of revolutionary leadership, hence having high seniority and elevated positions. Whereas some formidable politicians such as Zhou Enlai or Ye Jianying have had political bases both broad and deep, others have had bases that were deep but narrow (for example, Chen Boda), or broad but shallow (Hu Yaobang, for instance)—which has tended to limit their options. Since the passing of the Yanan generation in the 1990s, no Chinese political actor had a comparable broad and deep base.

How is an informal base assembled? It is put together through the incremental accretion of "connections". People have a large but finite number of potential affinities, including kinship, common geographic origin, former classmates, teachers or students, or common former Field Army affiliation—at least one of which is usually requisite to form a "connection" (*guanxi*). A cadre assigned to a new task or post will, as a matter of course, immediately canvass the area for politically opportune objective affinities as a priority, not just passively wait for them to emerge. An objective basis for an affinity does not necessarily create one, however, as demonstrated for example by Mao's wholesale purge of fellow Hunanese of his generation during the Cultural Revolution, or Chen Yun's loathing for Kang Sheng, whom he knew all too well: it is no more than a starting point. An informal base must be "cultivated", which involves investing gifts, time, and personal attention to the relationship. An initial bonding episode is also useful, such as the bond formed among certain "White" area cadres when Liu Shaoqi authorized confessions to spring them from KMT prisons, or the bond formed between fellow Shandong natives Kang Sheng and Jiang Qing when he vouched for her admission to the Party and her marriage to Mao (not to mention Kang Sheng's rumoured romantic relationship with the ambitious young woman in Shandong much earlier).[20]

If such bonding involves an experience common to a whole group of cadres, we might refer to this as categorical recruitment, an occasion that may later be publicly commemorated once the recruits become politically established. Thus 9 December is typically used to celebrate the so-called White area clique that emerged to lead the urban anti-Japanese student movement, just as 1 August, originally an occasion for celebrations among Nanchang Uprising alumni (and the cadres who helped organize it), became the anniversary of the founding of the PLA. But connections may also be recruited on an individual basis, as when Mao recruited Chen Boda at Yanan in the early 1940s or Hua Guofeng in Hunan in the mid-1950s. And of course it is quite possible to have connections with patrons who later have a falling out, thrusting a client into a cruel dilemma (as Chen Boda was forced to choose in late 1965 between Liu Shaoqi, his first patron, and Mao Zedong, his later but more powerful one).[21]

---

[20]   There is "plausible" but by no means conclusive evidence that Jiang Qing became Kang Sheng's lover when her mother was employed in the Zhang household in Shandong. See John Byron and Robert Pack, *The Claws of the Dragon: Kang Sheng* (New York: Simon and Schuster, 1992), pp. 18, 48–9; Ross Terrill, *The White-Boned Demon: A Biography of Madame Mao Zedong* (New York: William Morrow, 1984), pp. 18, 136. Despite the lack of any confirming evidence, the fact that such rumours are so widely credited by Chinese sources (for instance, Terrill cites Hu Yaobang on the "depravity" of the liaison) is in itself significant.

[21]   When Liu was in charge of the Northern Bureau during the anti-Japanese war period, he recruited Peng Zhen as director of the organization department and Chen Boda as director of the propaganda department, thus giving Chen his first important post since joining the Party. Chen's subsequent collaboration with Liu included helping to edit several of his manuscripts for publication. Chen became Mao's "pen" at Yanan, allegedly saving his life during a Nationalist air raid at Fuping in 1948, and much later compiled (with Kang

Cadres with an informal base may resort to this resource in the case of a serious threat to their careers, an "antagonistic contradiction" that would normally lead to purge or permanent sidelining. An informal base might be mobilized in the most extreme case via clandestine meetings or informant networks, as in the cases of Chen Duxiu's "Leninist Left-wing Opposition", Zhang Guotao's alleged organization of a rival Central Committee, Peng Dehuai's "Military Recreation Club" that Mao claimed conspired in Peng's critique of the Leap prior to the Lushan plenum, Zhang Chunqiao's "244 Secret Service Group", whose purpose was ironically to frame other leading cadres on charges of belonging to secret conspiracies, or Lin Biao's son Liguo setting up an alleged "Joint Fleet Command" to plot a coup d'état.[22] But because factional conspiracies are *ipso facto* illegitimate, more subtle tactics are often used, such as Aesopian public signals (as in the commissioning of rival writing groups to reconstrue Chinese history, a device used by both moderates and radicals in the mid-1970s)[23] or even a passive manifestation of support by withholding public criticism of the target (for instance, Ye Jianying, Xu Xiangqian et al. conspicuously failed to join in criticizing Deng Xiaoping in 1976). This last tactic was employed with increasing frequency and boldness during such mobilizational efforts as the Anti-Spiritual Pollution campaign of 1983–84 or the Anti-Bourgeois Liberalization campaigns of 1987 and 1989-90. These campaigns illustrated the waning capability of the Party to induce positive expressions of compliance. Because informal bases are not mobilized for the sake of routine bureaucratic policy-making but rather for reasons of personal power, the bases normally have no specific policy relevance—though given the assumption that politics is a moral crusade, the factional gist of a dispute may be disguised by ideological rhetoric alleging earth-shaking policy relevance. (Thus Deng Xiaoping, when asked in the 1980s about specific cases in the history of CCP "line struggles", dismissed the importance of diverging policy "lines".)[24]

Sheng) the "little red book" for publication. Chen was alerted to his dilemma in 1966 while editing the draft of the May 16 Circular (*Wuyiliu tongzhi*) in Hangzhou. When Chen and Kang Sheng found that Mao had added the phrase "Khrushchev-like persons sleeping beside us", Chen asked Jiang Qing for guidance. Jiang rolled her eyes and said, "You really don't know who China's Khrushchev is? You helped him edit and publish his *How to Be a Good Communist* . . . You should be cautious". See Ye Yonglie, *Chen Boda* (Hong Kong: Wenhua Jiaoyu Chubanshe, 1990), pp. 103–4, 157–9, 234–78.

22   This was a twenty-member network based at 244 Yongfu Road in Shanghai during the 1970s, which allegedly succeeded in destroying more than a thousand of Zhang's enemies. As cited in John Wilson Lewis, "Political Networks and Policy Implementation in China", unpublished paper (Stanford University, 1983), pp. 43–4.

23   Cf. Lowell Dittmer, *China's Continuous Revolution* (Berkeley: University of California Press, 1987), pp. 197–205.

24   "The struggle against Comrade Peng Dehuai cannot be viewed as a struggle between two lines. Nor can the struggle against Comrade Liu Shaoqi", he chided the authors of the 1981 Resolution on Party History. While absolving Chen Duxiu, Qu Qiubai, Li Lisan and others

The relationship between formal and informal politics is fluid and ambiguous—informal groups are often absorbed into formal structures, and formal structures in turn operate with a great deal of informality[25]—but the distinction remains relevant in at least three respects. First, the distinction appears in the recruitment and utilization of "base" members. There are two ideal types of base members: those who entail relatively pure cases of informal "connections", and those who have their own formal credentials (*zige*). An example of purely informal connections lies in the growing incidence of relatives in elite politics (for instance, Jiang Qing, Liu Shaoqi's wife Wang Guangmei, and the children of Lin Biao, Deng Xiaoping and Chen Yun). Still more "informal" would be Mao's extracurricular romantic attachments[26] (or Jiang Qing's, for that matter).[27] But personal secretaries may be included in this relatively pure form of informal recruitment as well (for example, Chen Boda and Hu Qiaomu had been Mao's secretaries; Deng Liqun was Liu Shaoqi's secretary; Zhang Chunqiao was Ke

---

of conspiracy, he did accuse Lin Biao, Gao Gang, Jiang Qing et al. of conspiracy—yet not of championing a divergent "line". As an example: "But so far as Gao Gang's real line is concerned, actually, I can't see that he had one, so it's hard to say whether we should call it a struggle between two lines". Deng Xiaoping, "Adhere to the Party Line and Improve Methods of Work" (29 February 1980), in *Selected Works of Deng Xiaoping* (Beijing: Foreign Languages Press, 1984), pp. 278–9.

[25]   Due to the members' long-term association with one another, their relative lack of lateral contact with members of parallel organizations, the comprehensive regulation of participants' roles, and a perceived sense of common threat from the "outgroup", informal bonds often develop among members of the same formal unit.

[26]   These reportedly included an actress introduced to him in 1948 by Wang Dongxing named Yu Shan, with whom Mao was so smitten that he installed her in the palace of Zhongnanhai and had Jiang Qing sent to the USSR for rest and recuperation (like her predecessor He Zichen); and a beautiful young woman (also introduced by Wang) named Zhang Yufeng, with whom he became infatuated in the 1970s. Both affairs had an impact on policy, the first by temporarily severing Kang Sheng's connection to Mao, the second by exacerbating the estrangement between Mao and Jiang Qing in the mid-1970s. See Roger Faligot and Remi Kauffer, *The Chinese Secret Service*, translated by Christine Donougher (London: Headline Books, 1989), pp. 216, 262, 389. The authoritative source on this dimension is of course Zhisui Li, *The Private Life of Chairman Mao: The Inside Story of the Man Who Made Modern China* (London: Chatto & Windus, 1994).

[27]   Aside from Kang Sheng, Jiang is alleged to have "became quite brazen about her intermittent bouts with Zhuang Zedong, the dashing young table tennis champion (who found himself rewarded with a meteoric rise to the post of Minister of Sports)". See Terrill, *The White-Boned Demon*, pp. 316–17. Other writers, however, dismiss the possibility of any extra-marital activity on Jiang Qing's part, due to her unpopularity and extreme dependence on Mao's favour; e.g., see Jin Qiu, *The Culture of Power: The Lin Biao Incident in the Cultural Revolution* (Stanford: Stanford University Press, 1999).

Qingshi's secretary;[28] after 1956 Jiang Qing became Mao's fifth secretary in charge of international affairs).[29] Also included are miscellaneous staff personnel, such as Mao's former bodyguard Wang Dongxing.[30] We may refer to the relatively purely informal recruit as the "favourite", as in monarchical court politics, and to the formal-informal mix as "regular" patronage.

An example of regular patronage was the coalescence of Bo Yibo, Peng Zhen, Yao Yilin, An Ziwen and the other cadres around Liu Shaoqi, who had recruited and led them in the White Areas; or the concatenation of Hu Qili, Rui Xingwen, Hu Jintao and others into Hu Yaobang's "Youth League Faction" (*Qingtuan pai*). The main difference between the two examples is that whereas favourites are exclusively dependent on their patron, clients in a regular patronage relationship may have other patrons, and in any case their own qualifications and background provide career insurance. Thus favourites are inclined to be more personally loyal, as their patron is their lifeline and they are apt to find it difficult to extend their base beyond him or her (cf. Chen Boda's catastrophic attempt to cultivate Lin Biao's support). This has certain advantages for their patron, who may more readily entrust a favourite with maverick personal missions that an established bureaucrat would not touch. In fact, favourites may deliberately cultivate those aspects of their patron's agenda apt to exacerbate friction with the bureaucratic apparatus and thus enhance their own indispensability to their patron (thus Chen Boda, Zhang Chunqiao, Yao Wenyuan and others enhanced their own strategic importance and informal career prospects by giving voice to Mao's anti-

---

[28]   Zhang Chunqiao utilized his connection to Ke Qingshi to gain access to Mao, Ke's patron. By reading Ke's reports to Mao, he was able to divine Mao's intellectual interests, and on this basis proceeded to draft an essay ("Destroy the Bourgeois Right") for publication in Shanghai's *Jiefang ribao* [Liberation Daily]. Mao read the essay, liked it, and instructed that it be published in *Renmin ribao* (People's Daily), 13 October 1958, with his own commentary attached. Ye Yonglie, *Chen Boda*, pp. 105, 208–9.

[29]   On Jiang Qing's appointment, see Ye Yonglie, *Chen Boda*, p. 163; on the more general importance of secretaries in Chinese politics, see Wei Li and Lucian Pye, "The Ubiquitous Role of the *Mishu* in Chinese Politics", *The China Quarterly*, No. 132 (December 1992), pp. 913–37; and Wei Li, *The Chinese Staff System: A Mechanism for Bureaucratic Control and Integration* (Berkeley: Center for Chinese Studies, Monograph No. 44, 1994).

[30]   Mao first recruited Wang as a personal bodyguard in the Jinggang Mountains when Wang was only 17, and Mao became almost a father to him. Wang cared for Mao when he was sick, and Mao taught Wang to read and write. As Mao's career advanced, he took Wang with him: first to lead the growing security contingent (eventually the "8341" team), then (upon Yang Shangkun's purge in the Cultural Revolution) to serve as director of the General Office of the Party Central Committee. Wang became an alternate Politburo member at the 9th Party Congress, and a full member at the 10th. See Du Feng, "Wang Dongxing, weishemma hui xiatai?" (Why did Wang Dongxing Fall?), *Zhengming* (Hong Kong), No. 30 (April 1980), pp. 34–40.

bureaucratic impulses).[31] Career officials are more likely to balance their patron's requests against their own bureaucratic interests.

The distinction is in reality not sharp and there are all sorts of mixed types. Take Kang Sheng, for example, who had a distinguished *zige* but exclusively in an area of secret police and cadre screening that alienated him from most of his colleagues. He therefore boosted his later career prospects by acting as a favourite, regaining access to the Chairman through Jiang Qing. An interesting mixed type to have emerged since the late 1980s is the so-called "third generation"—and, following them, the so-called princelings party (*taizi dang*). On the one hand, this younger generation of officials fits the category of formal, categorical recruitment, as their upward mobility was launched by the policy of bureaucratic rejuvenation introduced by Deng Xiaoping and Hu Yaobang in the mid-1980s. On the other hand, a rather conspicuous proportion of them are closely related to veteran cadres, beginning with Li Peng and Zou Jiahua, giving rise to suspicions of an underlying informal bias.[32] These "hybrids" may be expected to behave like favourites so long as their relatives are still in a political position to help them out, then to sink or swim based on the power bases and *zige* they have or have not been able to accumulate in the meantime.

Unlike most Western countries, where formal politics is clearly dominant over informal politics and the relationship is one of "imposition and resistance",[33] the Chinese informal sector has been historically dominant, with formal politics often providing no more than a façade for decisions made behind the scenes. Informal politics plays an important part in every organization at every level, but the higher the organization the more important it becomes. At the highest level, because the

---

[31] For example, Chen Boda reportedly promoted the concept of the "people's commune" in print even before Mao uttered his famous oral endorsement at Zhengzhou (in the article "Entirely New Society, Entirely New People", published in *Hongqi* [Red Flag], No. 3 (1 July 1958). Thus, when criticized by Peng Dehuai at Lushan, Mao declared: "I have no claim to the invention of the people's commune, though I made some suggestions". Ye Yonglie, *Chen Boda,* pp. 203, 208–9.

[32] Among the "third generation", Li Peng is Zhou Enlai and Deng Yingchao's adoptive son, and Zou Jiahua, Vice-Premier and (after the 14th Party Congress) full member of the Politburo, is Ye Jianying's son-in-law; Jiang Zemin's relationship to Li Xiannian was so close that Chinese rumours (inaccurately) imputed kinship. See *China Information,* Vol. 4, No. 1 (Summer 1989), pp. 64–68; and *South China Morning Post,* 11 April 1992. For a comprehensive analysis, see M. S. Tanner and M. J. Feder, "Family Politics, Elite Recruitment, and Succession in Post-Mao China", *The Australian Journal of Chinese Affairs,* No. 30 (July 1993), pp. 89–119; and He Ping and Gao Xin, *Zhong gong taizi dang* [Chinese Communist "Princeling" Party] (Hong Kong: Ming Qing, 1992). It should be noted that there is evidence of widespread resentment of the "princelings".

[33] Haruhiro Fukui and Shegeko Fukai, "Election Campaigning in Contemporary Japan", unpublished paper presented at the annual Association for Asian Studies meeting, 2–5 April 1992, Washington DC, p. 1.

tasks to be performed are relatively unstructured, the area of discretion large, personal judgment crucial, the demand for quick decisions great, and secrecy imperative, informal politics prevails. This informal sphere is distinguished from relations within the host organization as a whole by its more frequent contacts, greater degree of goal consensus, loyalty to the informal group, and ability to work together.

An adept leadership, while using informal politics to cobble together a majority within the formal apparatus, will then turn to formal politics to ensure rigorous public policy implementation. This is particularly so since the death of Mao, inasmuch as the diminution in the relative importance of ideology has led leaders to resort to formal-legal rationality as a potent means of legitimation. Whereas previously an official could be dismissed on the grounds of ideological deviation (as defined *ex cathedra* by a Caesero-papist leader), ideology in the post-Mao era has atrophied as grounds for dismissal. Now the exit ramps must be greased with elaborate bureaucratic machinations (as in the case of Hua Guofeng), sometimes even providing a legal façade (as in the trial of the "gang of ten"). Despite such interruptions as Tiananmen, the overall thrust in the reform era has been toward increasing formalization, as measured by the frequency, length and regularity of meeting sessions, and the number of people or procedural stages involved in drafting legislation.

Formal norms also serve a gate-keeping function, defining who can and cannot play. As noted above, without a formal position an informal base has little leverage; thus normally a factional network can be destroyed simply by removing its leader(s) from the formal positions in the organizational "trellis" along which loyalties and informal relations are extended. There are two fascinating exceptions to this generalization that warrant consideration: the two political resurrections of Deng Xiaoping, and the comeback of the veterans who had been "retired" in the mid-1980s to bring down first Hu Yaobang and then Zhao Ziyang. Deng's first and second comebacks, in 1973 and 1977, while greatly facilitated by his informal connections, were both achieved in conformance with the normative rules of the game (that is, by throwing himself upon the mercy of the Supreme Leader). True, neither of his self-criticisms (the letters, needless to say, have not been included in his official *Selected Works*) was sincere. After helping bring the PLA to heel by rotating military region commanders upon his first rehabilitation, Deng essentially abandoned Mao to work intensively with Zhou Enlai, promoting his Four Modernizations program in such a way as to undermine the radical program of "continuing the revolution under the dictatorship of the proletariat". He violated the terms of his second rehabilitation under Hua Guofeng by subtly differentiating his own position on various issues (for instance, on the treatment of intellectuals, on the personality cult, and on the treatment of Mao's legacy) from that of Hua, thereby presenting himself as an alternative and eventually wresting *de facto* leadership from Hua's grasp. Strictly speaking, neither comeback was a pure case of informal politics overcoming a formal verdict; instead, formal norms were skillfully massaged to legitimate a reversal of verdicts. Deng's informal base counted as a potent tool in this operation in two respects: some of his connections (notably Zhou Enlai in the first instance and Ye

Jianying in the second) undoubtedly lobbied on behalf of his return, and Deng's value to Mao (or to Hua) was not purely personal but an ensemble that took into account his vast military and civilian networks.

The second case, the comeback of the "sitting committee" from positions of nominal retirement in the Central Advisory Committee (or even from positions of complete withdrawal from all formal positions) to bring down Hu and Zhao can be explained by three circumstances. First, Deng's own retirement was only nominal, thereby setting an example that legitimized others' reactivation. Second, their retirements had been predicated on their right to name their own successors, in a tacit deal in which the latter continued to welcome their predecessors' "advice". Last but by no means least, their comeback was not a pure case of informal influence overcoming formal power but rather a convergence of informal and formal power. Their informal patron can be assumed to have been Deng Xiaoping, which explains their willingness to be pushed into retirement in the first place; and just as Deng obliged them to retire, he could now invite them back. This was formally legitimated by the device of the "expanded" meeting, which they could attend as observers at the invitation of the convener. In view of the fact that votes were sometimes not taken in such sessions the distinction between full members and observers was minimal.[34]

Thus at the January 1987 meeting urging Hu Yaobang to resign, no fewer than seventeen veteran leaders attended from the Central Advisory Committee and two from the Central Disciplinary Inspection Commission to augment eighteen Politburo members, two alternate members, and four Secretariat members. Bo Yibo, though no longer a member of the Politburo, was delegated to present the case for the prosecution. Deng, who convened the meeting, determined the roster and set the agenda. Ostensibly retired officials played an even more crucial role in the events leading to the crackdown at Tiananmen and the purge of Zhao Ziyang at the Fourth Plenum of the 13th Central Committee.[35]

It would appear that the long-term historical trend is toward political formalization: for example, compare the death of Lin Biao with the trial of the Gang of Four, or the unconstitutional demotion of Hu Yaobang with the Central Committee's plenary dismissal of Zhao Ziyang (actually, the dismissal of Zhao Ziyang and Hu Qili had already been decided upon by the elders a month before, but the fact that such pains were taken to hide this and to convey the impression

---

[34]   Chen Yizi et al (eds), *Zhengzhi tizhi gaige jianghua* [Talks on Political Restructuring] (Beijing: Renmin Chubanshe, 1987), p. 46.

[35]   However, according to recently available documentation, the decision to invoke martial law at Tiananmen Square in May 1989 was made by a formal vote of the Politburo Standing Committee and the informal members did not vote. See *The Tiananmen Papers*, compiled by Zhang Liang, edited by Andrew J. Nathan and Perry Link (New York: Public Affairs, 2001).

of legal procedure is in itself significant).[36] Overall, informal politics remains much more potent in China than in other countries and may be expected to prevail at the highest level well after formal-legal rationality has been superimposed in other areas. The formal rules of the game have the best chance of prevailing when they coincide with informal loyalties. When they do not, a clash may occur in which formal rules will be breached and the depth and breadth of one's informal base is likely to be the most decisive factor. Yet even in the event of such a clash, the winning faction will probably (1) use formal-legal norms and institutionalized expedients (such as Deng's self-criticisms) to augment informal resources prior to the clash, and (2) legitimize victory *post hoc*, via constitutional engineering and the proclamation of new formal norms.

Politics within the highest echelons of the Party is supposed to proceed according to what Teiwes calls "rules of the game", some of them written in such canonical texts as Mao's 1941 speech calling on cadres to rectify their methods of study and Liu Shaoqi's *On Inner-Party Struggle*, published the same year. Among these are the norms of collective leadership and democratic centralism. It is true that all Politburo members are formally equal in the sense that each (including the chair) has but one vote. Yet each member may be assumed to have not only a relatively broad and deep informal base, but to preside over a formal hierarchy as well. (Zhou Enlai for many years controlled the State Council and the foreign ministry; Mao the PLA; Liu and Deng the Party apparatus; Kang Sheng the security apparatus. From the October 1992 14th Party Congress to the 15th Congress five years later, Jiang Zemin was assumed to control the Party apparatus, Qiao Shi the National People's Congress and public security, Liu Huaqing the military, Qian Qichen the foreign ministry, Li Peng and perhaps Zhu Rongji the government bureaucracy.) Though the combination of formal and informal power bases rendered each member of the elite extremely powerful, there was an intra-elite balancing process, in which the functional division of labour and a rough equality consonant with the formal norm of collective leadership were in constant tension with the need for hierarchy.

This need for hierarchy is an informal norm cemented by patron-client relationships within the leadership and activated by a fear of "chaos" (*luan*) outside it: order means hierarchy. Paradoxically, although collective leadership is indeed a Party "norm", it is deemed unstable and a source of potential vulnerability (a "sheet of loose sand") even by many Chinese participant-observers. Thus the "normal" relationship among the Party elite is hierarchical, as indicated by the punctilious observance of protocol on ceremonial occasions (who appears, who mounts the dais in what order, who speaks in what sequence, who stands next to whom in photographs, the sequence in published name lists, and so

---

[36]   *Tiananmen Papers*, pp. 308–14. At the same meeting, on 27 May, the elders reportedly decided upon Jiang Zemin as Zhao's successor, all of which was inconsistent with the Party Statutes.

forth. The implicit cultural model for Chinese elite politics is the imperial court system,[37] the role of emperor being played by what Deng called the Party "core",[38] but which could be termed the "Supreme Leader". The Party hierarchy is somewhat looser than the imperial court, partly because it is informally based and in constant tension with the formal norm of collective leadership, partly because of the ongoing "musical chairs" competition for reallocation of formal hierarchies, and partly because the question of succession is never permanently settled. Yet the need for hierarchy has deep cultural roots, and any challenge to it is apt to provoke panic and extreme responses. *The perceived stability of this leadership hierarchy*, I submit, *is the decisive determinant of whether leadership differences will be settled through negotiated compromise or through a zero-sum struggle*, perchance involving mass publics and resulting in major organizational or "line" changes. Accordingly, I draw a clear analytical distinction between what I call "periods of hierarchical stability" and "periods of hierarchical turbulence". Leadership stability is in turn a function of the magnitude of the various elite cross-pressures alluded to above.

Second, it would seem that despite formal norms of collective leadership, the distribution of actual power within the Party leadership is steeply skewed, relative either to elected (or appointed) executives in pluralist systems or even to Communist Party leaderships in other socialist countries, such as the former East European "people's democracies" or the Soviet Union. There is ample evidence demonstrating that the Supreme Leader has greater access than anyone else at that level to both the intramural levers of bureaucratic power and to the media and symbolism capable of moving the masses in the public arena. In this sense we

---

[37]   Much of the responsibility for this lies with Mao Zedong, who immersed himself deeply in such dynastic histories as the *Shi ji* [Records of this Historian], which covers the period from the Yellow Emperor to the Han dynasty, and *Cu chi tang qian* [General Mirror for the Aid of Government], compiled in the eleventh century, which covers 1,300 years of imperial history, from 403 BC to AD 959). He quoted generously from the classics and generally modeled himself after China's great emperors. See Harrison Salisbury, *The New Emperors: China in the Era of Mao and Deng* (Boston: Little, Brown, 1992), pp. 8–9. In his final year, Mao was going through the *Cu chi tang qian* (which in its standard modern edition runs to 9,612 pages) for the eighteenth time, according to Guo Jinrong, *Mao Zedong de huanghun suiyue* [Mao Zedong's Twilight Years] (Hong Kong, 1990), as cited in W. J. F. Jenner, *The Tyranny of History: The Roots of China's Crisis* (London: Allen Lane, The Penguin Press, 1992), p. 38.

[38]   In an "internal" (*neibu*) speech on 16 June 1989, Deng classified Mao as the leadership core of the first generation and himself as the leadership core of the second generation and designated his client Jiang Zemin as the leadership core of the "third generation". *Zhongguo wenti ziliao zuokan*, Vol. 14, No. 392 (20 November 1989), p. 36.

would agree that the Chinese Communist Party indeed is governed by a Fuehrerprinzip, albeit an informal one.[39]

Inner-Party Debate: Mao expressed himself frequently on the need for full and open debates within the Party, and at the Lushan conference in 1959 he began his counterattack on Peng Dehuai by enjoining his supporters to "listen to bad words". He tried to maintain the impression that there had been full and free debate even at Lushan: "You have said what you have wanted to say, the minutes attest to that. If you do not agree with my views, you can refute them. I don't think it is right to say that one cannot refute the views of the Chairman". Yet close scrutiny of the available records reveals that there were many limits on freedom of discussion. First, Mao had an irascible and domineering personality. He could explode in anger and abuse, as he did in the summer of 1953 in response to some remarks by the venerable Liang Shuming, shouting that Liang had "stinking bones'; or as he did in response to Peng Dehuai's relatively mild and tactful criticisms in 1959 at Lushan.[40] Although Chen Yi claimed in his Cultural Revolution self-criticism that he had "opposed Chairman Mao several times", he

---

[39]   See Leonard Shapiro and John Wilson Lewis, "The Roles of the Monolithic Party under the Totalitarian Leader", in J. W. Lewis (ed.), *Party Leadership and Revolutionary Power in China* (London and New York: Cambridge University Press, 1970).

[40]   The system of hierarchy and the tradition of respect for one's superior put critics in a disadvantageous position. Those in a subordinate position assume a respectful attitude and understate their case, while those in a superior position can take advantage of their position to use forceful language to display their power or even temper. Thus, in his letter, Peng began by writing, "whether this letter is of value for reference or not is for you to decide. If what I say is wrong please correct me". He then confirmed the achievements made in the Great Leap Forward, before pointing out the shortcomings and errors committed by the Party. Even regarding the backyard furnaces, which everyone (including Mao) agreed were a disaster, he merely wrote "there have been some losses and some gains", making his point subtly by reversing the usual order. And he went out of his way to declare these shortcomings and errors were unavoidable and to observe that there were always shortcomings amid great achievements. He attributed these mistakes not to Mao but to the misinterpretation of Mao's instructions by officials and cadres. He asked for a systematic summing up of achievements and lessons gained in the several months since mid-1958 and wrote that "on the whole, there should be no investigation of personal responsibility". He noted finally that now the situation was under control and "we are embarking step by step on the right path". At the end of his letter he quoted Mao's assessment: "The achievements are tremendous, the problems are numerous, experience is rich, the future is bright". In contrast, Mao's criticism of Peng Dehuai was direct and blunt. Peng's letter "constituted an anti-Party outline of Rightist opportunism. It is by no means an accidental and individual error. It is planned, organized, prepared and purposeful. He attempted to seize control of the Party and they wanted to form their own opportunist Party. Peng Dehuai's letter is a program that opposes our general line although it superficially supports the people's communes ... His letter was designed to recruit followers to stage a rebellion. He was vicious and a hypocrite".

contradicted himself later: "Who dares to resist Chairman Mao? No one can do that, because Chairman Mao's prestige is too great". Indeed, if the conversations published in the *Mao Zedong sixiang wansui* volumes are analysed to determine the role of Mao's interlocutors, the Chairman rarely heard any discouraging words, even from those "XXX's", presumably so designated because they were later discovered to be his enemies. Zhang Wentian complained to Peng Dehuai that Politburo meetings "were only large-scale briefing meetings without any collective discussion", and Peng agreed that "in reporting to the Chairman on the current situation, one talks only about the possible and advantageous elements".

Deng disliked Mao's patriarchal leadership style so much that he never sat near him during meetings even though he was deaf in one ear (and when he did sit next to him it was with his deaf ear to Mao), a fact Mao took note of. Yet Deng himself, once rid of Hua, became much more respectful of Mao's legacy than before, and certainly showed in his tactical maneuvers that he had learned from the Helmsman.[41] Indeed, Deng was probably an even more proficient manipulator of bureaucratic levers than Mao, who repeatedly had to resort to outside forums (such as provincial officials, or the "broad masses") to get his way. Deng's gradual seizure of power from a seemingly solidly entrenched Hua Guofeng in 1978–82 was a masterpiece of bureaucratic intrigue. His very bureaucratic virtuosity ultimately made him a rather indifferent supporter of political reform, tearing down many of the reform institutions he had helped to construct when he found it expedient to do so. Thus, paradoxically, he left the paramount leadership role, whose prerogatives he originally decried (and whose formal position he never occupied), stronger and more autonomous than it was when he found it.

Public Contests: The Supreme Leader can use his formal authority to undercut the authority of an opposing faction. The clearest illustration of this is the way Mao handled the case of Lin Biao. At the Second Plenum of the 19th Central Committee at Lushan in August-September 1970, a dispute unexpectedly surfaced between Mao and Lin Biao-Chen Boda over whether the post of Chief-of-State should be abolished, after Mao thought he had disposed of the issue by disavowing interest in the post during preliminary negotiations. After that, Mao systematically used his control over the communication of important documents

---

[41]   "The second fall, it is known, took place at the beginning of the Cultural Revolution . . . Well, this time, too, Chairman Mao tried to protect me. Without success, though, because Lin Biao and the Gang of Four hated me too much. Not as much as they hated Liu Shaoqi, but enough to send me to Shanxi province to do manual labour . . . Even when I was sent to Shanxi . . . Chairman Mao had someone watching over my security. Foreign friends often ask me how it was possible for me to survive all those trials and tribulations, and I usually answer: 'Because I am the sort of person who does not get discouraged easily, because I am an optimist and know what politics is'. But this answer is not the real answer, the complete answer. I could survive because deep in my heart I always had faith in Chairman Mao". Cf. Deng's 1980 interview with Oriana Fallaci, reprinted in *Selected Works of Deng Xiaoping,* pp. 326–35.

to lower-level organizations and his power of appointment to undermine the influence of Lin and his supporters. "Throwing stones", as Mao phrased it, referred to Mao's strategic use of various documents that had an important bearing on the conflict. He took various documents written by Chen Boda, added his own critical comments, and distributed both to lower levels, and he approved the distribution of other documents such as the self-criticisms of military leaders under Lin—Huang Yongsheng, Wu Faxian, Li Zuopeng and Qiu Huizuo—with Mao's marginal criticisms. He also made an inspection trip during which he criticized Lin Biao and Chen Boda in speeches to local officials and commanders.[42] In contrast, the informal channels of communication available to the opposition reached only a very limited number of persons, as the need for secrecy constrained their communications. "Blending sand with soil", again quoting Mao's own wording, referred to Mao's use of his power of appointment to put his own men into the "management group" of the Central Military Commission, which had been staffed exclusively by Lin's followers. "Digging up the cornerstone" referred to his reorganization of the Beijing Military Region. Mao knew that informal groups depend on the formal organizational structure as a "trellis", in Nathan's words, and they can be undermined by invoking formal organizational sanctions to dismantle the trellis.

Though this was not Deng's preferred *modus operandi* and he had less need to do so in view of his consummate mastery of intramural political tactics, Deng was also quite capable of manipulating the *vox populi*. Thus he gladly accepted public support during the first Tiananmen incident of 1976 and in the early phase of the Democracy Wall movement, even giving the young participants clandestine backing. So, too, the article launching the summer 1978 "criterion of truth" debate was written in close collaboration with Hu Yaobang, just as Yao Wenyuan's article launching the Cultural Revolution had been reviewed by Mao. Deng's gradual retirement from formal positions after 1986 put him in a somewhat more awkward position to command public support, as access to the mass media is normally monopolized by formal incumbents. Yet just as Mao created an alternative channel to the media from his informal base in Shanghai, in 1991 Deng arranged through his daughter Maomao (Deng Rong) for a Shanghai newspaper to publish pseudonymous articles attacking conservative policy arguments.And just as Mao took advantage of the (somewhat misleading) impression that he had prematurely been shoved aside by ungrateful colleagues to justify his assault on them in the Cultural Revolution, in Deng's spring 1992 tour of the south (*nan xun*) he capitalized on his lack of formal positions to play the outsider to prod policy reversals by an entrenched centre. Though his conservative opposition did not surrender without resistance, Deng had chosen his symbolic weapons shrewdly, positioning himself in favour of "reform" and

---

[42] See Michael Y. M. Kao, *The Lin Piao Affair: Power Politics and Military Coup* (White Plains: International Arts and Sciences Press, 1975), *passim*, especially the "Introduction".

accelerated economic growth. His position was like that of an emperor, whom no one could openly challenge with impunity but must proceed by indirection (for instance, by impugning a surrogate, or heir apparent).

In sum, the informal role of Supreme Leader is endowed with the following assets: (1) a public image (symbolized since the imperial era by the sun) of not just goodwill but political flawlessness (thus Red Guards deemed any reference to "sun spots" evidence of *lèse majesté*); (2) the final word in the construal of official ideology; (3) a free ambit to act in concert with any combination of colleagues or subordinates at any level in any hierarchical network without fear of accusations of "factionalism"; and (4) privileged access to both internal bureaucratic document flows and public media networks. This has been true throughout the reigns of both Mao Zedong and Deng Xiaoping. The implication is that if and when a cleavage occurs, the Supreme Leader was far more likely to prevail than his challenger, and more likely to win than the incumbent in other Communist party-states in the maneuverings to determine a successor.

This is not to say that the other members of the leadership are completely powerless; were that the case, no elite cleavage would ever materialize. The resources of the Supreme Leader's colleagues are sufficient to stymie his initiatives in a protracted fashion during periods of hierarchical stability, or (at risk of purge) to mount a frontal challenge during a period of hierarchical unrest. The relative power of other Politburo members is a product of (1) their informal connections (*guanxi*) to the Supreme Leader, retaining his "favour'; (2) their formal executive positions beyond Politburo membership (such as Premier or National People's Congress Standing Committee chair); (3) their formal credentials (*zige*); (4) the depth and breadth of their informal bases; and (5) any adventitious situational opportunities that might arise (for example, the Supreme Leader's absence from the capital or serious illness). The Supreme Leader might be thought to control the first two of these resources by dint of his power of appointment and dismissal. But appointees are assumed to have a career-long tenure barring purge, and purge may be politically costly—particularly if a Politburo member has a relatively exalted prestige and a broad informal base (for example, the purges of Peng Dehuai, Liu Shaoqi and Lin Biao alienated many of the cadres in their respective "tails"). Thus a veteran leader may pose a sufficient challenge to a sitting Supreme Leader for the latter to postpone a showdown (as Deng Xiaoping and Chen Yun avoided a confrontation) or to wage a fairly fierce struggle if an open cleavage should eventuate. Yet the power balance is such that the ultimate outcome is not normally in doubt.

The basic leadership configuration within the Politburo may thus vary along two axes: the distribution of agreement and the distribution of power. Although both are continua with many intermediate positions, the polar alternatives may be depicted as shown in Figure 1.

Figure 1:   Patterns of Elite Alignment

Distribution of Agreement

		Cleavage	Solidarity
	Hierarchy	hierarchical discipline	primus inter pares
Distribution of Power	Collegiality	factionalism leadership	collective

Intra-elite cleavage necessarily emerges only when the Supreme Leader becomes engaged; otherwise rivalries may fester for years (like the Kang Sheng-Chen Yun or Jiang Qing-Wang Guangmei grudges). The single issue with the greatest potential to generate a cleavage is that of succession, a triangular affair pitting the Supreme Leader against his heir apparent and also implicating other potential successors. Yet the Supreme Leader is not necessarily the original focus of the dispute. If we review the ten "great line struggles" frequently listed during the Maoist era in Party history texts, few involved an immediate attempt to usurp power. The more typical pattern was for competition in the line of succession to focus on the designated heir apparent, leading the Supreme Leader to purge either the heir or the challengers. (As in traditional imperial court politics, which lacked Western primogeniture rules, maneuverings regarding succession are most likely during the time when a Supreme Leader is perceived to be approaching death, but they can emerge at any time). The purge of Gao Gang and Rao Shushi followed their attempt to displace Liu and Zhou at a time when Mao was introducing arrangements to retire to a "second front'; the Lushan plenum occurred immediately after the installation of Peng Dehuai's old nemesis Liu Shaoqi as heir apparent;[43] and the Cultural Revolution involved Lin Biao's displacement of Liu Shaoqi from that position.

The "September 13 incident" in which Lin Biao died in 1971 involved a more bipolar split between the sitting Supreme Leader and heir apparent, but

---

[43]   Peng's antipathy for Liu apparently dated back to 1940, when Liu presided over a long and gruelling criticism session of Peng after the failed Hundred Regiments campaign. (See Teiwes, *Politics at Mao's Court*, p. 68.) Of course, the purge of Peng Dehuai at Lushan involved many issues, some of them far more salient; the point is merely that succession was among them.

there was also conflict between the Gang of Four and the PLA, as well as friction within Lin's own family.[44] In the reform era, there have been two elite cleavages clearly involving succession. Whereas the purge of Hu Yaobang occurred in the context of a generalized resentment among veteran cadres toward Hu's Party reform program (which had moved them into retirement) and his anti-corruption drive (resulting in the prosecution of some of their children) and was reportedly preceded by friction between Hu and Zhao Ziyang (who criticized Hu's work style in a late 1984 letter to Deng that was read in the meeting deciding upon Hu's demotion),[45] the decisive factor in his fall was Deng's willingness to abandon him to his enemies, probably in response to Hu's attempts to ease Deng into retirement.[46] Zhao Ziyang's fall came in the context of clear signals of his sympathy for democracy activists who were publicly calling for Li Peng's purge and Deng's retirement, and was anticipated by a sharp Zhao-Li Peng rivalry dating from Li's takeover of Zhao's economic portfolio after an inflationary binge the previous summer. All of the above were pre-mortem succession struggles; a post-mortem conflict tends to involve more evenly balanced forces at a time when no Supreme Leader has yet emerged.

A second type of hierarchy disturbance may occur when the Supreme Leader seeks to delegate authority as a way of exploring policy options or circumventing bureaucratic impediments, testing loyalties, or even justifying an intended dismissal—a sort of "unguided missile" launch. The Supreme Leader may thus assign different elites to do contradictory things, delegate several people to perform the same task, violate the chain of command and hold briefings with subordinates without informing their chief. Mao did all of these and more.

---

[44] See the memoirs of Lin Biao's former secretary: Jiao Hua, *Ye Qun zhi mi: Ye Qun yu Lin Biao* (Hong Kong: Cosmos Books, 1993). Ye Qun, Lin Biao's wife, appears to have been a proud and ambitious woman, which may have helped precipitate the 1966 fall of of Lu Dingyi (due to friction between Ye Qun and Su Huiding) and later brought her into conflict with both Jiang Qing and her own daughter, "Doudou".

[45] See Ruan Ming, *Deng Xiaoping diguo* [Deng Xiaoping's Empire] (Taiwan: Shibao Wenhua Chuban Qiye Youxian Gongsi, 1992), pp. 188–91. Hu Qili reportedly also provided information for the January meeting critical of his erstwhile patron.

[46] Hu, having been appointed Party Secretary-General, was apparently under the delusion that he was really in command. So he reportedly went to Deng and asked him to cede his power: "Be an example. I cannot work efficiently while you are still in power". Moreover, he allowed his ambitions to become public. When Lu Deng asked him in 1986, "Why do you have to wait until Deng dies to become Central Military Commission chair?" he was silent. Not too long afterward, the *Washington Post* interviewed Hu: "Who is going to replace Deng as chair of the Central Military Commission?" Hu replied: "We will solve this problem once and for all at the Party's 13th Congress. No one can be in a post forever". See Pang Pang, *The Death of Hu Yaobang*, translated by Si Ren (Honolulu: University of Hawaii, Centre for Chinese Studies, 1989), pp. 42–3.

For example, Mao reportedly complained to Gao Gang about Liu Shaoqi, Zhou Enlai and other White area cadres at the time he was setting up the "two fronts" within the Politburo, giving Gao grounds to hope he might displace them.[47] The Chairman consorted with Bo Yibo in formulating the Ten Great Articles without first clearing this with Bo's superior, Zhou Enlai.[48] During the Cultural Revolution, Mao simultaneously delegated a central work conference in October 1965 to look into the case of Wu Han and instigated an informal group in Shanghai to launch its own inquiry and to write a polemical article assailing Wu (keeping his involvement with the Shanghai group secret). He set up the Cultural Revolution Group under Peng Zhen's chairmanship, and Peng circulated the "February (1966) Outline Report on the Current Academic Discussion" ("February Outline Report" [Eryue tigang]) only after travelling to Wuhan on 5 February to get Mao's approval. But meanwhile Mao personally supervised the February Summary (Eryue qiyao) based on a more radical meeting on literary and art work in the armed forces conducted by Lin Biao and Jiang Qing in the period 2-20 February 1966. Mao personally revised this latter the document three times before having it circulated through inner-Party channels, and a few months later he discredited the February Outline and disbanded the Cultural Revolution Group. At a time when he was covertly inspiring a Red Guard insurrection against the cadre work teams launched by the "bourgeois reactionary headquarters" of Liu Shaoqi and Deng Xiaoping, he was also apparently suspicious of his latest chosen successor, Lin Biao, as he confided in a confidential letter to Jiang Qing.[49] Three years later, while still naming Lin Biao his successor in the Constitution of the 9th Party Congress, he also made a bid to the radicals, telling Lin that as he was getting old, Lin, too, should have a successor—Zhang Chunqiao would be a good candidate.[50] Mao seems to have encouraged the Gang of Four to formulate a slate of government appointments for the 4th National People's Congress in early 1975, while to his senior colleagues he expressed nothing but scorn for these efforts. During Mao's final year in power his actions were typically ambivalent: he backed Deng's measures to carry out the Four Modernizations program and defended him from the Gang, but simultaneously he allowed his own inflammatory ideological comments to be propagated, while sanctioning the efforts of such would-be theorists as Zhang

---

[47]   Du Feng, "Can the Gao Gang Dilemma Be Resolved?" *Zhengming*, No. 37 (1 November 1980), pp. 18–19.

[48]   I am indebted to Professor Peter N. S. Lee for this point.

[49]   Mao wrote the letter revealing his uneasy state of mind on 8 July 1966, though it was not publicly revealed until after Lin Biao was killed on 13 September 1971. He was apparently perturbed by Lin Biao's speech at an extended meeting of the Politburo on 18 May 1966 warning against *coups d'état*. Ye Yonglie, *Chen Boda*, p. 280.

[50]   Wang Nianyi, *1949–1989 niande Zhongguo: datong luande niandai* [China in 1949–1989: An Era of Harmony and Chaos] (Henan: Henan Renmin Chubanshe, 1988), pp. 387–8.

Chunqiao and Yao Wenyuan, who wrote major exegeses on class struggle and proletarian dictatorship that could not have been so widely publicized without his endorsement. Both Liu Shaoqi during the various struggle sessions against him in the Cultural Revolution and Jiang Qing during her trial a decade later insisted resolutely that they were doing only what Mao had told them to do; though Mao had publicly repudiated one and not the other, both may have been right.

Deng Xiaoping seems to have been less apt to delegate various subordinates to conflicting (or identical) assignments, but no less willing to give them relatively "hot potatoes" for which he would then claim credit if they succeeded or scapegoat them if they failed. Certainly, Hu Yaobang had grounds to assume he had Deng's support in his campaign to rejuvenate the Party and to retire Party elders. Zhao Ziyang also claimed to have had Deng's authorization to pursue a soft line toward the protesters during the first two weeks of May 1989. Yet both found themselves abandoned when their opponents saw an opportunity to counterattack. Both the 1986 campaign for political reform and the summer 1988 experiment with price reform also appear to have originated with Deng, who left first Hu and then Zhao holding the bag.

A third type of elite cleavage consists of the continuation of policy debate by other means, to parody Clausewitz. Policy disputes tend to escalate when the leadership is in a quandary—an open-ended situation offering several feasible options, with chances for relative gains by various factions. Indeed, the more serious the problems confronting the Party, the greater the legitimacy of raising differing views and alternatives about which groups might differ. In the first half of 1962, in the wake of the Great Leap Forward's failure, redistributing land to the individual household was suggested, as was the foreign policy alternative of reconciliation with imperialists, revisionists and reactionaries, and cutting off aid to national liberation movements. As we now know, this was at a time of perhaps the gravest crisis in Party history, when millions of people were starving to death as a consequence of the Great Leap Forward (some thirteen and a half million, according to official PRC statistics).

The issues raised by the democracy marchers in April-May 1989 were also far-reaching, involving the legitimation of autonomous associations within a bounded civil society. Such policy issues provide the provocation for a dispute, but do not necessarily define the contending parties. Thus Zhou Enlai's position on the Cultural Revolution (as on most policy issues) coincided more closely with that of Liu and Deng than with Mao's, but he switched his position in time for the Eleventh Plenum of the 8th Central Committee and threw his lot in with the radicals.

In short, disagreement may begin over policy issues, but at some point fairly early in the struggle a weighing of the political capital controlled by the various contenders occurs and parties to the conflict choose sides strategically, eventually precipitating a bandwagon effect based on opportunistic considerations. The more evenly matched the factional contenders, the more protracted and bitter the struggle is likely to be (cf. the 1930s conflict between Mao and the so-called Returned Students); the more imbalanced, the shorter and more easily resolved (cf. the Deng-Hu and Deng-Zhao splits). In such confrontations, *ceteris paribus*, the faction chief with the broadest and deepest base and most distinguished *zige* will prevail. As noted above, this tends to skew the outcome in favour of the Supreme Leader. Yet even at the height of polarization there is a large group of individuals who do not belong to any of the principal factions. Most leading officials are neither "leftists" nor "rightists", but somewhere in between. The existence of this group of "free-floaters" (*zhuzhong tiaohe pai*) exercises a certain constraint on the "leftists" and "rightists", who are relatively few in number but exercise a disproportionate influence in politics. Finally, policy disagreements were "normally" resolved within the elite without including outside forces. That has been the norm since the publication of Liu's *On Inner-Party Struggle* in 1941, and after the Cultural Revolution and Mao's death the Party has sought to reaffirm that norm. The most explosive confrontations are those that are publicly vented, giving one faction the option of manipulating the masses against another. In such cases (cf. the 1966, 1976, 1978, 1986 and 1989 clashes), rhetorical and promotional skills may also play a role in the outcome.

The Impact of Reform

The question of the impact of reform is of course complex, deserving far more empirical research than has yet been conducted,[51] but a few preliminary hypotheses may be suggested. First, the overall decline in the perceived efficacy of ideology (with the inadvertent assistance of the regime) and the increasing importance of purpose-rational relationships have had both an emancipatory and a corrosive impact upon *guanxi*: emancipatory because with the relaxation of constraints on lateral communication brought about by the end of "class struggle" and the spread of the market economy, contacts of all types are multiplying. At the same time, the reform's impact is corrosive in the sense that such connections have become suffused with utilitarian considerations. As a consequence, the dichotomy introduced earlier between value-rational and purpose-rational relationships has tended to break down. A new type of connection has emerged that is at once more instrumental and less sentimental (see Figure 2).

In this figure, the "pure" or Weberian types of relationship are either purpose-rational (highly purposive, low in value: "commodified") or value-rational (low in purpose, high in value: "sentimental"). "Bureaucratism" (a term for relationships neither value- nor purpose-rational) has been (for obvious reasons) negatively valued in both the Maoist and reform eras. The new hybrid *guanxi* is, however, *both* value-rational and purpose-rational, to the consternation of more traditional types who deplore the adulteration of value-rational relationships with considerations of short-term material interest. Here, one uses

---

[51]   See Peter N. S. Lee, "Informal Politics and Leadership in Post-Mao China", unpublished paper presented at the annual Association for Asian Studies meeting, Washington DC, 2-5 April 1992.

Figure 2:   Reform and Informal Relationships

Mixed Relationships

Purpose

	High	Low
High *Value*	*guanxi* (new) "hybrid"	*guanxi* (old) "sentimental"
Low	market "commodified"	bureaucratic (neutral)

connections cultivated for their intrinsic value as an instrument to achieve other ends, or even cultivates "connections" with material gains in mind. This is particularly noticeable at lower levels, where cadres with direct responsibility for managing the economy are constantly offered new opportunities for rent-seeking behaviour. The other tendency is for networks of connections to metastasize throughout society at large, with the breakdown of the previously impermeable boundaries of the "basic work unit". The ultimate upshot remains to be seen, of course, but the trend is for *guanxi* to become indistinguishable from collegial or other superficially affective business associations.

At the highest elite levels, still protected from the market by a combination of reasonably high salaries and a comprehensive free-supply system, material interests have not yet adulterated value-rational relationships in any obvious way. Yet, an increasing purpose-rationality has also made its appearance here.

Previously, factions were primarily motivated by personal security considerations, as Pye has noted. But in the course of reform, security is no longer in such short supply; on the contrary, there has been an attempt to legalize tenure arrangements and to restore popular respect for officialdom. The bloody crackdown on the "masses" at Tiananmen should not blind us to the fact that disciplinary measures against members of the political elite have become much milder than before. The Liuist barriers shielding the Party from populist monitoring (from mass protests and big-character posters, for example) have been re-erected, and whereas rectification campaigns and purges have not been altogether discontinued, they have been far less sweeping than before, sparing the leading "targets" from public humiliation and other severe sanctions.[52] Hua

---

[52]   For a perceptive review of Party rectification under the 1980s reforms, see Ch'i Hsi-sheng, *Politics of Disillusionment: The Chinese Communist Party under Deng Xiaoping, 1978–*

Guofeng retained a seat on the Central Committee, Hu Yaobang died a full member of the Politburo, and even Zhao Ziyang retained Party membership and has been seen on the golf course. Moreover, the secularization of Mao Zedong Thought that has accompanied Deng's pragmatic focus on growth at any cost, and the attendant dismissal of the spectres of a "struggle between two lines" and "people in the Party taking the capitalist road", have reduced the ideological barriers to the operation of factions. Though still denied and forbidden,[53] factional behaviour has become somewhat less clandestine. The upshot is that contemporary elite factions have begun to engage in the active pursuit of policies that are perceived to enhance the interests of their constituencies, not merely in furtive self-defense and attack maneuvers.

Figure 3:   Reform and Elite Coalitions

		Action General	Particular
Structure	Formal	bureaucratic politics	independent kingdom
	Informal	policy group	faction

In the course of reform, though, the dominant trend has been, clockwise, from factions toward bureaucratic politics. Independent kingdoms have always been taboo, and their empirical incidence seems to have declined since Liberation, given the centre's enhanced power to rotate cadres. At present, the emergent operational form is the "policy group". This is informally constituted but takes coherent positions on policy issues of interest to its constituency. Take,

1989 (Armonk: M. E. Sharpe, 1991), pp. 170–257. In this connection, it is noteworthy that when Liu Shaoqi's works on Party rectification were republished after his posthumous rehabilitation, the "unity" (*tuanjie*) and conciliatory themes (already ascendant) were emphasized, while discussions of contradiction and inner-Party struggle were toned down.

53   Zhao Ziyang, Li Peng and Deng Xiaoping, for example, all emphasized the non-existence of factions within the Party leadership in speeches immediately after the 13th Party Congress in 1987. See Suisheng Zhao, "The Feeble Political Capacity of a Strong One-Party Regime: An Institutional Approach toward the Formulation and Implementation of Economic Policy in Post-Mao Mainland China" (Part One), *Issues and Studies*, Vol. 26, No. 1 (January 1990), pp. 47–81.

for example, the so-called petroleum faction (Yu Qiuli, Gu Mu, Li Shiguang, Kang Shi'en). Though classically constituted via loyalties formed while exploiting the Daqing oil fields in the early 1960s, this grouping cohered in defense of energy, heavy industry and central planning. Though purged in the mid-1980s, it was succeeded by a new functional grouping headed by Chen Yun. Or consider the 1980s coalition of Deng Liqun's propaganda apparatus with Chen Yun's planning and heavy industry group in defense of complementary bureaucratic interests.[54] A policy group is a hybrid association that is on its way to bureaucratic politics but has not yet arrived. Recruitment to a policy group still seems to be based on patronage rather than issue-orientation, and loyalty to the patron tends in the event of elite cleavage to override bureaucratic interests. This, then, is a "half-rationalized" (that is, policy-oriented but still personalistic) form of factionalism corresponding to the "half-reformed" status of the Chinese political system.

A second result of reform is that with increasing decentralization and market autonomy, there is growing latitude for various forms of cleavage to come into increasingly open competition. This may involve conflicts among informal relations: splits among groups based on repressed cleavages—class background, geographic origin, Tiananmen, Democracy Wall, the Cultural Revolution; or conflict between formal and informal bases (Deng Xiaoping mobilizing old cronies to purge Hu and Zhao). Decentralization opens the way to conflicts among formal bases: central versus local, region versus region (such as the rich and cosmopolitan eastern seaboard versus the poorer internal provinces), and market versus planning bureaucracies. At least three factors have made it likely that these conflicts will not be suppressed, as has often been the case in the past, but instead increasingly openly aired. First, the decline of ideology renders more options legitimate, more arguments open to discussion. The "pragmatization" of Mao's thought entails that nationalism, regionalism, avocational pursuits (stamp collectors, martial arts devotees) and other particular interests all operate according to their own "laws" and need no longer be repudiated. Second, the extraordinary growth of the market and the existence of extrabudgetary funds, independent financial accounting and so forth implies that there are ample resources available to the contending forces in any such cleavages. At the same time, marketization tends to remove from the political game the traffic in material commodities (these are now openly available through the price system), reserving

---

[54]   See Charles Burton, *Political and Social Change in China Since 1978* (New York: Greenwood, 1990), pp. 63–4. It soon became clear to Deng Liqun that most threatening to the interests of the constituency of propaganda workers was devolution of authority to lower levels, because maintaining an "orthodoxy" demands uniformity though central coordination (namely, the "Party's unified leadership"). This threw Deng Liqun into the arms of Chen Yun. The conditions defined by the reformers as necessary to economic development were seen to be antagonistic to those required for effective political and ideological work.

the use of factionalism more exclusively for political and other extra-market transactions. Third, the impact of Tiananmen haunts not only would-be protesters with the spectre of violent suppression; a national leadership increasingly dependent upon international capital and upon commodity and service markets also has become more sensitive to the need to avoid ostracism and sanctions.

Conclusions

To sum up, informal politics can be defined on the basis of a combination of behavioural, structural and cyclical criteria. Behaviourally, informal politics consists of value-rational as opposed to purpose-rational relationships functioning in the service of a personal base. Informal politics tends to be implicit and covert (*neibu*) rather than explicit and public. It tends to be flexible, casual and irregular rather than institutionalized. Structurally, informal politics may be assumed to affect the leadership strata more than routine administration, and high-level leadership more than low-level. This informality is a function of discretionary latitude and is limited to small, closed groups. The structural circumstances most conducive to informal politics are those in which the leadership is beset by a crisis not resolvable through standard operating procedures, permitting the existing hierarchical monopoly to break down into a more open competition among elites. Informal politics tends to occur at those times in the political cycle when this type of structural breakdown is most likely to occur—particularly leadership successions, of course, but other national crises as well.

Is the political cycle of stable hierarchy versus polarized conflict correlated to the business cycle that has materialized under the economic reforms?[55] Looking back in time for clues, elite cleavages appeared in the past at or near times of economic boom (Gao Gang, the Cultural Revolution, Hu Yaobang) and bust (Deng Xiaoping's second comeback in December 1978, Zhao Ziyang's fall). More important than the market's top or bottom, perhaps, is whether the cycle has reached an outer limit at which at least one faction within the leadership is prepared to fight "against the current" for a correction.

As a political form, informal politics in contemporary China is Janus-faced. It tends to be substantively "progressive", as its flexibility facilitates more rapid change by offering short-cuts to standard bureaucratic procedures. This has helped make China an extraordinarily well-led country compared to others in the Third World (albeit not always wisely governed). Paradoxically, it is at the same time "reactionary" in its procedural implications, tending to reinforce traditional hierarchical relationships (including the "cult" of leadership inherited from the empire) and culturally embedded political relationships more generally (for

---

[55]   This question is taken up in Lowell Dittmer, "Patterns of Leadership in Reform China", in Arthur L. Rosenbaum (ed.), *State and Society in China: The Consequences of Reform* (Boulder: Westview, 1992), pp. 529–36.

instance, time-honoured primordial "connections"), at the expense of rational-legal and meritocratic arrangements.

The outlook is further complicated by the fact that informal politics must be assumed to have been evolving along with everything else. Generally speaking, we would conclude that informal politics under Deng was undergoing a process of rationalization, with a tendency to backslide during periods of crisis. This is visible, first of all, in the growing institutionalization of various bureaucratic "systems" at all but the highest levels. These became increasingly dependent on explicit rules, procedural regularization, and so forth. Second, as noted above, informal groups have become increasingly oriented not merely to the maximization of power and the minimization of risk but to the promotion of policies designed to enhance their bureaucratic interests. Thus, at the mass level, informal groups seem to be undergoing a transition to professional, avocational and business groupings; and at the elite level, to political pressure groups or even quasi-parties (that is, "reformers" versus "conservatives"). Yet as indicated, myriad qualifications and exceptions are in order: this will be a "march of 10,000 li". That was plainly visible in the crises that provoked the ejection of first Hu Yaobang and then Zhao Ziyang from the line of succession, which involved a bureaucratically irrational splintering of the so-called reform grouping.

TWO

Factions and the Politics of *Guanxi*: Paradoxes in Chinese Administrative and Political Behaviour

Lucian W. Pye

Lowell Dittmer has provided a thoughtful and constructive review of various efforts to understand the workings of personal relationships in Chinese politics, and proposes an elegant analytical framework for future research. It is an important study above all because he seeks to bring order and analytical clarity to one of the most fundamental aspects of Chinese political behaviour. In the process he displays an impressive command of the details of elite relations during both the Mao Zedong and Deng Xiaoping eras.

Yet by pushing nearly to the limits the potential for theoretical neatness, he also, I believe, reveals the limitations of generalized analysis of the subject and why there is need for greater contextual sensitivity of a more particularistic nature. The rules of personal relationships in Chinese politics, and especially the workings of *guanxi*, do not follow precise or constant formulations but are rather nuanced and subtle, for they accord to the particular situation. Dittmer does, nevertheless, provide a clearer overview of some fundamental features of Chinese public life which have been under-appreciated or misunderstood. Thus, while there may be some problems with his formulations, there are also pay-offs from the effort which may be more significant than the issues he addresses.

Before discussing the conceptual problems I find in his formulations, let me first state that I greatly appreciate his acknowledgment of the merits of my theory that factional relations among cadres in the Mao era were very much driven by an anxious search for security in a danger-filled political environment. We now have extensive new documentation from the flood of memoirs, autobiographical writings and reports of participants and observers of life in the inner circle of the Chinese leadership which reveal the dark mood of personal insecurity that prevailed in the Party even while the public rhetoric was one of triumphal joy. China did not have Stalin's petrifying reign of state terror. Rather, Chinese politics operated in an atmosphere of tension in which everyone sensed the need always to be careful and calculating about what was done or said. Mao's doctor Li Zhisui tells of the anxieties and at times near panic which possessed those who inhabited Zhongnanhai, because everyone below the Chairman needed protectors and allies since they could never be sure that they would not become a target of suspicion.[1] The more vivid and detailed picture we now have of elite relations in both Beijing and in the provinces makes questionable the idea that the Chinese Communist Party ever had a "code of civility".[2]

In the same spirit of constructive criticism as Dittmer has displayed, let me turn to an evaluation of the two pairs of concepts that I believe are at the core of his proposal as to how we can best advance our understanding of Chinese political behaviour. The two pairs are, first, the distinction between "formal" and "informal" in politics, and second, his classification of relationships as being either "value-rational" or "purpose-rational". It seems to me that these concepts, when applied in the Chinese context, turn out to be less clear-cut and empirically testable than is desirable for theory building. The very problems, however, serve to illuminate significant features of Chinese politics that will increasingly demand more attention, especially as the cloak of ideology continues to fray.

Is There a Distinction between "Formal" and "Informal" in Politics?

As a start, I have some difficulties with the concepts of "formal" and "informal" as applied to politics. In political science the distinction between "formal" and "informal" came out of the study of administrative behaviour and the processes of decision-making in organizations. Chester Barnard, Robert Merton and Peter Blau, among others, initiated the idea that we need to look behind the formal structures of organizations and try to identify who in fact are the key

---

[1]   Li Zhisui, *The Private Life of Chairman Mao* (New York: Random House, 1994).

[2]   It is troubling that for a long time it was possible for China specialists to write of the "Round table spirit" that Mao, as the first among equals, presided over in Yanan when in fact the first four competing leaders to Mao were either killed or exiled. On this, see David Apter and Tony Saich, *Revolutionary Discourse in Mao's Republic* (Cambridge: Harvard University Press, 1994, p. 35). It is furthermore odd that while many China specialists have no trouble imagining that the McCarthy era was filled with paralysing fear for American academics, they have been strangely insensitive to the role of fear in Chinese elite relations. It is even stranger that political scientists in general have not picked up on Montesquieu's observation that fear is the key element in tyrannies, and therefore the discipline has never had a general theory of the psychodynamics of fear as a critical factor in various kinds of political systems. There have been numerous accounts of the use of terror and cruelty in particular situations, but not any general theories.

actors in any actual decision-making process.[3] In their writings, formal structures were defined by tables of organization and legally constituted arrangements, whereas informal structures involved the actual dealings among those who were in fact making the organization's decisions. One person or group might be formally in charge but informally others would in fact be making the decisions, and therefore power relationships usually do not conform to the lines of the official chain of command. Another way of stating this is that the informal is the "politics" of an organization while the formal is its legal arrangements or structures.

Politics, however, is not administration, and there are no neat boundaries between what might be thought of as official and unofficial politics. When the American president "works the phones" to get critical Congressional votes or when lobbyists walk the corridors of the Capitol to persuade legislators to support their interests, such activities are just ordinary politics, neither formal nor informal. Politics is the process of making authoritative decisions in which—using the currency of power—interests, values and preferences contend with each other. The "game" of "who gets what, when, and how" really has no formal or informal aspects.

At least in political science that is the way we have generally thought about politics as distinct from administration. The problem is that the People's Republic of China presents an awkward case precisely because its Leninist Party-state arrangement blurs any meaningful line between administration and politics. The intertwining of Party and state hierarchies in a setting that is not well institutionalized makes somewhat irrelevant any attempt to distinguish between formal legal structures and informal power relationships. Indeed, Chinese administration is essentially politics, and the constraints that do exist are not so much legal regulations as the realities of power relationships.

This is a problem, however, that goes deeper than just the Chinese adoption of a Leninist system because it was a part of the Confucian tradition in which law was not the basis of administration. Didn't we all learn in our first classes in Chinese politics that China follows the tradition of rule by men and not by laws? In imperial China there was, however, a strong sense of a moral order and there were powerful constraints based on rules of ritualized Confucian behaviour. Thus, while traditional Chinese culture did not instil in officials and citizens a sense of awe for the majesty of the law, it did have a body of moral precepts and rules of correct conduct that provided the mystique of legitimacy.

---

[3]   Chester I. Barnard, *The Functions of the Executive* (Cambridge, Mass.: Harvard University Press, 1938, 1962); Robert K. Merton, *Social Theory and Social Structure* (Glencoe, Ill.: The Free Press, 1949, revised and enlarged 1957); Peter Blau, *The Dynamics of Bureaucracy* (Chicago: University of Chicago Press, 1955, 1963).

Thus, with respect to traditional China it might be said that there was a distinction between formal and informal according to whether or not actions adhered to the established moral norms of the Confucian order or responded to private considerations. The Confucian moral order was in a sense the functional equivalent of the legal systems of the West. In both cases there were accepted differences between proper and improper conduct.

In today's China there is neither a legal system nor a moral order that has been adequately internalized so as to govern the behaviour of officials. It is true that Chinese political rhetoric is still highly moralistic, but today hypocrisy rests lightly on most officials. Indeed, one should not put much weight on the distinction between what the Chinese leaders pretend their system to be and what it is actually like.[4] Surely we all know by now that in the succession process, when the talk is of a "harmonious collective leadership" it means that the struggle for power has in fact become more intense. And we certainly know that pronouncements about "consensus" at the top are really a Chinese way of putting a gloss on authoritarianism.

Similarly, it is not very helpful to treat the distinction between formal and informal as that between what is open and what is secret in Chinese politics because, as everyone knows, China has one of the world's most secretive political systems and what is out in the open is usually not very significant.

At times Dittmer identifies the formal with the official organizational position and the informal with personal interests. But this is also a slippery distinction, as is apparent when he suggests that Deng Xiaoping out of principle "relied exclusively on official power". This hardly squares with the power wielded by China's paramount leader in ruling 1.2 billion Chinese by mumbling a few cryptic words when the only official title he had was that of Honorary Chairman of the All-China Bridge Players' Association. As his daughter made clear in her hagiography of him, Deng Xiaoping was never in his career constrained by any job description of his posts. He was much too active in building relationships.[5]

In any case, whatever the basis for the distinction between formal and informal one might choose to use, there is, I am afraid, simply not enough operational concreteness to the concepts or clear enough boundaries between them to allow one to test as hypotheses the question as to whether it is the "formal that influences the informal" or the "informal that shapes the formal". It

---

[4]   It does seem that Chinese officials have two contradictory responses to legal formalities. On the one hand, they are prone to totally ignore them, as for example the guarantees in their constitution for freedom of speech, assembly and the press. On the other hand, they are also quick to point out the failings of other parties to uphold international agreements and to extol their own righteousness in both moral and legalistic terms.

[5]   Deng Maomao, *Deng Xiaoping: My Father* (New York: Basic Books, 1994).

is true that among Anglo-Saxons hypocrisy did work for progress by making gentlemen behave better than they were wont to do, but it takes a great stretch of the imagination to believe that the rhetorical pretensions of the Chinese leaders will shortly become Chinese realities. The whole system is founded too firmly upon the art of feigned compliance, and the practice of comfortably saying one thing while doing another, for pretensions to change actual behaviour. The leadership appreciates far too much the advantages of operating in the shadows of a closed system to want to bring their decision-making processes out into the open.

Therefore, instead of trying to treat "informal" politics as somehow an elusive and hard-to-get-at dimension of Chinese politics, it is, I believe, necessary to acknowledge that the "informal" is very nearly the sum total of Chinese politics. Which is to say that the Chinese political system (1) is not well institutionalized, (2) is not government by a binding legal system and (3) largely operates in secret and out of public scrutiny.

Yet (and here we come to a positive pay-off) the very limitations of Dittmer's formulation point to a very fundamental feature of Chinese politics that goes well beyond the domain of elite personal relationships. The fact that it is so hard to make any meaningful distinctions between "formal" and "informal" shows that China lacks an institutionalized administrative system that is based on either a moral or a legal order. The behaviour of high-level officials is not constrained by any sense of awe either of the majesty of the law or of a system of ethical virtues. They are constrained by the power of others, that is to say, by the play of politics. Thus, Chinese administration is politics, but politics of a peculiar and highly personalized nature. Even during Mao's rule, when ideology was supposedly all important, the structure of authority was not disciplined by generalized rules or precise regulations but rather by a shared understanding about the importance of experience, status, seniority and particularistic relationships. Starting with admission into the ranks of the Party, which required the recommendations and personal vouching of two established members, career advancement and the accumulation of power depended upon the dynamics of acquaintanceships and of personal and professional relationships. The flat edict that this should not be the case only made the personal networking the more essential for everyone's security.

In operational terms the Chinese concept of administration entails a structure of authority which is governed by human relationships that extend from the "leading figure" to his deputies and on down a chain of status relationships. Superiors and subordinates fit together, not by a book of rules but by the more deeply ingrained rules of proper human relationships. Authority lies not in an objectified body of laws or moral codes, but in subjective understandings of the meaning of leadership, superior-subordinate relationships, and the rewards of showing deference to higher status and in return accepting command over inferiors. In a system of rule by men, not by laws, successful governance requires skills in reading character, building and maintaining personal relationships, and meticulously performing one's expected roles.

The Quagmire of Rationality and the Denial of Interests

A second theoretical distinction that Lowell Dittmer employs which gives me trouble is that between "value-rational" and "purpose-rational" relationships. The former is a relationship in which "the other is valued as an end in itself"—presumably like a true friendship or love—and the latter is a relationship "in which the other is merely a means to other ends"—as is standard in *guanxi* connections.[6] My problem here, as with the first pair of concepts, lies both at the level of general theoretical analysis and at the more particularistic level of Chinese realities.

At the general level the concept of rationality presupposes that actors have coherent motives, and this leads directly into a quagmire of having to fathom what in fact are the purposes or motives of those being studied. What makes the social sciences inherently different from the physical sciences is that the objects of analysis, human beings, possess the capacity to act in terms of willpower and commitment of purpose. The pay-offs from correctly knowing the purposes of those being studied are so great that we are always tempted to believe that we in fact know what they are. For example, if you can see the calendar of even the most peripatetic scholar, you can make some astonishingly accurate predictions as to precisely where he or she will be at various particular dates in the future. But of course the trouble is that it is extremely difficult to judge motives, especially in the realm of politics where actors have good reasons for masking their purposes, even if they do know what these are. The analyst has to fall back upon the rather unreliable tests of either plausibility ("his actions *make sense* if such-and-such were his motives") or empathy ("regardless of the consequences of his actions, he must have had such-and-such worthy intentions"). The fact that purpose is a subjective and always hidden matter means that it is possible to arrive at what can be outlandish "explanations" based on "what makes sense".[7]

---

6   Dittmer is correct in saying that although he borrowed the terms from Max Weber, he gives them a different meaning. For Weber "ends rational" behaviour or *Wertrationbalitaet* are actions in which there is a direct causal relationship between the ends and the means employed toward a goal, while "instrumental rational" behaviour entails actions which are not purposeful when seen in isolation but which become meaningful when seen in a larger context—such as the apparently "irrational" behaviour of a man tightening bolts on a "rational" assembly line—behaviour which Charlie Chaplin in *Modern Times* made into a memorable satire of the irrationality of factory work.

7   To show how treacherous the problem of motivation can be, let me suggest that it is possible to make the case that Mao Zedong's actions from 1956 on can be explained as

The problem in the Chinese case is peculiarly difficult because the concept of rationality also presupposes that the actors have interests, but in both traditional and Communist cultures there has been a powerful taboo against asserting any particularistic or private interests. The cardinal sin has always been any behaviour that might suggest selfishness; and thus politically the articulation of interests has been severely suppressed. The wisdom and benevolence of the rulers is supposed to take care of everyone's interests, and therefore nobody is supposed to have to advance any particular interests. Individualism is out, and only the claims of the group—be it family, lineage or nation—can have legitimacy.

All of which means that it is peculiarly difficult to determine the rationale for public acts, and hence the basis of any particular relationship. It is therefore not surprising that Dittmer has problems distinguishing between the two types of relationships and that he is led to conclude that with the Deng reforms the dichotomy "has tended to break down". Indeed, he goes further and says that relationships can be *both* value-rational and purpose-rational. But for him this is only a "new hybrid *guanxi*" that has come with the reforms. If his theory allows for a relationship to be of both types, then I would think that one should concede that just about all relationships among the leadership have probably had elements of both at all times.[8]

"making sense", and thus totally "rational", if it is assumed that he was operating under the guidance of the CIA: first he deprived China of its intellectuals during the Anti-Rightist Campaign, then he went after the peasants with the Great Leap Forward, then he tore the Party and government apart and destroyed faith in ideology with the Cultural Revolution, and then he broke with the Soviet Union and avoided involvement in the Vietnam War by insisting that revisionism was worse than imperialism, and finally he invited President Nixon to China. It all fits a "reasonable" pattern, right? And of course his anti-American rhetoric was just his cover.

It is puzzling that as scholars we can be so glib in identifying the motivations of public figures when in terms of our own lives most of us would be hard put to explain our motives, for example in writing books and articles. Is it because we really believe that we are advancing knowledge (Dittmer's "value-rational"), or is it to get tenure (his "purpose-rational"), or is it to show off, or is it just because we are conforming to our peer group and doing what is expected of us? Who knows?

[8]   Dittmer seems a bit more sympathetic to the politics of ideology of the Mao era and appears to look down on the relationships of the reform era. Thus he suggests that in the earlier period relationships were more value-rational and that they became more purpose-rational starting with Deng's reforms. The fact that the role of *guanxi* is more openly recognized now does not mean that it did not play an equally significant role behind the mask of ideological rhetoric. Back in the Mao period the cadres were just as eager to get ahead, find security, and improve their status, both politically and materially, as they are today. From what we are now learning about life among the Chinese elite under Mao, it is naive to believe any longer that the officials were simple-

Yet, just as the problem of the dichotomy between formal and informal pointed to a larger issue about Chinese administrative behaviour, so this problem with the two types of rationality illuminates an even bigger problem of Chinese politics: the persistent denial of people's rights and needs to articulate their diverse interests. The consequence of this pretence that private interests are shameful and illegitimate has been that China never developed a genuine political process. The very essence of politics is the contending of competing interests, and when interests cannot be acknowledged openly there can be no true politics. For as Bernard Crick, in the spirit of Aristotle, has eloquently argued, "politics is a great and civilizing human activity" precisely because it is an activity through which contending interests are conciliated, differences are expressed and reconciled, and the survival of the whole community is protected.[9]

In traditional China the lack of legitimate channels for the articulation of interests meant that China never developed a mature political economy, in the sense that geographically-based economic interests were never allowed to surface. Rural China and urban China, rice-growing South China and wheat-growing North China, coastal China and interior China were all supposed to have the same interests which the benevolence of the rulers would take care of without any prompting from society. Thus, both Confucian and Marxist-Leninist China have operated without benefit of true politics. The denial of the legitimacy of interests has meant that China has had at best a distorted, limited and, one might say, crippled form of politics.

This Chinese tradition of denying the legitimacy of interests also helps to explain the historic failure of China to develop a strong civil society and why, for all the impressive economic development under the reforms, China still lags in the emergence of interest groups that might be expected to form with the greater differentiation of the economy and society. The establishment of various federations and associations presumably to look after the interests of labour, women and the like have tended to be creatures of the supposedly benevolent state and not challengers of the state. The potential for interest articulation, and hence of real politics, has thus been stifled by a political culture that has made it more natural for China to move toward forms of state corporatism.[10]

---

minded idealists who were unprepared to use their relationships to better their lot. They knew what it took to get better housing, access to a car, and all the other things that went with the privileges of rank.

[9] Bernard Crick, *In Defense of Politics* (Chicago: University of Chicago Press, 1972), pp. 15–22.

[10] In recent years there has been significant research on questions of state and civil society in China that have illuminated some of China's core problems in democratic development. Tony Saich has pointed to the Chinese tendency toward state corporatism

In sum then, instead of an open articulation of interests, the Chinese political system has had to mask any hint of private interests through the stealthy use of personal connections. The idea that the rational advancement of one's own self-interest is fundamentally shameful and indicates greediness was derived from a Confucian ethic that despised the activities of the merchants and was reinforced by the imperatives of ideological conformity basic to Maoism. Interests can only be advanced surreptitiously and hence the current paradox that those who are doing best as entrepreneurs are happy with their indirect methods of influence and are against any movement toward more open politics. They proclaim the ideal of "political stability", which is only another way of praising authoritarian rule.

The Substitute Role of *Guanxi* in Both Administration and Politics

Thus we have a double paradox: Chinese administration has been a form of "politics", but China has never had true politics. In an astonishing way, China has been able to get along with a system of government that, first, practises administration without the benefit of a binding legal system. Second, it has had a version of politics that operates without the open articulation of interests. Instead, in China the functions that legal norms perform in administration and that interests serve for politics in most other political systems have been largely met in China by the extraordinary powers of *guanxi*. This substitution has been possible because for most Chinese the structuring of human relationships has such a vivid quality as to be a very substantive part of physical reality.[11] In practice, *guanxi* in action has thus structured authority and

---

in his article "The Search for Civil Society and Democracy in China", *Current History* (September 1994), pp. 260–4. Instead of thinking in terms of the European models of corporatism it may be more profitable for understanding likely Chinese developments to look to the Japanese experience. See, for example, T.J. Pemple and Keiichi Tsunekawa, "Corporatism Without Labor? The Japanese Anomaly", in Gerhard Lehmbruch and Philippe C. Schmitter (eds), *Patterns of Corporatist Policy-Making* (London: Sage Publications, 1982); and Arend J. Lijphart and Markus M. L. Crepaz, "Corporatism and Consensus Democracy in Eighteen Countries", *The British Journal of Political Science*, Vol. 21, No. 2 (April 1991).

[11]   There is an odd general assumption that the Chinese concept of *guanxi* is self-evident, and so it has not received the analytical attention it deserves. Bruce Jacobs has sought to explicate the concept, but he gives it more of an affective dimension than I believe it generally has. See J. Bruce Jacobs, "A Preliminary Model of Particularistic Ties in Chinese Political Alliances: *Kan-ch'ing* and *Kuan-hsi* in a Rural Taiwanese Township", *The China Quarterly*, No. 78 (June 1979), pp. 237–73. See also Barbara Pillsbury, "Factionalism Observed: Behind the Face of Harmony in a Chinese Community", *The China Quarterly*, No. 74 (June 1978), pp. 241–72. Part of the problem in understanding the phenomenon is that to the Western mind a bonding tie which clearly is very effective must have a strong emotional base, but in fact *guanxi* is a more pragmatic and

given order and form to Chinese governance and to what passes as both administration and politics. It has been particularism in the service of generalized institution-building—which helps explain why Chinese public life can be so orderly without being institutionalized.

I must note here that Dittmer has misconstrued my understanding of "primordial sentiments", and hence of *guanxi*. I did not mean to dismiss in any way the bonding powers of *guanxi*, but rather my point was that the particularistic basis of a relationship does not in itself provide a clear clue for predicting the purposes for which the relationship might be directed. People might be associated with each other, for example, because they came from the same town or province, but this would almost never mean that they would therefore work together for the interests of that place. The Shanghai cliques, both the earlier Gang of Four and the current Jiang Zemin et al., have been mutually supportive in advancing their group's power but not for the sake of Shanghai. Schoolmates may apply their *guanxi* politically but not usually for the interests of their school. In short, the particularistic basis of the relationship is not a guide as to what it may be applied toward. Indeed, the very power of *guanxi* is that its workings are not limited to its ostensible basis but rather it can be universally directed and used for multiple and diverse purposes. It is true, as I shall shortly note, that Overseas Chinese have tended to invest in their ancestral localities but this is because that is where they have their trusted ties.

Before we get carried away on the theme of Chinese exceptionalism, it needs to be noted that factionalism is not unique to the Chinese Communist Party, for it has been endemic with nearly all Communist parties. The story of the Russian Social Democratic Party before the Revolution was largely one of factional battles between the Bolsheviks and Mensheviks, and such struggles, of course, also characterized the early years under both Lenin and Stalin. Even the American Communist Party was fraught with factional divisions.[12] There are several reasons for this propensity toward factional strife among Communists. First, the ideology has the character of a religion in which there is the presumption of a single truth that guides the Party line at all times.

---

socially-defined relationship. Two people who have almost no feelings of attachment to each other may be bound by *guanxi* because it is expected of them.

[12]   Daniel Bell in a personal communication tells the wonderful story of a time when the American Communists were going through a factional fight that was demoralizing the rank and file. It was decided that there should be a meeting of three representatives of each faction, but when it was discovered that no resolution of differences was possible the leaders agreed that one member of one of the factions would shift over to the other faction, thereby giving the rank and file the impression of positive movement; but to keep the power balance, a member of the other faction shifted the other way, so the *status quo* remained. I doubt if the Chinese comrades in all their convoluted maneuvering ever came up with such a manipulation of power.

Therefore, anyone who does not openly support the line must, "objectively speaking", be against the Party and therefore working for the enemy, and hence a subversive element. Second, the tradition of secrecy means that conflicts take place in a sealed atmosphere and consequently they tend to become highly personalized. Differences cannot be aired out, diluted, and balanced by other considerations. The focus of action cannot escape considerations of personalities, much as in any small inward-looking community.

In China, however, the phenomenon of factions has had to operate under an additional burden because both traditional and contemporary Chinese political cultures have made the very idea of factions an abomination. Honest officials were never supposed to band together, and any hint of the existence of factions was taken as a sign of trouble for the political system. Whereas in other countries factions have a normal, even honoured, place in politics, in China there is a general conspiracy either to deny their existence or to denigrate opponents by calling them a faction.

By drawing a curtain to hide the reality of factions, the Chinese have erected a major obstacle to democratic development. Were the Chinese to overcome their taboo about factions and admit to their existence, the Chinese political system would become dramatically more transparent. Indeed, if the factions were required to come out into the open and publicly debate their different views, the country might take a significant step forward toward becoming a stable, pluralistic system. Instead of people having to speculate about possible elite differences, it would be possible for the public to learn where their different leaders stand on matters of general concern. If, instead of the behind-the-scenes jockeying for power, the factions were forced to make their cases in public, China might well be on its way to having nascent political parties. The factional line-ups of the highest officials would gradually become manifest in the National People's Congress and their different positions would rapidly be transmitted down the line, and in time local elections would begin to revolve around the issues that divide the top elite. Imagine what China would be today if Deng Xiaoping and Chen Yun had had to openly mobilize their respective followers as publicly acknowledged factions; or if Li Peng and Zhao Ziyang had had to debate their differences in public.

But this is dreaming the impossible, because the cultural taboo about factions is far too strong to be so easily wished away. It is a profound taboo because it is encased in an even stronger taboo, that against giving any legitimacy to *guanxi*. The need to pretend that factions do not exist, or that they are only the mischief of bad officials, is fundamentally related to the profound ambivalence that Chinese have about *guanxi*. They know that they have to use it, but they also have a deep sense of shame over that need. The tradition of denying legitimacy to all forms of *guanxi* has meant that the Chinese have never been able to discriminate between its honourable and dishonourable forms.[13] Ultimately, the test of maturity of China as a modernizing society will be the ability of the Chinese people to arrive at a shared understanding as to what kinds of *guanxi* behaviour should be seen as honourable and decent qualities of human relations and what practices of *guanxi* should remain shameful and dishonourable. Trust in human connections is the very essence of civility, which in turn is the absolutely critical foundation for any well-functioning society and polity. As long as the very mention of *guanxi* is treated by most Chinese as a black mark on Chinese national character, it will be impossible for them to forthrightly determine which forms of human bonding are legitimate and which are not acceptable. As long as *guanxi* is seen as inherently bad the entire realm of personal interchanges, with its attendant considerations of reciprocity, will be tainted as questionable, if not shameful. But of course no society can function without forms of trusted exchanges. Therefore, as long as the Chinese continue to class actions as shadowy that should be able to stand the light of day, they will be driven to believe that current conditions are worse than in fact they are.

A historical reason why the Chinese have not been able to acknowledge any honourable forms of *guanxi* is that China never experienced the loyalty traditions of feudalism which Europe and Japan had with the personal bonding of lord and knight, of *daimyo* and *samurai*, with all their emotionally charged pledges of fealty, allegiance and undying fidelity. Instead of the European and Japanese traditions of heroically carrying the colours of one's master and of boldly defending his interests, the Chinese had a bureaucratic tradition in which there were supposed to be no personal loyalties among superiors and subordinates.

The feudal traditions of Europe and Japan also implanted in those cultures an idealistic and heroic dimension to personal loyalty relationships that is generally lacking in the Chinese concept of *guanxi*. Instead, in China *guanxi* has always had a strongly utilitarian and pragmatic rationale. That is why it was more heavily masked during the ideological era of Maoism and less hidden with Deng Xiaoping's more pragmatic politics.

From "Politics in Command" to "To Get Rich is Glorious"

What all of this means is that *guanxi* has and will continue to play a fundamental but concealed role in shaping Chinese politics, particularly as it operates as the bonding power for factionalism. Therefore, if we are to seek more generalized formulations about the workings of personal relationships in Chinese politics, we should look for schemes in which the parameters are

---

[13] Andrew Nathan demonstrated how dishonourable forms of *guanxi* undermined China's early constitutional republic in *Peking Politics, 1918–1923: Factionalism and the Failure of Constitutionalism* (Berkeley: University of California Press, 1976).

highly sensitive to objective conditions and to the realities of power considerations. For, as Dittmer acknowledges, by citing Liang Shuming, Chinese society is not only based on relationships that are highly particularistic, but its culture is also strongly situationally oriented, in that behaviour is expected to vary with the circumstances. When conditions change new considerations should take over and relationships are expected to adjust, both in character and in relative importance. Indeed, because of the situation-oriented nature of Chinese culture the practices of administration and politics, and hence the role of *guanxi*, have been quite different during the Mao and Deng eras.

If we want to compare practices in the two eras according to a generalized model of factionalism, we might have to create a three-dimensional model. The first dimension would focus on the structure of power for the system as a whole, which would mean distinguishing between whether the general structure is highly centralized or decentralized, whether it is being tightened (*shou*) or letting go (*fang*).[14] With respect to the pole of decentralization we might need to add a special sub-category of "local empires" or "separate kingdoms" to deal with those factions that prefer to be like "big fish in a little pool" rather than being like little fish in the big, national pond. A second dimension would take note of the power orientations among the factions as they seek to preserve or maximize their power, and to do this we might usefully employ Avery Goldstein's distinctions between bandwagoning and balance-of-power, of the factions wanting to position themselves behind a dominant leader or of needing to form alliances to ward off threats.[15] Thirdly, we need to take account of how the factions respond to the collective problems of both system legitimization and system maintenance. In the Mao era these functions were met by a combination of stressing ideological correctness and applying coercion. In Deng's time it was material satisfaction and playing upon the fears of political instability and anarchy.

This, however, is not the place for a detailed comparison of factionalism under Mao's "Politics in Command" system of rule and Deng's "To Get Rich is Glorious" approach. The great break came with the aftershock of the Cultural Revolution, which included, first, the erosion of faith in ideology and, second, the counterbalancing fear of anarchy and hence an unquestioning worship of political stability.[16]

---

[14]   See Richard Baum, *Burying Mao: Chinese Politics in the Age of Deng Xiaoping* (Princeton: Princeton University Press, 1994), Ch. 1.

[15]   Avery Goldstein, *From Bandwagon to Balance-of-Power Politics* (Stanford: Stanford University Press, 1991).

[16]   As historians and political scientists we have probably tended to exaggerate the differences between Mao's and Deng's China. In a provocative and sophisticated

Initially, there was little difference between the late Mao years and the early Deng period. Indeed, the story of Deng Xiaoping's maneuvering to return from his third purge after the death of Zhou Enlai to become the paramount ruler and his successful purging of Hua Guofeng, and then later of Hu Yaobang and Zhao Ziyang, followed very much the Mao style of factional struggle.[17] Just a listing of the code words that were used to signal who was with whom can serve as a reminder of those battles: "The Two Whatevers", "Uphold the Four Cardinal Principles", "Practice as the Sole Criterion of Truth", "Promote Proletarian Ideology and Eliminate Bourgeois Ideas", "Eliminate the Influence of Feudalism", "Struggle Against Bourgeois Liberalism", "Oppose Humanism and Alienation", "Clean Up Spiritual Pollution", and "Build Socialism with Chinese Characteristics".

Over time, however, the decline in reliance on ideology, the increased decentralization of the entire system, and the loosening of discipline produced a significantly different pattern of factional activities. We Western analysts, with our propensity to emphasize the importance of public policy rhetoric, tried to establish some intellectual order in the confusing relationships by writing about the "reformist" faction being opposed by the "leftists" and/or "conservative" faction. The problem with the latter two labels shows how confused ideology had become. The line-up usually consisted of the Chen Yun *jituan* or clique, which included Hu Qiaomu, Wang Zhen, Deng Liqun, Yao Yilin and Song Ping, confronting the reformists led by Hu Yaobang, Wan Li, Zhao Ziyuan, Xi Zhongxun, Zhou Yang, Li Chang, Hu Jiwei and many others, with Deng himself as either a reformer or as a swing element.[18]

Yet increasingly over time, and particularly after Tiananmen, the problem with factions ran much deeper than just issues of public policy. The Chinese political system was increasingly caught in a state of political paralysis. After

---

philosophically-oriented analysis, Jiwei Ci has insightfully argued that China easily went from utopianism, to nihilism, to hedonism in part because in essence Maoism was more an appeal of materialism than idealism. See Jiwei Ci, *Dialectic of the Chinese Revolution: From Utopianism to Hedonism* (Stanford: Stanford University Press, 1994).

[17]   For a detailed analysis of factions under Deng from the perspective of one who was centrally involved, see Ruan Ming, *Deng Xiaoping: Chronicle of an Empire* (Boulder: Westview Press, 1994).

[18]   Among the many studies of these clashes are Ruan Ming, *Deng Xiaoping*; Jonathan Unger (ed.), *Using the Past to Serve the Present: Historiography and Politics in Contemporary China* (Armonk: M. E. Sharpe, 1993); Merle Goldman, *Sowing the Seeds of Democracy in China* (Cambridge, Mass.: Harvard University Press, 1994); Chu-yuan Cheng, *Behind the Tiananmen Massacre: Social, Political, and Economic Ferment in China* (Boulder: Westview Press, 1990); Susan Shirk, *The Political Logic of Economic Reform in China* (Berkeley: University of California Press, 1993); and Joseph Fewsmith, *Dilemmas of Reform in China* (Armonk: M. E. Sharpe, 1994).

more than a decade and a half of the reforms, it was not prudent for any element of the leadership to employ the standard Chinese Communist rhetoric of joy and optimism, because there was too much social unrest and too many unhappy people in both the countryside and the cities. Yet no leadership faction was willing to take the risk of giving voice to discontent, for that would be like lighting a match to a powder keg. The divisions among the cadres thus became less about strategic differences over the making of a "New China" and more about tactical differences in preserving their collective position as China's ruling elite. For some, preserving the system has meant the advantages of decentralization, but for others the importance of the centre has remained paramount, for it is only the centre that can pass on subsidies to failing industries and tighten or loosen the money supply.

The succession struggle for leadership in the immediate post-Deng era involved contending factions since there were no other institutionalized procedures for allocating power. Yet, none of the main contenders was ready to show his hand for fear of giving cause to the others to mobilize a collective opposition. The situation is one of a balance-of-power game, since no one is in a position to set off a bandwagon movement.[19]

Under the then guiding principle of Chinese politics, that "To Get Rich Is Glorious", there was a shameless exploiting of connections for material benefits. That is to say, what in other societies would be called "corruption" abounded in China, and in no small measure precisely because, once again, there was no distinguishing between honourable and dishonourable forms of *guanxi*. With personal connections having only utilitarian and almost no idealistic dimensions, the result is a pragmatism that rejoices in the idea that it is all right to get rich.[20]

It is no secret that officials were using their positions in various ways for personal profit. Indeed, the most publicized political campaign of the mid-1990s was the "Anti-Corruption Struggle", which brought forth a rhetoric reminiscent of the mass campaigns under Chairman Mao: "Get a firm grasp on making anti-corruption a reality"; "Rely on the masses, proceed according to

---

[19]   The latter phenomenon during the Mao era is discussed at length in Avery Goldstein's *From Bandwagon to Balance-of-Power Politics*.

[20]   The spirit of the times in China is well summarized in the following quote from Jiwei Ci, *Dialectic of the Chinese Revolution*, p. 247: "One popular catchphrase, though wildly hyperbolic and, for the sake of linguistic effect, not quite accurate about the total population figure, captures China's present ethos well. Out of a population of one billion, it goes, nine hundred million have set up shop as businessmen, and the remaining one hundred million are poised to follow suit (*shiyi renmin jiuyi shang, haiyou yiyi dai kaizhang*)".

law, and grasp hold of major cases"; "Solve all disciplinary violations one by one with an across-the-board clean-up".[21]

The Chinese people shook their heads as they talked about the *taizi dang* or "princes' party" composed of the sons and daughters of high-level cadres, who were busily engaged in using their connections to become directors of trading firms, banks and joint ventures. With only a few conspicuous exceptions the offspring of all the top leaders used their family status to make money. Some of them definitely had individual talent and were well educated and thus could make it on their own, but the road to success for all of them was made easier by the Chinese cultural beliefs about the potency of connections and the workings of *guanxi*.

Some analysts, believing in the importance of stability and the need for economic growth before political liberalization, saw the emergence of the "princes' party" as not necessarily a bad development for China. They argued that the personal interests of these sons and daughters ensured that there would be strong commitments to preserving the monopoly of power of the Chinese Communist Party after Deng died, and this will mean that the economic reforms would remain in place. Initially, the "princes' party" emerged mainly in the economic realm as the sons and daughters followed the precept of "To Get Rich is Glorious", but as the end of Deng's rule approached they became ever more active in government and politics. Chen Yuan, the vice-governor of the central bank and the son of Chen Yun, was seen as the group's natural political leader, and Li Peng's son, Li Xiaoyong, was a dominant voice in managing the power sector.[22]

During the transition from Deng to Jiang Zemin the majority of the Chinese population seemingly believed that political stability was all important and liberalization could wait. History may prove them right. Indeed, those who held to "neo-authoritarian" views insisted that corruption need not be a sign of political decay and the death knell of a regime. After all, throughout history, tolerance of corruption has often given strength to the position of rulers and thus served as a source of legitimacy. This has been the case especially when a population has become cynical and lacks any compelling basis for defining and justifying morality.

Melanie Manion, in a study that combines game theory and interviewing, has ingeniously illuminated the logic that links corruption and the Deng

---

[21]   In the spirit of the campaign, the PLA in the fall of 1994 opened an exhibit at the Beijing military museum on civilian corruption which drew 10,000 visitors a day. There was something possibly ominous about such an exhibition because in the developing world the military have often used the issue of "corrupt politicians" to justify taking over power.

[22]   *The Economist*, 22–28 October 1994, p. 37.

economic reforms.[23] The paradox behind the relationship is that cadres interested in liberalizing the economy also find that it is to their advantage to increase the numbers of permits or licences that an entrepreneur needed from the government in order to set up and operate a business. Simply put, if only one or two permits are necessary then it makes sense for a businessman to follow the formal procedures, but if the number increases to, say, 80 or 100, which was often the case, then it is to everyone's interest to use the "back door". Moreover, in the tacit negotiating to set the sum to be paid, the total amount of bribes, as even a child would understand, naturally goes up as the number of permits increases. Hence the enthusiasm of cadres to liberalize the economy but also to increase the numbers of regulations.[24]

This logic suggests that officials interested in expanding investments in their jurisdictions needed to get the word out that they were ready and willing to do business. This has produced another problem that the Chinese government had to struggle with, that of ballooning expenditures for entertainment. In 1988 more than 81 billion *yuan* was reportedly spent by officials on banquets and food and drink, which was more than the central government's combined expenditures for health, education, science and welfare. And the government announced that by 1993 the figure had grown to over 100 billion *yuan* in spite of a campaign to curtail expenditures. [25] This is confirmation not only of the well-known fact that the Chinese national pastime is enjoying good food, but is also proof of the vigour with which Chinese cadres with access to public funds were seeking to put people in their debt and thereby increase their *guanxi* ties.

Furthermore, one cannot understand the geographical pattern of growth of the Chinese economy without an appreciation of the role that personalistic ties have played in investment decisions. The dramatic contrast between the dynamically developing coastal areas and the sluggish interior regions cannot be understood in terms of the standard Western theories about industrial

---

[23]   Melanie Manion, "Corruption by Design: Bribery in Chinese Enterprise Licensing", *The Journal of Law, Economics, and Organization*, Vol. 12, No. 1 (1996), pp. 167–96.

[24]   The *guanxi* relationships between officials and entrepreneurs is also now working to make the merchants anxious for the Party-state not to be further weakened or for liberalization to go further because they are happy with their sheltered arrangements. See Dorothy Solinger, "Urban Entrepreneurs and the State: The Merger of State and Society", in Arthur Lewis Rosenbaum (ed.), *State and Society in China: The Consequences of Reform* (Boulder: Westview Press, 1992).

[25]   In am indebted to Anne F. Thurston for bringing to my attention these official Chinese government figures. I believe it prudent to take with a grain of salt most official Chinese statistics but since, almost by definition, an economist is a scholar who treats such numbers seriously, we should not dismiss out of hand the government's attempt to say how bad corruption has become.

location which hold that the three key factors in such decisions are proximity to large market demand, cheap production factors, and a favourable political climate.[26] To believe that these are the critical considerations in explaining the political economy of the Chinese "miracle" would show ignorance of Chinese ways. In the case of China, the key variable has been the particularistic bonding of Overseas Chinese to specific communities and kinship groupings. Nearly all the active investors from Taiwan, Hong Kong and the Overseas Chinese communities of Southeast Asia and elsewhere have personal ties with the coastal regions of the mother country, and that is why their money has flowed to those locations. Officials in interior China desire just as much to attract foreign investments as cadres in coastal China, but hardly any of their former residents went abroad and did well financially, hence the lack of potential entrepreneurs with a natural interest in investing in their communities.[27]

Guanxi as the Basis of Legitimacy

The shift in the focus of *guanxi* ties from the Mao era to the period of the Deng reforms had profound consequences for the nature of Chinese politics. In particular, the way was opened for the emergence of a Chinese political economy in which real interests are more openly acknowledged, and thus the leadership no longer needs to pretend it is benevolently taking care of everyone's interests. The traditional denial of legitimacy to interest articulation may thus fade away as cadres feel they must act in the interest of the local concerns that they have personally helped to establish.

Officials at the county and township levels have had to become promoters of local investments, and if successful they need to continue to protect what has been established. Localities with large but inefficient state enterprises need to have *guanxi* ties to make sure that the subsidies continue and that their interests are not forgotten. Thus there will be strains between the imperative to have good connections in the higher ranks of the government and the need to

---

26   Paul Krugman, *Geography and Trade* (Cambridge, Mass.: MIT Press, 1991), pp. 14–15, 23; and David Pearce, *The MIT Dictionary of Modern Economics* (Cambridge, Mass.: MIT Press, 1989), p. 250.

27   When I inquired of a Taiwan businessman, who was in the midst of setting up investments on the Chinese mainland, as to how important personal connections might be in such decisions, he replied it would be impossible to find a single investment that was not founded on the kind of trust that only *guanxi* ties can produce. Another Taiwan entrepreneur said that he was confident it would only take one intermediary at the most to bring together a Taiwan investor and a PRC official to arrange a deal. The greater the amount of money to be invested the higher the official would have to be, but there are always ways to find the right official with the right *guanxi* to make the deal secure. Overseas Chinese investors simply do not trust the Chinese legal system and therefore need to place their trust in particularistic connections.

champion what has been developed locally. But these are the strains that are common to representative and pluralistic systems of government.

Under Jiang Zemin *guanxi* has proven to be an even more important ingredient in governing than it was during the Mao and Deng eras. With the erosion of ideology and the lack of clearly defined nationalistic ideals, the personalistic bonding of the political elite has turned out to be the most critical factor in holding the system together.[28] The triumph of pragmatism that came with Deng's reforms has left China without any ideals or myths for legitimizing the state. State authority has had to depend more than ever on the personal power and status of a self-perpetuating elite.

As the Chinese Communist Party comes ever closer to abandoning the need to give even lip service to ideology, it may become the first Communist Party to preserve its structure and authority through the power of the personal bonding of its members. Marxism-Leninism-Mao Zedong Thought is dead; long live the band of self-serving, pragmatic, power-hungry cadres! Yes, it may at first seem to be stretching the limits of the plausible to suggest that the entire Chinese political system could come to rest on the bonding powers of the personal relations of its rulers, but we need to remember that China would not be the first country in history to be held together by the personal connections of its elite.[29] The very pragmatic, utilitarian character of *guanxi* can help it to serve the function of institutionalizing power relationships, and thereby give the system a degree of stability. It is not just that the cadres will band together to preserve their collective interests, but the people at large may also find it not unnatural that their leaders should have their bonding relationships, and therefore the political elite's claim to status and personal authority will be enough to justify its right to rule the country. Many Chinese will be unhappy that idealism is gone, that there is no grand vision for the country, but daily life

---

[28]   One of the great surprises about China in its post-ideological stage is that the country has at best an inchoate and poorly developed sense of modern nationalism. It of course has a rich body of traditions which go with its great civilization, but there has not been a selective process of identifying specific ideals, values and myths that can serve as the basis for identification with the nation as a modern state. See such works as Lowell Dittmer and Samuel S. Kim (eds), *China's Quest for National Identity* (Ithaca: Cornell University Press, 1993); and Lucian W. Pye, "How China's Nationalism Was Shanghaied", *The Australian Journal of Chinese Affairs*, No. 29 (January 1993), pp. 107–34.

[29]   Indeed, some would argue that the Japanese system of factional politics based on that culture's particularistic bonds of *on* and *giri*, of obligation and indebtedness, comes close to being just such a system. I make this argument in *Asian Power and Politics: The Cultural Dimensions of Authority* (Cambridge, Mass.: Harvard University Press, 1985), pp. 163–6.

could go on under the authority of rulers who operate out of the security of their personal connections.

Thus, in the post-Deng period the prime imperative has been the need to hold together the ruling class, which already had a caste-like character. Without a strong system of laws or a well-articulated popular faith to uphold the mystique of legitimacy, coercion may have to play a key role. It is significant that the PLA is in fact the only well-functioning national institution, and that it is constantly being indoctrinated to carry out the will of the political rulers.

If such a jerry-built system survives, then it can be expected that the different interests of the elite will drive the whole structure toward factional competition. If the system is without a new ideological basis, as seems likely, then the factions may have to come out into the open and seek popular acceptance. The result would be the beginning of an elementary form of competitive politics. Thus, through a painful, complicated process China may be slowly working its way toward a more pluralistic political system and thereby joining the ranks of the modern nation-states. For this to happen, however, the Chinese will have to sort out which forms of *guanxi* are to be seen as honourable and which dishonourable. The choice will decide whether the country is to be ruled by a respectable establishment or by a mafia.

THREE

The Paradoxical Post-Mao Transition: From Obeying the Leader to "Normal Politics"*

Frederick C. Teiwes

There has been much speculation (on the question of Hua Guofeng's position) but it hasn't any significance. These kinds of changes happen in any country. There is nothing strange about that.
—Deng Xiaoping, February 1981.[1]

Everyone listened to Mao and then to Deng. ... No one can stand against Deng's political line, but the change of leadership (after Deng's death) will be the end of one-man rule.
—Significant reform official of the post-Mao era.[2]

Chinese politics is too complicated to understand; some things can never be made clear.
—Former member of the Central Committee (1982-85) and the Central Advisory Committee (1985-92).[3]

Lowell Dittmer's lead contribution to this book correctly emphasizes both the continued great salience of informal elite politics and a secular trend toward a

* Lucien Bianco, Tim Cheek, Bruce Dickson, Keith Forster, David Goodman, Carol Hamrin, Bruce Jacobs, Tony Saich, Susan Shirk, K. K. Shum, Dorothy Solinger, Jon Unger, Graham Young and especially Warren Sun (who also provided additional important contributions) commented on earlier versions of this chapter. I gratefully acknowledge the financial support of the Australian Research Council, the Ian Potter Foundation, and the University of Sydney's research grants scheme and its Research Institute for Asia and the Pacific, which made possible the research on which this is based.

[1] Reuters dispatch on Deng's press conference, *The Sydney Morning Herald*, 14 February 1981, p. 5.

[2] Interview, Beijing, 1994.

[3] Interview, Beijing, 1991.

more institutionalized political process during the post-Mao period.[4] In this discussion I propose to examine some of the paradoxical features that arose during this period of transition under Deng Xiaoping. The focus will be firmly on the top level of the central elite, although the very changes under Deng rendered the leadership ever more responsive to pressures from within the far-flung official apparatus and society more broadly. I will offer some general observations about continuities and changes since the Maoist period, and then consider in greater detail key issues concerning authority, norms and conflict in the Deng era.

An important methodological point must be made first, however. Any valid overview of elite Party politics must be based on a painstaking gathering of detailed information concerning events, and ideally a careful weighing of the reliability of each discrete piece of evidence before a general interpretation is put forward. Analysis of the Maoist period has suffered greatly from a failure to observe this approach, with studies often accepting flawed official interpretive models however much they may have been recast in social science concepts. The most obvious example is the discredited but perversely still influential "two line struggle" interpretation of the pre-Cultural Revolution period. This view of Mao Zedong having to contend with various Politburo "opponents" is increasingly unsustainable in the face of a flood of new information from Party history publications and less official sources that depict an absolutely dominant Mao.[5] More specifically, Western analysis has largely accepted the official view of Lin Biao as an ambitious politician who sought military dominance of the political system, pushed forward the Cultural Revolution for his own power interests, and engaged in a bitter political struggle with Mao at least during the last year of his life. New detailed evidence, however, points to a very different picture: a Lin Biao who did not seek enhanced power, adopted a largely passive role, tended to take initiatives only to moderate the Cultural Revolution, and never challenged Mao politically.[6]

---

[4] While many of Lucian Pye's comments concerning the difficulty of distinguishing formal from informal politics in the Chinese context are valid, there can be little doubt that such a distinction exists and that institutional factors have become increasingly important. This is also the judgment of former middle-level officials now in exile, as seen in the various contributions in Carol Lee Hamrin and Suisheng Zhao (eds), *Decision-Making in Deng's China: Perspectives from Insiders* (Armonk: M. E. Sharpe, 1995). See especially Zhao's conclusion that "personal and institutional authority has become more distinguishable in Deng Xiaoping's China" (pp. 233–4).

[5] For a survey of such evidence, see the introduction to the second edition of Frederick C. Teiwes, *Politics and Purges in China: Rectification and the Decline of Party Norms 1950–1965* (Armonk: M. E. Sharpe, 1993).

[6] See Frederick C. Teiwes and Warren Sun, *The Tragedy of Lin Biao: Riding the Tiger During the Cultural Revolution, 1966–1971* (London: C. Hurst & Co., 1996). My own earlier analysis of Lin Biao in *Leadership, Legitimacy, and Conflict in China: From a*

The problem is even greater concerning the post-Mao period. Here I not only endorse Dittmer's call for more empirical research, but go further in identifying the methodological problems involved. Despite the unprecedented openness of the 1980s and a surfeit of purported inside information, in crucial respects we know less about contemporary politics at the top than we now know for the Maoist era.[7] Given the secretive nature of the top leadership, it is hardly surprising that participants in the system often express the view that "nobody knows" what goes on "up there".[8] As the final quotation at the head of this chapter indicates, even highly placed figures, including those with personal knowledge of the very top leaders, feel limited in what they know, and their assessments sometimes are at variance in significant ways with those of younger, more middle-level officials either in China or living in exile. Given these limitations, scholarship has unfortunately relied extensively and often indiscriminately on suspect Hong Kong sources to fill the gap. As Lyman Miller has observed, the Hong Kong press has recorded "a flood of reports, stories, rumours, and sometimes speculations and fantasies about political events in China".[9] The key problem is that in the effort to create a coherent picture, analysts use Hong Kong reports to fill out a picture based on assumptions that may be as misleading as notions of "two line struggle" or a Bonapartist Lin Biao. Given these severe methodological difficulties, what follows must necessarily be more tentative than my historical studies on the Maoist era.

Continuity and Change from the Maoist Era: An Overview

A number of striking continuities marked elite politics under Mao and Deng, albeit these are continuities that disguise significant differences. First is the crucial role of the pre-eminent leader himself, something highlighted by Dittmer.

Charismatic Mao to the Politics of Succession (Armonk: M. E. Sharpe, 1984), pp. 105–13, was seriously flawed for reasons similar to those criticized here.

[7] In terms of Party history sources, compare the rich insights into the fears, motives and interactions of the top elite in the first three volumes of the "China 1949–1989" series with the largely sterile final volume by Wang Hongmo et al., *1949–1989 nian de Zhongguo: Gaige kaifang de licheng* [China 1949–1989: The Course of Reform and Opening] (Henan: Henan Renmin Chubanshe, 1989).

[8] Cf. the assessment of H. Lyman Miller, "Politics Inside the Ring Road: On Sources and Comparisons", in Hamrin and Zhao, *Decision-Making in Deng's China*, p. 229, that "we do not appear to learn very much (from emigré cadres) about the interactions among the top leaders themselves".

[9] Miller, "Politics Inside the Ring Road", p. 212. A dubious example widely cited in Western analyses focuses on the alleged votes in Politburo Standing Committee meetings during the Tiananmen crisis in May 1989. A source very close to one of the principals in these meetings dismissed such reports with the scornful remark that no one sticks up their hand in such situations.

In both periods the leader was the ultimate source of major new departures and the final arbiter of political conflict. In ways that will be examined in greater detail here, Deng Xiaoping not only had less—although still enormous—authority than Mao, but was less individually prominent in the design of new programs than the Chairman and more consultative in style, particularly in comparison with Mao's last twenty years. Nevertheless, I will argue that for Deng as well as for Mao, the leadership was permeated with a sense that his words had to be obeyed. Other members of the leadership who wished to pursue their own personal or institutional interests had to engage in a "court politics" of accepting the paramount leader's orders, pandering to his preferences, seeking his ear to advance their projects and, at most, skewing his often vague and ambiguous guidelines to enhance their respective causes.[10]

The difference between the two great leaders is indicated by Yan Jiaqi's observation that "Whatever Deng Xiaoping says must be carried out, *unless it is not feasible*".[11] This is reflected in the weeks it took to reverse Deng's impetuous and virtually one-man effort in 1988 to achieve a breakthrough in price reform, compared with the nearly three years it took to begin a genuine retreat from Mao's Great Leap Forward. In this, Deng's style facilitated the attempts by other leaders to persuade him of another course, whereas Mao's fury intimidated his colleagues all the while his prestige engendered considerable blind faith among them.[12] Deng's pragmatism entailed a wish to avoid the social disruption that pressing ahead guaranteed, while Mao clung to his policies in the face of mounting evidence of disaster. Moreover, the overall cast of the utilitarian reform era created a completely different context from Mao's time, when the combination of ideology and coercion had held both the elite and population in its grip. The contrast was both in the nature of the two leaders and the situations they created, but in neither case was the leader's authority challenged.

A second continuity, largely ignored by Dittmer, involves the immense significance of revolutionary status.[13] All top leaders in the pre-Cultural

---

[10] For a discussion of court politics in the most benign period of Mao's rule, see Frederick C. Teiwes, *Politics at Mao's Court: Gao Gang and Party Factionalism in the Early 1950s* (Armonk: M. E. Sharpe, 1990). For an inside (albeit flawed) account of a far more threatening court life over a longer period, see Li Zhisui, *The Private Life of Chairman Mao: The Memoirs of Mao's Personal Physician* (London: Chatto & Windus, 1994).

[11] Yan Jiaqi, "The Nature of Chinese Authoritarianism", in Hamrin and Zhao, *Decision-Making in Deng's China*, p. 7 (emphasis added).

[12] On this peculiar mix of fear and belief in early 1958, see the concluding section of Frederick C. Teiwes with Warren Sun, "The Politics of an 'Un-Maoist' Period: The Case of Opposing Rash Advance, 1956–1957", in Timothy Cheek and Tony Saich (eds), *New Perspectives on State Socialism in China* (Armonk: M. E. Sharpe, 1997).

[13] Dittmer comes closest to acknowledging status in his discussion of the *depth* of informal ties, which he characterizes as connections with supporters "going all the way back to the

Revolution period owed their power to their status as heroes of the revolution. Yet arguably the importance of revolutionary prestige has been even more important during the reform era. While the charismatic Mao could set aside the claims of revolutionary seniority of other leaders at will, Deng—whose own authority was based on a less exalted status—had neither the inclination nor the ability to do so. This has been reflected in differences within two related further continuities: the operation of "two fronts" of leadership and the personalized nature of authority. While the leaders in charge of daily work on the "first front" during the reform era have faced the same dilemma of how to please more authoritative but less involved figures on the "second front", their task in some ways has been easier and in some respects harder than that of their "first front" predecessors under Mao.

An essential difference is that under Mao the "second front" was effectively limited to the Chairman himself. This left "first front" leaders vulnerable to his increasingly unpredictable moods and views, but at least there was no ambiguity concerning his overwhelming power. Moreover, in a real sense Mao never retired to the "second front" but retained all power in his hands, something eminently more feasible in an era dominated by ideological concerns.[14] In contrast, the "second front" of the reform period has consisted of an array of Party elders of different views and, apart from Deng and Chen Yun, unclear relative authority. While the elders' interventions have been more predictable and less disruptive than those of Mao, and they have been more constrained by the reform-period understanding that they should not interfere too much, these Party elders inevitably complicated the lives of the officials in charge of running the country. Finally, while authority was clearly ultimately personal under Mao, other leaders in nearly all cases had official posts reflecting their individual status, thus validating Pye's observation *for this period* that it was virtually impossible to separate the formal from the informal. But during the reform period, the ability of key figures to continue to exert a critical influence with few or no official posts, as in the case of the post-1989 Deng, in this respect indicates even less institutionalization of authority than earlier.

Another prominent feature of reform-period politics with complex links to the past involves the pursuit of consensus. At the heart of this effort has been a desire for Party unity, a value at the very centre of the Party's "fine traditions"

---

early generations of revolutionary leadership". The difference is that he focuses on the ties that bind the members of the groups concerned, rather than on the status and prestige derived from revolutionary achievements that has sustained individual leaders well beyond their particular "factions".

[14]   This is not to deny that Mao delegated authority or, under the chaotic conditions of the Cultural Revolution, created a situation where it was impossible to keep tight control. What I do claim is that Mao both made a much more conscious effort than Deng to control everything, and that the more political and less technical focus of his policies allowed him considerable success in the effort.

(that is, the official norms that have been strongly reasserted, particularly in the early reform period),[15] giving rise to a repeated emphasis on "stability and unity" since Mao's death. In this, of course, there was both a nostalgic harking back to the earlier periods of Mao's leadership, when consultation and consensus were a genuine although inconstant feature of politics at the top, and a reaction to the arbitrary rule and conflict-ridden politics of the Chairman's last two decades. For the surviving first-generation leaders[16] in particular, consensual politics not only was part and parcel of a successful revolutionary endeavour, it also guaranteed a predictable politics that protected the interests of the elite as a whole. Yet in seeking to sustain consensual politics under the reforms—indeed introducing far more consultative practices than had existed under Mao—the Party leadership created a less unified Party than had existed before the Cultural Revolution, for a number of reasons.

First, in the period up to 1966 a bedrock of leadership unity existed due to common experience in the successful revolution and loyalty to Mao, even when there were significant diverse views. This, in turn, was mirrored in the Party as a whole due to the mix of belief and coercion engendered by the Party's totalistic ideology and organization. In contrast, the leadership of the reform period deliberately reduced the Party's demands on society, and at the same time the demands of the Party on its members, thus shifting the system from a totalitarian to an authoritarian one. This has dramatically eased pressure for conformity and has allowed individuals and groups within leadership circles to hold to and advocate their own particular versions of the reform program. While this situation is consistent with the letter of traditional democratic centralism, in fact it represents a much looser unity than what was demanded under Mao even in his most benign periods.

A second factor that made unity a more elusive goal than during the pre-Cultural Revolution period involved the objectives of Deng and his colleagues, which were more open-ended, far-reaching, and difficult to accomplish than those held by the pre-1966 Mao. While Mao's endeavour to "continue the revolution" contained disruptive utopian strands, before the Cultural Revolution this did not involve any clear challenge to the core values of the revolution or to the dominant

---

[15] See especially the "Guiding Principles for Inner Party Life" approved by the Central Committee in February 1980, in *Beijing Review*, No. 14 (1980).

[16] The usage here is at variance with that officially adopted after the leadership change of 1989, which identified a first generation led by Mao, a second generation led by Deng, and a third generation headed by Jiang Zemin. While clearly a valid distinction can be made between the Mao and Deng "generations" in terms of Party seniority and historical roles, for our purposes their common involvement in the revolutionary and post-revolution periods at high levels is more relevant. The official usage is more dubious in its designation of a third generation under Jiang since this passes over the Hu Yaobang-Zhao Ziyang "generation".

institutions of the Party-state.[17] But the Deng regime sought both to restore the "fine traditions" of the pre-Cultural Revolution period and to introduce innovations in pursuit of a modern China that were in profound tension with the basic assumptions of the earlier period.[18] Such measures as encouraging private economic activity, disbanding the collectivized agricultural system, greatly expanding the role of the market at the expense of the established central planning authorities, allowing access to non-Marxist ideas and foreign influences on an unprecedented scale, and weakening the concrete guiding role of Party organizations sharply challenge the values and practices of the Party. It is hardly surprising that such radical departures engendered considerable controversy and dissent within the elite. Rather, what is remarkable is that a significant degree of consensus on central features of the reforms was maintained despite sharp differences on specific aspects of the program.

A third factor complicating the pursuit of consensus is that post-Mao politics has eliminated the vulnerability of the elite to the whims of the leader, while at the same time producing a more normal politics where one's official position, in the "first front" at least, is more closely tied to policy advocacy and results. This has normative as well as pragmatic aspects. In the Maoist period Party norms or, in Andrew Nathan's terminology, a "code of civility" affirming the rights of Party leaders did exist in practice as well as in theory, notwithstanding repeated and often horrific violations. This is demonstrated clearly by the widespread dismay within the elite following Mao's gross violation of those standards at the pivotal 1959 Lushan conference, and by the fact that (notwithstanding Lushan) on the very eve of the Cultural Revolution the vast majority of Party veterans could not conceive of what was coming and retained their faith that the Chairman would observe the code.[19] At the same time, it is important to recognize that the norms also included the Party's culture of struggle: that is, severe criticism could be meted out to erring comrades even while rectification principles served to reduce the degree of punishment and to retain a measure of civility. But while the moderating aspects of the norms and the shared informal sense of respect owed to the revolutionary heroes supported the unusual leadership stability that existed under Mao before the Cultural Revolution, the elite turmoil of 1966–76 led Deng and his elderly comrades to reaffirm traditional norms and to diminish (but not eliminate) the culture of struggle precisely so as to protect the interests of the

---

[17] During the 1949–65 period only the short-lived Great Leap Forward produced a general program that was clearly beyond the capabilities of the regime, but even this program did not threaten basic Party values or the general—as opposed to various specific—institutional interests of the Party.

[18] For an early discussion of this tension, see Frederick C. Teiwes, "Restoration and Innovation", *The Australian Journal of Chinese Affairs*, No. 5 (January 1981).

[19] On these developments and the reality of Party norms more generally, see Teiwes, *Politics and Purges in China*, especially pp. xliv–lxvii.

larger leadership elite. During the reform period, however, they clearly expected the "first front" leaders (officials who lack truly imposing revolutionary credentials and therefore have to rely to a great extent on their official positions) to produce successful outcomes or suffer the consequences in terms of dismissal.[20] In comparison with the inherently conservative politics of the revolutionary elite before 1966,[21] Chinese leaders under the reforms necessarily must be more aggressive in building support for policy preferences and must run greater risks to protect and further their political interests. I shall examine this development— together with its paradoxical relationship to formal norms—in the final section of this chapter.

Political Authority: Deng Xiaoping, Chen Yun and the "Older Generation of Revolutionaries"

Undoubtedly the most striking continuities between the Maoist and Deng periods concern the central role of the leader and the importance of revolutionary status. As noted, revolutionary status was clearly the crucial source for the power and authority of the pre-eminent leader, Deng Xiaoping, as well as for the second most influential figure in the Party, Chen Yun, and for the Party elders as a group. While this is hardly surprising given the Party's elite political culture, more startling are the similarities in the roles of Mao and Deng. As argued above, nothwithstanding both the widespread desire to avoid the arbitrariness of Mao's rule and significant differences in leadership style, a court politics within which the leading figure has the final say while various courtiers vie for his approval remained at the centre of elite interaction. What is the evidence for this assertion? On what basis was Deng raised above Chen Yun and Peng Zhen, who could claim at least equal revolutionary status? What was the relationship of Deng and Chen Yun in policy and political terms, as well as the relationships within the larger group of Party elders, between them and Deng as the paramount leader, and between them and the "first front" leaders?

The clearest testimony concerning Deng's critical policy role, political clout, and ultimate authority has come from leaders on the "first front". In an assessment echoed by various individual leaders throughout the 1980s and into the 1990s, the Central Committee declared at the time of his formal retirement in November 1989 that during "the past ten years, Deng Xiaoping is worthy of being the chief architect in all aspects of our Party's and army's work, in economic

---

[20]   Deng has explicitly made this point by observing that those who did not work out could be discarded after several years' testing. See, for example, *Selected Works of Deng Xiaoping (1975–1982)*, (Vol. II) (Beijing: Foreign Languages Press, 1984), p. 216.

[21]   While this period was marked by radical policies and disruptive movements, it was conservative in the sense that not only was there little change in the top elite but the name of the game was simply to retain one's status rather than climb higher, and the key to this was avoiding political trouble rather than promoting bold initiatives.

construction, reform and opening to the outside world".[22] Two years earlier, when Deng vacated all but his military posts, Zhao Ziyang acknowledged his enduring authority: "not one person (among Party leaders) can compare favourably with Comrade Deng Xiaoping in political experience and wisdom. ... If we seek his advice when facing important problems, we can manage these affairs even better".[23] And two years before that, Hu Yaobang graphically illustrated Deng's clout *vis-à-vis* the PLA, by commenting that "With Comrade Deng Xiaoping taking charge, it is sufficient for him to say one sentence, but we have to say five sentences".[24]

Similar statements could be cited many times over, but in and of themselves they suggest only Deng's pre-eminent status, not a Mao-like capacity to have his words obeyed regardless of their effect on his subordinates. Given the degree of consensus on Deng's overall program, which never threatened the fundamental power interests of the elite despite the tension with Party values, and his consultative style (see below), it is impossible to demonstrate the degree to which political outcomes manifested reflexive obedience to the leader's wishes or the extent to which they involved give and take. Indeed, the dominant Western interpretation and, in a more confused fashion, the judgement of mid-level emigré cadres[25] have perceived Deng more as the first among equals in an oligarchy rather than as an unchallenged leader. In such analyses, Deng's paramount role was a result of political balancing, a politics where Deng retained his position by arbitrating between reformers and conservatives, successors and Party elders and through administrative arrangements which dispersed executive authority so that no one had sufficient power to challenge him.[26] Thus Deng's power assertedly

---

[22]   "Communiqué of the Fifth Plenary Session of the 13th CPC Central Committee", *Beijing Review*, No. 47 (1989), p. 17.

[23]   *Renmin ribao* [People's Daily], 3 November 1987, p. 3.

[24]   Interview with Hong Kong journalist Lu Keng, 10 May 1985, as translated in An-chia Wu, "Hu Yao-pang's Downfall: Its Causes and Impact", *Issues & Studies*, Vol. 23, No. 7 (July 1987), pp. 18–19.

[25]   The emigré contributions in Hamrin and Zhao, *Decision-Making in Deng's China*, often propose an oligarchic model and interpret policy changes in terms of Deng's concessions to conservative elders (see, for example, pp. 5, 26, 55, 133, 236–7, 241). However, the reflections of these authors are sprinkled with such sentiments as "Deng's every word, in particular, must be obeyed by the Politburo" (p. 5); "If Deng said something was 'good', no one would say otherwise'"(p. 146); and "Whether the members of the Standing Committee agreed with Deng's ideas or not, they first had to obey him politically" (p. 193). Moreover, *when discussing matters they are directly familiar with*, these emigrés tend to adopt the "Deng must be obeyed" perspective.

[26]   See, for instance, Carol Lee Hamrin, *China and the Challenge of the Future: Changing Political Patterns* (Boulder: Westview Press, 1990), pp. 5, 188; and Lowell Dittmer,

depended on his skill—in Dittmer's words, "his consummate mastery of intramural political tactics"[27]—in keeping a dominant coalition behind him, through a series of trade-offs and concessions and by positioning himself so that he became the balancer required to guarantee Party unity among the contending camps. Clearly, as will be discussed, Deng did play a balancing role, but to attribute his position to such a role or to political legerdemain understates the authority he actually exercised.

Given the limitations of reliable materials concerning the elite's interactions, it is difficult to demonstrate the subordination to Deng's wishes, which is so richly documented by Party history sources for Mao. Moreover, although it apparently involved no determined resistance on his part, at least in the case of Zhao Ziyang during the Beijing spring of 1989 there was a refusal to go along with the directives of the paramount leader, causing an exasperated Yang Shangkun to confront Zhao with the remark that "Comrade Xiaoping did speak on this question. ... So are you for Comrade Xiaoping or against him?"[28] Yet apart from that single exception,[29] there is little unambiguous evidence of Deng being disobeyed in any case where he had clearly stated his position. Instead, there are many examples, in the classic manner of court politics, of different leaders and groups using Deng's views to push their particular perspectives, seeking to persuade him of their positions in order to pre-empt collective decisions, or of the leader's intervention ending a contentious debate where significant interests were engaged or even where other major leaders—including Chen Yun—had staked out contrary positions. A few cases by way of illustration will demonstrate these points.

An example of different groups using and attempting to influence Deng's views occurred during the theory conference shortly after the 1978 Third Plenum. In the first half of the conference in January-February 1979, reformist

---

"Patterns of Elite Strife and Succession in Chinese Politics", *The China Quarterly*, No. 123 (1990), p. 408.

[27] Dittmer is actually inconsistent in his treatment of Deng's power, on the one hand picturing him as an emperor-like figure that "no one can openly challenge", yet on the other hand seeing him as having had to contend with challenges from various "strong rivals". The specific point at issue here is whether Deng's power was based on political maneuvering or on an unchallengeable authority based on status.

[28] See Yang Shangkun's speech of 22 May 1989, in James Tong (ed.), "Death at the Gate of Heavenly Peace: The Democracy Movement in Beijing, April-June 1989 (I)", *Chinese Law and Government* (Spring 1990), p. 71. While Zhao dissented from the decision to impose martial law during the Tiananmen protests, there is no reliable information that he did anything to rally opposition to Deng's course of action.

[29] Other instances where a case for disobedience to Deng's orders could be made concern Hu Yaobang's activities in 1986 and the price reform issue in 1988. For my interpretation of these cases, see below.

intellectuals were encouraged by the results of the Third Plenum, the direct patronage of Hu Yaobang, and Deng's remarks at both the plenum and conference on the need for greater democracy (which even noted "the good points of the bourgeoisie"). In response, these intellectuals mustered the courage to launch sweeping criticisms of past and existing practices. During the spring festival break, however, more conservative theorists led by Hu Qiaomu brought to Deng's attention some of the radical criticisms, which predictably shocked the leader. This led to his famous statement in March 1979 laying down the "four cardinal principles",[30] which significantly reinforced ideological orthodoxy. A significant hardening in policy towards intellectuals and political life more broadly followed the shifting views of the leader.[31]

Top "first front" leaders, moreover, consistently sought Deng's backing. Hu Yaobang visited Deng many times in late 1983 before convincing him of the need to curb the campaign against spiritual pollution.[32] In drafting a political reform program from September 1986 to mid-1987, Zhao Ziyang linked all policy proposals to Deng's ideas, discussed decisions with Deng before meetings of the responsible leadership group, and sought his approval well before any major new concepts went to the Politburo. Zhao's general practice at Politburo meetings was to prejudice the discussion by beginning with the observation that "I have already talked to Comrade Xiaoping about this issue".[33] Li Peng and Yao Yilin went to Deng in the late summer of 1988 and convinced him of the seriousness of the economy's overheating, thus aborting price reform plans and launching an austerity program.[34] And in the spring of 1989 Zhao used Deng's confidant Yang Shangkun as an intermediary in an effort to persuade Deng to reverse his judgement of the student demonstrations, only to receive his leader's fiat that this was not allowed (*bu xing*).[35]

Examples abound of Deng forthrightly settling contentious debates. A debate raged in late 1983 over whether to retain and expand the Special Economic Zones (SEZs), a topic on which Chen Yun had taken a decidedly cautious line. In the event, Deng toured the SEZs in January-February 1984 and gave his personal blessing. Upon returning to Beijing Deng convened a high-level meeting to recommend the creation of a number of open cities on China's coast and, in the words of an oral source, after Deng spoke "of course" no one opposed it, while

---

[30]   These were: the need to uphold the socialist road, the dictatorship of the proletariat, the leadership of the Communist Party, and Marxism-Leninism and Mao Zedong Thought.

[31]   Merle Goldman, "Hu Yaobang's Intellectual Network and the Theory Conference of 1979", *The China Quarterly*, No. 126 (1991), especially pp. 230–7; and oral sources.

[32]   Interview with a senior reform official well positioned to know of the matter.

[33]   Hamrin and Zhao, *Decision-Making in Deng's China*, pp. 143–6, 236.

[34]   Interview with a senior Party historian who has written on economic policy in the reform era.

[35]   Source cited in the note above.

Chen Yun absented himself from further participation. Subsequent debate apparently focused on the particulars of the new policy, the end result being an expansion to fourteen open cities.[36] Several years later Deng's power was again demonstrated in an even more sensitive area. Following the early 1987 resignation of Hu Yaobang and the launching of intense criticism against "bourgeois liberalization", Zhao Ziyang persuaded Deng of the need to curb the campaign and set about drafting his critical 13 May statement to that effect. Once Deng approved, even the most fervent advocate of attacks on "liberalization", Deng Liqun, could do no more than suggest the addition of a single word during the relevant discussions.[37] Later that same year, the presentation of a blueprint for political reform to a Central Committee plenum produced different opinions. In the account of a State Council official of the time, "as soon as (those concerned) saw Deng's (approving) assessment, no further opinions were expressed".[38] And in the most dramatic case, more than two years after his formal retirement Deng again toured southern China in early 1992 to advocate a speeding up of reform and economic development. In an account of the public reaction reminiscent of responses to the pronouncements of Chairman Mao, people assertedly "hailed and digested" Deng's words while the Politburo adopted his program and Party elders including Chen Yun, Peng Zhen and Bo Yibo, alleged conservatives all, voiced their support.[39] In all these and other cases, there was a clear downward flow of authority and a willingness to accept Deng's directives by those with reservations, a process that surely went beyond political balancing.

---

[36]   Hamrin, *China and the Challenge of the Future*, pp. 82–3; Ruan Ming, "The Evolution of the Central Secretariat and Its Authority", in Hamrin and Zhao, *Decision-Making in Deng's China*, pp. 18–21; *Chen Yun wenxuan (1956–1985)* [Selected Works of Chen Yun, 1956–1985] (Beijing: Renmin Chubanshe, 1986), pp. 276, 280; Deng Xiaoping, *Fundamental Issues in Present-Day China* (Beijing: Foreign Languages Press, 1987), pp. 43–5; and oral sources. This is not to say that Chen had no impact on the shape of the decision, as several senior Party figures attribute the failure to extend the open cities to Shanghai to his influence, but the decision clearly went against his argument for no expansion.

[37]   This was the only "essential criticism" offered by any participant. Guoguang Wu, "'Documentary Politics': Hypotheses, Process, and Case Studies", in Hamrin and Zhao, *Decision-Making in Deng's China*, pp. 30–3.

[38]   Chen Yizi, *Zhongguo: shinian gaige yu bajiu minyun—Beijing liusi tushade beihou* [China: Ten Years of Reform and the 1989 Movement—Background to the 4 June Beijing Massacre] (Taipei: Lianjing Chubanshe, 1991), p. 112.

[39]   *Beijing Review*, No. 12 (1992), p. 5, No. 15 (1992), p. 4; and Xinhua Domestic Service, 31 March, 4 April and 1 May 1992, in *Foreign Broadcast Information Service*, 1 April 1992, pp. 19–20, 6 April 1992, pp. 36–7, 1 May 1992, pp. 18–19. It is not clear whether Deng consulted with other leaders before his tour, while an account in the Hong Kong daily, *Ming bao*, 20 February 1992, claims that Deng's proposals were accepted by the Politburo without discussion; *Inside China Mainland* (April 1992), pp. 3–4.

The question remains why Deng had such extraordinary authority. A key factor here was assuredly his revolutionary status as one of the highest ranking associates of Mao Zedong.[40] Yet this cannot explain why Deng stood so clearly above both Chen Yun and Peng Zhen in actual authority. Not only were these figures of nearly equal seniority in Party membership, but Chen and Peng had preceded Deng on the Politburo by twenty and nine years respectively. Moreover, according to an authoritative oral source, mainly by virtue of his opinions concerning the Great Leap Forward, Chen Yun entered the post-Mao period with a deserved reputation of having been more consistently correct in his policy views than any other leader. Yet a number of factors appear to have worked in Deng's favour. First, among the three men Deng had served the longest since 1949 as a member of the core group around Mao, despite his two "purges" in 1966–72 and 1976. In contrast, when the post-Mao era began, Chen Yun had basically been on the sidelines since 1962, while Peng Zhen was still classified as an anti-Party element who would not be rehabilitated until 1979. Moreover, ironically in view of Deng's two falls at the hands of Mao, he was more highly assessed by the Chairman than either Chen or Peng, as revealed in Mao's praise at the time of Deng's recall to office in 1973.[41] Even after he was ousted by Mao a second time three years later, this subsequent judgement could more readily be explained away in terms of Mao's deteriorating health and manipulation by the "Gang of Four" than could his earlier negative conclusions on Chen and Peng. In another sense, Deng's active role in combatting the hated "Gang" during the period before Mao's death and the fact that, prior to the Chairman's last change of heart, Deng had the endorsement of both Mao and the admired Zhou Enlai as *de facto* successor gave Deng an especially potent claim to leadership, albeit one that would be confused by Mao's subsequent designation of Hua Guofeng in the same role. Thus Deng's restoration to office became a prime mission of veteran revolutionaries in the immediate post-Mao period, a mission that implicitly recognized his pre-eminence among the older generation.

Finally, a critical factor was Deng's military prestige. As one of the co-leaders of the Second Field Army and a key figure in the crucial Huai-Hai battle of 1948, Deng was one of the true heroes of the military struggle, a status in no way challenged by the essentially civilian careers of Chen and Peng. Indeed, when military ranks were granted in 1955, it had originally been planned to name Deng a marshal, a proposal that was dropped because it was decided no "civilian"

---

[40]   Again, the crucial status factor is ignored by Dittmer. See his discussion of the sources of power of the "Supreme Leader"—namely, of Mao as well as Deng—which emphasizes access to "levers of bureaucratic power and to the media and symbolism" without acknowledging the prestige on which such access was predicated.

[41]   For this assessment and Mao-Deng relations generally, see Frederick C. Teiwes, "Mao and His Lieutenants", *The Australian Journal of Chinese Affairs*, Nos 19 and 20 (1988), especially pp. 68–72. Senior oral sources, moreover, emphasize that among the leadership group Deng, along with Lin Biao, was Mao's favourite.

leader would hold the rank.[42] Deng's military prestige was perhaps most graphically illustrated when he visited the home of Defense Minister Ye Jianying in spring 1977—in other words, before resuming official duties. During this private meeting Deng respectfully addressed Ye as "old marshal", and Ye quickly replied that "you too are an old marshal, you are the *leader* of us old marshals".[43] Such a perception by the leading military figures of the revolution makes credible the reports that Deng subsequently was placed under considerable PLA pressure to retain ultimate military authority as head of the Central Military Commission when he may have wished to appoint Hu Yaobang and then Zhao Ziyang to the position.[44] In any case, it clearly was a vital factor in Deng's unquestioned status as *the* leader of the Party.

While the above factors explain Deng's status, they only go part of the way in determining his capacity to claim a large degree of obedience. Here the need for someone to be in charge (*zhuchi*) (a need similar to that facilitating Mao's expanding powers in revolutionary times) seems crucial. Nothwithstanding the real desire for leadership collegiality, the impulse for decisive leadership has ultimately been stronger, particularly for old revolutionaries. This impulse, as well as an evaluation that Deng had satisfactorily filled the role, was reflected in the 1989 Central Committee decision on his resignation:

> After the downfall of the "Gang of Four" and especially through the Third Plenary Session of the 11th Party Central Committee, Comrade Deng Xiaoping became the nucleus of our Party's second-generation[45] leading collective. At that time, China was confronted with a very grave situation and arduous tasks: It had to extricate itself swiftly from the calamities wrought by the "Cultural Revolution" and moreover a

---

[42]   According to a senior Party historian, the original plan was to name Mao "Generalissimo", thus placing him on the same level as Chiang Kai-shek (and incidentally Stalin), while Zhou Enlai was to be declared a marshal along with Deng, but Mao decided against both steps. An exception to the no civilian stipulation was Chen Yi, who by that time was largely performing a foreign affairs role, but who had been a key *commander* during the revolution, in contrast to *political commissar* Deng. For further information on Deng's role in the PLA in this and other periods, see David S. G. Goodman, *Deng Xiaoping and the Chinese Revolution: A Political Biography* (London: Routledge, 1994), pp. 117–19; and *Zhonghua Renmin Gongheguo dang zheng jun qun lingdao renminglu* [Namelists of PRC Party, Government, Military and Mass Organization Leaders] (Beijing: Zhonggong dangshi chubanshe, 1990), pp. 13–14.

[43]   Hu Hua (ed.), *Zhonggong dangshi renwuzhuan* [Biographies of Personalities in CCP History], Vol. 44 (Xi'an: Shaanxi Renmin Chubanshe, 1989), p. 107 (emphasis added).

[44]   The sources are a Hong Kong report in the case of Hu and, apparently, oral sources concerning Zhao. See *Zhengming* [Contention] (August 1981), in *Foreign Broadcast Information Service*, 14 August 1981, p. W6; and Stuart R. Schram, "China After the 13th Congress", *The China Quarterly*, No. 114 (1988), pp. 194–5.

[45]   See above, note 16.

new blueprint had to be charted to advance in the years to come. Comrade Deng Xiaoping lived up to the great expectations of the Party and the people.[46]

Such an evaluation clearly has charismatic overtones, although it would be more appropriate to conclude that Deng was thrust into the leading role more on the basis of his previously achieved status than by demonstrating an ongoing ability to solve the Party's crises as had been the case with the pre-Liberation Mao. Yet like Mao, once Deng was in the role of unchallenged leader, his ongoing authority was not affected by any of the setbacks endured by the Party under his policies.

While Deng's actual authority was substantially above that of the collective, and some of the instances examined above suggest that he may have acted unilaterally from time to time, on the whole his style of leadership reflected the loose conception of collective rule valued by the broader elite and actually implemented to a significant degree by Mao up to 1957. There is ample evidence of Deng consulting other senior leaders in the process of shaping policies or handling crisis situations, even seeking out Chen Yun in his home, and incorporating their views in his speeches.[47] Clearly this was designed to build a consensus. Undoubtedly the most elaborate example involving not only key veteran revolutionaries but large numbers of Party leaders and historians was the drafting of the 1981 Resolution on Party History. With the explicit aim of "closing ranks and looking to the future", this resolution illustrated both Deng's consultative approach and his ultimate authority. Broad consultation over a 20-month period, involving 4,000 participants and more than twenty actual drafters, achieved an acceptable middle ground on such sensitive issues as the evaluation of Mao, but a middle ground that significantly conformed to Deng's guidelines on substance, methodology and style.[48] This was reminiscent of the best of the pre-1957 Mao—open to suggestion, normally holding to a centrist position, yet at the same time having firm control of the overall direction. Even where he may have acted unilaterally concerning SEZs in 1984 or the acceleration of reform in 1992, it was within the parameters of an existing policy debate rather than the unpredictable, disruptive interventions of the later Mao.

Most though not all of the evidence of Deng's consultative style comes from his more active period in the early 1980s, with the evidence naturally becoming less clear as he moved progressively further onto the "second front". But this

---

[46]   Beijing Review, No. 47 (1989), p. 19.

[47]   See, for example, Selected Works of Deng, pp. 289, 365; and Dangshi tongxun [Party History Bulletin], No. 17 (1983), pp. 2–3.

[48]   Selected Works of Deng, pp. 277, 282–3, 287, 291; and Dangshi huiyi baogaoji [Collection of Reports to the Party History Conference] (Beijing: Zhonggong Zhongyang Dangxiao Chubanshe, 1982), pp. 119–21, 127–8.

retreat points to central features of Deng's long-term plan for China, involving an increasing institutionalization of power, the cultivation of a successor generation, and the transfer of power to that generation. There is little to suggest anything but a serious commitment to these goals, but at the same time, Deng recognized that the process would have to be gradual. While it is likely that Deng was ambivalent about the prospect, which arguably influenced Hu Yaobang's fall,[49] he nevertheless declared his (and also Chen Yun's) desire to retire on various occasions beginning in 1979.[50] That it took ten years before his official retirement was undoubtedly due in large measure to the demands of his colleagues, his realization that his political muscle was the ultimate guarantor of his program, and—as particularly revealed during spring 1989—a patrimonial sense shared by his generation of a special responsibility for the survival of *their* revolution.

Yet short of ceding final authority and apart from his consultations with other elders, Deng did grant his "first front" comrades considerable scope in policy design as well as daily administration. In 1984 he noted that most of the work had been done by others, that during the previous year he had only concerned himself with the crackdown on crime, that at present he was limiting himself to the Hong Kong question and the opening of fourteen new cities, and that he had contributed not one word to the crucial decision on urban economic reform.[51] More than four years later, in March 1989 he declared he had retired (sic) "so as to let others assume responsibility", as he did not wish to create "pressure over the heads" of new leaders. Two years later Li Peng claimed that Deng "always encourages the new collective leadership to make decisions and to deal with things independently".[52] While Deng clearly was not willing to remove pressure from above in a crisis or, as events at the start of 1992 indicate, forever allow the "first front" to manage the policy agenda independently, overall his style encouraged a much greater degree of initiative than Mao ever countenanced from his position on the "second front". Nevertheless, Deng's ongoing ultimate authority, whether by Party decision after the 1987 13th Congress or, apparently, by general acceptance after his formal retirement, greatly complicated the task of those on the "first front" who required his support or his tolerance for major policies, and who had to judge repeatedly the appropriate level of consultation with a leader who asked them to take the initiative but obviously was unwilling to give up the final say. Their dilemma was further complicated by Deng's advanced years, a

---

[49]   While Dittmer argues in Chapter 1 that Hu attempted to pressure Deng into full retirement, a more credible version of this incident is that Hu took up *Deng's* proposal, but that elders such as Wang Zhen took even this as inexcusable; see Ruan Ming, *Deng Xiaoping: Chronicle of an Empire* (Boulder: Westview Press, 1994), pp. 164–5.

[50]   See *Selected Works of Deng*, pp. 220, 365.

[51]   Deng, *Fundamental Issues in Present-Day China*, pp. 72–4.

[52]   *Renmin ribao*, 24 March 1989, p. 1; and *Beijing Review*, No. 16 (1991) p. 18.

situation inevitably limiting his ability to focus on issues and marked by an erratic memory—thus increasing the possibilities of misunderstanding.[53]

While Deng's authority within the leadership was secure throughout the reform period, his political *modus operandi* inevitably involved concern with maximizing political support for his objectives. Clearly, like Mao, Deng was also concerned with personal loyalty, as reflected in the retention of fellow octogenarian Yang Shangkun on the "first front" and in a key operational military role after the 13th Congress.[54] More broadly, despite an apparent relative impartiality in spreading positions among historical Party groupings, reminiscent of Mao during the initial post-1949 period,[55] a degree of "factional" favouritism on Deng's part in the PLA is suggested by a seeming partiality in promoting members of Deng's Second Field Army.[56] But while Deng's role as balancer arguably also encompassed a desire to sustain personal support, there is no convincing evidence of his position ever being under threat from any grouping within the higher echelons of the elite. Rather, as shall be discussed at greater length in the concluding section, Deng's balancing role is better explained as reflecting his pursuit of consensus and the diverse strands of his own political preferences. Indeed, the judgment of Tang Tsou more than a decade and a half ago remains valid: Deng "was subjected to cross-pressure from all sides (but he) responded to these pressures in his own way, according to his own convictions, and in pursuit of his own purposes".[57] Simply put, while Deng made tactical concessions, the swings in the Party's policy during the reform era, in another similarity to Mao's time, are most easily understood as reflecting strategic adjustments on the part of a leader whose thought encompassed both far-reaching reform goals and an unbending commitment to Party rule.

---

[53]   As early as 1982 Deng indicated he was unable to work an eight-hour day, and the situation certainly deteriorated in the subsequent period; *Selected Works of Deng*, p. 378. With regard to Deng's memory, according to an authoritative oral source, on one occasion Deng requested a meeting with provincial leaders but when they gathered at his home he demanded to know what they were doing there and sent them away.

[54]   While Yang was not close to Deng during the revolutionary period, they apparently developed close relations while serving in the central Party apparatus from the early 1950s onward.

[55]   For Mao in this regard, see Teiwes, *Politics at Mao's Court*, pp. 98–101, 134–40.

[56]   This was particularly apparent in the disproportionate number of Second Field Army veterans holding the rank of general in 1988, and there are many unverified reports of resentment on the part of those who served in other army units during the revolution; see, for instance, Ian Wilson and You Ji, "Leadership by 'Lines': China's Unresolved Succession", *Problems of Communism*, Vol. 39, No. 1 (January-February 1990), pp. 38–41.

[57]   Tang Tsou, "The Historic Change in Direction and Continuity with the Past", *The China Quarterly*, No. 98 (1984), pp. 338–9.

Deng Xiaoping and Chen Yun: Political Cooperation and Policy Divergence

While Deng's ideas and especially his authority have been crucial to reform era politics, enormous influence was also exerted by Chen Yun. As a leading reform intellectual put it in the mid-1980s, "there are only two superpowers in Chinese politics, Deng Xiaoping and Chen Yun; when they speak everyone feels they must obey".[58] While this statement overstates the degree of obedience felt necessary in response to Chen's words, it reflects the enormity of his prestige and power that was widely assumed by attentive audiences in the PRC.[59] In particular, Chen's influence was manifest in the two areas he had been connected with historically, Party organization and the economy, in the latter case especially through the State Planning Commission. However, it is also widely believed, both within China and by outside observers including Dittmer, that Chen Yun was the head of a "conservative" leadership faction that often opposed Deng's policies, or even was involved in a power struggle with Deng.[60] Although much cannot be known about the Deng-Chen relationship, at the very least such a view is grossly oversimplified. A more adequate view would note a period of close cooperation, undoubted differences both on some issues and in the men's temperaments, but a willingness on Chen's part to accept Deng's ultimate authority. As a senior figure with a close personal knowledge of Chen declared, he was "not the sort of man" to oppose the Party's leader.[61]

The importance of Chen Yun's support for Deng Xiaoping in the initial post-Mao period cannot be exaggerated. Chen was one of the earliest and most forceful voices demanding the return of Deng to office, particularly (with Wang Zhen) at the major March 1977 central work conference.[62] Moreover, at the late 1978 work conference preceding the Third Plenum, Chen was a dominant force in altering the agenda and raising issues on which Hua Guofeng was vulnerable; he took the lead on such questions as the rehabilitation of veteran leaders and the "reversal of the verdict" on the 1976 Tiananmen incident. Indeed, in some ways he seemed more prominent than Deng at this critical juncture.[63] Equally

---

58   Interview, Sydney, 1986.

59   Awareness of Chen's clout was a particular feature of emigré cadre accounts, some of which tended to see him as virtually on a par with Deng; see Hamrin and Zhao, *Decision-Making in Deng's China*, pp. 51, 55, 198–9, 241.

60   For example, see ibid., pp. 135, 236–7; and Richard Baum, *Burying Mao: Chinese Politics in the Age of Deng Xiaoping* (Princeton: Princeton University Press, 1994), pp. 10–11, 319–20, 352–5 and *passim*.

61   Interview, Sydney, 1993. The person in question is not a conservative, and indeed was critical of Chen's policy preferences.

62   *Guoshi yanjiu tongxun* [National History Research Bulletin], 10 April 1993, p. 1; and oral sources.

63   Wang Hongmo et al., *Gaige kaifang*, pp. 122–7; and oral sources.

important, once installed as a Party vice chairman at the Third Plenum in late 1978, Chen played a major role in shaping the emerging reform program and managing the accompanying political problems. For this period up to the mid-1980s, he could justly be called the co-architect of reform, even though this accolade was never officially bestowed.[64] In fact, on many occasions it was difficult to determine whether Deng or Chen was the initiator of key programs, with Chen frequently appearing to be the prime mover. This was reflected in Deng's statements of support for various views advocated by Chen, views that went well beyond Chen's acknowledged economic expertise. Of particular importance was Chen's role in personnel policy and Party discipline, areas where as Party organization chief in Yan'an he also had imposing credentials. Chen more than anyone else appears to have been the designer of the program to promote younger, better educated and professionally competent cadres who would both modernize public administration and become the successor generations of leaders.[65] Moreover, he demonstrated acute sensitivity to the popular alienation caused by the abuse of official privileges and economic crime, and Deng forcefully endorsed his view that improving the Party's work style was "a matter of life and death".[66] And on the crucial issue of evaluating the Party's history and especially Mao Zedong, Chen and Deng seemingly coordinated their activities to produce what was deemed a satisfactory result.[67] Given that Deng was essentially endorsing Chen's economic views in this initial period,[68] the cooperation between the two veteran leaders could hardly have been closer or more significant for the overall reform program.

The contentious issue involves the degree to which there was a parting of the ways between Deng and Chen from the mid-1980s onward and, to the extent there was any rift, its political significance. Any assessment must be speculative because of the relative lack of hard evidence concerning Chen's beliefs, activities and role after 1985. Always one of the less public figures in the leadership, not only were Chen's appearances infrequent but his known statements were few and far between during that period. When Chen's thoughts were made public it was usually in the form of recycling his old statements, congratulatory inscriptions, or

---

[64]   According to Robert Delfs in *Far Eastern Economic Review*, 8 November 1990, p. 19, Chen's supporters in Beijing were trying to make precisely this claim at that time.

[65]   See *Chen Yun wenxuan*, pp. 262–73; *Selected Works of Deng*, pp. 308, 362, 365, 378; and Deng, *Fundamental Issues in Present-Day China*, p. 81.

[66]   *Hongqi* [Red Flag], No. 3 (1982), p. 4; and *Selected Works of Deng*, p. 340.

[67]   See *Selected Works of Deng*, p. 289; *Chen Yun wenxuan*, pp. 218, 255–6; and *Dangshi huiyi baogaoji*, pp. 119–20.

[68]   See *Selected Works of Deng*, pp. 335–6, 343. Cf. Tsou, "The Historic Change in Direction", p. 336.

very brief letters addressing issues far from the top of the Party's agenda.[69] Frail in health, Chen apparently was also a less regular provider of guidance than Deng in his declining years.[70] This, however, might partially be explained by the fact that, unlike Deng's case, there was no formal decision at the 13th Congress to require the referral of key decisions to Chen.[71]

Chen's fundamental elusiveness after 1985 notwithstanding, there is no clear evidence of *determined opposition* to Deng on Chen Yun's part concerning either overall policy or specific issues. While the record is similarly scanty with regard to statements of support, and both rumour and deduction can lead one to believe that Chen was less than impressed with Deng's positions or performance at key junctures, he nevertheless did provide support during the 1989 Tiananmen crisis and for Deng's re-emphasis on reform in early 1992.[72] Moreover, whatever reservations Chen may have had on specific points, in July 1987 he unambiguously declared that "at present the number one leader is Comrade Xiaoping".[73] Finally, whatever their differences on specifics, in considering their many earlier areas of close collaboration there is little reason to posit any post-1985 discordance on the strategy of orderly generational change, the need to deal with corruption and limit arbitrary power, and the desirability of an experimental step-by-step approach to policy. In general terms, Deng, Chen and most of their fellow Party veterans surely retained fundamental agreement on the centrality of Party rule, the importance of ideological education to support that rule, the need for "stability and unity" within the leadership, economic growth as the over-riding task, the necessity for significant reform of the existing economic structure, a belief that economic reform in some way needed to be linked to a less well understood process of political reform, and the necessity for China to open up to the outside world.

The differences that seemingly emerged between Chen and Deng largely concerned economic policy as the Party moved further down the reform path. Chen Yun's core economic opinions have remained remarkably consistent over

---

[69]   See *Renmin ribao*, 18 January 1991, p. 1, 20 April 1992, p. 4; and *Shisanda yilai zhongyao wenxian xuanbian* [Selected Important Documents Since the 13th Congress], Vol. 1 (Beijing: Renmin Chubanshe, 1991), p. 252, Vol. 2, pp. 881–4, 1045, 1122.

[70]   See Cheng Xiaonong, "Decision and Miscarriage: Radical Price Reform in the Summer of 1988", in Hamrin and Zhao, *Decision-Making in Deng's China*, pp. 190, 199.

[71]   According to a high-ranking participant at the Congress. Cf. Zhao Ziyang's 13th Congress remarks in *Yanhua zisun* [Chinese Descendants] (March 1988), p. 9.

[72]   While in both cases Chen's support may have been grudging, it was not necessarily consistently "conservative". As Baum, in *Burying Mao*, p. 10, has skillfully argued, Chen's views (as in 1989) concerning the use of coercion may have been more restrained than those of Deng.

[73]   *Dang de wenxian*, No. 4 (1990), p. 5.

the entire post-1949 period.[74] Chen was an early critic of the Stalinist economic model who saw the need for greater decentralization and a larger role for the market, albeit under the overall guidance of central planning and central financial controls. He thus advocated restructuring the economic system, with greater economic efficiency as the over-riding objective. He further believed that to sustain economic growth it was crucial to guarantee balanced growth among the economic sectors, and his readjustment policies, whether in the early 1960s or early 1980s, were designed to achieve this goal. Perhaps most crucial, Chen has been a consistent advocate of economic caution, of not setting unrealistic, disruptive targets, and of steering clear of any pursuit of maximum growth in order to guarantee steady, stable long-term development.

These economic ideas were the basis not only of his readjustment policies, but also of the basic thrust of economic reform as it initially evolved in the late 1970s and early 1980s.[75] There is not only irrefutable evidence of Deng's support for Chen's economic views, but also much evidence that the pre-eminent economic reformer of the mid and late 1980s, Zhao Ziyang, was also closely following Chen's line during this initial early 1980s period.[76] The question really becomes how sharply economic policy departed from Chen's views from about the time of the October 1984 decision on urban economic reform. On the one hand, there can be no doubt that experiments with the market and the weakening of the planning system went far beyond anything Chen Yun had contemplated in the Maoist period or publicly advocated under the reforms. On the other hand, apart from a few warnings on specific matters like China's neglect of grain— warnings subsequently echoed by Deng[77]—Chen did not openly oppose any policies and in fact gave his assent to the 1984 package.[78] Finally, during the post-June 1989 period, when it is generally assumed that Chen's influence on economic policy was greatest, and readjustment, balance and caution were the themes of the day, the state sector continued to shrink, market experiments were

---

[74]   See, for example, David M. Bachman, *Chen Yun and the Chinese Political System*, China Research Monograph No. 29 (Berkeley: University of California, 1985), Ch. III; and the Introduction to Nicholas R. Lardy and Kenneth Lieberthal (eds), *Chen Yun's Strategy for China's Development: A Non-Maoist Alternative* (Armonk: M. E. Sharpe, 1983).

[75]   Nearly all of the crucial reform themes can be traced to the 1979 and early 1980 period when Chen was in direct overall charge of the economy. That responsibility became Zhao Ziyang's in March 1980.

[76]   See *Chen Yun wenxuan*, pp. 250, 254, 276, 277, 285; *Selected Works of Deng*, pp. 335, 343; and Ruan Ming, *Deng Xiaoping*, pp. 129–30.

[77]   See, for example, Deng, *Fundamental Issues in Present-Day China*, pp. 141–2. Chen's views on the grain question had been most forcefully expressed at the 1985 National Party Conference; see *Chen Yun wenxuan*, pp. 303–4.

[78]   See Deng's assertion that all Central Committee leaders had approved the decision; *Fundamental Issues in Present-Day China*, p. 81.

pushed further and, despite the emphasis on planning, no return to the old-style planning system was contemplated.[79] The slim record suggests that Chen was willing to go along with or at least not openly oppose many of the innovations which went further than his long-held beliefs, that he was not overly tied to any specific concept of planning or socialism, but that he continued to prefer a cautious approach to economic management.[80] Indeed, in discussing Chen Yun's role with Chinese Party historians, the more senior the individual concerned, including those of manifest reformist sympathies, the more likely that the person will view Chen and Deng as having been united on the reform course but differing concerning methods.[81]

Two specific cases of possible Deng-Chen conflict—the 1988 price reform and Deng's renewed reform push of 1992—require examination, however. In the former case, Deng's authority was reflected in his virtual one-man initiative, which caught nearly everyone by surprise. While initially the "first front" leaders attempted to respond with a leisurely five-year plan, Deng's insistence (largely expressed through conversations with foreigners) led to hasty proposals without the benefit of any prior planning, with even reformist think tanks divided among themselves. In a classic case of court politics, the various actors sought to use Deng's unexpected and simplistic intervention to push their own larger programs—Zhao Ziyang to advocate more comprehensive economic reform measures, and Li Peng and Yao Yilin to design a price reform compatible with the interests of the State Planning Commission. Chen Yun did intervene in this context not to oppose price reform but to instruct Yao Yilin on the dangers of overheating. With the development of panic-buying, Deng subsequently consented

---

[79] See David Bachman, "Planning and Politics in Mainland China Since the Massacre", *Issues & Studies*, Vol. 26, No. 8 (August 1990); Nina P. Halpern, "The Impact of Tiananmen on the Political Climate of Economic Reform", *Issues & Studies*, Vol. 27, No. 3 (March 1991); and Nicholas R. Lardy, "Is China Different? The Fate of Its Economic Reform", in Daniel Chirot (ed.), *The Crisis of Leninism and the Decline of the Left: The Revolutions of 1989* (Seattle: University of Washington Press, 1991).

[80] See the spate of praise for Chen's economic thought in 1990, especially Liu Guoguang's article in *Renmin ribao*, 14 September 1990, p. 5. Here Liu basically praised Chen's pragmatic and steady approach to economic policy. Of particular note was his claim that the problems in economic work since 1984 were due to "blind optimism" and "seeking quick results", precisely the type of program that Chen had consistently opposed. Liu also praised Chen's famous "bird cage" analogy, which emphasized the overall primacy of planning, but the specifics of his discussion emphasized the measures Chen had advocated in the 1950s to *relax* planning controls. It is also worth noting that Liu, the acolyte of the "conservative" Chen, was a major proponent of one of the most risky reform measures— price reform.

[81] In this regard, one senior historian observed that Chen was quite practical in his economic views and not a rigid advocate of planning, and that his concept of socialism centred on the state sector remaining the dominant factor in the economy.

to an austerity program, which also saw the sidelining of radical price reform. But while Chen's actions had the effect of complicating price-reform efforts (something arguably more affected by the technical difficulties involved and by popular discontent with rising prices), at no time did he oppose Deng's initiative.[82]

Deng's 1992 southern tour occurred under even more unusual circumstances: more than two years after his formal retirement; in the context of his statements about not placing pressure on the "first front" leaders; and at a time when Chen Yun's austerity views (which reflected economic realities) were dominant in economic thinking. Deng seemingly concluded that this situation was damaging reform and took the Mao-like step of mobilizing support in the localities. In contrast to Dittmer, however, I believe that as in Mao's case[83] this did *not* mean that Deng could not get his way at the Centre and had to rely on outside support. Rather, given his explicit posture of not overly interfering in the affairs of the "first front", it seemed more appropriate to him to demonstrate support than to issue direct commands. As Deng's daughter, Deng Rong, put it, when big issues arose her father would speak out, and his words carried greater weight than those of others.[84] With the "first front" falling into line (albeit not without reservations even on the part of reformers such as Zhu Rongji),[85] Chen Yun soon voiced support, endorsing Deng's initiative and calling for "emancipating the mind" and "bold steps" to guarantee development. Whatever reservations Chen undoubtedly had, he supported his leader.[86]

Overall, for all the differences of context, Chen's relationship to Deng bears a remarkable similarity to his relationship with Mao. In both cases there were differences in policy preference, although far less dramatic in the case of Chen and

---

[82]   See Cheng Xiaonong, "Decision and Miscarriage", pp. 192–7. Cheng, however, has a different interpretation which posits that both Deng and Chen avoided openly contradicting the other, thus suggesting a more equal relationship of the two (see p. 199). While I agree that Deng has generally sought to avoid public stances at variance with those of Chen, this has not stopped him from advocating, and seeing implemented, policies at odds with Chen's on-the-record views, as in the case of Special Economic Zones.

[83]   See the discussion of Mao's use of provincial leaders during the 1955 agricultural cooperativization campaign in Frederick C. Teiwes and Warren Sun, *The Politics of Agricultural Cooperativization: Mao, Deng Zihui and the 'High Tide' of 1955* (Armonk: M. E. Sharpe, 1993), p. 20.

[84]   As related by a senior reform figure during an interview.

[85]   See Tony Saich, "The Fourteenth Party Congress: A Programme for Authoritarian Rule", *The China Quarterly*, No. 132 (1992), p. 1142n.

[86]   Xinhua Domestic Service, 1 May 1992, in *Foreign Broadcast Information Service*, 1 May 1992, pp. 18–19. For much more conflictual accounts relying heavily on Hong Kong sources, see Baum, *Burying Mao*, Ch.14; and Suisheng Zhao, "Deng Xiaoping's Southern Tour: Elite Politics in Post-Tiananmen China", *Asian Survey*, Vol. 33, No. 8 (August 1993).

Deng, and even more significantly, differences in temperament. The essential contrast in both periods was between Chen's inherent caution and his leader's propensity to boldness. In the reform context, this was reflected in Chen's concern with economic overheating and a far more restrictive approach than Deng to specific policies such as the SEZs and rural enterprises, even when he approved these in principle.[87] While there were many occasions on which Deng too warned of overheating, endorsed steady and stable growth, and echoed Chen's approach of testing innovations and quickly correcting any destabilizing side effects,[88] he repeatedly made un-Chen-like appeals for daring and a willingness to take risks.[89] This was most startlingly expressed in Deng's early 1992 criticism of those who acted like "women with bound feet",[90] a deliberate use of the pointed phrase that Mao had used against those skeptical of speeding up agricultural cooperativization in 1955—and precisely the kind of campaign approach that both Deng and Chen had so forcefully rejected throughout the reform era. Yet a crucial continuity linked Chen's style in dealing with his supreme leader. Mao had observed that Chen "observes discipline", and Chen did not speak out in disagreement in Mao's time.[91] In the view of a senior Party historian, that crucial uncodified norm of the Maoist period, the duty to obey the leader, was carried forward by Chen Yun in strikingly different times.

The Role of the Party Elders

The same pattern seemingly existed in the relations between Deng and the other gerontocrats. Nothwithstanding the more conservative views of some elders,[92] there is a dearth of hard evidence of any veteran figure actually opposing a position staked out by Deng. Indeed, from their known views there appeared to have been a broad commonality of opinions on fundamental *political* issues and a willingness to follow or at least not oppose Deng's lead on economic questions. Most importantly, in critical situations such as the spring of 1989, the impulse of this generation was to rally around its leader. While differences of emphasis clearly existed, in political terms the older generation apparently maintained a high degree of cohesion.

---

[87]   See, for instance, *Chen Yun wenxuan*, pp. 276, 280, 304, 305.

[88]   See, for instance, Deng, *Fundamental Issues in Present-Day China*, pp. 56, 69, 119, 128–9, 177.

[89]   For example, see ibid., pp. 89, 128, 169, 191.

[90]   *Beijing Review*, No. 15 (1992), p. 4.

[91]   See Teiwes, *Politics and Purges in China*, pp. xxvi–xxi; and Bachman, *Chen Yun*, p. 147.

[92]   Despite the conservative label often applied indiscriminately to the elders, Yang Shangkun in particular was a consistent supporter of reform, while Bo Yibo's position seemingly fluctuated.

Although not systematically addressed by Dittmer, the role of the older generation as a whole over the past decade and a half has clearly been crucial. While part of Deng's strategic design from early on included the need for that generation to pass power on to successor generations, he always saw the veterans as playing a vital role in selecting and training their successors. This was not simply a concession to keep their support; he felt it was essential, that the transition to a successor generation could be resolved relatively smoothly "while we are still around", but that chaos would result if the elders did not act and the problem was left to the future leaders themselves. The elders' retreat from power, in Deng's view, had to be gradual so that the designated successors who did not measure up could be removed in good time and better choices made.[93] The leaders on the "first front", moreover, acknowledged the continuing influence of the older generation. Hu Yaobang did so in 1981 upon assuming the Party Chairmanship, while in 1987 Zhao Ziyang marked his election as General Secretary by observing that the new leaders could be confident "because the elders are still in good health and around us".[94] This clearly left some grey areas for all concerned: the elders were to withdraw gradually, but at what pace? Even after "half retirement"[95] they would still be influential, but what authority would it be appropriate for them to exercise? The need to retain the good will of the elders as a group remained an important political requirement for the "first front", but a difficult one to realize.

The whole question of retiring from active political involvement raised uncertainties. First, it has frequently been assumed that key elderly leaders resisted retirement in order to "thwart" Deng and his reform program, but there is little to indicate that this has been the case at the very highest level. For example, Ye Jianying, one of those sometimes cited as refusing to retire in order to obstruct Deng, in fact submitted his resignation on several occasions beginning in 1979.[96] In contrast, the most intense reaction from the elders came in opposition to suggestions that Deng *himself* should completely retire.[97] More broadly, throughout the 1980s key leaders did withdraw from everyday authority as Deng required, be it from State Council posts in 1980 or from the Politburo and/or Central Committee in 1985 and 1987.[98] The latter resignations were in large

---

[93]   See *Selected Works of Deng*, pp. 198–9, 214–16, 309, 325, 361–2, 378–9. 389; and Michael Schoenhals, "The 1978 Truth Criterion Controversy", *The China Quarterly*, No. 126 (1991), p. 267.

[94]   Tian Guoliang et al., *Hu Yaobang zhuan* [Biography of Hu Yaobang] (Beijing: Zhonggong Dangshi Ziliao Chubanshe, 1989), p. 136; and *Yanhua zisun* (March 1988), p. 9.

[95]   This was Zhao Ziyang's term at the 13th Congress; see *Yanhua zisun* (March 1988), p. 9.

[96]   Tian Guoliang, *Hu Yaobang zhuan*, p. 114.

[97]   See Yan Jiaqi, "Chinese Authoritarianism", p. 7; and above, note 49.

[98]   See *Selected Works of Deng*, p. 302; *Beijing Review*, No. 39 (1985), pp. 6–7; and Stanley Rosen, "China in 1987: The Year of the Thirteenth Party Congress", *Asian Survey*, Vol.

measure "half retirements" to the Central Advisory Committee, which Deng had designed precisely for that purpose until he demanded its abolition in 1992. Yet some leaders—notably the "conservative" Peng Zhen[99]—were willing to go even further and surrender all official posts. While it is likely that some veteran leaders were at least ambivalent about the reduction of their formal power, there is little on which to base the notion of significant resistance to retirement, and knowledgeable oral sources deny that it was a major problem. While retirement did not affect power based on informal status, the reduction or elimination of their formal posts subtly affected the overall clout of the veteran leadership generation as a group.[100]

How, then, did the elders operate in retirement? The view of an assertive, interfering older generation was perhaps most colourfully expressed by the dissident intellectual Fang Lizhi, who declared in 1988 that "Those old guys just get on the phone and say 'do this'".[101] While this cannot be ruled out, such direct interference must have been sharply restricted given Deng's expressed desire that the "first front" operate as independently as possible and the obvious fact that the numbers of potential callers of extremely high status were of a decidedly limited and decreasing quantity. Further, it appears the elders seldom came together as a group; when they did meet during the 1989 Tiananmen crisis Yang Shangkun remarked that it was "the first time these octogenarians had gotten together to discuss central affairs in many years".[102]

In normal times two main avenues for the elders' influence existed. The first was through any influence they individually might have had with Deng Xiaoping. There were numerous reports backed up by reliable oral sources of various elders expressing their discontent to Deng about Hu Yaobang or Zhao Ziyang. Such links to Deng were based on personal intimacy as in the case of Wang Zhen, or because of an identification with Deng's program. Thus a senior Party historian,

---

28, No. 1 (January 1988), p. 43. Significantly, of Deng's generation only his close supporter, Yang Shangkun, remained on the "first front" after the 13th Congress.

[99]   Peng did not join the Central Advisory Committee at the 13th Congress, and after resigning as Chairman of the National People's Congress Standing Committee in 1988, he held no formal posts.

[100]   According to a senior Party historian, for the great bulk of older cadres of Central Advisory Committee level there has been relatively little scope to interfere, apart from military cadres where the legacy of command relationships between superiors and subordinates is particularly strong.

[101]   *New York Times* interview cited in June Teufel Dreyer, "The PLA Since the Thirteenth Party Congress", *Issues & Studies*, Vol. 25, No. 1 (January 1989), p. 101.

[102]   See Yang's speech of 24 May 1989, in Tong, "Death at the Gate of Heavenly Peace", p. 82.

when questioned about the continuing influence of Wan Li, commented that it was due to Deng's high regard for Wan as a "banner of reform".[103]

The second major method for influencing affairs available to retired veteran leaders was through direct contact with leaders on the "first front" whom they had sponsored or otherwise developed close relations with. Here the basic co-opting role of the older generation in selecting successors was central.[104] In this process older leaders sometimes picked out younger officials who had almost randomly come to their attention,[105] but more often they chose, as Deng put it, people "from within the circle of their own acquaintances".[106] These were most frequently individuals who had worked with them in official organizations, but it also involved the appointment of secretaries, bodyguards and relatives to high office. Whatever the specific circumstances, the patron-client relationships so central to Nathan's original model clearly existed on a substantial scale and greatly facilitated the ability of the elders to exert influence.

An inevitable result of the elders' advanced years, their often ill-informed ideas, the diversity of their views, and the irregularity of their involvement was not only that difficulties were created for the "first front", but also opportunities for officials to appeal to and manipulate this "higher authority" during their own

---

[103]   During the 1980s a small number of elderly leaders—usually eight—were, according to Beijing gossip as reflected in Hong Kong sources, considered of particular importance. These were Deng, Chen Yun, Li Xiannian, Peng Zhen, Yang Shangkun, Wang Zhen, Bo Yibo and Song Renqiong; see *Inside China Mainland* (September 1990), p. 5. Apart from Chen and Peng, whose historical status is clear, and Li and Bo, who achieved Politburo status in 1956, and Yang, who had a particularly significant pre-1949 role (as well as an intimate relationship with Deng), the remaining two—Wang Zhen and Song Renqiong—had no exceptional status but close personal ties to Deng. Cf. the fascinating group photo at the 14th Congress which included, in addition to Deng and the new and just replaced Standing Committees, the retired Yang Shangkun, Bo Yibo, Song Renqiong and Wan Li; *Renmin ribao*, 20 October 1992, p. 2.

[104]   While it is simplistic to say, as Dittmer among others does, that veteran leaders chose their own successors as part of some bargain with Deng, it is nevertheless clear that both before and after their retirement key elders played an inordinantly influential role in personnel matters. However, the claim of Chen Yizi in *Zhongguo*, p. 124, that control over appointments was vested in a "personnel small group" of Chen Yun and eight other elders even after the 13th Congress appears erroneous. According to a senior figure from the central organization department, no such group existed, although a similar body headed by Bo Yibo did handle the personnel fallout from Hu Yaobang's dismissal.

[105]   The classic case is Deng's favourable impression of Wang Zhaoguo during an inspection of a factory in 1980; see *Selected Works of Deng*, p. 389. Wang was raised from his position as factory deputy director to first secretary of the Youth League in 1982, and then became a secretary of the Party Secretariat in 1985 before being demoted to the post of vice governor of Fujian in 1987.

[106]   *Selected Works of Deng*, p. 392.

conflicts. This often led to counter-intuitive results, as in the case of reform intellectual Su Shaozhi mobilizing personal networks to persuade "conservative" Bo Yibo to save his threatened Marxism-Leninism Institute.[107] Zhao Ziyang's methods for dealing with the elders are also instructive. According to one of Zhao's advisers, Zhao paid great attention to the elders (showing an understanding of Chinese politics that Hu Yaobang lacked), always seeking their support, since "Those old folks need to be respected and what they fear most is to be ignored". Thus Bo Yibo was invited to give speeches, and was given a prior look at documents so that "If he does not come up with explicit opposition views" it would then be "very difficult for (him) to publicly oppose (Zhao's position) later". Zhao's adviser disdainfully remarked that this tactic reflected the fact that the elders lacked "real wisdom and (were) unable to come up with specific agendas".[108] Nevertheless, the very existence of such a "higher authority" greatly complicated the political game for the "first front" leaders.

In sum, political authority during the Deng era clearly rested primarily with the ultimate leader, and the evidence suggests this was the case to an extraordinary degree. The second most authoritative figure, Chen Yun, exercised enormous political clout and initially played a key role shaping the reforms—but from the mid-1980s onward, Chen, along with the Party elders more widely, developed reservations about aspects of the reforms yet never opposed Deng politically. Overall, the older generation headed by Deng appeared to have genuinely learned the lesson of the Maoist period as to the importance of Party unity, but ironically a lesson still encompassing the impulse to obey the leader—a trait in which they found the "first front" leaders deficient.[109]

Party Norms, Consensus and Conflict: The Problematics of "Stability and Unity"

The longing for Party unity was not the sole preserve of the Party elders. It has also been shared widely by the post-Mao leadership as a whole for a variety of reasons. First, Party unity is a core value underlying the whole structure of the Party's organizational norms; it is believed to have crucially contributed to the success of the revolution, and its violation is held responsible for the disasters of the Cultural Revolution period. Informed Chinese observers, including those who perceived a sharp factional struggle at the top, observe that no group wants to be

---

[107]   Su Shaozhi, "A Decade of Crises at the Institute of Marxism-Leninism-Mao Zedong Thought, 1979–89", *The China Quarterly*, No. 134 (1993), pp. 343–4.

[108]   See Ruan Ming, *Deng Xiaoping*, pp. 206–7.

[109]   The failure to obey Deng was raised by Party elders as perhaps the key mistakes of Hu Yaobang and Zhao Ziyang. On Hu, see Ruan Ming, *Deng Xiaoping*, p. 112. On Zhao, see above (footnote 28).

responsible for a Party split.[110] This, of course, is a matter of self-interest as well as a Party norm. They had witnessed during 1966–76 that unregulated conflict can severely affect the well-being of the whole elite. Moreover, pragmatism required "stability and unity", as it was frequently called by Deng and others, to support the leadership's broad goals of economic development and continued Party rule. This did not normally result in a stifling of differences—indeed, it was widely assumed that bad policies could be prevented if the prohibitions on contrary opinions that had increasingly marked Mao's one-man rule were cast aside. It meant instead a broad recognition of the need to regulate political conflict and keep it within non-disruptive bounds. In this effort, the leaders believed, traditional Party norms had a critical role to play.

A major aspect of the effort to revive the Party's "fine traditions" involved "reversing the verdicts" on those who had suffered in the Cultural Revolution and earlier campaigns. This process reinstated large numbers of expelled Party members and, at the highest levels, restored the reputations of virtually all past Party leaders and leadership groupings in a manner that abjured narrow political advantage.[111] This, then, had the effect of providing justice to those wronged, upholding the integrity of the norms, and alleviating deep discontent within powerful Party circles, thus facilitating their support for the reform program. Of course, restoring traditional constituencies within the Party in an even-handed manner also enhanced the prestige of leaders such as Deng, whose authority was based on revolutionary status, while undermining those like Hua Guofeng whose high position was solely a product of Cultural Revolution developments.

Meanwhile, despite the elements of the culture of struggle that remained in the reformulated norms, Deng's ban on Party-sponsored political campaigns, which has been substantially observed,[112] fundamentally altered the dynamics of inner-Party life, as well as life in society generally. While there have been periodic political-ideological tightenings during the past two decades, as well as harsh struggles,[113] or severe individual sanctions such as jailings (particularly in

---

[110]   See Yan Huai, "Organizational Hierarchy and the Cadre Management System", in Hamrin and Zhao, *Decision-Making in Deng's China*, p. 50.

[111]   For a comprehensive examination of the process of political rehabilitation, see Hong Yung Lee, *From Revolutionary Cadres to Party Technocrats in Socialist China* (Berkeley: University of California Press, 1991), Ch. 8.

[112]   The main exceptions occurred in 1983 and 1989. The late 1983 drive against spiritual pollution, which one senior reform figure compared to the 1957 Anti-Rightist Campaign, was, however, as ideological conservatives complained, aborted after 28 days. For an insightful discussion of the failure of campaign methods during the post-Tiananmen repression in 1989, see Hong Shi, "China's Political Development After Tiananmen: Tranquility by Default", *Asian Survey*, Vol. 30, No. 12 (December 1990).

[113]   This was particularly witnessed in the weeding out of the so-called "three types of persons" within official organizations in the early 1980s. The "three types" referred to several

1989), political campaigns as they were understood from the 1950s to the 1970s have basically not occurred during the reform era. The practice has been more to apply pressure to particular individuals,[114] and usually the pressure has been applied with a substantial degree of restraint. In this manner the leadership has attempted to curb perceived troublemakers without launching a campaign, while "Party life" as a whole has become lax and the coercive element of Party discipline has dramatically diminished in comparison to the Maoist era. The net effect of all this has been to lessen the force behind "Party rectification", reducing the pressure on those holding discordant policy views, and weakening ideological uniformity and organizational discipline within the Party generally.[115]

As Dittmer has noted, the same impulse to limit excessive punishment has affected politics at the top. Yet the culture of struggle has resurfaced upon occasion. In the context of Hu Yaobang's resignation and the subsequent struggle against "bourgeois liberalization", Hu was subjected to an unpleasant "Party life meeting" (shenghuo hui) in 1987. Yet Bo Yibo could conclude that "it was a good meeting, better than any similar meeting in our Party's history (and conducted in an) atmosphere of equality, civility and lack of pressure".[116] This should not be taken as mere hypocrisy, for despite harsh criticism the consequences were very different from the later Mao period—Hu was allowed to retain his Politburo Standing Committee seat and was subsequently re-elected to the Politburo. To be sure, in the anti-bourgeois liberalization campaign of 1987, Party theoretician Yu Guangyuan suffered "Cultural Revolution-style" criticism,

---

categories of people who emerged during the Cultural Revolution and managed to remain in official bodies: followers of Lin Biao and the "Gang of Four", those seriously affected by factional ideas, and people who "smashed and grabbed" during the 1966–76 period. For an analysis of the weeding out process in one locality, see Keith Forster, "Repudiation of the Cultural Revolution in China: The Case of Zhejiang", *Pacific Affairs*, Vol. 59, No. 1 (Spring 1986).

[114] An early example is the case of the army novelist Bai Hua in 1981. Deng himself joined in criticizing Bai Hua, but at the same time warned against turning the case into a campaign. See *Selected Works of Deng*, pp. 359, 367–71.

[115] Interviews with Party members indicate that in the Mao era the leadership stipulated relatively clear deviations to be criticized. Work-unit heads often selected individual targets according to quotas, and a general atmosphere of tension was created. In contrast, during the reform era the work-unit leaders often find themselves isolated if they attempt to enforce Party discipline, targets receive more or less open sympathy from their colleagues, and the unit leaders themselves often systematically shield their subordinates. In addition, the growth of the private sector has meant the Party can no longer manipulate tangible rewards to the extent it could under Mao—now that there were many "exits" from political life where previously there had been none.

[116] "Report of Comrade Bo Yibo to the Enlarged Politburo Meeting on the the Central Committee Top-Level Party-Life Meeting (Excerpts)", *Zhongfa* (Central Document), No. 3 (16 January 1987), in *Chinese Law and Government* (Spring 1988), p. 24.

and at the time I personally witnessed the extreme distress of a leading Party intellectual whose position was then under threat. Nevertheless, even under these circumstances—in sharp contrast to the Maoist period—people could resist, as in the case of theoretician Su Shaozhi, who refused to bow to pressure yet was allowed to retain his Party membership.[117] Two years later Zhao Ziyang was also subjected to severe criticism at a Party life meeting after the suppression of the Tiananmen protests for, among other things, supporting counter-revolutionary turmoil and splitting the Party, yet he retained his Party membership and by all accounts has continued to lead a comfortable life. More broadly, even during the period of cruel post-Tiananmen repression, discipline within the Party remained strikingly lax, with many work units routinely clearing their members of any wrongdoing unless they were unfortunate enough to have been caught by the cameras around Tiananmen.[118]

Apart from this markedly greater tolerance toward political losers, Deng sought to enhance inner-Party discussion by allowing a degree of discordant public and inner-Party debate that goes beyond the formal grant of minority rights. Deng tolerated a vigorous articulation of opinions critical of reform. In the view of one of the leading advocates of reform of the 1980s, rather than merely reflecting an ongoing factional struggle, this was a deliberate practice on Deng's part to avoid the excessive curbs on expression of the past and to let everyone (among the Party faithful) have their say. According to this source, Deng believed it was best not to engage in disputes with, or criticize, the reforms' critics. He would not, for example, agree to ideologue Deng Liqun assuming a truly powerful post such as General Secretary, but was willing to tolerate his conservative advocacy.[119] This analysis minimizes the damage that could be done through the propaganda posts Deng Liqun and his supporters sometimes dominated and ignores such occasions as 1992 when Deng Xiaoping's tolerance reached the breaking point, but it captures an essential aspect of Deng's effort to promote freer debate within the Party—ironically by allowing a measure of ideological polemics.

The reform program has also involved an effort to create a more institutionalized political process and to limit arbitrary power—an approach that is the very antithesis of the campaign style. Deng Xiaoping placed great weight on this effort, declaring that "systems and institutions are the decisive factor" and, at his most expansive, indicating that the abuses of both Stalin and the Cultural Revolution could not have occurred in Western capitalist countries where

---

[117]   Su Shaozhi, "Decade of Crises", pp. 347–9; Ruan Ming, *Deng Xiaoping*, pp. 182–4; and oral sources.

[118]   *Beijing Review*, No. 32 (1989), pp. 9–10; Hong Shi, "Tranquility by Default", pp. 1210–11; and oral sources.

[119]   Interview, Beijing, 1994.

institutions were more developed.[120] The concrete measures that were adopted, with mixed results, included a more consultative policy process involving an increased use of scholars and specialists both inside and outside the government, a more regularized drafting process for official documents, the use of educational and other meritocratic criteria in the recruitment and promotion of personnel, and an attempt to define more precisely the responsibilities of different institutions, with a particular aim to limit the intrusion of the Party organization into the affairs of other bodies.[121]

Such measures, with a technocratic and procedural emphasis, stand in contradiction to the traditional primacy of politics that remains present in the recodified norms. Moreover, in actual practice they have coexisted with the explicitly rejected method whereby a word or note from a leader is considered authoritative and participants in the system feel there are no basic rules to follow. This sentiment was echoed within the Politburo in 1986 when, well into the regularization process, Wan Li complained that Party policy-making was still dominated by the "personal likes and dislikes" of leading officials, their individual past experiences, and the invocation of unrepresentative successful "models", while what was needed were scientific methods, consultation with affected groups, objective analysis before decisions were adopted, and careful monitoring and consultation during their implementation.[122] Nevertheless, it is clear that the policy process as a whole has become more consultative and systematic than previously—but the fundamental obstacle to further institutionalization remained the authority of the retired leader and the older generation more broadly.

While policy formulation became more regularized, even more significant have been changes in the *political* process as they affected the "first front". Under Mao prior to the Cultural Revolution, the Chairman's ranking colleagues either had unusual security of office based on revolutionary status or faced sudden dismissal as a result of his displeasure. This was reflected in the life tenure system whereby only death or serious political errors normally could remove a leader from office. In effect, leaders (and lower level officials to a lesser degree) had an understanding that if they stayed out of political trouble they would retain their positions (or at least their rank) regardless of competence or performance.

---

[120]   *Selected Works of Deng*, pp. 295, 316. Ironically, the reference to Stalin was a paraphrase of Mao.

[121]   See, for example, Harry Harding, *China's Second Revolution: Reform after Mao* (Washington DC: The Brookings Institution, 1987), pp. 211 ff; A. Doak Barnett, *The Making of Foreign Policy in China: Structure and Process* (Boulder: Westview Press, 1985); Hamrin and Zhao, *Decision-Making in Deng's China*, pp. 153 ff and *passim*; and Tony Saich, "The Chinese Communist Party at the Thirteenth National Congress: Policies and Prospects for Reform", *Issues & Studies*, Vol. 25, No. 1 (January 1989).

[122]   As cited in Harding, *China's Second Revolution*, pp. 213–14.

During the Deng era, in contrast, the "first front" became involved in a more normal politics of a type found in most countries, as Deng put it when speaking of Hua Guofeng's ouster. That is, the power and position of senior leaders became subject to change depending on their performance. Unlike the Great Leap Forward, when no Politburo member faced sanctions for mismanagement, which caused tens of millions of deaths by starvation,[123] since the Third Plenum of 1978 top "first front" leaders have been held responsible for the results of their policies. This has been reflected in experiments with multi-candidate elections to Party and government offices,[124] while measures such as the rejection of life tenure, limiting top state posts to two terms, and setting up a retirement system further underlined the reduced circumstances of "first front" leaders. The new pattern was fundamentally due to the relative lack of revolutionary contributions of these figures; even Hu Yaobang and Zhao Ziyang were junior participants in the pre-1949 struggle and could not draw on their historical contributions to offset attacks on their positions. They had to achieve successes by gaining the support of peers and subordinates—which increasingly required persuasion rather than commands, as well as the all-important courting of their elders. While Deng, like Mao before him, could avoid the consequences of his mistakes, more junior leaders would suffer from society's backlash against failed policies and opposition from significant Party constituencies.

A case in point is the ouster of Hu Yaobang. While Hu was paying the price for Deng's renewed 1986 emphasis on political reform and the final denouement had "unconstitutional" aspects, as Dittmer has noted, Hu's fall is best understood as a product of his own deficiences as a politician. Although his prospects had been significantly compromised both by the difficulty of his task in pushing reform forward and the late 1986 student demonstrations, which was a factor beyond his control, Hu had also alienated virtually every key constituency within the Party leadership. Despite Deng Xiaoping's earlier observation that Hu was more enlightened than himself, by the latter part of 1986 the relationship was clearly under strain. Whether this was largely due to differences over bourgeois liberalization as officially claimed or even over Deng's retirement is difficult to assess,[125] but it does appear that Hu had let the relationship wither due to insufficient cultivation. According to a senior reform figure, in contrast to Hu Qiaomu, who visited Deng "almost every day", Hu Yaobang normally chose to

---

[123]   Of course, this reflected the fact that Mao was the ultimate source of the mismanagement, but given the scale of the problems caused it is remarkable that no senior scapegoats were found.

[124]   A significant case of such elections was the selection of the new Party leadership at the 13th Congress; see Ruan Ming, *Deng Xiaoping*, pp. 184–7.

[125]   See Deng, *Fundamental Issues in Present-Day China*, pp. 154–5, 161ff; and above, note 49. With regard to bourgeois liberalization, Hu appears to have attempted to tread a middle course between the critics of bourgeois liberalization and those who strongly opposed any critique. See Ruan Ming, *Deng Xiaoping*, pp. 160–3.

liaise with Deng through his son, Deng Pufang, leading Deng Pufang to comment, "Uncle Hu, your way won't accomplish much; you should talk to the old man directly".[126] Similarly, Hu Yaobang alienated Chen Yun, who initially had been favourably disposed to him. But Chen frowned upon Hu's habit of touring the country and giving repeated on-the-spot directives. Chen Yun reportedly observed in exasperation that when he himself conducted on-site investigations he would stay in a single county for a long time, whereas Hu made quick forays everywhere, visiting several counties in a day.[127]

Hu Yaobang also alienated the Party elders as a group by pursuing some of their children during the anti-corruption drive in 1986. While this may have been a "no win" situation for Hu, his manner of conducting the crackdown was bound to increase discontent. In particular, Hu Yaobang lured Hu Qiaomu from his home to a meeting so that the arrest of his son could be effected in his absence.[128] But Hu Yaobang's difficulties were not limited to the "second front". Apart from his inevitable conflict with the conservatives in the propaganda apparatus (who might have been isolated in other circumstances), Hu's penchant for issuing directives on a wide variety of matters offended the responsible bureaucracies and their leaders. This was nowhere more important than in the economic realm, where state rather than Party organs were supposed to take the lead. In late 1986, Song Ping openly criticized Hu for issuing orders on his tours that contravened those of the State Planning Commission.[129] But Hu's interference in economic matters caused problems with an even more important figure—and a key *reformist* leader—Zhao Ziyang. This tension led Zhao to complain to Deng and arguably contributed to the nastiness of Zhao's contribution during the January 1987 meeting dealing with Hu.[130] Hu was thus vulnerable to charges of having violated the Party norm of collective leadership and the reform principle of reducing Party interference in government affairs. Given all of this, the view that Hu's removal was forced upon Deng by a conservative faction has little persuasiveness. Hu, like Hua Guofeng before him, fell victim to something akin to the normal political pressures found elsewhere, albeit with the peculiar Chinese feature of Party elders in the wings.

While holding leaders responsible for the results of their policies opened the way to intensified "normal" political competition, the concern with "stability and unity" served to dampen conflict in several respects. After the ravages and

---

[126]   Interview, Beijing, 1994.

[127]   Interview with a senior Party historian, Beijing, 1994.

[128]   Ruan Ming, *Deng Xiaoping*, p. 165; and oral source familiar with Hu Qiaomu.

[129]   Wang Lixin and Joseph Fewsmith, "Bulwark of the Planned Economy: The Structure and Role of the State Planning Commission", in Hamrin and Zhao, *Decision-Making in Deng's China*, p. 62.

[130]   Ruan Ming, *Deng Xiaoping*, pp. 165–6, 168; and oral sources.

uncertainty of the Cultural Revolution, Party unity has meant an effort to keep personnel changes gradual at the top, although much less so at lower levels,[131] and especially to limit the numbers of those removed (apart from retirements) while cushioning the consequences for those ousted. In most cases considerable effort was taken to provide a soft landing even for those tainted with "leftist" ideology. A case in point was the old peasant and model of Maoist rural virtue, Chen Yonggui, who apparently held to these values after Mao's death, although he was not directly involved with the so-called "whateverist" group that allegedly supported Hua Guofeng. When Chen Yonggui was forced to resign as vice premier in 1980 Deng Xiaoping visited him to offer consolation, while after Chen's failure to be re-elected to the Politburo in 1982 Hu Yaobang also offered reassuring words and made arrangements to guarantee Chen's living standards.[132] More generally, from the Third Plenum in 1978 to the 14th Congress in 1992, once the retirements of old revolutionaries are excluded, personnel movements out of the Politburo bear a considerable if incomplete similarity to pre-Cultural Revolution times: in both periods the relatively small proportion of leaders removed for "errors" comprised the largest category of Politburo leavers. Among the 49 leaders serving as full Politburo members in this period, only a handful of departures involved factors other than retirement, death or serious political mistakes—and these presumably were for the reasons of unsatisfactory performance or backing the wrong political horse. The fact that exclusions from the top body for these reasons seem to have increased gradually by the time of the 14th Congress was arguably another modest sign of the trend toward normal politics.[133]

---

[131]   The turnover of leading personnel at the Central Committee, ministerial, provincial Party, and regional military levels has been both more extensive and rapid than within the Politburo. A number of factors appear to have been involved. First, the same process of retirements was implemented, but on apparently an even more sweeping basis. Second, particularly at the local levels, the process of weeding out Cultural Revolution remnants was more protracted. Third, the lesser status of those involved apparently made such figures more vulnerable to shifting political winds and anti-corruption crackdowns. Finally, the involvement of such figures in daily administration probably made their performance even more salient than for top policy makers. For details on the scope of these changes, see Harding, *China's Second Revolution*, pp. 204–9; Lee, *From Revolutionary Cadres*, Ch. 11; and Christopher M. Clarke, "Changing The Context for Policy Implementation: Organizational and Personnel Reform in Post-Mao China", in David M. Lampton (ed.), *Policy Implementation in Post-Mao China* (Berkeley: University of California Press, 1987), pp. 33–46.

[132]   Zhongguo xinwenshe (China News Agency) (ed.), *Shehui mingliu jianfanglu* [Record of Interviews with Celebrities in Society] (Beijing: Tuanjie Chubanshe, 1989), p. 57.

[133]   Of these 49 members, only four (or five if Chen Yonggui is included) of those leaving the Politburo did not join the Central Advisory Commission (CAC) or obviously retire, were not subjected to criticism for major errors, or had not passed away: Peng Chong (1982), Ni

"Stability and unity" has also meant a politics of consensus and compromise on policy issues—a clear break with the last period of Mao's rule. This statement in no way denies that sharp differences have marked the policy process, as one would expect given the breadth of change involved, or that it became increasingly difficult to maintain a consensus from the mid-1980s onward with the onset of urban reform, attempts at political reform, marketization and the need to respond to popular discontent dominating the Party's agenda. What it does assert is that the pursuit of consensus has been a significant impulse in reform politics, as already seen in Deng's consultative style. This approach to policy making was even written into the 1982 Party constitution, which stipulated that when Party organizations found themselves nearly equally divided on a matter, "the decision should be put off to allow for further investigation, study and exchange of opinions followed by another discussion".[134] It is also a familiar theme in the growing body of literature dealing with bureaucratic behaviour during the Deng era, which emphasizes extensive consultation, consensus building and bargaining. This literature explains the prevalence of these phenomena by such factors as a cultural proclivity for persuasion and consensus, a propensity to recognize the interests of subordinates and an unwillingness to impose "unfair" decisions on them, the dispersion of economic resources among diverse bureaucratic actors under the reforms, the dependence of generalist officials upon a consensus of experts before new projects are approved, and the fragmentation of authority whereby—short of the highest levels—actors generally lack the capacity to enforce their preferences on others.[135]

Many of these considerations are undoubtedly relevant to the politics of consensus at the top although, as Carol Hamrin and Suisheng Zhao conclude on the basis of detailed case studies, "there was less real bargaining ... than persuasion or even intimidation".[136] Certainly, when Deng Xiaoping was

---

Zhifu (1987), and Li Ximing and Yang Rudai (1992). The complete figures are: retained on the 14th Politburo—6; died in office—3; retired/joined CAC—28; removed for political mistakes—7 or 8; and others—4 or 5. Of course, some of those who moved to the CAC may have been persuaded to do so based on perceived deficiences in their performance. See *Zhonghua Renmin Gongheguo*, pp. 5–9; and *Who's Who in China: Current Leaders* (Beijing: Foreign Languages Press, 1989).

[134] *Beijing Review*, No. 38 (1982), p. 14.

[135] See David M. Lampton, "Chinese Politics: The Bargaining Treadmill", *Issues & Studies*, Vol. 23, No. 3 (March 1987); *idem*, "The Implementation Problem in Post-Mao China", in Lampton, *Policy Implementation*; and Kenneth Lieberthal and Michel Oksenberg, *Policy Making in China: Leaders, Structures, and Processes* (Princeton: Princeton University Press, 1988), pp. 22–3, 158, 229, 270, 334, 389, 412 and *passim*.

[136] See their introduction in *Decision-Making in Deng's China*, p. xxxv. Recall Zhao Ziyang's practice of beginning Politburo meetings with references to his visits to Deng. Another questionable implication from the bureaucratic literature is the notion of systemic immobilism, the reduced capacity of the leadership to initiate change, and its increasing

involved, the fundamental mode entailed authoritative directives rather than bargained trade-offs. As with Mao, those dealing with Deng sought to accommodate his wishes and to attempt to sway him toward their favoured positions by force of argument and through demonstrations of broad support for these positions. On Deng's part, consensual politics is best explained by his awareness that the successful implementation of any policy required as wide a basis of support as possible, his calculation that concessions on particularly controversial issues like political reform might prevent the coalescence of opposition to economic reforms, the complexity of the problems faced and the diversity of the specialist advice received, the different strands in his own preferences, and not least his overarching belief in the desirability of Party unity. Deng played a "balancing" role, not because such a role was necessary to preserve his ultimate authority, but to provide maximum leverage to achieve his specific goals when he decided one or another strand of his centrist program required emphasis. The effect of this, however, was to build an ongoing competition among diverse and sometimes hostile groups. Various leaders not only appealed to the patriarch in the tried and true method of court politics, but also sought to build more broadly-based support as dictated by a more normal politics, which naturally included enhancing one's own prospects at the expense of others.

The contrary pulls of a more open policy debate, diverse opinions within the "first front" (and diverse elders to appeal to), and vulnerability to poor performance on the one hand, and efforts to mute conflict in the name of Party unity on the other, created major uncertainties about how the political game should be played. At its most basic, Party norms still do not accept competition for power as legitimate. There is not only no approved process by which a leader can campaign for higher office,[137] but the ban on factions means efforts to undermine those of opposing views are highly suspect. The situation during the Deng era was further complicated by the fact that while "first front" leaders

---

dependence on bureaucratic exchanges to achieve results. For all the difficulties with specific policies, a leadership that decollectivized agriculture, reduced the state share of the economy to less than half, extensively decentralized economic power, opened Chinese society to unprecedented outside contact, and radically altered the pattern of state-society relations can hardly be considered "immobile". For a persuasive analysis challenging the bargaining and immobilism theses, see Dorothy J. Solinger, *From Lathes to Looms: China's Industrial Policy in Comparative Perspective, 1979–1982* (Stanford: Stanford University Press, 1991), Ch. 5.

[137] Thus efforts to stake a claim to a particular office must be circumspect, at least in public. Consider the dilemma of Li Peng, who, following the June 1989 repression, was obviously concerned with his prospects for re-election when the new Party and state leaderships were selected in 1992 and 1993. In a 1991 press conference, Li awkwardly raised the question of his own position, but he could only say that he would stay at his post as premier for the remainder of the government's term in the interests of political stability, thereby leaving the issue of his future open. *Beijing Review*, No. 16 (1991), p. 18.

needed to build support within China's leadership elite more broadly than ever before, both on specific policies and on behalf of their own future prospects, up through the 14th Congress in 1992 the crucial constituency that selected the "first front" leadership remained Deng Xiaoping and the elderly revolutionaries.[138] This led to a further paradox, since to the extent that concern with Party unity was overriding among the older generation, any attempt to undercut perceived rivals too aggressively could backfire, while in situations where Party elders and especially Deng were particularly unhappy with a "first front" figure, others had an incentive to attack. Arguably, the overall result was a politics with an enhanced but still somewhat restrained level of "normal" conflict but, as in Mao's day, one where the leader's displeasure greatly raised the stakes.

Clearly, despite the impulse to maintain a consensus, there were periods of sharp conflict on the "first front". But in contrast to analyses positing repeated or almost constant succession struggles,[139] the paradoxical nature of the post-Mao transition resulted in few manifestations of such politics, or at most psuedo-succession struggles that did not involve competition among clearly identifiable leading figures for a specific leading post. Given the failure of Hua Guofeng after early 1977 to defend his position, the alleged Hua-Deng struggle is better viewed as having been an almost inevitable process of restoring proper statuses within the Party.[140] With Deng unambiguously in charge after the Third Plenum of late 1978 and Hu Yaobang's pre-eminent position on the "first front" under threat by 1986, conditions for a succession struggle ostensibly existed. Indeed, there is some evidence that Deng Liqun desired the post—and was jokingly referred to as the "underground General Secretary". Deng Liqun certainly clashed sharply with Hu over policy within the Party Secretariat and assertedly sought to undermine Hu and further his own candidacy through direct and indirect approaches to Deng Xiaoping. Moreover, once Hu fell, some elders reportedly supported him as Hu's replacement. This, however, could never have been a realistic prospect given both Deng Xiaoping's disapproval of Deng Liqun's critical posture toward reform and the fact that Deng Liqun did not have a seat on the Politburo.[141]

Another suggestion posited a Hu Yaobang-Zhao Ziyang succession struggle.[142] Notwithstanding the tensions over Hu's interference in Zhao's

---

[138]   This analysis directly contradicts the emphasis of Susan L. Shirk, *The Political Logic of Economic Reform in China* (Berkeley: University of California Press, 1993), especially pp. 79 ff, on the importance of "the Central Committee selectorate", which, in my view, has played only the most indirect role, if any, in leadership changes.

[139]   See especially Shirk, *The Political Logic*, p. 14.

[140]   Cf. the preliminary analysis in Teiwes, *Leadership, Legitimacy, and Conflict*, pp. 118–27.

[141]   Ruan Ming, *Deng Xiaoping*, pp. 112–13, 151; and interviews with senior Party historians.

[142]   See Ruan Ming, *Deng Xiaoping*, pp. 165–6, 190; and Shirk, *The Political Logic*, pp. 14, 89, 221–2, 308.

economic portfolio, the political logic of dividing the reform forces was questionable, and reportedly Hu had no knowledge of any such intention on Zhao's part.[143] Moreover, the evidence strongly indicates that Zhao tried until mid-1987 to avoid taking up the General Secretaryship, a post which despite its nominal number-one status was clearly subordinate to Deng and, due to the reform emphasis on separating Party and government functions, had limited say in the crucial area of economic reform. But Zhao had to accept the post given Deng's insistence that the image of Party unity would be damaged by two changes of General Secretary in one year.[144] In Zhao's own case his support for separating the Party from the government ironically weakened his subsequent capacity as Party General Secretary to influence economic affairs, which played a key role in an intensified leadership conflict from mid-1988 up to Zhao's ouster in the Tiananmen crisis.[145] Yet even here, despite suggestions that the new Premier, Li Peng, was now challenging Zhao for primacy on the "first front",[146] there was no way Li Peng or anyone else could campaign for leadership. In the event, under the crisis conditions of spring 1989, a rank outsider, junior Politburo member Jiang Zemin, was thrust into the "top" post by the *dictat* of Deng Xiaoping.

With the question of succession again at the forefront, in one profound sense there was no succession to Deng's leadership position since no one possessed the revolutionary status to assume Deng's role. Contrary to Dittmer's statement that Deng Xiaoping "left the paramount leadership role ... stronger and more autonomous than it was when he found it", the role itself could not outlive Deng. Competition among "first front" leaders was inevitable after 1989 although muted by a number of factors—not least an awareness that unbridled struggle would weaken the Party as a whole *vis-à-vis* dissatisfied forces in society. Other complicating factors included the continued albeit fading presence of the Party elders, who retained their historical prestige and wanted their say, as well as the Party norm of collective leadership, the tradition of dismissing a number-one leader only for serious political errors, and the reform principle of separating Party and government affairs.

A crucial aspect of the post-Mao transition was the emergence of two different conceptions of Party unity reflecting the different outlooks and circumstances of the revolutionary and successor generations. For the old revolutionaries Party unity had a sacred dimension, involving a belief that the

---

[143]   Ruan Ming, *Deng Xiaoping*, p. 166.

[144]   Chen Yizi, "The Decision Process Behind the 1986–1989 Political Reforms", in Hamrin and Zhao, *Decision-Making in Deng's China*, p. 148. The issue was Zhao resigning the Premiership at the 13th Congress to become full rather than acting General Secretary as he had been since Hu's resignation.

[145]   See Cheng Xiaonong, "Decision and Miscarriage", p. 190.

[146]   See Ruan Ming, *Deng Xiaoping*, p. 204; and Zhu Xiaoqun, "Political Reform in Beijing City", in Hamrin and Zhao, *Decision-Making in Deng's China*, p. 181.

revolution's and China's welfare required a unity based on following the leader and burying differences. For the successor generation, unity is more managerial in nature. The members of this generation are more diverse in background and lack the bonding of revolutionary struggle; they are politicians thrown together by fortuitous circumstances.[147] As in normal politics elsewhere, unity is desirable to maximize the strength of the organization but there is nothing permanent in any particular leadership arrangement—no claims are based on unchallengeable status. Normal political jockeying has ensued. Party unity, then, is less a restraining general principle (although it remains that to some extent) than a political calculation, and this became ever more a rationale, in fact if not in theory, as the old revolutionaries faded away. By the mid-1990s the "first front" leaders had entered a period when the key uncertainty was less the opinions of aged revolutionaries than the emergent forces in their own society.

---

[147] Cf. Alan P. L. Liu, "Aspects of Beijing's Crisis Management: The Tiananmen Square Demonstration", *Asian Survey*, Vol. 30, No. 5 (May 1990), p. 519.

FOUR

Chinese Politics at the Top:
Factionalism or Informal Politics?
Balance-of-Power Politics or a Game to Win All?*

Tang Tsou

In the study of contemporary China, the sub-field that analyses elite Party politics is the least developed, in spite of the existence of many outstanding monographs. It lags behind studies on villages, the economy, foreign policy, the bureaucracy, and histories of the Chinese revolution. Until recently, it held less promise in theoretical sophistication than the emerging field of state-society relations. This state of affairs is due not only to the secrecy shrouding the Chinese leadership and thus the dearth of reliable information, but also results from a paucity of serious endeavours to provide a system of clearly defined concepts, a theoretical framework, explicitly stated assumptions, and carefully designed research programs aimed at developing a model or a theory. In the 1970s, Andrew Nathan took the first step in this direction[1] and I tried to respond.[2] But unfortunately, neither of us continued our endeavour. It is fitting that Lowell Dittmer has taken

* Over the years I have benefitted from discussions with my colleagues and students on theoretical and methodological problems related to ideas expressed in this paper. I wish to express my thanks to Jon Elster, Ira Katznelson, Joseph Cropsey, David Laitin, Christopher Achen, Glenn H. Snyder, Brantly Womack, Duncan Snidal, Charles Lipson, James Fearon, Joseph Fewsmith, Zhiyuan Cui, and Gaochao He. The support of the East Asian Center of the University of Chicago over many years is greatly appreciated. I should like also to express special appreciation to Ms Kathy Anderson, who, as the only person who can read my handwriting, turned my messy draft into a readable piece and patiently made revisions several times afterwards.

[1] Andrew Nathan, "A Factionalist Model of CCP Politics", *The China Quarterly*, No. 53 (January/March 1973), p. 38.

[2] Tang Tsou, "Prolegomenon to the Study of Informal Groups in CCP Politics", *The China Quarterly*, No. 65 (March 1976); reprinted in Tang Tsou, *The Cultural Revolution and Post-Mao Reforms* (Chicago: University of Chicago Press, 1986), p. 100.

up this task now that many memoirs, biographies, docudramas, autobiographies, and Chinese documents as well as what H. Lyman Miller calls "emigré cadre literature"[3] have been published. Meanwhile, our mother discipline, political science, has moved ahead rapidly both in the fields of methodology and theory.

Dittmer's chapter opens with a recap of the exchange of ideas between Nathan and me. But Dittmer's new endeavour stands in contrast to Nathan's in methodology. Whereas Nathan's seminal article comprised the first endeavour to build a model, Dittmer abjures, to use his words, "prematurely ambitious conceptualizations" or "abstract model-building" (p. 9). His method is to make extensive use of recently available materials on twenty to thirty top Chinese leaders[4] and then to place the information systematically into a conceptual framework, whereas Nathan's model is necessarily and intentionally a simplification of a complex reality,[5] dealing with the complex real world only when he tries to test the model. That is, Dittmer starts from the data and tries to systematize or make sense of the complex world by fitting these into his conceptual scheme. He provides an elaborate picture of Chinese reality and a vast parade of factual information; but ultimately, his contribution depends on whether or not the general propositions derived from his conceptual synthesis provide for a deeper understanding of current reality, the historical development of Chinese

---

[3] See, for example, the important book by Carol Lee Hamrin and Suisheng Zhao (eds), *Decision-Making in Deng's China: Perspectives from Insiders* (Armonk: M. E. Sharpe, 1995).

[4] Neither Dittmer nor Nathan makes any explicit or systematic differentiation among these 20 to 30 leaders, whereas the essays in the book edited by Hamrin and Zhao (footnote 3) distinguish between four groups: first, the supreme leader; second, the rest of the revolutionary elders; third, top leaders in the Party Politburo and its standing committee; and fourth, other top office holders and bureaucrats. One of the emphases in that book is on the "revolutionary elders" as a distinct political stratum in the Deng era. Their special role is somewhat analogous to the *genro* in the years after Japan's Meji restoration but entirely different from the *dang guo yuan lao* (the founding members of the state and the party) under Chiang Kai-shek's rule, who had high status but no power. There are, however, several basic problems to be resolved. The writers disagree among themselves as to whether China under Deng was a one-man dictatorship, an "autocracy" or "an oligarchy", as they understand these terms. And when Yan Jiaqi posits "cyclical swings" between oligarchy and one-man dictatorship, can it truly be that during periods when an oligarchy purportedly prevails and China has a "collective leadership", Deng is merely the "first among equals" (p. 241)? The various book chapters generally agree that below the first three top levels of leaders, there has been a tendency toward increasingly greater degrees of professionalism in foreign and economic affairs. Suisheng Zhao even believes that a long-term trend toward "institutional pluralism" seems "inevitable" (p. 243), in contrast to the emphasis in Chen Yizi's and Hsiao Pen's chapters.

[5] On the need to simplify in building a model, see Gary King, Robert O. Keohane and Sidney Verba, *Designing Social Inquiry* (Princeton: Princeton University Press, 1994), p. 49.

politics, and the future reshaping of the Chinese state—and whether or not the general propositions have any validity, too, when applied to other cases.

I. Methodological Questions

Rather than concentrate on the substantive problems, as Lucian Pye does in his forceful and insightful chapter, I shall focus on the methodological aspects of Dittmer's and Nathan's papers. But I do hold to several substantive theses that have developed out of a critique of both of their papers and my immersion in Chinese history. I rather vaguely stated the most important of these theses two decades ago in my exchange with Nathan. To use the formulation that I finally arrived at, I suggest that at irregular intervals the struggle for power among the Chinese elite, involving either supreme political power or power one level below that, always involves one side winning all and/or the other side losing all. This is a feature not only of elite CCP politics but of Chinese politics throughout the twentieth century.

It is startling to think that this phenomenon, of such momentous consequences, has not become the centre of our analysis of CCP politics. I would urge colleagues to consider it the central feature of Chinese politics. Its effects on all other aspects of elite politics should be analysed, including the insecurity and fear of *luan* that Lucian Pye so perceptively pointed to long ago. Its foundations should be sought in China's imperial past, in the Nationalist and Communist revolutions, in the Nationalist ideology as defined by such men as Dai Jitao, the Communist ideology of class struggle, and even Liu Shaoqi's *On Inner-Party Struggle*,[6] and ultimately in the Chinese conception of political power itself. We can never understand elite Party politics unless we focus our attention on this central feature. Unless we know why, how and under what conditions it persists, we cannot know in what direction the Chinese system will evolve or whether and how it can be changed.

The Building Blocks: Nathan's Clientelist Leader-Follower Ties and Dittmer's Informal Relationships

The model Nathan built in his initial paper consists of three parts: first, the building blocks or elementary particles; second, the units or unit-actors; and third, the system of elite politics and indeed the political system itself. The building blocks or elementary particles are the clientelist leader-follower ties, and the unit

---

6   Liu's book was written with the aim of moderating inner-Party struggle and establishing some normative rules to govern it. But its basic ideological and political assumption is still that the right line must win and the wrong line must lose.

actors are the "factions".[7] At the time Nathan built his model, the concept of clientelist ties and the study of how these built into political factions was already widely known, as he himself noted. But out of this general literature, he succinctly provided a list of seven formal characteristics of clientelist ties which served well his purpose of building a "factionalism model". This is one of the merits of his method. He clearly distinguished clientelist ties from authority relationships (or what he called "the power relationships of 'imperative coordination'")[8] on the one hand and from "the generic exchange relationship" on the other. He was also aware of the notion of "networks", a sub-field of study that had just begun its rapid development, and of what the Chinese call *guanxi*, which is the foundation of Lucian Pye's structural edifice and the core of his analysis. The elevation to a theoretical level of the notion of the "clientelist" *cum* "leader-follower" relationship as a building block in the construction of a "faction", and the depiction of a "factionalism model of CCP politics" as the central part of the Chinese political system, are Nathan's most important and lasting contributions.

But Nathan's clientelist leader-follower ties are not substantial enough to serve as adequate building blocks of what many observers and the actors themselves believe to be factions, because there are also factions based on personal relationships between equals. Besides clientelist leader-follower ties, there exist many other kinds of informal relationships that directly affect elite politics, as Dittmer points out. There are also too many other phenomena which cannot be explained in terms of "factions", as we shall see in section III of this chapter.

By replacing Nathan's concept of clientelist leader-follower ties with the notion of a "relationship" or "connection" of an informal or personal character and by broadening the focus of the discourse from a "factionalism model" to "informal politics", Dittmer provides a foundation solid and broad enough to build a synthesis of the newly available data on the one hand and ideas, concepts and a theory of the politics of CCP elites on the other. Lucien Pye's notion of *guanxi* can also be rightly considered as one type of Dittmer's informal relationships or connections. In his constructive criticism of Dittmer's enterprise, Pye pays an unintended compliment to the usefulness of Dittmer's concept by noting that the informal "is *very nearly* the sum total of Chinese politics" (my emphasis) (p. 42).

Yet Pye poses a fundamental challenge to Dittmer's concept of informal politics. He casts doubt on the appropriateness or fruitfulness of applying a pair of concepts developed first in the field of public administration to the study of politics. But I believe that Dittmer's transposition of this concept is methodologically sound. Scholars working in the field of public administration

---

[7]   For purposes of clarity, whenever I use the term faction in Nathan's sense, I will put it in quotation marks so as to distinguish it from the same term used by journalists and other scholars.

[8]   Andrew Nathan, "A Factionalist Model of CCP Politics", p. 38.

recognized long ago that in some areas, administration and politics cannot be sharply distinguished. Although the foci of administration and politics are different, there is a large sphere of activities in which the two overlap. Even more to the point is that according to some neo-Weberian scholars, a bureaucracy is working at its best when formal authority is supplemented and supported but not corrupted by a set of informal relationships. There are many cases of successful transpositions of concepts and theories in one field to another, provided necessary modifications and adaptations can be made.

Still, Dittmer must give us an adequate definition of the "informal" and, as a necessary logical complement, the "formal" in politics. Informal politics cannot be understood without understanding formal politics. After all, Nathan clearly states that formal hierarchy is the trellis on which "factions" extend their influence,[9] and indeed one can go further and say that it helps to establish, shape and strengthen the clientelist ties and many other kinds of informal ties, and turns them into "factions". Dittmer is right when he states that "formal positions are normally a *prerequisite* to informal power" (my emphasis) (p. 14).

Most importantly, when we look at Chinese elite politics, particularly the relations between formal and informal politics, we must maintain a long historical perspective on the political development of China. One must remember that the Chinese revolution was initiated by persons with informal relationships, which grew into associations such as the *Xinmin xuehui*, the Marxist small groups, the Party, the rudimentary base-area government and army, and then finally the whole formal and informal structure of power relationships. In the Communists' project of rebuilding the state and the reconstruction of the whole society, the process of institutionalization has never been completed. It has had its periods of progress and retrogression and is now again in a state of flux.

Dittmer chooses the concept of "informal politics" as the key to his synthesis because he believes that informal politics overshadowed formal politics. The choice of this concept will enable him to raise fundamental historical questions about the processes of state-rebuilding and institutionalization in China. In one sense, institutionalization can be conceived as the process in which formal politics and formal relationships regularly prevail over informal politics and informal relationships, with the former complemented without being corrupted by the latter. From this perspective, he can explore in the Chinese setting how informal and formal politics are transformed into each other, and how they interact at any particular time.

Take for example what Deng Xiaoping calls the "core" of the Party (Mao in the first generation and he himself in the second), which constitutes the most important part of the whole political system. The bases of the power and influence of the "core" leader were fundamentally but not exclusively informal. Deng, for instance, played the role of the "core" at different times on the basis of different

---

[9]   Nathan, "A Factionalist Model of CCP Politics", p. 44.

sources of "formal" authority. In 1977 he was the Vice-Chairman of the Party and its Military Commission, and in 1981 became Chairman of the latter. On 9 November 1989, five months after the Tiananmen tragedy, he resigned from this latter post, and after 1990, when he resigned as Chairman of the Military Commission, he had no official position at all. Yet it was he who made the final decisions and took the major initiative in policy-making even after his official retirement, as indicated by his influential remarks on his tour of the southern provinces in 1992. In Mao's case, the relationship between his formal authority and informal power changed over a period of forty-one years from the Zunyi Conference of 1935 to his death in 1976. The present "core", Jiang Zemin, unites in his person the three most important positions of official authority but the question was whether he could use these formal powers and the informal influence derived from Deng's anointment to build up his informal relationships and power. This is indispensable for him to retain his formal positions and to function as the "core"—a task that Hua Guofeng failed to accomplish.

But Dittmer must first of all define what is the informal and the formal. As Pye notes perceptively, Dittmer's distinctions between a "value-rational" and "purpose-rational" relationship are unsatisfactory. I agree. To begin with, the term "rational" has no specific meaning in Dittmer's usage, except as a residue of Weber's terminology.[10] The terms "values" and "purpose" are vague and imprecise. Sometimes, one's value is one's purpose and *vice versa*. As Dittmer writes in his conclusion, "Behaviourally, informal politics consists of value-rational as opposed to purpose-rational relationships functioning in service to a personal base". And he equates "value-rational" relationships with a "relationship with other" which is "valued as an end in itself". This can be reworded as: "informal politics consists in making the 'relationship with other' (that is, informal connections or relationships) an end in itself, in order to serve a personal base (in other words, a set of informal connections or relationships)".[11] Rephrased more simply, one may say that informal politics is, in the final analysis, politics in which personal relationships with others or a set of such relationships constitute an end in itself.

Dittmer's notion of informal politics is more useful than Nathan's concept of clientelist leader-follower ties, "faction", and "factionalism". It includes Nathan's notions as one of the concepts in the synthesis along with other notions. What it loses in simplicity, it gains in its greater usefulness and its applicability to the

---

[10]   With the rise of rational choice theory, the term "reason" has taken on new meaning and has become controversial in connection with the application of that theory to non-Western nations. See Chalmers Johnson and E. G. Keehn, "A Disaster in the Making: Rational Choice and Asian Studies", *The National Interest*, No. 30 (Summer 1994), pp. 14–22; Reid Cushman, "Rational Fears", *Lingua Franca* (November/December 1994), pp. 42–54.

[11]   The implication of this sentence is that everything else is a means to this end, including ideals, policies, issues and authority relationships.

complex Chinese scene. More significantly, it points directly to a whole set of important origins of clientelist leader-follower ties besides Nathan's "trellis". One of these sources of informal politics or "factionalism" was particularly prominent during the Cultural Revolution and even more so during Mao's last years. To underscore this point, one need only mention the names of Jiang Qing, Mao Yuanxin, Wang Hairong, and perhaps even Zhang Yufeng.

Most importantly, Dittmer's notion of informal politics raises the question of the relationship between informal and formal politics, informal power and formal authority, the transformation of one into the other, and the relative weight of each in different periods. All this leads us to the question of "formalization" as a precondition for institutionalization, which in turn is a condition and necessary ingredient of the rule of law and democratization.

Dittmer mentions the social "attributes" that form the basis of Chinese relationships. From his discussion, we can construct a continuum of informal relationships in terms of the degree of their closeness, intimacy and spatial propinquity. For our purposes, we may begin with the husband-wife relationship, father-children relationships, kinship, the parochial village, school ties, and relationships established in "basic work units". But to develop a conceptual synthesis about Chinese politics we must join this continuum of informal politics to a continuum of formal politics. One of the ways to construct the latter continuum is to use as our criterion the question: how fundamental and how comprehensive are these relationships with regard to the professed purposes and/or presumptive operations of the political process? It may begin with relationships that arise from and are governed by the constitution of the state (written or unwritten), the Party constitution, Party rules (such as the CCP's "On Certain Rules Governing the Political Life Inside the Party"), legislated laws, executive orders, rules and regulations, Party documents, editorials in the official newspaper of the Party, and so on. In Chinese elite politics, this list should be headed by ideology accepted as authoritative. These two continua may be linked into one, with a middle zone in which the formal and informal overlap each other.[12]

This allows us to raise two questions. The first is: which of the categories of informal relationships will influence formal politics and relationships in what different ways and with what general consequences and why? Trying to answer this set of questions will lead to some interesting factual propositions and some normative judgments. Second, we are particularly interested in the middle zone where the formal and informal are intertwined, penetrate each other or simply overlap. It is in this middle zone that we find relationships among top party leaders which are shaped by the expectation of an outcome of winning all or losing all in inner-Party struggles over supreme political power or at one level removed from it.

---

[12]   Complementarity or conflict may both comprise the content of this overlapping.

The above continuum is structured on the basis of the denotations of the terms "formal" and "informal". But "formal" and "informal" can also be distinguished and indeed contrasted with the following dichotomies. The first is the contrast between *universalistic* relationships among specific *categories* of people explicitly defined with regard to *specific* issues and arenas of action and *particularistic* relationships, typically between two or a small number of persons on some basis of social or political attributes with regard to a range of *unspecified* and *diffuse* issues and arenas. The second pair of features is the quality of publicity and openness on the one hand and privacy and secrecy on the other. The third pair is the relationship governed by regular procedures and schedules and relationships which are not. The fourth comprises relationships which are usually defined in public documents as against those relationships that usually are not. Finally, there is the familiar contrast between relationships based on achievement and those based on ascription.

Although all of this does not constitute a full conceptualization of informal politics in China, allow me to follow Dittmer's lead and formulate a *provisional* definition, as follows: informal politics consists of political interactions among persons with different types of informal relationships and their networks, which play an important part and sometimes even serve as a nucleus of "political action groups"[13] in the struggle, conflict, or contestation over significant policy issues or personnel changes. These networks assume at different times and in different periods a dominant, co-equal, or complementary role to formal politics based on formal relationships. In elite politics in the CCP, these personal, informal networks are linked directly or indirectly to the "core" of the Party. The "core" is itself the centre of an intricate pattern of informal and formal relationships. Those of us interested in state-rebuilding and the process of institutionalization in China should focus on the interconnection and the changing properties between the "formal" and "informal" relationships in this pattern of personal networks with a "core".

This provisional concept can be refined through further empirical and theoretical testing, and one should in addition examine politics in some other country selected for its comparative value. Only then can we derive a reliable concept on which to build a conceptual synthesis.

When we examine the Chinese data again with this in mind, we discover it inadequate in at least two respects. First it does not take into account the personalities[14] of the twenty to forty top leaders, particularly that of the core

---

[13]   I use this term in a special sense; see section IV.

[14]   All of the essays in the volume edited by Hamrin and Zhao (footnote 3) emphasize the personalistic factor in Chinese elite politics, particularly among the elders and, above all, Mao and Deng. That the personality of the leaders inevitably affects the operation of the system is obvious in the difference between the Mao and Deng periods. But the less obvious point is that it also serves as a selective mechanism, what Ding Xueliang calls a sieve, for selecting potential leaders. Compare Zhu Houze and Yuan Ming under Hu Yaobang, Bao

leader. The personality of the core leader affects all his decisions and, together with the personalities of subordinates, also shapes what Lucian Pye calls the quality of *guanxi*. Mao, for example, was a radical, an ideologist, a utopian, a romantic and, most importantly, a man with an earth-shaking rage which he could suppress when it was necessary to adopt moderate, rational policies, friendly relations with his colleagues and even his enemies. But the suppressed rage could also flare into the open when the political situation permitted or demanded, and lead to irrational actions that he rationalized with his ideology. His irregular working habits, the ambiguity of his spoken words, and the depth of his hidden motives also created unstable and unpredictable formal and informal relationships with his colleagues, friends and those around him.

Deng was a very different kind of person. He was basically a "pragmatist".[15] He was a strong disciplinarian. He acted decisively. He made his views clear when he made up his mind. The operation of the informal networks was quite different under Deng, who strove for stability while seeking down-to-earth changes, and who was attentive to routine affairs and had regular habits. An even clearer contrast is between the effects of Jiang Qing's and Ye Qun's active participation in politics and that of Deng Yingchao (Mme Zhou Enlai). The former were deeply disruptive of formal politics and formal authority while the latter supported and strengthened them.

The second inadequacy arises from the failure to take account of the possibility that there existed rules of the game in the middle zone where informal and formal politics overlap. In his earlier works, Frederick Teiwes mentions the existence of normative rules of the game. In addition to these rules, which may or may not be followed or even blatantly violated, one must try to discover the unwritten or even unacknowledged rules of the game, or what Teiwes calls the prudential rules. I believe that we may be able to find some of these by focusing on the most significant phenomenon with the most grievous and pernicious consequences for China. This central phenomenon is, let me repeat, the fact that whenever there was an intra-Party struggle for supreme power or at one level below, the outcome was consistently, from the very beginning of the founding of the Party, that one side has eventually won all and the other side has lost all. Up through Mao's death, these are what were known as the "ten major line struggles" of Party history. They were followed by the arrest of the Gang of Four and many years later the removal of Zhao Ziyang from all positions after the 1989 Tiananmen tragedy.[16] This recurrent outcome must have created corresponding

---

Tong and Wu Guoguang under Zhao Ziyang, and Chen Xitong and Yuan Mu under Li Peng.

[15] This term "pragmatist" here designates a person who stresses the consequences of action rather than merely its intrinsic value.

[16] Tang Tsou, "The Tiananmen Tragedy: The State-Society Relationship, Choices, and the Mechanisms in Historical Perspective", in Brantly Womack (ed.), *Contemporary Chinese*

expectations among the top leaders, which in turn cannot but have influenced their informal relationships.

They face at least two options. One is that the participants will anticipate the outcome and from the beginning play a game to win all or lose all. Or, second, they can adjust their behaviour in order to avoid being involved in such an outcome. For example, even though Chen Yun disagreed with Deng Xiaoping after the latter decided to accelerate economic reforms toward a market system as far and as fast as circumstances permitted, thus abandoning his earlier reliance on Chen Yun's advice on economic matters, Chen Yun took care not to openly challenge Deng's economic policies when Deng took a public position. He would make his views public only when Deng had left some loopholes in his public pronouncements. When Deng stumbled, as in the de-control of prices in 1988, Chen Yun's views prevailed for a time. But he never publicly challenged Deng's power as the "core".[17] It is these kinds of rules of the game that we want to discover and incorporate as a part of our analysis of elite politics in the Party, informal or formal.

My provisional delineation of the relationship between formal and informal politics is summed up by the following two tables.

If Dittmer does intend to define informal politics as politics in which a set of personal relationships constitute an end in themselves, then he overstates his case for the importance of informal politics in China. Informal or personal relationships are ends in themselves only under certain conditions and at specific times, when the goal of a participant or a group of participants is the pursuit of personal power pure and simple, the preservation of power and status, or the quest for personal survival. In many cases and at different times, though, they are means to other goals. Thus, there is a need for a Table 2 to illustrate the possible relations between various kinds of goals and personal informal relationships as a means.

Politics in Historical Perspectives (Cambridge: Cambridge University Press, 1991), pp. 289–94, 319–21. The account about the Tiananmen tragedy is generally confirmed by Zhao Ziyang's defense of his action, made at the 4th Plenum of the 13th Central Committee. The full text in Chinese is available in *Xinbao caijing yuekan* (Hong Kong) (July 1994), pp. 129–37.

17   On this, see the preceding chapter by Frederick Teiwes, which is one of the most balanced, accurate and impressive descriptions of Chinese Party politics that I have read. See also Cheng Xiaonong in Hamrin and Zhao, *Decision-Making in Deng's China*, p. 199.

Table 1: Formal and Informal Politics

Relations between (A) persons occupying formal institutional roles or linked by formal institutional ties and (B) those playing informal roles or linked by informal, personal ties.

	HARMONY	**CONFLICT**
	consensus agreement convergence parallelism	hidden disagreement friction covert conflict open conflict
(A) prevails over (B)	(I) Mao prevailed over Liu (1949-56).	(II) Mao prevailed over Liu (1959, summer 1962, 1964, 1965); Mao prevailed over Peng (1959); Mao prevailed over Deng (1966, 1975); Mao prevailed over Lin Biao (1970–71); Jiang Zemin prevailed over the generals of the Yang clan
(B) prevails over (A)	(IV) Deng prevailed over Hu (before summer 1986); over Zhao (before May 1989); over Jiang (1989-)	(III) Jiang Qing (supported by Mao) prevailed over Liu, Deng, Tao, etc. (1966–67); Deng prevailed over Hu (after summer 1986); over Zhao (during late May 1989)

Notes:

1.   Chinese political development since 1949 can be described as starting from square (I) to (II), to (III), to (IV). Whether it will move back to (I) under Jiang or another leader remains to be seen.

2.   This table shows the dominating power, particularly the informal power, of the "core" leader. Formalization and institutionalization of the power of the "core" would be the most important first step for political reform in China.

Table 2: Ideals and Power Interests as Goals and Formal and Informal Politics as the Means

	Pure Ideals	Both Ideals and Power Interests with Ideals as the Primary Goal	Both Power Interests and Ideals, with Power Interests as the Primary Goal	Pure Power Interests
Formal Relationships as the Primary Means and Formal Procedures as the Usual Path	Early Revolutionaries Chen Duxiu Early Mao	Mao Liu Deng (before 1980-81) Hu Zhao	Zhang Guotao (1935) Chen Boda (1969-70)	Lin Biao Kang Sheng
Informal Relationships as the Primary Means and Informal Routes as the Usual Path	Mme Sun Yat-sen before 1949 Liao Chengzhi before he joined the CCP in 1924	Deng (after 1980-81)	Deng Liqun (after 1981)	Jiang Qing Ye Qun

Notes:

1. If one construes Dittmer's informal politics as politics that take personal relationships as an end in itself, then this is concentrated in the right-hand column. But it also is scattered here and there throughout the two other columns to its left.

2. The entries to this table are highly subjective and based on personal judgements.

In imagery, formal politics is best represented as a hierarchical pyramid, while informal politics is best represented by a spider's web with the "core" at the centre and with a series of irregularly shaped concentric circles linked by a series of irregularly shaped radii.[18] Chinese elite politics works well when each supports the other and the "core" is not challenged. In this case it does not matter much whether formal politics dominates informal politics or *vice versa*. The more important factor is the personality and work style of the "core" leader, which may lead to the adoption of disastrous policies. For the purposes of institutionalization and long-term stability, the pyramidal hierarchy should be supplemented and not dominated by the spider's web.

If we turn to Dittmer's perception of "collective leadership" in Party politics (*vide* Dittmer's first table), we find that collective leadership has, in the past, proved to be a transitional phase.[19] As a game played by an unspecified and varying number of top leaders, it is inherently unstable. It tends to be polarized and then one side wins and the other side loses. Finally, a "core" is established. "Collective leadership" can be made stable only if there are a series of institutional reforms and a change in the attitudes and perception of how the game of power struggle is played or should be played. In Dittmer's terms, the British Cabinet system could be described as "collective leadership" *cum* "primus inter pares". Its unity and stability is maintained by its institutional responsibility to the Parliament and by the anticipation of the next election. Cabinet unity and stability under the Prime Minister are necessary for remaining in power and for the success of the party. To make "collective leadership" into a system, the CCP would need to make innovations in its institutions and change the expectations of players.

---

[18]   I notice a parallelism between my imagery and Nathan's in his preface to *The Private Life of Chairman Mao* by Li Zhisui (New York: Random House, 1994), p. xii. His use of the imagery of "the spider's position at the centre" is identical to mine. But he describes the spider's web as the Party's *factional* web (p. xii, my emphasis), while I do not use the word factional for reasons that will become clear. In recognizing now the special role of Mao and in using the imagery of "the spider's position at the centre", he has moved a long way from the imagery projected by his factionalism model, despite his effort to maintain continuity by using the phrase "factional web".

[19]   Yan Jiaqi writes, "In the early 1980s Deng Xiaoping, Chen Yun and Li Xiannian formed a collective leadership which evolved into dictatorship by Deng". (See Hamrin and Zhao, *Decision-Making in Deng's China*, p. 5.) So, too, after the Zunyi conference of 1935, a collective leadership emerged with Mao as the director of the Military Affairs Committee, with Zhang Wentian, one of the "28½ Bolsheviks", and Zhang Guotao wielding enormous influence. Mao was the first among equals in this collective leadership. But after the Rectification campaign in 1942, the "collective leadership" was gradually superseded by a system in which the Thought of Mao Zedong became the guide for all the work of the Party, and Mao usually made the final decision in all important matters. This system was formalized at the Seventh Party Congress in 1945.

Having begun my discussion with Dittmer's building blocks, his "informal relationships" and his "value-rational" relationships, and having proceeded with suggestions on how he could define informal politics and a proposal that he needs to link informal politics with formal politics, let us now turn to a discussion of Nathan's "factions".

II. "Factions"

As noted, from the building blocks of the "clientelist, leader-followers" relationship, Nathan constructed "factions" as the unit-actors of his "factionalism model of CCP politics". According to Nathan, a "faction" consists of a "one-to-one, rather than corporate, pattern of relationships between leaders (or subleaders) and followers ... the hierarchy and established communications and authority flow of the existing organization provides the trellis upon which the complex faction is able to extend its own informal personal loyalties and relations". Once established, these "clientelist ties should not be confused with "the power relationship of 'imperative coordination'".[20] Inferentially, this type of power relationship is not included in his concept of "factions". Such an analytically clear distinction is necessary in all scholarly study of China, and not only in building "a factionalism model". But in reality, at all institutional and bureaucratic levels the actions of a leader frequently involve both types of relationships. No matter how clearly the concept of "faction" is defined, in testing the model and the utility of the concept, it is incumbent to show what roles are played by these two kinds of relationships, what is their relative significance and consequences, and hence what is the force and limits of their explanatory and predictive power.

According to Nathan, there are two types of "factions": "simple factions" and "complex factions" that consist of many simple factions ultimately linked through sub-leaders to the same leader.[21] By definition, Nathan's "factions" are not "corporatized". Therefore, one cannot think of them in the imagery of the quasi-corporatized factions in Japan's Liberal Democratic Party, or even the semi-secretive Blue Shirts, the Fuxing She, and the elusive CC Clique in the Kuomintang.[22] Nathan called his "faction" a "structure", presumably because it is a

---

[20] Nathan, "A Factionalism Model for CCP Politics", pp. 41–2, 44. Nathan wrote: "Structurally, the faction is articulated through one or more nodes; it is recruited and coordinated on the basis of the personal exchange relationship I have called clientelist ties" (p. 42).

[21] Ibid., pp. 40–2.

[22] The leaders of the CC Clique consistently denied that it ever existed. For the retrospective account of Ch'en Li-fu on the origins of the term "CC Clique", see Chen Li-fu, *The Storm Clouds Clear over China: The Memoir of Chen Li-fu, 1900–1993* (Stanford: Hoover Press, 1994), p. 215. But political actors in China seldom failed to know who were members in good standing or not. They formed small cliques in various bureaucratic organizations at all levels.

structure of "clientelist ties" or "leader-follower ties". But to come to term with the general usage, I shall reserve the term "structure" to designate the whole political structure or system and label Nathan's "factions" as one type of unit-actor in my analysis.

Nathan's simple and elegant concept of "faction" must, of course, be confronted with the Chinese reality. He himself tested his "factionalism model" against Party politics during the Cultural Revolution. After concluding that his model passed the test, he then tried to demonstrate the vast explanatory power of his model in "sketching the interpretation that would flow from the maximum assumption: factionalism since the earliest day".[23] He believed that it held up well. We shall examine both of these claims of Nathan's in the next section.

As I suggested in 1973, "Nathan's model fits certain periods of CCP politics (e.g., the Cultural Revolution) better than other periods (e.g., 1945–56)".[24] This is still my opinion. There were at least two factions, "the Gang of Four" and Lin Biao's faction, that came as close as possible in real life during this period to Nathan's "factions".

Both explicitly and implicitly, Nathan designated Mao as the leader of a faction and discussed the Cultural Revolution according to this characterization. This was in line, even in scholarly circles, with the most popular and most widely accepted interpretation both before and during the Cultural Revolution and followed a long-standing interpretation of Party politics as almost exclusively involving factional struggles for power, be these analyses from Taiwan and Hong Kong or earlier on the mainland from 1927 to 1949.

But can Mao's position in elite politics or in the Chinese political system be understood simply as the head of one of many factions? As is well known, after his dismissal of Peng Dehuai in 1959, Mao promoted the return of Lin Biao from semi-retirement to a position of real power as Defense Minister and as the leader in charge of the Party's Military Commission. Lin used these positions to build up a very powerful faction in the army, as well as a political faction with Chen Boda as the most important recruit. But Mao himself personally weakened, isolated and destroyed Lin Biao and his faction after Lin tried to promote himself to become Chairman of the Republic against Mao's expressed wish not to re-establish that position, which would have diluted Mao's absolute power.

It is also perfectly true that Mao was instrumental in creating what was subsequently known as "the Gang of Four". Indeed, many people in Taiwan and Hong Kong have invoked the term "Gang of Five" to include Mao. But Mao never wholeheartedly supported the Gang of Four. On crucial occasions, he personally prevented it from grasping additional power.[25] According to one report,

---

[23]   Nathan, "A Factionalism Model for CCP Politics", p. 58.

[24]   Tang Tsou, "Prolegomenon to the Study of Informal Groups in CCP Politics", p. 100.

[25]   The clearest example is Mao's letter to Jiang Qing dated 12 November 1974 asking her not to try to "organize the Cabinet (to become the boss behind the scene)". On 3 May 1975,

"Jiang Qing believed that the person preventing her from obtaining supreme power is the Chairman".[26]

The simple fact is that Mao occupied the unique position as the "core" and practiced the traditional tactics of divide and rule, using the Lin Biao "faction" and the Gang of Four "faction" first to balance and then destroy the rising power of Liu Shaoqi and other leaders who did not share his visions, did not absolutely obey him, did not agree with him on many important issues, and were, he suspected, not totally loyal to him. He also mobilized the students and the masses outside the Party to attack the "factions" dominating the Party and government bureaucracies. Naturally, both the "factions" and the individual leaders in turn used Mao to gain additional power, to attack their opponents, and to advance their careers. Mao clearly knew this and said so.[27]

More importantly, it was Mao who made all the final decisions on such momentous events as the Hundred Flowers Campaign, the Anti-Rightist Campaign, the programs of cooperativization and collectivization, the Great Leap Forward, the Socialist Education Movement, and the Cultural Revolution, in pursuit of his unrealistic, radical, utopian ideas and to keep or retain absolute power in his own hands.

Mao's ability to play one faction against another or even to create a faction overnight, as it were, and to make the final decisions depended on his charismatic authority, his formal authority as Chairman of the Central Committee and his informal power, which, in combination, overshadowed the Politburo[28] and its standing committee as collective bodies. His vast network of what Dittmer calls "informal relationships" was a part of his informal power. This power and its bases constituted the central reality of Party politics under Mao. Nathan did grasp one aspect of this key reality that did not fit comfortably with his notion of Mao as a leader of a "faction" or more precisely a "complex faction". He wrote that Mao's

---

Mao said at a meeting of the Politburo: "Don't behave as a gang of four, don't carry on in the way you have been". Quoted in Ye Yonglie, *Jiang Qing Zhuan* (A Biography of Jiang Qing) (Zhangchun: Shidai Chubanshe, 1993), pp. 523, 520.

[26] This was the remark of Wang Dongxing, the head of the General Office of the Party Central Committee, and the Party Secretary of the Guard Regiment of the Party Centre, as reported by Li Zhisui in *Mao Zedong siren yisheng* (Mao Zedong's Private Doctor) (Taipei: Shibao Chuban, 1994).

[27] The best evidence is Mao's letter to Jiang Qing dated 8 July 1966 at the beginning of the Cultural Revolution. He pointed out that Lin Biao wanted to use him as Zhong Kui, the ghostbuster in traditional folklore, to bust the ghosts (namely, the enemies of Lin who were also opponents of Mao). So, too, on 10 February 1967 Mao criticized Chen Boda to his face, noting that "In the past, you always played the role of an opportunist between Liu Shaoqi and me". Quoted in Wang Li, *Xianchang lishi* [The Scenes of History] (Hong Kong: Oxford University Press, 1993), p. 29.

[28] Mao said to his doctor that "the decision made by the Politburo can be changed by me". Li Zhisui, *Mao Zedong siren yisheng*, p. 169.

"goal" in the Cultural Revolution was no longer merely "an improved position of his faction in the elite, but an end to factionalism and its associated policy oscillations and an institutionalization of the Party as an instrument of Mao's will".[29]

Nathan's characterization of Mao's goal is not only plausible but may even be downright correct. But Mao could espouse this goal because his power depended not only or even primarily on his "faction" of the Gang of Four or that of Lin Biao but also on the other generally recognized sources of power and authority mentioned above as well as the fact that the Party for a long period of time had been "an instrument of his will".

More basically, there is a methodological lesson to be learned here. In his endeavour to build a simple, elegant model by abstracting it from an extraordinarily complex reality, and probably coming under the influence of widely accepted views and extensively circulated writings on factional struggles in the Party, Nathan simply designated Mao as the leader of a faction and did not incorporate in his model the most important and central reality of Party politics— the special role of Mao or, more broadly, the role of what has become known as the "core" of the Party since Deng's speech of June 1989.

Kenneth N. Waltz distinguishes two senses of the term "model". He writes: "In one sense a model represents a theory. In another sense a model pictures a reality while simplifying it. ... If such a model departs too far from reality, it becomes useless. A model airplane should look like a real airplane. Explanatory power, however, is gained by moving away from 'reality', not by staying close to it. A full description would be of least explanatory power; an elegant theory, of most".[30] In their discussion of building a model, King, Koehane and Verba underscore "the importance of abstracting the correct features ... for a particular problem".[31]

However, Nathan was so anxious to follow simplicity as a methodological principle, as stressed in the last sentence of the quotation from Waltz, that he was not conscious of the principle laid down by King et. al. that the value of a model also depends on which aspect or feature of the reality it is built upon or which aspects or features it discards or ignores. Consequently, for certain problems such as the analysis of an ordinary policy conflict and its resolution, in which the ultimate direction of the regime and supreme political power are not at stake, Nathan's model selected one of the appropriate features.[32] But for that most

---

[29]   Nathan, "A Factionalism Model for CCP Politics", p. 60.

[30]   Kenneth N. Waltz, *Theory of International Politics* (New York: Random House, 1979), p. 7.

[31]   King, Keohane and Verba, *Designing Social Inquiry*, p. 49.

[32]   I assume that this is one of the bases for Dittmer's appreciation of Nathan's model.

important question of supreme political power, he missed the key feature of Party politics.

Strictly applying Nathan's notion of "faction", one would also have serious trouble in explaining the relationship between Mao on the one hand and leaders such as Zhou Enlai, Liu Shaoqi and Deng Xiaoping *etcetera* on the other, particularly their changing relationships going back to the revolutionary period. All China scholars know that in the Jiangxi period, Zhou Enlai was the instrument used by the "28½ Bolsheviks" to weaken Mao's control over the army and thus his political power. At the Ningdu Conference in 1932, Zhou took over most of Mao's authority with respect to military affairs.[33] It was only at the Zunyi Conference of January 1935 that Zhou openly supported Mao's military policy in opposition to that of Bo Gu and Otto Braun and took the initiative to admit a share of responsibility for the mistakes that had led to the Red Army's defeat in the Kuomintang's fifth campaign of encirclement and annihilation.[34] It was only on 10 March of that year that Mao and Zhou worked together in a "three-man military command small group".[35] For his collaboration with the "28½ Bolsheviks", Zhou suffered repeated criticism and undertook several self-criticisms, particularly during the 1942 Zhengfeng movement.[36]

From 1943 onwards, Zhou always followed Mao's policy closely when the latter arrived at a final decision. Sometimes, he honestly believed in the judgment of Mao, but even when he disagreed or had serious reservations he went along with Mao as a loyal supporter, implementing Mao's policies as best he could while trying to modify them in the light of his judgment of whether Mao would accept his suggestions.

The relationship between Zhou and Mao was a mixture of both Nathan's "leader-follower" relationship and his "power relationship of 'imperative coordination'". But it was the latter that predominated, particularly after 1949, when Zhou served as the premier of the government in a system where the Party had authority over the government. After 1956 Zhou became the second ranking Vice-Chairman after Liu Shaoqi, but the line of authority was clear. Zhou did not enjoy a close informal relationship with Mao, even given that Mao believed him indispensable during the Cultural Revolution.

Mao's relationship with Deng and Liu was different from the Zhou-Mao relationship. Both Deng and Liu had been leading members of Mao's "faction". The first demotion of Deng occurred during the Jiangxi period, when he supported

---

[33]   Zhongyang wenxian yanjiushi (ed.), *Zhou Enlai nianpu* [The Chronological Biography of Zhou Enlai] (Beijing: Renmin Chubanshe, 1990), pp. 560–9.

[34]   Ibid., p. 273.

[35]   Ibid., p. 277. The third person was Wang Jiaxiang.

[36]   Zhongyang wenxian yanjiushi (ed.), *Zhou Enlai zhuan* [A Biography of Zhou Enlai] (Beijing: Renmin Chubanshe, 1989), pp. 561–3.

Mao's policy and was characterized by his enemies as a "chief of the Mao faction".[37] Liu was the most effective advocate of the cult of Mao in the Yanan period. But after 1949, the "power relationship of 'imperative coordination'" gradually overshadowed the "factional" clientelist tie. Mao charged that Liu acted on many occasions without consulting him or even reporting to him. On 19 May 1953, Mao wrote a formal circular, criticizing Liu and Yang Shangkun "for a breach of discipline in issuing documents in the name of the Central Committee without (Mao's) authorization".[38] Mao also complained that Deng did not come to see him as often as he should and that in meetings he sat far away from Mao in spite of Deng's deafness.

One can, of course, analyse these developments in terms of Nathan's concept of "faction" in the following way. Prior to 1945, Mao was the leader of a "complex faction", with Liu and Deng, among others, as his followers. They in turn were leaders of "complex factions" at the next lower level, with supporting structures and subordinate simple factions. After Mao's "complex faction", which had captured complete control of the Party in 1945, became in 1949 the ruling group in the national government, the "complex factions" of both Liu and Deng gradually achieved independence from Mao and stood opposed to Mao on some issues. Their opposition to the "cult of personality" at the 8th Party Congress of 1956, which led to the elimination of the statement in the Party Constitution of 1945 that Mao Zedong Thought provided the guiding principles for all the Party's work, was a watershed in their relationship with Mao.[39] It was one of the most important roots leading ultimately to the Cultural Revolution. But whether this use of Nathan's terms and framework is the best way to analyse Chinese elite politics is an open question.

What Nathan designated as the "trellis", which enabled a "faction" to extend "its informal personal loyalties and relations", turned out to have a life of its own. The trellis of institutions and bureaucracies is more like a tree that can grow both vertically and horizontally and that develops new branches and leaves. It adds a "power relationship of 'imperative coordination'" to the personal, informal ones, and it shapes and transforms the latter. At the very least, it strengthens the former and weakens the latter. Frequently, a person's assumption of a formal role changes the relationship with his erstwhile leaders, friends and colleagues.

Moreover, Nathan's concept of "faction" cannot be employed easily to account for the transformation of informal groups into formal institutions and the

---

[37]   These are Mao's own words when he acknowledged his long political relationship with Deng in his comment on Deng's letter to Mao after Lin Biao had defected. See Mao Mao, *Wo de fuqin Deng Xiaoping* [My Father Deng Xiaoping] (Hong Kong: Sanlian Shudian, 1993), p. 278.

[38]   Mao Zedong, *Selected Works*, Vol. V (Beijing: Foreign Languages Press, 1977), p. 92.

[39]   For Mao's strong private reaction to Liu and Deng's actions regarding the cult of personality, see Li Zhisui, *Mao Zedong siren yisheng*, pp. 172–5.

development of bureaucratic groups, institutional interest groups, unorganized opinion groups (groups constituted by persons with no face-to-face relationships, and groups which cut across institutional bureaucratic lines) and what Hong Yung Lee once called "situational groups" (that is, persons and groups that find themselves in the same political situation in spite of different bureaucratic, "factional", personal affiliations and economic interests, such as those who were pushed aside during the Cultural Revolution (*wenge shousun pai*) by those gaining in political power *(wenge shouyi pai)*. In other words, Nathan's concept of "factions" is too narrow to encompass the variety of groups that participate in the political process. It does not lend itself easily to the study of political development, the "rebuilding of the state", and the progress and retrogression of institutionalization in a political system.

In short, while "factions" as one type of personal network or informal group are admittedly one of the most important unit-actors in Party politics, political decisions are not made by "factions" alone. There are many other important actors which Nathan ignored. There are many socio-political cleavages that are activated by disputes over fundamental issues.[40] Focusing on "factions" alone as the unit-actors, Nathan succeeded in building a simple and elegant model of one aspect of factionalism in Party politics, but it is not a model of elite Party politics.

To illustrate these remarks, let me note two turning points in CCP politics. The first occurred before the publication of Nathan's paper and the other after its appearance. In the first case, Mao easily set a trap for Lin Biao and his "faction". Mao used his authority both as a charismatic leader and as Chairman of the Party and its Military Commission to undermine Lin's power and prestige.[41] In Mao's trip to the south in 1971 he mobilized the regional and local commanders to oppose Lin. These commanders could not be said to form a faction. Instead, they can be designated a bureaucratic interest group in the army. Mao used the

---

[40]   Writing on the question of succession to Deng, Yan Jiaqi observes: "The game of hide and seek (in the struggle for succession) frequently transcends the factor of factions". He asserts that many social, economic and political cleavages will influence the formation of factions and their coalition or combination. His remarks apply to many of the political struggles in the past, such as the Lushan meeting in 1959. Yan Jiaqi, "Quanli zhuomicang: gejiu gewei" (The Game of Hide and Seek of Power (Struggles): On Your Mark!), *Shijie ribao zhoukan* [The Weekly Magazine of the World Journal (NY)], 26 February 1995, p. 3.

[41]   Mao used three colourful figures of speech to describe his methods in weakening Lin's power, all of which were based on Mao's formal authority: (1) "Throwing stones"—that is, making comments critical of Lin and his followers on reports submitted to him and circulating them to high level officials; (2) "Digging up the foundations"—that is, removing Lin's men from key positions and replacing them with men loyal to Mao himself; and (3) "Mixing in sand to loosen up a solid situation"—that is, putting men loyal to Mao in Lin's general office. These famous figures of speech are cited by Dittmer and many other scholars.

opportunity to activate his intensive informal relationships with the military leaders, which also bolstered his formal authority.[42]

The second event was the arrest of the Gang of Four on 6 October 1976.[43] The final decision to act was made by only three persons: Hua Guofeng, the first Vice-Chairman of the Party; Ye Jianying, another Vice-Chairman of the Party, Vice-Chairman of the Party's Military Commission, and Defense Minister who, though in semi-retirement by order of Mao, retained tremendous prestige as the most senior Marshal in good health; and Wang Dongxing, the head of the General Office of the Central Committee and the Party secretary of the division-strength 8341 unit which guarded the places where the top leaders worked and lived. The central figure was Ye Jianying, who had extensive informal relationships with top military figures, but he was not known as a "factional" leader in Nathan's sense or in common usage.[44] In the days just before the arrest of the "Gang of Four", it was he who contacted, on a one-by-one basis, a number of leaders who had survived the Cultural Revolution. These leaders, ranging from Deng Yingchao (Mme Zhou Enlai) to Chen Yun, cannot be said to form a "faction" in Nathan's sense, because their relationship was not that of a vertical leader-follower type but a horizontal relationship of equals or near equals. After Mao's death, they talked secretly and discreetly about the political situation—but individually, not as a group. Deng Xiaoping, the indomitable warrior, was one of the first to take the initiative to see Ye alone. General Wang Zhen, the aggressive and blunt former commander of the 359 brigade in the Yanan period, served as Ye's intermediary in these one-to-one contacts, earning him the nickname of "the staff officer for liaison".[45] This collection of veteran political leaders has been called an "opinion group" by Franz Schurmann and a "situational group" by Hong Yung Lee, but it did not qualify as a "faction" in Nathan's sense. Dittmer's notion of informal relationships is much more directly useful.

These leaders were confronted with three alternatives: (1) to follow regular procedures, convoke a regular or enlarged meeting of the Politburo and adopt a decision to dismiss the Gang of Four; (2) for a few top leaders to make a decision

---

[42] There is no need to document this point beyond drawing attention to the following document—"A Summary of Important Points of Chairman Mao's Remarks to Responsible Officials during the Period of his Tour outside Beijing" (from the middle ten days of August to 12 September 1977) (in Chinese), reprinted in *Zhonggong nianbao 1993* [Yearbook for the Study of the Chinese Communist Party, 1993] (Taiwan), Section 7, pp. 5–8.

[43] The following account is based on the best book so far available on the subject—Fan Shuo, *Ye Jianying zai 1976* [Ye Jianging in 1976] (Beijing: Zhonggong Zhongyang Dangxiao, 1990), p. 270.

[44] Ye said that throughout his life he did not establish a "mountain top", nor did he have a *dixi*, personal clique or troops loyal to him as an individual. Ibid., p. 204.

[45] Ibid., p. 208.

and take resolute, drastic action against them, and only then convoke a meeting of the Politburo to ratify the action; and (3) to use the army to arrest them in a sudden strike and then deal with them according to law. Wang Zhen advocated the third alternative. Chen Yun thought this would not be legal and indicated his preference to solve the problem legally. Deng Yingchao told Ye Jianying that to act legally, "one person", meaning Hua, must stand up first.

Deng Yingchao's remarks suggested that Hua was important to the enterprise because of his formal authority as the first Vice-Chairman, legally the top leader after the death of Mao, not because of his political power or the "faction" under his control. Before the Cultural Revolution, Hua had been merely the Vice-Governor of Hunan province and Secretary of the provincial secretariat. He had been elected as a member of the Central Committee only in 1969, and became a member of the Politburo only in 1973. He had not had time to build a powerful "faction" in Nathan's sense. Most of his colleagues in the Politburo were either his equals or had been senior to him in Party rank in the recent past. His indispensability on this occasion came from his formal authority and his informal influence as the designated heir of Mao, who had scribbled three sentences with his trembling hand on 30 April 1976, the last sentence being "with you in charge, my mind is at ease". This last fact and Mao's last gestures to Ye Jianying just before Mao's death greatly influenced Ye's attitude.[46]

The final decision by the three conspirators was to choose the second alternative. The arrests were all accomplished within one hour on the night of 6 October 1976. The Politburo met immediately afterwards and through the early morning of 7 October and elected Hua as Chairman of the Party and its Military Commission. Thus the destruction of the "faction" of the "Gang of Four" was accomplished by a final decision made by three men with formal authority over the Party, army, and leadership guard unit. They were supported by no more than a few dozen political and military leaders, who had been contacted one by one. There was no caucus, no meeting of a "faction". Long-standing informal personal relationships facilitated the process of securing support in great secrecy. The leadership group of three and the "situational group" of a small number of leaders dared to stage what we would call a pre-emptive strike[47] in a life and death struggle (an action whose legality was doubted even by some of the supporters) because they realized that they had the support of many bureaucratic groups in the Party and government bureaucracy, as well as the larger "situational group" in the upper political levels, the totally amorphous opinion groups in society at large, and a submerged mass opinion that reacted against the extremism and cruelty of the "Gang of Four". At this turning point in Party politics, the destruction of a "faction" in Nathan's sense was accomplished overnight by a collection of

---

[46]   Ye's unflagging loyalty to Hua as Mao's designated heir was the subject of his self-criticism years later.

[47]   Ibid., pp. 236, 285.

different types of political actors and forces, some acting directly and others giving their support.

While his concept of "faction" does apply quite adequately to the "Gang of Four", the concept does not suffice to describe the collection of persons and forces which destroyed the Gang. The Chinese political system, in fact, has a bias against "factions" in Nathan's sense or in the common parlance. They do exist, sometimes even for a long period of time. But they must bear the onus of being "factions" and do not have the status of legitimate unit-actors in the system. They are at a disadvantage when the struggle over power and policy intensifies in circumstances in which the defeated are always eliminated in a game of winning all or losing all. This is one of the reasons that Chinese leaders always claim that they have "working relationships" with each other and do not form a "faction". This is also the reason that the leaders always deny with a straight face that factions exist.

Those writers who focus their attention almost exclusively on factions must face one of the most salient facts about factions that do not have supreme political authority or the tacit support or acquiescence of its holder. They are very fragile entities. Lin Biao was destroyed without much effort. Before Mao's death, the veteran leaders did not remove Jiang Qing from power due purely to consideration of Mao's power and authority or out of affection for him. After Mao scolded Jiang Qing in a Politburo meeting on 3 May 1975 for acting as a "Gang of Four" and after Kang Sheng indirectly told Mao that Jiang Qing and Zhang Chunqiao had been "renegades" (*pantu*) in the 1930s, some leaders apparently had the thought of taking action to strike down the Gang. Premier Zhou, always the realist, told them that "up to now the Chairman has not bent (sufficiently) to ask for the striking down of Jiang Qing's group of four persons through criticism. ... It is not that easy to overthrow them".[48] Marshal Ye also hesitated to act when Mao was still breathing. But as soon as Mao died, the four were easily removed by a pre-emptive strike.

This fragility of "factions" which do not form a part of a political action group enjoying legitimate control over, or the willing cooperation or toleration of, the top authoritative Party organs, particularly that of the "core" leader, is a characteristic of CCP politics throughout its history. This proposition seems a tautology but it is not. One of the clearest cases is provided by Mao himself. Mao could be considered and was considered by the "28½ Bolsheviks" as the leader of a "faction". After the authoritative organs of the Central Committee moved one after another to the Jiangxi-Fujian base area, which had been built up by Mao, he progressively lost his power, authority and influence to the Central Committee. This was controlled by Bo Gu, who had played no part in building up the Red Army and its base. Insofar as the so-called ten line-struggles involved factions, these factions proved to be very fragile. If we follow Nathan and consider Liu, Deng, Tao Zhu and all the others as leaders of "factions", then it is not true that

---

[48]   Li Zhisui, *Mao Zedong siren yisheng*, p. 575.

these leaders actively mobilized their "factions" to defend themselves, or that they did their best to protect their followers under attack, as Dittmer's remarks imply. If they did, their feeble efforts were futile and almost invisible.[49] In contrast to the fragility of "factions", a leader or a group of leaders with widespread informal connections, high prestige, great informal power and general popular support can capture or recapture power in times of crisis or before a poltical leadership has stabilized itself.

The above effort to re-examine Nathan's concept of "factions" illuminates the basic question of the principle of simplicity and parsimony in the construction of models and/or theory. Nathan follows the principle that a model, to be useful, must simplify reality, but there is a question of when, how, and how far one can follow this principle. The following passages in the book by King, Keohane and Verba deserve to be quoted extensively:

> Parsimony is therefore a judgment, or even assumption, about the nature of the world: it is assumed to be simple. ... In the social sciences ... we believe (parsimony) is only occasionally appropriate ... we would never insist on parsimony as a general principle in designing theories, but it is useful in those situations where we have some knowledge of the simplicity of the world we are studying.

> Our point is that we do not advise researchers to seek parsimony as an essential good, since there seems little reason to adopt it unless we already know a lot about a subject. We do not need parsimony to avoid excessively complicated theories since it is indirectly implied by the maxim that theory should be just as complicated as all our evidence suggest.[50]

Since Nathan himself admitted that "it remains impossible to delineate with any confidence who the major factional leaders have been, much less their followers", there is, all the more, no sound reason that parsimony should be taken as "an essential good". If Nathan really tried to build his model on the basis of available information about CCP politics, his effort was premature. But did he really build his model on that basis? We shall answer this question in the next section.

By broadening the focus of our attention from "factions" in Nathan's sense to "informal politics", Dittmer adopts a central concept that is broad enough to take

---

[49]   In Hamrin and Zhao, *Decision-Making in Deng's China*, Yan Guai more generally observes, "Opposition factions that could seriously upset order rarely arise in the system, since no faction wants to be responsible for splitting the party. The defeated party in a given power struggle swiftly loses its legitimacy, as it is denounced as ideologically flawed".

[50]   King, Keohane and Verba, *Designing Social Inquiry*, p. 20. I interpret the phrase "just as complicated" to mean that it should be as simple as possible but as complicated as necessary.

into account the complexity of Chinese politics, particularly if he takes advantage of the advances in organizational theory in the last twenty years and tries to develop a sharp operational distinction between the formal and the informal and to distinguish different kinds of informal relationships and their roles and operation in Party politics, as suggested in the last section. His attempt at "a synthesis" will help to deal with this extraordinarily complex entity called Party politics, which, moreover, has been and will continue to be in a state of flux. To study a changing phenomenon, he must have a historical and developmental perspective. In so doing, he should reassess, in the light of new information available in the past two decades and particularly the last half-dozen years, the validity of the "Mao-in-command" model, "the policy making under Mao" interpretation, and Schurmann's notion of "opinion groups", as well as Nathan's flat rejection of the preceding.

Dittmer and all of us must squarely confront the problem of what are the similarities and differences between the role of the "core" leader and the other systems of one-man rule, such as the traditional imperial system in China and the *Fuerhrerprinzip* that he mentions. We could start with the simple commonsense observation that under the imperial system, the rule of succession was clearly defined. More basically, we could, using our continuum mentioned in Section II, assert that in the imperial system, family relationships comprised a part of the formal institution, whereas in Party theory and ideology, there should be a clear separation between family relationships and formal political authority. This was one of the unspoken principles that Mao broke and that made Jiang Qing such a hated person. The term "princelings Party" was coined in Taiwan and Hong Kong to delegitimize the current regime.

As Dittmer notes, the Party is governed by a *Fuerhrerprinzip*, however informal (p. 24). But one must also point out that in Chinese elite politics, voting in the Central Committee still counts and the legitimacy of the "core" leader must still be maintained on the surface through all sorts of manipulations. According to Yan Jiaqi, "In 1966, Mao himself believed that he was in the minority in the Central Committee". Hence he started the "Great Cultural Revolution". Through the "cult of personality" and the Red Guard movement,[51] Mao did obtain a majority in the 11th Central Committee convened in August 1966 by these outside pressures and some underhanded manoeuvres. To gain a majority may also have been behind the move whereby Liu and Deng were merely downgraded to the eighth and sixth positions in the standing committee of the Politburo. This lenient treatment stood in sharp contrast to their later fate.

As preliminary steps to the building of a model, the best way to study CCP politics—whether one uses the concept of Nathan's "faction" or Dittmer's "informal politics"—is, as I see it, to analyse the debate over an important policy

---

[51]   Yan Jiaqi, "Quanli zhuomicang: gejiu gewei".

and its resolution,[52] as well as the actual events surrounding a power struggle and its resolution, as Teiwes has done in his book on the Gao-Rao affair.[53] This type of research or case study could be premised on explicit or implicit theoretical assumptions with the aim of developing a model or theory or, more modestly, some general propositions applicable to other cases. But ultimately, we must follow Nathan's example of building a model that simplifies reality. We must do so, though, on the basis of a real knowledge and appreciation of its complexity.

III. Testing Nathan's "Factionalism Model"

Nathan built his model deductively. He began with a very restrictive definition of "faction" and a clear delineation of its structure. He then discussed his "ideal-typical *political system* which is primarily organized by factions" or "the pure case of an all-factional *system*" (my emphasis).[54] His model, or "ideal-typical political system", consisted of fifteen propositions on the characteristic mode of conflict. Methodologically, the most important point is that the first two sets of propositions are derived from (or to use Nathan's own term, "based upon") attributes of the units of the model,[55] that is, "the factions".

Of Nathan's fifteen characteristics of factional politics (or the informal rules of conflict and conflict resolution, as I would prefer to call them), several were flatly contradicted by events.[56] The existence of "a code of civility" was disproved by the public struggle meetings staged by the Red Guards against "Peng, Lu, Luo, and Yang", and against Wang Guangmei and Liu Shaoqi, as well as the circumstances surrounding the deaths of Marshal He Long and Liu Shaoqi. These and many other events contradict Nathan's remark about the lack of "severity of treatment" against losing factions by the victorious ones.

---

[52]   Debates are public events and they are the most reliable sources, the anchor of all studies of elite politics. See Joseph Fewsmith, *The Dilemmas of Reform in China* (Armonk: M. E. Sharpe, 1994), the works of Michel Oksenberg, Kenneth Lieberthal and David M. Lampton, and the articles in Hamrin and Zhao, *Decision-Making in Deng's China*.

[53]   Frederick C. Teiwes, *Politics at Mao's Court: Gao Gang and Party Factionalism in the Early 1950s* (Armonk: M. E. Sharpe, 1990).

[54]   Nathan, "A Factionalism Model for CCP Politics", p. 45.

[55]   The terms "attributes" and "units" as well as one of the ideas used to reinforce my earlier criticism of Nathan's model come from Waltz, *Theory of International Politics*; and Avery Goldstein, *From Bandwagon to Balance-of-Power Politics: Structural Constraints and Politics in China, 1949–1978* (Stanford: Stanford University Press, 1991).

[56]   If I were to subject my own piece to the same kind of strict methodological criticism, I am not sure whether it would fare better than Nathan's more creative piece. In any case, criticism in the social sciences is always easier than creative work, although original ideas can, sometimes but not very often, be expressed through criticism.

The two characteristics discussed by Nathan on policy-making were also contradicted by materials already available at the time. Policy-making since 1949 has never been characterized by *immobilism*. After a period of discussion, dispute, or fierce struggle, the "core"—that is, Mao—always made the final decision, even if it was a decision to accept a policy that he disliked. During the Cultural Revolution, Mao still made the most momentous decisions such as to dispatch workers and PLA propaganda teams to control the student movement, the sending of students off to settle in the countryside, the establishment of contacts with the United States, the initiation of criticisms against Lin Biao, the second dismissal of Deng Xiaoping, and the appointment of Hua Guofeng as his heir.

The impressions of *immobilism* during the Cultural Revolution arose from the difficulty or impossibility of implementing decisions or the immensity and intractability of problems rather than from a lack of ability to make a decision. Examples are the slow process of establishing Revolutionary Committees in the various provinces and restructuring provincial Party Committees. There was no policy cycle of the type described by Nathan. Policy was not made by "consensus" among the "factions", which were forced by "crisis" to make a decision and act on it, and then, after the "crisis" was over, to see *immobilism* return. On the contrary, the final decision was made by the "core" leader, particularly when there was a "crisis", or conflict among "factions", or when the policy adopted in favour of the "core" leader was challenged. His decision may have promoted the power or supported the views of one "faction" against another, but whether or not genuine consensus was established, as distinguished from compliance, is another question.

In discussing "doctrinalism", Nathan asserted that "no faction is likely to be able to carry out an innovative political program".[57] But the politics of the Party after 1949, including the Cultural Revolution, was and still is characterized by many innovative programs, good or bad, successful or disastrous. Since Mao was, in Nathan's model, the head of a faction, the innovative programs must, in Nathan's view, have been carried out by a "faction" in a "factional system". If Nathan's model cannot explain all the innovations under Mao, his model also cannot predict those undertaken by Deng.

In his insightful discussion of the impossibility of making ideological agreement a primary condition for alliance with other factions, Nathan nevertheless downgraded, to an unwarranted degree, the importance of ideology in his model, dismissing it as either a means or an end in the struggle for power— in a period when the prominence of ideology was actually at its peak. Many Chinese, then and now, believe that Mao was a utopian who was as much motivated by his own ideology as by his quest for, or unwillingness to relinquish, absolute power. This is one aspect of Chinese reality (or at least one aspect of the Chinese perception of Mao) that Nathan's model does not take sufficiently into account. Even if ideology was frequently subordinated to power interests, it was

---

57   Nathan, "A Factionalism Model for CCP Politics", p. 49.

still a very powerful weapon for attack or defence. How else can we explain the importance of Yao Wenyuan's article "On the Social Basis of the Lin Biao Anti-Party Clique" (7 March 1975) and Zhang Chunqiao's "On Exercising All-Round Dictatorship over the Bourgeoisie" (4 April 1975).[58] These were part of a campaign to counteract the influence of Deng, an oblique attack on Zhou Enlai and the whole bureaucratic establishment, and a tactical move within the field of ideology in the on-going struggle to succeed Mao.[59]

The reason why many of Nathan's assertions about the "characteristics" of "factional" politics fail to pass the test is that they are related directly or indirectly to his central thesis, which he derived from the features of the "faction", that is, "the power limitations typical of factions". This central thesis is that: "the several factions in a given factional arena will tend, over time, to enjoy relative power equality; for no faction will be able to achieve and maintain overwhelmingly superior power. ... A faction engaging in conflict with other factions must therefore operate on the assumption that it will not be able to decisively and finally eliminate its rivals".[60] We shall discuss the applicability of Nathan's model in the light of the events before 1966 in the next section. But when we test his thesis against elite Chinese politics during the Cultural Revolution up to the early 1970s, when Nathan completed his article, Liu Shaoqi's "faction" had already been destroyed; Peng Zhen and his colleagues and friends in Beijing had been dispersed and disgraced; so too had Tao Zhu and his group in Guangdong and Central South China, and Luo Ruiqing had suffered "serious persecution" and his followers had lost their positions. Then came the demise of Lin Biao and his "faction". In view of his later rehabilitation, Deng Xiaoping seems to have been treated differently; but there is little doubt that his followers no longer functioned as a "faction", since even according to Nathan's model "a faction cannot survive its leader".[61] Nor can Nathan's model predict events thereafter, namely the easy destruction of the Gang of Four after Mao's death. Thus, the model has no explanatory and predictive power insofar as the outcome of "factional struggle" is concerned, although it is useful in explaining a part of the structure of elite Chinese politics and, in some cases, some aspects of the processes.

---

[58]   These pieces were published long after the appearance of Nathan's article, but Mao's attacks on Chen Boda and Lin Biao were known about before Nathan's article went to print.

[59]   The continued importance of ideology is taken into account by most of the authors in Hamrin and Zhao, *Decision-Making in Deng's China*. For example, Zhao writes: "an ideological policy issue becomes a 'high politics' arena that has direct implications for the status and power of the top leaders or their factions. They (the top leaders) get involved personally in economic policy debate only if the policy becomes ideologically sensitive" (p. 239).

[60]   Nathan, "A Factionalism Model for CCP Politics", p. 46.

[61]   Ibid., p. 43.

In short, Nathan's model explains only a small part of Chinese elite politics. Nathan admitted that "A more complete explanation of behavior in any political system would have to take into account not only what might be called 'organizational structural' constraints on behavior which have been discussed in this paper, but also cultural constraints, institutional constraints, and ideological constraints".[62] This tells us that his "factionalism model" has a very narrow focus.

In trying to build up his "conceptual synthesis", Dittmer distills what he believes to be correct in Nathan's model. Nathan's idea that a victorious "faction" cannot eliminate its rival is taken up by Dittmer but formulated with a greater degree of precision and subtlety. But in doing so, Dittmer succeeds in misconstruing my points and omits some others. He asks rhetorically: "Yet does (Tsou's view) necessarily imply that intra-elite conflict inevitably culminates in a showdown resulting in the clear-cut victory of one group and its establishment in a position of hegemony?" (p. 10). I did not use the terms "necessarily" and "inevitably" in my paper and I have questioned the notion of "necessity" and "inevitability" in general. But I do believe that *recurrently* and at irregular intervals, political struggles directly or indirectly involving supreme political power result in the clear-cut victory of "one group", or more precisely of one side, over the other. But I also suggested that this victory does not always result *immediately* in the establishment of the victorious group's hegemony. I took into account the possibility of "collective leadership"[63] in a transitional period and, to use Dittmer's term, "a certain level of elite pluralism" during the period of stalemate. I mentioned specifically Mao's policy of "divide and rule". Without "a certain level of elite pluralism", there is no need for a policy of "divide and rule"; or one could say that even if there were a "monolithic" elite, this tactic of the "core" could create "elite pluralism". As mentioned before, Mao deliberately promoted Lin Biao and created what was subsequently called "the Gang of Four" so that he could practise the traditional statecraft of divide and rule. But the point I was making was simply that all these states of affairs either culminate in the hegemony of the "core" leader or represent phases in the degeneration of his hegemony. It is a mistake to juxtapose hegemony with "factionalism" or "elite pluralism". Indeed, it is frequently the case that the hegemony of the "core" leader is needed partly because of the existence of "factionalism" and "elite pluralism" and that "factionalism" and "elite pluralism" may even be considered one of the conditions necessary for the preservation of political stability. Factional struggles or political conflicts in general are involved in all efforts to adapt and implement a policy or uphold a principle. The crux of the problem of political stability is whether or not the relationships among the various groups or factions can be institutionalized and how they can be managed without exploding into a life and death struggle.

---

[62]   Ibid., p. 66.

[63]   Tsou, *The Cultural Revolution*, p. 105.

Nathan made the point that the "factions" do not eliminate each other and are "condemned to live together".[64] Dittmer tries to preserve this argument by changing its meaning in two ways. One is that despite the victory of one faction and the destruction of its rival, the political "line" (Dittmer's term) persisted, or more precisely a certain general political tendency and view. Together with the survival or re-emergence of the line, some of the defeated leaders also survived. He cites the purge of Zhao Ziyang as an example and says his line survived with the help of Li Ruihuan, Zhu Rongji and Tian Jiyun (p. 11). But what he fails to mention is that the "faction" of Zhao, as a "faction", no longer existed. The political struggle focussed on the issue of how to deal with the democratic movement of 1989 and whether to suppress it with the PLA or to persuade it to withdraw from Tiananmen though concessions and accommodations. It did not involve Zhao Ziyang's line on economic reform, which was also Deng's line.[65] Zhao's policy toward the democratic movement was duly repudiated but the economic line survived. Hu Qili and Yan Mingfu, who were involved in implementing Zhao's policy toward the democratic movement, were demoted to insignificant positions in the bureaucracy. Li Ruihuan did not openly support Zhao but handled the democratic movement in Tianjin with considerable tact; Zhu Rongji was in Shanghai handling municipal economic affairs; and Tian Jiyun was concentrating on economic affairs in spite of his long association with Zhao. One of my methodological points is that in the discussion of "faction" and "factionalism", one must not confuse the "faction" as a *unit-actor* and the *persons* involved in the "factions". The *"faction"* disappears but the *persons* survive and are sometimes co-opted by the winning side or given honourable positions without any real power after performing the ritual of self-criticism.

With Dittmer's basic building block of informal relationships, which is broader than Nathan's concept of clientelist leader-follower ties, and with his concept of informal politics, which is more basic than Nathan's "factionalism", Dittmer is in a much better position to make this distinction between "factions" and members of the factions, or between the unit and the individuals within the unit. He could easily assert that while Mao destroyed Deng's "faction", Mao's informal relationship with Deng remained a part of his memory, tattered but not destroyed. This informal relationship of the past, together with political necessity after the defection of Lin Biao, were factors leading Mao to bring Deng back to be a prospective replacement for the terminally ill Zhou Enlai. It is unfortunate that Dittmer does not exploit the advantages of his basic concept.

More importantly, this brief discussion of the post-Zhou Enlai and post-Zhao Ziyang personnel changes underscores a basic methodological procedure proposed earlier in this essay. We must always go back and forth between our conceptual

---

[64]   Nathan, "A Factionalism Model for CCP Politics", p. 46.

[65]   If indeed it is true that Deng himself made the decision to free prices in 1988, Zhao was simply the scapegoat for this disastrous, premature move.

schema and empirical facts, and in doing so we may encounter information that cannot be easily fitted into our conceptual schema. In 1989 we discover that the "factional" struggle in the first instance revolved around a specific issue—that is, the policy toward the democratic movement—although there were other background factors, including the problem of succession and differences in economic thinking; we also discover that not all persons in Zhao's "faction" or with long leader-follower ties with Zhao such as Tian Jiyun were involved in the struggle over this specific issue, and that only a few among the top leaders were purged or demoted, even though several scores of Zhao's advisers and intellectuals and students taking part in the democratic movement were arrested or escaped from China with outside help. The total victory and total defeat took place between those aligned on two different sides on a specific issue under dispute. It did not involve a wholesale purge of a "faction" or of persons with intimate personal relationships with Zhao, and the punishment for the defeated among the elite was relatively mild. Thus our conceptual schema must more fully take into account another two variables. One is whether the total victory or total defeat developed out of a struggle over a specific issue or over a diffuse and general issue like "Thoroughly Criticizing the Reactionary Bourgeois Line" proposed by Mao in October 1966, or the opposition to Right opportunism in 1959. The second variable involves severity or leniency in the treatment of individuals after the defeat of a "faction". Adding such variables through a series of case studies, we shall be able to see the rise and fall of "factionalism" or "informal politics" and progress or retrogression in the process of institutionalization.

Another way in which Dittmer tries to save Nathan's argument is to note that although one side wins and the other side loses, the factional system remains because new factions will emerge and/or the old faction will re-emerge in a new form or under new leadership. But we are here discussing the model of conflict and the characteristics of "factionalism", not the problem of eliminating the "factional" system as such, which is another question altogether. I do not share Mao's utopian dream, as described by Nathan, that the factional system can be eliminated. Factional conflicts can have both beneficial and harmful consequences, depending on the primary objective of the struggle: policy and principle on the one hand and purely personal power interests on the other. It also depends on the formal and informal rules governing the process.

Dittmer makes the point that in trying to understand elite Party politics, it is unwarranted to "privilege" or to give "a higher level of 'reality'" to the struggle for power that involves victory by one side and defeat by another, as against normal periods of "factional" conflicts or elite pluralism (p. 10). It is here that I disagree with Dittmer most strongly. One of the two criteria in choosing a research project is that it "should pose a question that is important in the real world".[66] Total victory and total defeat, as distinguished from elite pluralism or day-to-day struggles for power or over policy, frequently signifies important turning points in Party history. Mao's ultimate total victory over Wang Ming in 1938 at the 6th Plenum of the 6th Central Committee meant Mao's policy of "both struggle and unity" with Chiang Kai-shek triumphed over Wang Ming's policy of following a more conciliatory line toward the Kuomintang. Mao's destruction of Liu Shaoqi heralded a partial disintegration of the Party system. The arrest of the Gang of Four marked the end of a ten-year period of chaos started by the Cultural Revolution. The total triumph of Deng and the elimination of Hua Guofeng's "faction" as an effective political force signified the beginning of a new era of economic reform and growth. It is by analysing such struggles that we can truly understand the nature of a regime in which supreme political power is considered one and indivisible and the leaders believe that the marginal utility of power is always increasing.[67] The accompanying mind-set does not accede easily to the erosion of absolute power and the establishment of democracy.

Total victory and ultimate total defeat in political struggle has been a recurrent phenomenon in twentieth century China under four different kinds of regime: the failed experiment with democracy after the fall of the empire, the near anarchy under the warlord system, the Kuomintang Party tutelage, and the Communist regime. The first and the most pressing precondition for political reform today is to try to understand the "causes" of the recurrence of "life and death struggle", the mentality leading to it, and the processes and conditions which turn ordinary struggles over policy and power into a quest for total victory for one side and a fear of total defeat for the other.

I have tried to show the problems with Nathan's model and of Dittmer's generous attempts to defend it. The reason is not far to seek. The basic methodological problem is that although *in form* Nathan deduced his model of Party politics from the features of the faction, his *actual* method was very different. In fact, Nathan built his model on the basis of his earlier meticulous PhD research on Chinese elite politics in 1918-23 in the era of warlordism. This was eventually presented in an outstanding book that combined good political science with good history.[68] Chapter II of the book was a *tour de force* and constructed an adequate model of "factional" politics for that period. Having creatively built that simple and elegant model, Nathan's next methodological task should have been to test it against other cases, particularly the hard cases that might disprove it. To do

[66] King, Keohane and Verba, *Designing Social Inquiry*, p. 15.

[67] Tang Tsou, *Ershi shiji Zhongguo zhengzhi* [Twentieth-Century Chinese Politics] (Hong Kong: Oxford University Press, 1994), p. 261.

[68] Andrew Nathan, *Peking Politics, 1918–1923: Factionalism and the Failure of Constitutionalism* (Berkeley: University of California Press, 1976). The chart on "Portion of Personal Faction of Tuan Ch'i-jui" in Appendix 21 (p. 227) can serve as an exemplar for any future case studies of major "factional" struggles among the Party elite.

so, he would have had to look very hard at the events since the founding of the Party and the events of the Cultural Revolution and to test the fifteen characteristics and particularly his central thesis that no faction can have such great power as "to be able to expunge its rivals" as well as the factions' assumption that "it will not be able decisively and finally to eliminate its rival".[69] If he had really done this and if my reading of the events in Party politics is correct, he would have found his model failed to pass the test. But unfortunately, Nathan simply used sections of his dissertation/book chapter in his article in *The China Quarterly* almost without any substantive change and flatly declared that the model fits elite Party politics. In effect, Nathan concludes that the system of "factions" and "factionalism" had undergone no change despite the fact that the political system of China had shifted from warlordism to Kuomintang tutelage and finally to the so-called "people's democratic dictatorship" of the CCP.

Another more difficult methodological problem with Nathan's enterprise, for which I do not have a direct answer, is whether a model or "an ideal-typical political system which is primarily organized by factions"[70] can be built or deduced from the features of its units. If we interpret his term "an ideal-typical political system" from the viewpoint of systems theory, then the answer is emphatically in the negative. As Kenneth Waltz writes: "A system consists of a structure. ... Definitions of structure must omit the attributes and relations of units".[71] Following Waltz's lead, Avery Goldstein warns us not to explain political outcomes "by focusing on the nature of the actors". He points out that "Factional approaches focus on the attributes of the actors (that is, essential characteristics of a faction), and the process by which they interact (that is, rules of the game)",[72] and he quotes A. Angyal to the effect that "the system cannot be derived from the parts; the system is an independent framework in which the parts are placed".[73]

Nathan may have used the term "system" casually: he was, after all, attempting to build a "model" as distinguished from a "system". But can this distinction be validly drawn? If so, can a model be built by deducing it from the attributes of its units? I do not know the answer to this question, but it raises an important substantive issue—namely, whether and to what extent the structure as depicted by the model imposes constraints on the behaviour of the units and their relationships (insofar as these relationships can be distinguished from the structure).

As I see it, Party leaders made a series of choices on the political structure, units and rules of the game in the light of the socio-economic conditions

---

[69] Nathan, "A Factionalism Model for CCP Politics", p. 46.

[70] Ibid., p. 45.

[71] Waltz, *Theory of International Politics*, p. 40.

[72] Goldstein, *From Bandwagon to Balance-of-Power Politics*, p. 12.

[73] A. Angyal, "A Logic of Systems", pp. 26–7, quoted in ibid., p. 16.

confronting them, in response to the influence and example provided by the Comintern, and under the influence of traditional Chinese statecraft. These choices hardened after 1949 into a formal political structure, in which the three formal positions with the highest authority were, in the following order, the Chairman of the Party, the Chairman of the Republic, and Chairman of the Military Commission. In short, the formal structure is a hierarchy with a leader at the top, and the informal political structure consists of a network of informal relations shaped like a spider's irregular web with the "core" leader at the centre. The formal structure and informal network interacted but did not need to correspond exactly with each other, as reflected in the fact that Deng held informal authority beyond his formal position. But this combination of a formal hierarchy and an informal network with its "core" became a structure which exercised different kinds of constraints on the units of the formal hierarchy and on the informal networks in their handling of different issues at different times.[74] At the moment, we have too little knowledge of the types and nature of these constraints, and only a series of research projects on crucial decisions and decisive struggles for power can give us the information to make systematic statements. This type of research is what I call theoretically informed and relevant case studies or what Verba calls "disciplined-configurative studies".[75] It is theoretically informed because the data are fitted into a conceptual scheme; it is theoretically relevant because, hopefully, the propositions reached are applicable to other cases. Finally, through luck and the mysterious processes of abstraction and simplification, a model or theory could be developed out of the complex sets of propositions and data.

IV. Balance-of-Power Politics or a Game to Win All?

In my earlier critique in *The China Quarterly*, I wrote that Nathan's model "reminds his readers of the system of multiple balance of power in international political theory".[76] Avery Goldstein writes, without specific reference to names, that "it became popular (especially among those adopting one of the many group conflict or *factional* models) to depict what is going on by employing language reminiscent of the balance-of-power literature from the study of international relations" (my emphasis).[77] Goldstein's book, *From Bandwagon to Balance-of-*

---

[74] Yan Jiaqi's notions of "speech space" and "decision space", which represent the limits of the spheres of discretion "for leaders at every level beneath the supreme leaders", reflect one of the constraints of the structure on the units. See Hamrin and Zhao, *Decision-Making in Deng's China*, p. 8.

[75] Sidney Verba, "Some Dilemmas in Comparative Research", *World Politics*, No. 20 (1967), pp. 111–27. The practice of my research has not gone much beyond the ideas expressed there.

[76] Reprinted in Tsou, *The Cultural Revolution*, pp. 99, 100.

[77] Goldstein, *From Bandwagon to Balance-of-Power Politics*, p. 5.

Power Politics: Structural Constraints and Politics in China, 1949-78, is the most methodologically sophisticated book on elite Party politics published thus far. He extends Kenneth Waltz's formulation of the theory of balance of power and develops the latter's undeveloped notion of bandwagon politics into a theoretical concept and applies it to China.

Goldstein adopts the approach of systems theory in his theoretical formulations. He makes two points that are fundamental to elite Party politics: that the structure of the system exerts constraints on the behaviour of the unit-actors and decisively affects the outcome of their interactions; and second, as already noted, that the structure itself cannot be deduced from the attributes of the unit-actors or the "characteristics" of the units. These two points form the basis of his criticism of "factional explanations", of which Nathan's model is one.

Goldstein's application of his systems approach produces one of the best analyses of the structure of elite Party politics *before 1966* in his theory of bandwagon politics. It represents a simplification of a complex reality in the best sense of the term. He suggests that the structure of Chinese politics from 1949 to 1966 was characterized by three features. First, there was an established hierarchy in which relations of political authority functioned quite well, and authority based on position or on expertise was generally respected, while sanctions served only in a supplementary capacity.[78] Second, the Party was a "functionally undifferentiated political institution" and "the decisive actors were still members of the technically non-expert CCP elite (especially Mao)".[79] Third, the distribution of capabilities was skewed or power was tightly concentrated in the hands of super-ordinate actors.

In terms of Goldstein's theory, the first feature is the opposite of anarchy, in a dichotomy with which he explains the difference between the periods before and after 1966, and the third feature is a variable that helps to account for the change from a hierarchic structure into an anarchic realm, from bandwagon politics into balance-of-power politics. This is a change from a relatively well-functioning, well-ordered political system through a process of disintegration or self-destruction into a fractured system where the authority relationships are in disarray but not totally destroyed. Goldstein's analysis of the period from 1949 to 1966 stands in sharp contrast to the popular views that found academic and theoretical expression in Nathan's "maximum assumption: factionalism since the earliest days of the party".[80] Goldstein suggests that the hierarchic authority relationship was the main ingredient in elite Party politics before 1966. Formal authority was supplemented by informal authority, and there was a commitment to

---

[78]   Ibid., pp. 29, 59, 64.

[79]   Ibid., p. 65.

[80]   Nathan, "A Factionalism Model for CCP Politics", p. 58.

the organization and the vitality of the Party.[81] Factional power interests did not run wild. Ideology and policy issues and the basic political perspectives of the actors were matters of importance in the conflicts and conflict resolution among them. He writes: "In hierarchically ordered politics of the specific type, ideological and other substantive interests are not so thoroughly subordinate to strategic considerations".[82] Mao's special role in the system was recognized. Not only was his preference likely to prevail, but the very expectation of this likelihood had a self-fulfilling effect—an observation which is not only grounded in strategic theory in the West but more importantly is in accord with Mao's own thinking. The ideological basis of Mao's political authority is given due weight, contrary to the general tendency of our time to dismiss ideology as of no practical significance except as rationalization. All these analyses are basic propositions about the main components of the hierarchic structure, the skewed distribution of its capacity, and the low degree of differentiation of functions.

I will examine Goldstein's book not primarily as an exercise in political theory or a test of that political theory as he himself would wish, but as a work in the study of Chinese elite politics. The purpose is to see how we can reach a better understanding of elite CCP politics, the necessary groundwork for building a model, a system, or a theory.

First, let us examine what Goldstein labels "bandwagon politics" in China between 1949 and 1966. Here, his originality lies in identifying an almost unique phenomenon in Chinese politics, which he explains in terms of the theory that he has developed from Waltz's simple notion. The phenomenon is that as soon as it becomes clear that one side in a conflict over fundamentally important policy issues is winning or appears to be winning, those on the opposite side or those not directly involved in the confrontation will readily abandon their former position and hop on the wagon of the winning side. He explains: "Bandwagon politics prevails in those hierarchically ordered, functionally undifferentiated realms in which power is tightly concentrated in the hands of super-ordinate actors".[83] In addition, he points to two specific factors that contributed to this phenomenon. One was "the commitment to the long-term vitality of the political community" or, more specifically for Party leaders, "a commitment to the organizational vitality of the Party as opposed to more narrowly defined short-term individual interests" and "the overriding interest in preserving the image of a unified vanguard party to which their fortunes were tied eventually".[84]

The second factor is perhaps more basic in terms of his theoretical schema: "With some exceptions, those who failed to hop on the bandwagon soon enough

---

[81]   Goldstein, *From Bandwagon to Balance-of-Power Politics*, pp. 70 and 80.

[82]   Ibid., p. 49.

[83]   Ibid., p. 57.

[84]   Ibid., p. 80.

to avoid the stigma of defeat confronted not the prospect of elimination by purge but rather a choice between face-saving self-criticism to gain reacceptance by the winning coalition (the approach encouraged by the CCP regime), providing the Party leaders and members a sense of security; reserving their opinion while conforming with the will of the majority; or accepting relatively mild political setbacks for errors committed, as long as there was no evidence of organized conspiratorial activity in support of the defeated position".[85] This provided the Party leaders and members a sense of security.[86] They could reserve their opinion while conforming with the will of the majority, or accept relatively mild political setbacks for errors committed, as long as they did not engage in conspiratorial activity in support of the defeated position. One may call it a special kind of "code of civility", to borrow a term from Nathan. But for Nathan this "code of civility" existed even during the Cultural Revolution and was a built-in feature of the "factionalism model"; whereas for Goldstein it is a feature of a specific type of hierarchic structure, a complementary part of the bandwagon politics that prevailed before 1966.

These conclusions are supported by Teiwes's writings, particularly his *Politics at Mao's Court*, published a year before Goldstein's book. Teiwes's book is a meticulously researched work of history whereas Goldstein develops a theory and tests it with the Chinese case, but both should be taken seriously for understanding elite politics before the Cultural Revolution.

Teiwes's work on the so-called Gao-Rao Anti-Party Alliance provides one of the most concrete and purest examples of Nathan's notion of a simple "faction" and more generally his idea of "leader-follower" clientelist ties arising out of a bureaucratic structure headed by the leader.[87] There is little doubt that Gao and Rao each led a "simple faction" or an "anti-Party clique"[88] as Mao called it. Teiwes's book lists the main official posts of those disciplined in the early 1950s, and all of them were either subordinates of Gao in the Northeast Great Administrative Region or the State Planning Commission or subordinates of Rao in the East China region.[89] These apparently formed the nuclei of the two "simple factions", and the other people named by Teiwes complete the structure of their "factions" or cliques.

---

[85] Ibid., pp. 78–9.

[86] The sense of security plays a very important part in Goldstein's theoretical schema. The balance-of-power politics in the anarchic realm is, according to him, driven by the insecurity of the actors.

[87] In this sense, the bureaucratic or institutional structure is more than a "trellis".

[88] Teiwes, *Politics at Mao's Court*, p. 263.

[89] See the informative Table IV: "Officials Disciplined as a Result of the Gao-Rao Affair", ibid., pp. 132–3.

Teiwes himself does not give us any definition of a faction or any model of factionalism, but uses the term very broadly. He considers "the common identification of different revolutionary groups (during 1927-49) as one type of 'factionalism'". In his table on "The Factional Balance: Key Party and State Positions, 1954-1956", the main "factional associations" listed are: "North China White Areas, the Four Field Armies, Mongol progressive circles, North Shaanxi base, North China Field Army".[90] But these are political, geographical and, indirectly and incidentally, social cleavages. They themselves did not form factions. What Teiwes meant to say is that these are cleavages that can become the basis of factions. So we still need a term for political entities broader than Nathan's "factions" and narrower than Teiwes' usage of the word.

Trying to incorporate some of the useful insights in Nathan's "factions" and "factionalism", Dittmer's informal politics and Goldstein's bandwagon and balance-of-power politics, I arrive at the simple but fundamental term "political action groups" as the units of elite Party politics. This term will hopefully lead us to ask new questions. For example, how was the political action group headed by Mao structured? What were its components, both in terms of individuals and groups? How did its composition change at different times and on different issues? How did formal authority intermix with informal politics in this particular group at different periods of time? What were its relations with political action groups headed by Liu Shaoqi, Deng Xiaoping, Zhou Enlai, Peng Zhen, Lin Biao and others? How did these relationships change? How did these groups reflect economic, social and cultural interests? What were their constituencies or, more precisely in the Chinese context, reference groups? What were the rules of the game governing their conflicts and conflict resolution? How can these political groups, each of which perform the diverse political functions that in the West are performed by bureaucratic interest groups, pressure groups and spokespeople for various economic and social interests with different ideological affinities and intensities, be institutionalized and given a recognized and legitimate status in the political system? What kind of structure for these political groups would give China political stability and economic, social and cultural progress?

At the top, the political action group headed by Mao was in a special category by itself because of Mao's charismatic personality, his status as the formulator and authoritative interpreter of the ideology bearing his name, his repeatedly demonstrated skill as a political and military strategist, his fixed position as the Chairman of the Party, his historic contribution in bringing the Party from near annihilation to total victory, his indomitable will and his penchant for making final decisions on vital matters in all fields in a regime characterized by what Goldstein calls a "low degree of functional differentiation".

His group consisted of a variety of sub-groups based on different kinds of relationships and diverse social, political and ideological cleavages. Before the

---

[90]   Ibid., pp. 136–9.

Cultural Revolution was formally launched on 16 May 1966, in November 1965 he used his informal relationship with Jiang Qing to initiate the attack on Wu Han and in February 1966 to attack the general tendencies in the field of literature and the arts. In so doing, he violated an understanding with his colleagues in Yanan when they consented for him to marry Jiang, who was reportedly pregnant with his child. Before the Cultural Revolution, Jiang had not been given any important political position. She was only a deputy director of an office dealing with literature and the arts in the Department of Propaganda, a position two levels below that of a minister, although she had begun to intervene on various controversial issues in literature and the arts, relying on her informal position as the wife of the Chairman. She was also officially appointed in 1956 as one of Mao's private secretaries. But in 1966, six months after her successful organizational efforts in stirring up the attack on Wu Han,[91] the informal group which she organized around her was anointed part of the Cultural Revolution Small Group under the Standing Committee of the Politburo. This was a decisive step in the transformation of an informal group into a formal group. Thereafter, it progressively expanded its political authority until, in effect, it acted as if it were the Party General Secretariat. Its members became participants in unscheduled meetings that took over some of the functions of the Politburo after the "February Adverse Current" of 1967.[92] In May 1975, Mao labelled Jiang and her three

---

[91]   Jiang Qing first conceived of the idea of writing an article critical of Wu Han's play "The Dismissal of Hui Jui". Mao suggested that she go to the Shanghai Party Committee to secure support for her effort. Jiang contacted Zhang Chunqiao, who assigned the task to Yao Wenyuan, then only a member of the editorial board of the newspaper *Wen hui bao* in charge of the literature and arts section. At the beginning of the Cultural Revolution, this informal personalistic network was given an institutional base, the newly organized Cultural Revolutionary Small Group. See Ye Yonglie, *Jiang Qing zhuan* (The Biography of Jiang Qing), Chs 13 and 14 (Changchun: Shidai Wenyi Chubanshe, 1993); Wang Li, *Xianchang lishi*, p. 36. Wang Li, a member of the Cultural Revolution Small Group, took part in the meeting that ushered in the so-called "February Adverse Current". He was under house arrest starting in late August 1967 and imprisoned from 1968 to 1982. Li Zhisui, *The Private Life of Chairman Mao*, pp. 440–1.

[92]   In this period, the Politburo and the Secretariat were paralysed. While the Cultural Revolution Small Group took over the functions of the Secretariat, the *peng tou huiyi* (unscheduled, irregular meeting), which consisted of a group of selected officials chaired by Zhou Enlai, with the members of the Revolutionary Small Group as regular participants, served in effect as a substitute for the Politburo on some matters. Finally, in April 1969, the 1st Plenum of the 9th Central Committee elected a new Politburo that included Jiang Qing, Chen Boda, Kang Sheng, Zhang Chunqiao and Yao Wenyuan. This completed the process of transformation of members of an informal group into members of the highest organ of the Party. On many issues, they overshadowed the other veteran leaders or new beneficiaries of the Cultural Revolution in that august body. See, for example, *"Wenhua da geming" yanjiu ziliao* [Research Materials on "The Great Cultural Revolution"], edited and published by the Teaching and Research Office for Political Work on Party History and

closest collaborators "the Gang of Four". This was the process of an informal group becoming a "faction" in Nathan's sense.

The Lin Biao group was a purer "faction" in Nathan's sense. The nucleus consisted of the top military leaders at the PLA headquarters. But it was diluted by the presence of Lin's wife Ye Qun and his son Lin Liguo, both of whom were given high and responsible positions in spite of their lack of any military experience and qualifications.

The position of Zhou Enlai and his colleagues in the political action group headed by Mao was different. As already noted, the relationship between Mao and Zhou was primarily "a power relationship of 'imperative coordination'", to use Nathan's term, between the Chairman of the Party and a Vice-Chairman of the Party *cum* Premier of the government. Having pledged his loyalty to Mao in the Rectification Movement of 1942, he had not deviated from this, in many cases leaning over backwards to please Mao against his better judgment. But in cooperating with Mao and flattering Jiang Qing (Zhou shouted during a meeting with the Red Guards, "Learn from Comrade Jiang Qing"), he gained the ability to protect some of his trusted colleagues, such as Chen Yi, from the harassments and attacks of the Red Guards. He could also exercise some restraint on Mao. But even he could not protect three of his trusted colleagues from Mao's wrath after the "February Adverse Current", nor could he prevent the Red Guards from disrupting the operations of the Seventh Machinery Ministry.

Mao's political action group also included many bureaucratic interest groups. The clearest example comprised the local military commanders over whom he held formal authority as Chairman of the Party's Military Commission. He also had long-standing informal relationships with many of them, and seemed in their eyes the person who had "saved the Red Army" during the Long March and developed it into a mighty force to defeat Chiang Kai-shek.

Then there were the Red Guards, whom Mao mobilized to destroy the authority of the Party leaders who were his targets. In so doing, he utilized not only his ideological authority but exploited the youngsters' feelings of being suffocated under the strict control of the Party organization over every aspect of their lives, as well as the grievances of the most disadvantaged groups in Chinese society, such as the temporary workers, the workers in small ill-equipped factories, and urban residents who had been sent to the countryside by the state. Their submerged grievances marked deep political and economic cleavages in society.

In sum, Nathan's "factions" formed a part of Mao's political action group, but that concept is too narrow to be the basis for an analysis of politics among the top elite. Mao's political action group was a complex of groups that stood on both sides of deep political and socio-economic cleavages. Mao had been a political

---

Party Construction of the Defense University of the PLA (Beijing, 1988), Vol. II, p. 338. Hereafter cited as *Research Materials on "The Great Cultural Revolution"*.

entrepreneur who tried to "expand the feasible set" of alternatives by interpreting, articulating and shaping the desires of people.[93]

The same type of analysis should be applied to other major political action groups before, during and after the Cultural Revolution, paying special attention to their conflicts and their modes of conflict resolution (that is, the acknowledged and unacknowledged rules of the game).

In order to make my points absolutely clear and to link my concept more closely with Dittmer's synthesis and Nathan's model, let me reverse the above order of presentation and restate the same points as follows: All the top leaders, the twenty to forty persons in Dittmer's and Nathan's universe, developed their own networks of persons connected by both formal and informal relationships, and Nathan's "faction" is an important and sometimes the most important part of these networks. Everyone has "his own men or women", their *banzi*, the basic members of the network, some of whom may be members of Nathan's "faction" and some not. This informal personal network forms the nucleus of a political action group that is composed, in different cases, of groups of the various kinds mentioned above and that reflect the different economic, social, political and ideological cleavages of the society in different proportions. These political groups are of two major types and several sub-types. There are formal and informal rules of the game governing conflict and conflict resolution among them. In conflicts over supreme political power or at one level below this, the outcome that recurs at irregular intervals is that one side wins all and the other side loses all.

To follow this thought process, we must begin with a tentative list of political, economic, social and cultural cleavages that can underpin the formation of political-action groups. These include, for example, ideological affinities, regional differences, political tendencies (that is, basic political attitudes among persons with no face-to-face relationship and no common institutional base), opinion groupings over specific issues (sometimes but not always with institutional linkages), institutional interest groups (based by definition on authority and bureaucratic structures), and informal ties of all kinds. A political action group may coalesce based on each one of these cleavages or on the basis of a combination of cleavages. The group occupies varying degrees of importance when it works together to fight on a *specific* issue or to seize a *particular* position of power. When confronted with another specific issue or attempting to seize another position of power, a different faction or political action group will form. This is a weak form of political action group.

There is another kind of political action group. Such groups are concerned not with a single specific issue or a particular position of power at a low level. Instead, they deal with all of the important issues, and always line up on the opposite side on each issue. Intentionally or not, they find themselves involved in

---

[93]   These characterizations of a political entrepreneur are drawn from Jon Elster, *Explaining Technical Changes* (Cambridge: Cambridge University Press, 1983), p. 102.

conflicts that have immediate implications for supreme political power or one step removed from that. It is this second type of political action group that should be the primary subject of our study of politics among the top Party elite. The Gao-Rao Anti-Party Alliance of 1953-55 is a good example for the period up to 1966. In this case, the political action group was a "faction". The Gang of Four is the prime example during Avery Goldstein's second post-1966 period, although it formed a part of Mao's political action group.

Thus a political action group is usually based on both formal institutional structure and informal networks. Sometimes, the latter serves as a nucleus to rally and organize the various groups based on different cleavages and interests. This personal network can be labelled a faction. But it need not be identical with Nathan's "faction", for this personal network may consist of many kinds of formal and informal ties. Political action groups of both types, as well as personal networks, exist everywhere in the world. But in China, their status and mode of operation are different from what is found in many other countries. In the United States, they are legitimate, and their actions and operations are governed by constitutional, legal or formal (written or unwritten) rules that everyone recognizes. They range from the two parties, caucuses such as the Southern Democrats within the Democratic Party, pressure groups, lobbies, political action committees, the Kitchen Cabinet, the Irish Mafia, the Black Caucus, the Boll Weevils, the Christian Right, and so on. In China, factions and political action groups of various kinds have no recognized status in the formal structure. They are *supposed* to work only within the Party and government organizations and to follow the formal procedures. These formal norms did impose considerable restraints on their behaviour both before and after the Cultural Revolution. Naturally, it is the Party leader at the top, particularly Mao and later Deng— namely, the "core" of the Party—who decided whether the norms were followed and whether their activities were legitimate. But in the last analysis, what counts is who wins and who loses at the end. In the struggle for political power the outcome has always been that the winner takes all and the defeated group will be labelled a faction; and the faction or group as an entity, but not the individual followers, loses all.[94]

The ten so-called "line struggles" up to Mao's death all ended in a similar manner, as did the struggles against the Gang of Four and the unwillingness of Zhao Ziyang to go along with Deng's decision to use the PLA against the students. But sometimes leaders or groups which at one period were regarded as following the wrong line or as having committed serious errors or as organizing

---

[94] The term "all" is inherently ambiguous. Tentatively, the meaning of "all" must be understood in relation to the contested object in question, or more specifically the issue that causes the deadlock. Our interest insofar as Party politics is concerned lies primarily in supreme political power and power positions one step removed from it. To lose "all" means losing all political power and disappearing as a meaningful political entity in the subsequent political games.

factions were subsequently hailed as leaders of the Party, as was Mao after 1935 and Deng after 1977-80.

This pattern, coupled with the lenient treatment of those who hopped on the bandwagon, produced "bandwagon politics". The former was the stick while the latter was the carrot.[95] "Bandwagon politics" was produced by a hierarchic system of a particular type, in which, to use Goldstein's term, the political, military and other "capacities" are concentrated at the very top, either in one person or in a closely-knit oligarchy or collective leadership that generally converts into the rule of a single person known as the "core".

This rearranged pattern of events in a hierarchic system of this particular variant is the opposite of balance-of-power politics, which is rooted in an anarchic realm. This brings us to the fundamental question raised by Goldstein's analysis: whether or not the hierarchic realm disappeared entirely during the Cultural Revolution and was replaced by an anarchic realm. My view is that the hierarchic system which functioned quite well in its own terms before 1966 was badly fractured and the formal authority relations and the informal personal relationships were in disarray, but that the system, however much weakened, remained hierarchic at its pinnacle. The realm of Chinese politics was not totally anarchic. Throughout the Cultural Revolution, Mao retained in his hands the ultimate power of decision-making, although many of his decisions were not carried out as effectively as before and sometimes even sparked off powerful resistance and backlashes.

Even after Mao had violated many of the most important written and unwritten norms of the Party, there was no organized opposition that seriously threatened his rule. This strange phenomenon suggests that the regime was still hierarchic, not anarchic. In the so-called "February Adverse Current", the targets of attack were Jiang Qing, Zhang Chunqiao and Lin Biao. Of all the seven vice-premiers and marshals who took part at the meeting on 16 February 1967, only Marshal Chen Yi criticized Mao.[96] An angry Mao called a meeting five days later at which three of the most outspoken persons were told to take a vacation in order to make self-criticisms. In the second episode, the so-called "mutiny at Wuhan", Mao himself was present at Wuhan. The military leaders could easily have arrested him, just as Zhang Xueliang kidnapped Chiang Kai-shek in December 1936. But Mao was allowed to leave Wuhan without harm.[97] After he arrived in Shanghai, he asked rhetorically: "If Chen Zaidao (the commander of the Wuhan military

---

[95]   The availability of the carrot and the escape route is one of the features that differentiates Chinese Communist politics from Stalinist rule. Goldstein mentions the different ways in which terror, the ultimate stick, occurred under the two systems.

[96]   Wang Li, *Xianchang lishi*, p. 31.

[97]   Ibid., pp. 39–42.

district) had staged a mutiny, could we have left there"?[98] Wang Li, who had been kidnapped by the military and the conservative Red Guards, quoted Mao as saying later that the military "wanted to take Wang Li as a hostage and to force the Party Centre to alter its method in dealing with the problems in Wuhan" (the violent conflict between the Rebel Red Guards who were directly and openly supported by the Cultural Revolution Small Group and indirectly by Mao and the Conservative Red Guards who were supported by the Wuhan Military District).[99] A final episode was the Lin Biao Affair. Mao won easily in all three instances of organized or unorganized opposition.

Thus, given Mao's capacity to make the most important decisions on domestic and foreign policies and an absence of any open opposition threatening his rule, China's hierarchic political structure did not totally collapse and China even during the Cultural Revolution was not in a state of total anarchy. Since in the Waltz-Goldstein theory, balance-of-power politics is a pattern in an anarchic realm, balance-of-power politics in its pure form as postulated in international theory could not have been the fundamental characteristic of Chinese elite politics between 1966 and 1977.

If the hierarchic realm did not totally disappear, bandwagon politics must have still existed in some form. Goldstein tries hard but not very convincingly to explain away the Red Guards' response to the call of Mao that to rebel is justified, as dramatically symbolized by the eight Red Guard rallies at which Mao personally appeared. Even at the level of elite politics, the bandwagon phenomenon still occurred. At the 12th Plenum of the 8th Central Committee meeting in 1968, the resolution branding Liu Shaoqi as a renegade, traitor and scab and expelling him permanently from the Party was adopted with only one member, a relatively unknown person, failing to raise his hand and bending his head toward his desk without showing his attitude. Even Li Fuchun, Li Xiannian and Marshals Chen Yi, Ye Jianying, Xu Xiangqian and Ye Rongzhen, who had all been criticized and struggled against, raised their hands and voted for the resolution.[100] Bandwagon politics was alive but not well during the period of the Cultural Revolution.

Moreover, balance-of-power politics cannot explain the elimination of a long series of leaders or "factions" as effective actors in a very short period of time. In the first nine months from 16 May 1966 to 2 February 1967, Mao effectively removed the following top leaders from power in the following order: Luo Ruiqing, Lu Dingyi, Yang Shangkun, Peng Zhen, He Long, Liu Shaoqi, Deng Xiaoping, Zhou Yang, Tao Zhu, Chen Yi, Tan Zhenlin and Xu Xiangqian. After the January Revolution in Shanghai, a large number of secretaries and first secretaries of the provincial and city Party Committees were deprived of their

---

[98]   "Wuhan 7/20 shijian shimmo" (The Beginning and End of the 20 July Affair in Wuhan), *Research Materials on "The Great Cultural Revolution"*, Vol. I, p. 518.

[99]   Wang Li, *Xianchang lishi*, p. 42.

[100]   Yan Jiaqi, "Quanli zhuo micang: gejiu gewei", p. 3.

posts in the movement to seize power, beginning with Shanxi, Qingdao, Guizhou, and Heilongjiang. Zhao Ziyang in Guangdong peacefully and dutifully handed over his office to the Red Guards. The seizure-of-power movement reached the brigades and teams in the rural areas in some cases.

All of these events do not fit the balance-of-power politics model. According to Morton Kaplan's version of the "balance of power" system, one of the "essential rules" is to "stop fighting rather than eliminate an essential actor".[101] The Waltz-Goldstein theory of balance-of-power disputes that any "rules of the game" such as those suggested by Kaplan are necessary conditions for the existence of a pattern of balance-of-power politics. The two minimal conditions required are simply "that the social order be anarchic" and "it be populated by at least two interacting units waiting to ensure their political survival".[102] Goldstein's argument is that "the elimination of actors (provided at least two remain) does not undermine the theory's relevance".[103] He also points out that the "altruistic" treatment accorded the losers in the period between 1966 and 1978 lends support to his analysis.

Without going into arguments about the theoretical status of "rules of the game", one can raise the following questions. In the international realm, the actor-units are the states. The structure of international relations acts on the states. It affects, at least in political affairs, the individuals in the states only indirectly.[104] Then one must raise the question: What were the unit-actors in the period of the Cultural Revolution? If the unit actors were "factions" in Nathan's sense or whatever units enter into Goldstein's balance-of-power politics, many of these "factions" qua "factions" and many units as units were eliminated, even if some of the individuals in these "factions" and units were treated leniently. If the actors in this "balance-of-power" politics were individuals, then "balance-of-power" is merely a metaphor, because according to the theory the structure exercises its constraints on the state or the units and does not directly affect individuals, whereas politics during the Cultural Revolution affected not only leaders but also many individuals directly, rather than indirectly through their "factions" or "units". It is true that some nation-states disappeared in the balance-of-power system. But their destruction occurred infrequently over a long period of time and is nothing like the elimination of the leaders and groups that I listed. Moreover, at first glance they seem to have been destroyed by the combined efforts of a Lin Biao-Jiang Qing coalition, as the theory of coalition in international politics posits. But without Mao's backing, hints, suggestions and direct interventions, the latter

---

[101]   Morton A. Kaplan, *System and Process in International Politics* (New York: John Wiley, 1957), p. 23.

[102]   Goldstein, *From Bandwagon to Balance-of-Power Politics*, p. 37.

[103]   Ibid., p. 40.

[104]   I am not unmindful of the operations of the multinational corporation.

could not have succeeded so easily in eliminating their rivals in such a short time. As Goldstein himself writes: "Mao's special role in the Chinese polity allowed him to take steps to eventually destroy the nexus of political authority in the PRC".[105]

The more obvious, less profound interpretation is that the relatively well-functioning hierarchic system had been weakened since 1956, and it badly fractured but did not totally collapse in 1966. This fracturing of the system was not the unforeseen consequence of a series of *ad hoc* actions. The basic source was two-fold. First was Mao's unwillingness to relinquish absolute power. Dr Li Zhisui has confirmed the widely known but seldom expressed fact of Mao's private reactions toward the substantive actions taken by Liu Shaoqi and Deng Xiaoping during the 8th Party Congress meeting in September 1956.[106] The Congress, following Khrushchev's denunciation of Stalin, criticized the cult of personality and removed the words "Mao Zedong Thought" from the sentence "The CCP takes Marxism-Leninism and Mao Zedong Thought as the guiding principles of its work". These words were subsequently restored in the Party Constitution adopted in 1969 by the 9th Party Congress after Liu and Deng had been removed from their positions of power. Although in the 1950s Mao wanted to retreat to the "second line" and let Liu Shaoqi and others man the first line and though he agreed to the election of Liu as Chairman of the Republic to replace him, he afterwards must have been uncomfortable with the existence of a second centre of power (Liu as Chairman of the Republic), even though the government was subordinate to the Party. This was suggested by his opposition to the re-establishment of the position of Chairman of the Republic after the downfall of Liu. As noted, this was one of the issues over which Mao broke with and destroyed Lin Biao.

Yet Mao's determination to hold onto absolute power was not the only impetus for the Cultural Revolution. An equally if not more important factor involved the long series of policies in the 1950s and 1960s that emerged from Mao's radical and even utopian visions. During the revolutionary war and in the first few years of the People's Republic, his radical, utopian vision had enabled him to create a new China with a degree of unprecedented equality, even if it was equality in poverty, and a higher level of mass participation, even if it entailed participation under strict control and with great political and personal risks attached to non-compliance. But Mao's vision also led to many adventurous policies, particularly in the economic arena, that were opposed or silently resisted by his colleagues.[107] To stress the struggle for power without an equal emphasis on ideology and vision would produce a partial picture of Chinese elite or mass

---

[105]   Goldstein, *From Bandwagon to Balance-of-Power Politics*, p. 158.

[106]   Li Zhisui, *The Private Life of Chairman Mao*, pp. 182–4.

[107]   The best account can be found in Bo Yibo, *Ruogan zhongda juece yu shijian di huigu* [A Review of Certain Important Decisions and Affairs], Vols I and II (Beijing: Press of the Party School of the Central Committee, 1991, 1993).

politics.[108] The Cultural Revolution was adumbrated and actually began when the informal relationship between Mao and Jiang Qing had merged with Mao Zedong Thought. This merger of informal relationships with ideology prevailed over formal politics and official procedures and norms and enabled Mao to destroy parts of the Party system. This suggests the importance of emphasizing *both* ideology *and* informal relationships rather than just one or the other in our study of elite CCP politics.

Goldstein is engaged in a theoretical endeavour, while I am trying to cross-fertilize history and the social sciences. I have to bring in events "at the level of units" to supplement his account of the "structural transformation from hierarchy to anarchy" at the level of the system. Still, the balance-of-power theory does have great explanatory and predictive power at a secondary level. Goldstein succinctly identifies the key "players" (note he does not use the term faction): "the veteran cadres, Mao Zedong himself, the Chairman's ideological followers, the Cultural Revolution's less fanatical beneficiaries, the small cliques in the military personally loyal to Lin Biao, and the much larger corps of professional military commanders".[109] He then invokes one of his basic postulates, that the insecurity of the states in an anarchic realm leads the weaker states threatened by a stronger state to form an alliance or coalition to oppose the latter, and when the latter is checked or defeated, the alliance/coalition disintegrates. This furnishes one of his basic explanations for the tacit alliance that developed between Zhou Enlai and the Gang of Four in opposition to Lin Biao when Lin maneuvred in 1970 to become Chairman of the Republic. After Lin's demise, Zhou and the Gang of Four almost immediately began a debate whether Lin had committed a Leftist error—a formulation that would bolster Zhou's position—or a Rightist error, a characterization that would favour the Gang of Four. Ultimately, the compromise formula was "Left in form but Right in essence", but the Gang of Four soon

---

[108]   The arguments among American scholars over the importance or lack of importance of ideology in China often overlook several variables. One is the level of politics. The higher the level of politics, the more important it was both as an end and a means. Among the masses, it is much less important. The other variable involves the personality, proclivities and aptitudes of the leader. For a person who said that a cat which catches mice is a good cat whether it is a yellow cat or a black cat, and who does not read much other than the official documents, ideology is not very important except as an obstacle to be overcome or as a means to an end. Finally, in times of crisis when people seek a rough road map to guide them through unknown territory, ideology will be important. This was so when Mao Zedong Thought was developed and became accepted. Deng plunged ahead with his economic reform without developing any systematic and convincing ideology. Hence the present ideological confusion in China as exemplified during the 1990s by the "Mao Zedong fever" and the book entitled *Seeing China Through a Third Eye* (supposedly translated into Chinese from German but actually written by a Chinese), and finally the forum sponsored by the Capital Steel Corporation in the summer of 1994.

[109]   Ibid., pp. 183–4.

thereafter launched a campaign to criticize Lin Biao and Confucius, an allusion to Zhou. The postulate also fits the tacit cooperation between the Gang of Four and the relatively moderate beneficiaries of the Cultural Revolution to oppose Deng Xiaoping after his rehabilitation.

But two qualifications about the usefulness of this postulate must be made. First, the decisive blows against both Lin Biao and Deng Xiaoping were dealt by Mao himself. It was he who made the final decision. Second, the arrest of the Gang of Four took place soon after the death of Mao; no one was willing or able to act against them even when Mao was dying.

It should be noted, too, that all of the most important confrontations that became polarized ended in one side losing all and the other side winning all. This stands in contrast to one side checking the growing power of the other side to maintain a balance as in international relations, where the breakup of an alliance frequently but not always occurs before the other side has lost all or been eliminated.

Instead, the above phenomenon of alliances and their breakups can best be explained in terms of a system in which a supreme leader plays a game of divide and rule, and acts at a decisive moment to preserve his absolute power and to press on with his vision. In his heart, Mao favoured many of the radical views of the Cultural Revolution Small Group and the Gang of Four but he also found the veteran cadres led by Zhou Enlai indispensable in running China's day-to-day affairs. Many of the radical ideas came from him, although when these ran into difficulty or created serious opposition some of the radicals were made the scapegoats. For example, it was Mao who expressed, in July 1967, the view that the workers and students in Wuhan should be given arms,[110] but the impression was created that Wang Li and Jiang Qing were the originators of this view. Paradoxically, the "February Adverse Current" of 1967 was triggered by Mao's suggestion to criticize Chen Boda and Jiang Qing, whereby several of the Vice-Premiers and Marshals took advantage of Mao's opposition to the Left and pressed on with the attack. They went too far and misunderstood Mao's intention (just as Gao Gang had misconstrued Mao's complaints against Liu Shaoqi in 1952-53, as Teiwes reports). Mao ended the "February Adverse Current" by stepping in to right the balance, disciplining the three top veteran leaders.[111]

---

[110] Wang Li, *Xianchang lishi*, pp. 40, 53–4.

[111] Wang Li believes that throughout the Cultural Revolution, Mao's primary action was to oppose the Right. Although he continuously raised the question of opposing the Left, characteristically every time he began to do so he ended up opposing the Right. Wang Li, pp. 49–50. Another series of clear incidents suggests this tendency. Mao's criticism of the "Gang of Four" on 3 May 1975 was followed by his comments on the novel *Shui hu zhuan* [Water Margin] in August 1975, by his criticism of the educational views of the Deputy Party Secretary Liu Bing of Qinghua University in September, and by his "important instructions" made between October 1975 to January 1976 to the effect that "Stability and unity do not mean writing off class struggle; class struggle is the key link and everything

Mao was not only very well versed in traditional statecraft;[112] he was also an extraordinarily complicated person. The recently published memoir of Hu Qiaomu, his one-time personal secretary, enables us to document one very important aspect. He was an extremely emotional man. But in the prime of his life, he could suppress his strong emotions and act rationally in the light of the political situation confronting him. In 1941, before the formal launching of the Zhengfeng movement, he wrote nine articles to criticize nine important documents that had embodied the "Left line" between 1931 and 1932. His articles were piquant, aggressive and rude. His personal delight and anger, sarcasms and curses jumped from the pages. But when he drafted a document that became the basis of the famous "Resolution on Questions in Party History" (adopted on 20 April 1945), he controlled his emotions and distilled the substantive, reasonable contents of the nine essays. In Hu's opinion, this document summed up the historical lessons systematically and in a comparatively all-rounded fashion. It was, as Hu said, a product of a process of sublimation from emotionality to rationality.[113] This dual aspect of his personality has only begun to be realized by the outside world. When Mao was angry, nobody dared to oppose him. But one must be impressed by how rationally he planned his political and military strategies and tactics as well as his political and economic programs when confronted by the superior power of the Kuomintang.

From this traditional and commonsensical perspective, the phenomenon of balance-of-power politics during the Cultural Revolution was a reflection of Mao's strategy of divide and rule and of the exploitation of his strategy by his subordinates, the various "factions", groups, or players in their defensive or offensive actions to maintain or maximize their own power. Obviously, I have not found a good theory or theoretical schema to cope with these richly complex data, so as to make sense of the integration and disintegration of a hierarchical system of authority that was supported by a concentric circle of informal networks. But Goldstein's analysis of China before 1966 is a good start, and parts of the balance-of-power theory can be absorbed into the prospective framework.

In an earlier section, I pointed out that the recurrent pattern of winning all or losing all should be the focus of our empirical research and our theorizing about elite Party politics because of its enormous consequences. I want to underscore this point by noting its course throughout the twentieth century. It began with Yuan Shikai's attempt to win all by assassinating Song Jiaoren in 1913, dissolving the Kuomintang and cancelling its parliamentary membership, and his preparations

---

else hinges on it". All of those remarks were directed against the Right, and the last specifically was aimed at Deng Xiaoping.

112   Ibid., pp. 49–50.

113   Hu Qiaomu, *Hu Qiaomu huiyi Mao Zedong* [Hu Qiaomu's Reminiscences about Mao Zedong] (Beijing: People's Publishing Press. 1994), p. 231. Unfortunately, these "nine pieces" have never been published.

to make himself emperor of a new dynasty in 1915. By trying to win all, he lost all. Yuan's death ushered in a period of warlordism. It was a period of near anarchy in China. There were many parties, many factions, many warlords, and a succession of presidents, cabinets, parliaments and constitutions. Nathan's model of "factionalism", as noted, was based on this period of history. With a few possible exceptions such as Duan Qirui and Wu Peifu, the warlords merely wanted to keep what they had or to slightly expand their holdings. But the Kuomintang based in Guangdong had the ambition of unifying China. This is the weak form of the game to win all. That is, one side wants to win all while the others merely want to keep what they had. But they were too disunited among themselves to establish a coalition against a player with hegemonic ambitions. The result was the unification of China under the Kuomintang in 1928 after the success of the Northern Expedition. The idea of one China was one of the factors that accounts for the collapse of the balance-of-power system in this period.[114]

The political system established by the Kuomintang entailed "Party tutelage". Chiang Kai-shek, as the *Zongcai* (General Director) of the Party, possessed an absolute veto over the decisions of the Central Committee and a suspensive veto over those of the Kuomintang's Party Congress. As Chairman of the Military Commission, he had control over the preponderance of military power in China. He oppressed or suppressed all other parties, even the innocuous China Youth Party, for many years. He eliminated his rivals inside the Kuomintang as effective political forces, one after another, through one method or another, and sooner or later. These included Feng Yuxiang, Hu Hanmin, Cai Tingkai, Zhang Xueliang, Chen Jitang, Sheng Shicai and Long Yun, and he made Acting President Li Zongren's position so untenable in the face of the onslaught of the Communist forces that Li left China a defeated man and later sought reconciliation with Mao rather than Chiang. Among his personal following, Chiang played the age-old game of divide and rule *vis-à-vis* the CC Clique, the Whampoa faction and the Political Science Group, using each against the others so as to make himself the indispensable man.[115]

The strong version of the game to win all can be found in the life-and-death struggle between the KMT and the CCP. It began on 12 April 1927 when Chiang staged a sudden and well-prepared blow against the Communists, killing at least 2,000 in Shanghai alone. The Kuomintang then staged five "campaigns of encirclement and annihilation" against the CCP in the Jiangxi and Fujian area, pursued the decimated Red Army in the so-called 25,000 *li* Long March, again surrounded its remnants in northern Shaanxi and completed preparations to launch

---

[114]   See Hsi-sheng Ch'i, *Warlord Politics in China, 1916–1928* (Stanford: Stanford University Press, 1976). This is still the best book on the subject. It has been translated into Chinese.

[115]   The leader of the CC Clique describes one episode of Chiang's strategy in his memoirs. Ch'en Li-fu, *The Storm Clouds Clear Over China*, pp. 142–4.

what was supposed to be the final campaign against them.[116] Chiang waged all of these military campaigns against his fellow Chinese in spite of the step-by-step aggression by Japan against China from the occupation of Manchuria in 1931 to the planned invasion of the Northwest in 1935-36. His policy was that "to resist foreign aggression, the nation must first pacify itself internally". The Japanese were regarded by some KMT leaders as a disease of the skin while the CCP was a disease that attacked the heart. The CCP was waging a class struggle in a social revolution, and by definition, the aim of a social revolution is to win all.

But the large-scale military invasion and attacks by the Japanese armies first in Manchuria and then in North and Northwest China aroused fierce Chinese nationalism and strong demands for the cessation of the civil war so as to concentrate on resisting Japan. Nevertheless, it took the kidnapping of Chiang Kai-shek himself on 12 December 1936 by troops of his second-in-command Zhang Xueliang to force on him a tacit agreement to end the civil war and step up negotiations with the CCP to conclude a United Front against Japanese aggression. This marked the end of the pure form of a game to win all.

The occupation of a large part of North and East China as well as of the main lines of communications and large and medium-sized cities separated the main forces of the Kuomintang from the regular and irregular Communist forces at most places. This imposed a stalemate between the two Chinese antagonists, which enabled the CCP to expand rapidly and recover its military capacity to defend itself. This new phase, which lasted until Japan's surrender, can be termed a stalemated game.

During this period of stalemate, both sides showed signs that they might give up the game to win all. Mao adopted a policy of establishing "a new democracy" and a "coalition government" with the Kuomintang, although asserting that the CCP's maximum program was still to seek Communism. Chiang told the People's Political Council in Chongqing (Chungking) in 1943 that he would use a "political method" to solve the Communist problem. In spite of frequent armed clashes and political conflicts, as well as continuation of deep distrust, this period suggests that a prolonged stalemate may provide one of the conditions that could eventually lead two sides to abandon the game to win all. Mutual exhaustion would be another.

The surrender of Japan, as we know, ended the stalemate. The CCP could have quickly seized all of North China and a large part of China if the Japanese troops had not followed Chiang's order to resist any Communist efforts to seize the cities and territories under their control until the Kuomintang armies could be airlifted and shipped in by the American armed forces under General Wedemeyer.

---

[116]   It is said that when Chiang was later held in captivity by Zhang Xueliang he told Zhou Enlai that his final campaign did not aim at eliminating the Communist forces but only at driving them from their position and confining them to a small area. I am not sure of the accuracy of this information, but if it is correct, one cannot know whether Chiang was sincere, and whether in his estimation he could not totally eliminate the CCP forces.

Again both sides resumed the game to win all. General Marshall at first succeeded in inducing the two sides to agree to a cessation of hostilities, a common political program and a plan to integrate the two armed forces into a national army, by deliberately applying the tactics of playing on the uncertainty of both sides about American policy.[117]

Yet Chiang questioned Marshall's judgment from the very beginning. He wrote in his diary on 22 January 1946 that Marshall had "no understanding of our domestic situation and the conspiracy of the CCP".[118] But American policy soon revealed itself by transporting Kuomintang forces into Manchuria so as to deny it to the Communists. This move in the incipient Cold War[119] was followed by a series of actions favouring the Kuomintang. Chiang's initial uncertainty was replaced by a belief that the United States had no alternative but to back him, given the prospects of the intensification of the Cold War. Marshall could no longer effectively restrain Chiang. The Kuomintang first reneged on carrying out the common political program. Its armies swept deep into Manchuria in spite of the danger of over-extension and against Marshall's advice. Chiang also endeavoured to alter to his advantage the agreement on the merger and disposition of the two forces.

At this point the game to win all took a slightly different shape. Chiang began to realize that he no longer could win all and he also wanted to obtain continued American aid by not totally alienating Marshall. In his final offer to the CCP, made under Marshall's persuasion, he would allow the CCP forces to occupy five remote areas in Manchuria on the Soviet border and a few isolated and strategically unimportant areas in North China.[120] The CCP's deep distrust of the Kuomintang and the expectations created by the repeated pattern of winning all or losing all contributed to the CCP's insistence on implementing the original political agreement and rejecting Chiang's increasingly harsh demands on military organization. This was clearly revealed in a little noted extract from a larger document. In it, Mao said as early as April 1946: "The principle of the reactionary forces in dealing with the democratic forces of the people (in other words, the

---

[117]   See Marshall's memorandum of his conversation with Truman, Byrnes and Leaky on 11 December 1945, printed in *Foreign Relations of the U.S. 1945, Vol. 7, The Far East and China*, pp. 767–8.

[118]   Qin Xiaoyi, *Zongtong Jianggong dashi changpian chugao* [Draft of a Long Chronology about President Chiang], Vol. 6, Bk1 (1978), p. 2776.

[119]   See Odd Arne Westad, *Cold War and Revolution: Soviet-American Rivalry and the Origins of the Civil War, 1944–1946* (New York: Columbia University Press, 1993).

[120]   The government's proposal can be found in "American Preliminary Agreement of Committee of Three dated June . . . 1946 to Govern the Amendment and Execution of the Army Reorganization Plan of February 25, 1946" in *Marshall's Mission to China*, Vol. II (Arlington: University Publications of America, 1976), p. 376. (The blank space in the date is in the original document.)

Communist forces) is definitely to destroy all they can and to prepare to destroy later whatever they cannot destroy now. Face to face with this situation, the democratic forces of the people should likewise apply the same principle to the reactionary forces".[121]

Even if by this time Chiang had been sincere in his offer, and had given up his hope of totally annihilating the Communist forces because they were already too strong and had the Soviet Union at their rear, Mao could not have trusted him. In this "mixed form" of the game of winning all or losing all, what is decisive is at first both sides' perception and then one side's perception of the other side's capability and ultimate intentions, rather than the latest offers. As Zhou Enlai told Marshall, the Generalissimo's idea was to assign the Communist forces to such areas that they "would constitute the least threat to his position and that he could wipe them out at his leisure".[122] Last but not least, Mao had developed a political-military-social strategy "to build up his forces from zero to something and from a small size to a large size", and he was confident that it would work even more effectively now because his forces had grown by leaps and bounds since 1937. Not long afterwards, he ordered his troops "to smash Chiang Kai-shek's offensive by a war of self-defense".[123] Mao's military success went far beyond everyone's expectations, including his own. By January 1949, Mao's Central Plain and East China Field Armies had wiped out the best equipped and strongest forces of the Kuomintang. In April, the Communist forces crossed the Yangzi River. After the capture of Nanjing on 20 April, Mao wrote a poem to celebrate the event that includes the following lines:

The sky is spinning and the earth upside down.
We are elated.
Yet we must use our courage to chase the hopeless enemy.
We must not stoop to fame like the overlord Hsiang Yu (Xiang Yu).[124]

Mao's evocation of an event in ancient history raises the question of whether the game of winning or losing all has been played since before the establishment of the Han dynasty. I hope my colleagues in the field of history will open a discussion on whether or not the Chinese under the imperial system, a system where absolute power was concentrated in the Emperor and his court, had always played this

---

[121]   Mao Zedong, *Selected Works*, Vol. IV, pp. 87–8. I searched in vain for the whole text of this document.

[122]   *Marshall's Mission*, Vol. I, p. 156. See also ibid., pp. 162–3.

[123]   Ibid., pp. 89–92

[124]   The translation was taken from Willis Bernstone in collaboration with Ko Ching-po, *The Poems of Mao Tse-tung* (New York: Harper & Row, 1972), p. 77. In the third century BC, Xiang Yu, at the moment of his greatest power, granted seventeen titles and territories to his subordinates and allies. One of them, Liu Bang, later allied with some of the others to defeat him and established the long-lasting Han dynasty.

game. Popular lore and conventional wisdom suggest that this was the case. As the popular sayings go: "There cannot be two suns in the heaven nor two kings among men" and "the victor becomes the king, and the losers become bandits". It is true that for long periods of time China was divided into two or more parts. But the relevant point is that in each of these parts, absolute power was still concentrated in the hands of one man or one small group and outcomes of the games played still entailed winning all or losing all in the end.

Looking at elite Party politics from this long historical perspective, it is not surprising that the recurrent outcome is still one of winning all and losing all. A centuries-long tradition, a modern ideology of class struggle in a social revolution, the perception of the military and political reality and practices of twentieth-century China, converged on Mao to make him the player *par excellence* of the game to win all. But in the twentieth century, the cost of losing all political power has not been as harsh on the individuals concerned. In the case of the Party, it was Mao himself who introduced the principle of "curing the disease and saving the patient". In cooperation with Lui Shaoqi, one of whose most celebrated contributions to the Party was his book *On Inner-Party Struggle* (July 1944), he developed the practice of allowing the followers and sometimes even the leaders of the defeated "faction" or group to continue to participate in the activities of the Party in various individual capacities through a process of conversion to the views of the winning side and the practice of co-optation of the repentant leaders—a practice that was one of two factors underlying Goldstein's bandwagon politics. In the process, Mao countermanded Kang Sheng's so-called "rescue movement", which imposed heavy punishments on many of the Communists whose loyalty and orthodoxy were suspect, particularly those who had had some sort of relationship in the past with the Kuomintang.

In analysing this new development of elite Chinese politics, one comes across still another variable to take into account. This involves relations exogenous to the Party: in this period, the existence of a militarily much stronger Kuomintang. In order to survive and then win, the Communist leadership had to build up the solidarity and morale of the Party—what Goldstein calls the integrity of the political community and the Party—on which the individual Party members must rely for their individual survival and welfare. Furthermore, the opportunity to defect to the Kuomintang was always open, which the KMT offered as a very attractive option, the most famous cases being Zhang Guotao and Ye Qing. Hence, "the code of civility", insofar as it existed, was partly the product of the countervailing force of the Kuomintang.

After 1949, particularly after the "suppression of the counter-revolutionary movement" of 1950, the remaining influence of the Kuomintang in China was totally wiped out. After the derailment of the 1956 Hundred Flowers campaign and the launching of the Anti-Rightist campaign of 1957, intellectuals outside the Party no longer dared to express any dissenting opinions. After the Lushan Conference in 1959, no other Party leader would openly oppose Mao. Power tends to corrupt and absolute power tends to corrupt absolutely, and the corruption of absolute political power took the form of the arbitrary suppression by Mao of the policies and policy proposals of his subordinates in charge of specific areas of activities, forcing his own visionary and unrealistic policies on them, particularly the Great Leap and People's Communes.[125] This political corruption reached its most unbridled form during the Cultural Revolution, when he destroyed all of his imaginary opponents one after another and violated almost all the written and unwritten rules and norms of the Party. It was during the Cultural Revolution, particularly in the last years of his life, that informal politics prevailed over formal politics, almost completely reversing the trend toward institutionalization.

If in the 1940s the exogenous variable of the existence of the Kuomintang induced the CCP to adopt moderate policies and restrained inner-Party struggle, the exogenous variable of disagreement and then open dispute with the Soviet Union had the opposite effect of creating and then exacerbating intra-Party tensions, leading to an almost total disruption and reversal of the "code of civility". We have already mentioned the impact of Khrushchev's speech on the relationship between Mao on the one hand and Liu and Deng on the other. One of the charges against Peng Dehuai was that he had established an illicit liaison with the Soviet Union. In the 1960s, the preparation of the nine essays criticizing revisionism in the Soviet Union accelerated the rise of Kang Sheng after a long period of relative political unimportance. More significantly, it stirred up Mao's fear of the development of revisionism in China.[126] One may even hazard the guess that when Mao could do nothing about "revisionism" in the USSR, he displaced his anger toward "China's Khrushchev" and the latter's supporters. It is also possible that as he grew older and as his hubris was further strengthened by his monopoly of power and the cult of personality, he was much less able to suppress his emotions in order to adopt and follow rational policies. Thus, in the political system the exogenous factor imploded. In Mao's psyche, emotionality triumphed over rationality.

In the preceding pages, I have discussed the historicity of the game to win or lose all in twentieth-century Chinese elite politics. The question ought to be asked how this repeated pattern can be understood in terms of the rapidly developing field of game theory.

The "game of win all or lose all" or "winner-takes-all" is a commonsense term. There is no such game in the technical literature on game theory. It begins with or reaches a point that Glenn Snyder and Paul Diesing called the "Deadlock

---

[125]   For the events leading from the "Opposition to Rash Advances" proposed by Zhou Enlai and Bo Yibo to the adoption of the Great Leap, see Bo Yibo, *Ruogan zhongda juece*, Vol. I, pp. 531–41, Vol. II, pp. 635–726.

[126]   For Hu Yaobang's assessment of the impact of the nine essays on the internal development of elite CCP politics, see Yuan Ming, *Lishi zuanzhe diansheng de Hu Yaobang* [Hu Yaobang at the Turning Point of History] (River Edge: Global Publishing Co., 1991), p. 5.

Game".[127] As Snyder has explained to me, "one or both sides believes that after bargaining breakdown, and perhaps in the military action which follows, the game will be Bully Chicken or Bull-PD (Prisoners' Dilemma) with themselves in the Bully role". In other words, compromise is unacceptable at the present time because of a belief that a period of hostilities will shift the bargaining power in one's favour and hostilities are not seen as terribly costly.[128] His sentence is an apt summary of the thinking of the leaders of both the Kuomintang and the CCP during the negotiations under Marshall's auspices.

The game to win all or lose all is different from a zero sum game. The final payoff for the losing side is always zero or minus and for the winning side it is always positive even if one takes into account the costs of winning. The payoffs to the two sides do not add up to zero. A game in which the final payoffs for both sides are zero is theoretically possible through mutual annihilation, or exhaustion, as well as absorption by a third party, in which case it is a game of three players—not a two-player game. The pure form of the game of win all or lose all between the Kuomintang and the CCP that occurred in the period from April 1927 to December 1936 seems similar to what two-game theorists call a "repeated two-player game with ruin".[129] In presenting the game of win or lose all, any ordinal ranking, which is generally used in the matrix of theoretical literature on many types of games, may be misleading because a similar ordinal ranking cannot reflect the difference in outcome in real life when the worst payoff for the losing side may be some very small positive number or can be zero or some large negative number.[130]

A problem is that although the game of win all or lose all has been a recurrent outcome in twentieth-century Chinese politics, particularly in politics at the very top, we do not know whether the players consciously play this game from the very beginning or start doing so at a certain point in the process, or whether circumstances beyond their control push them toward the recurrent outcome. This problem can perhaps be resolved through in-depth historical research. But if the political actors consciously play this game from the beginning, then they are less likely than players of other games to be inclined to compromise, even if the objective balance-of-forces and other factors such as third party mediation favour a settlement short of total victory. They are also less likely to accept a settlement

---

[127]   Glenn Snyder and Paul Diesing, *Conflict Among Nations* (Princeton: Princeton University Press, 1977), p. 45.

[128]   Letter from Professor Snyder, dated 7 June 1991.

[129]   R. W. Rosenthal and A. Rubinstein, "Repeated Two-Player Games with Ruin", *International Journal of Game Theory*, Vol. 13, No. 3, pp. 155–79. I am indebted to Zhiyuan Cui, who alerted me to this extremely technical article.

[130]   I am indebted to Charles Lipson for this point and to Duncan Snidal for initiating me into the mysteries of game theory.

even when they suffer a serious defeat, because in this game "the payoffs in the last game will dominate those of all the preceding games put together" and "all the preceding games will be played almost entirely with the last game in mind".[131] Did this last sentence correctly portray the mentality of the founder of a dynasty, a great strategist, and a far-sighted leader as seen through the eyes of the Chinese?

After laying so much stress on the historicity of the pattern of winning or losing all as well as the fundamental concepts underlying it, it would seem that the same pattern should inevitably be repeated in future. But this is not my point and not my hope. I not only repudiate any "objective" macro-historical law of development but also shy away from the notions of inevitability and necessity. I subscribe to Thomas C. Schelling's view of polarized behaviour:

> What is most directly perceived as inevitable is not the final result but the expectation of it, which, in turn, makes the result inevitable. Everyone expects everyone else to expect everyone else to expect the result, and everyone is powerless to deny it. There is no stable focal point except at the extremes. Nobody can expect the tacit process to stop at 10, 30, or 60 percent; no particular percentage commands agreement or provides a rallying point. ... (I)f coordination has to be tacit, compromise may be impossible.[132]

But on the same page he also writes: "If tradition suggests 100 percent, tradition could be contradicted only by explicit agreement". This analysis can be applied to the tradition of the game of win all or lose all. To break the tradition and its expectations, structural conditions and explicit agreements must converge to make winning all or losing all impossible or too costly even for the stronger side.

This may very well be the familiar problem or *non-problem* of chicken and egg. Besides total exhaustion, one structural condition is that each side is confronted with a situation where it cannot win and cannot maintain all political power in its own hands at acceptable costs now or in the foreseeable future. So, too, there must be explicit agreements about the fundamental principles and procedures for sharing power. Short of this, unilaterally proclaimed declarations of principles that are accepted by the opponent would also do, though these rest on less solid ground. Sooner or later, both sides would have to reach explicit agreements. A guarantee by a third force is highly desirable. The process of democratization in Taiwan seems to have begun in these circumstances. But this situation does not presently exist on the mainland. As a result of the mistaken strategy of a few radical student leaders during the Tiananmen tragedy, which played into the hands of the hard-liners in the Party, there are now no significant opposition and reformist forces on the mainland.

---

[131]   Letter from Christopher Achen, dated 8 June 1991.

[132]   Thomas C. Schelling, *The Strategy of Conflict* (Cambridge: Harvard University Press, 1960), p. 91.

But a total break with the traditions of winning all or losing all must be a *sine qua non* for any political progress—progress from the re-establishment of political stability as it existed in the early 1950s, through the establishment of a collective leadership with an accompanying set of institutions and practices to stabilize it, to the initiation of a necessarily long process of gradual democratization. To avoid recurrence of a total disruption of unity among the Party elite, a first step must be to develop further the idea that "class struggle is no longer the principal contradiction", to drop the constitutional provisos that weaken this declaration,[133] and, when possible, replace it with a theory of class accommodation. Even more urgently needed is an explicit and total repudiation of the thesis that conflicts within the Party are a reflection of class struggle in the society at large. A large part of Liu Shaoqi's *On Inner-Party Struggle* must be replaced by the development of what Wan Li advocated in 1985 and 1986 as "scientific decision-making". Under this slogan, problem-solving would replace class struggle. Firmly enforced written rules regarding the expression of opinion, debates and resolution of conflicts over policy and personnel issues must be laid down to facilitate the expression of interests, dialogue, bargaining, negotiation and compromises. In addition, research projects must be undertaken to document and analyse the processes and the indigenous and endogenous factors that in the past have turned ordinary conflicts in the Party into a game to win all or lose all. A central problem in the study of these processes would involve a detailed study of informal politics and its relationship to formal politics and how the latter affected conflict and its resolution in elite politics. Summing up these tragic experiences might help the leaders to seek a less destructive approach to conflict resolution.

Fundamentally, all of these intellectual and political endeavours must produce a set of Party institutions that provide for the existence of a "loyal opposition" within the Party, a system of devils' advocates in the policy-making organizations, a respected place for those who lose out in the conflicts over policy and power,[134] and a legitimate place for informal groups who take an unpopular stand on policy and personnel issues. All of these necessary steps toward further progress in elite

---

[133] "'The Constitution of the Communist Party of China' adopted by the 12th National Congress on September 6, 1982", *Beijing Review*, Vol. 25, No. 28 (20 September 1982), p. 9.

[134] Under the dark shadow of the dominant pattern of winning all and losing all, there has been a weak, contrapunctual, subordinate theme that points to the possibility of the development envisaged in this sentence. In 1981, Hua Guofeng resigned his position as Chairman of the Central Committee and Chairman of its Military Commission. Since 1982, he has remained a member of the Central Committee. After Hu Yaobang resigned as General Secretary in January 1986, he remained on the Politburo and was quite active until his death. This development has been tentative and reversible, as seen in the dismissal of Zhao Ziyang in June 1989. The Tiananmen tragedy not only inflicted serious damage on the democratic movement but also represented a reversal of a trend favourable to long-term political stability.

politics should precede or at least accompany the broad reforms in economic, social and political structures.

V. The Reformist Implications of Dittmer's Concept of Informal Politics: Reversing the Relations between Informal and Formal

Dittmer and other commentators have discussed the sources of the informal power of Mao that enabled him to capture formal authority and which in turn strengthened his informal power: his charisma, the ideology that he formulated, his indomitable will, his political and military skill. But ultimately all of these sources had only one fountainhead: success in the life-and-death struggles with Chiang Kai-shek. Success leading to political power is a commonplace phenomenon, but in China, where the traditional political, ideological and social systems had in various degrees disintegrated and the Kuomintang had failed to re-establish them fast enough to fill the institutional void, political success was the primary, if not the only, criterion for the legitimacy of a leader and the ultimate source of his charisma. After having lost much of his formal and informal authority from 1932 to 1934, Mao rebuilt his informal power and captured supreme formal authority between 1935 and 1945 as a result of his success in saving the Red Army from annihilation and in developing the Party into a formidable force capable of contesting the supreme power of the Kuomintang.

Deng's informal power rested ultimately on his development of a new political and ideological line, later symbolized and enshrined in the 3rd Plenum of the 11th Central Committee in 1978, in direct opposition to the Gang of Four and in indirect challenge to Mao. His success also occurred at a time of a profound crisis of faith in the aftermath of the Cultural Revolution. Deng used a fundamental postulate of Mao's ideology, "seek truth from facts", to refute Mao's concrete policies and many parts of his ideology, whereas, in contrast, Mao had put together a systematic set of ideas concerning every area of life.

Goldstein makes two basic points which enable us to understand why disastrous failures could occur in a hierarchic system with a "core" leader. The first, involving the low degree of functional differentiation, has had a long tradition in China. It was further aggravated by the successful efforts to stage a social revolution through protracted guerrilla warfare. It created an initial expectation, not only among the leaders but among all the followers and the masses, that a successful military-political leader could handle the entirely different tasks of economic development. Hence, it was Mao himself rather than those specializing in managing economic affairs who made the final decisions on economic policies that culminated in the Great Leap Forward and the commune system.

While success was the ultimate source of the informal power and formal authority of the "core" leader, even failure of such catastrophic proportions as the Great Leap did not lead to a change in the "core". This failure can be easily explained with another of Goldstein's points—a severely skewed distribution of capacities—and, one should add, the concentration of most of the informal and formal leverage of power in the hands of the "core" leader. In the realm of formal politics, even the Party Constitution of 1956, adopted at the low ebb of the cult of personality, did not provide for term limits on the Chairman of the Central Committee—although he would have to be re-elected and a new position of Honorary Chairman was to be established. Presumably, this position was reserved for Mao and perhaps was even a hint for him to retire not only to the second line but completely.

The merit of Dittmer's notion of informal politics and his conclusion that informal politics overshadowed formal politics is that it tells us that all the provisions in the Party Constitution are irrelevant if they come into conflict with informal politics, particularly the informal power of the "core" leader. To dramatize the difference in outcomes in cases where formal politics overshadowed informal politics and where formal political relationships overshadowed informal relationships, let us recall that Churchill made incalculable contributions to the British victory over Nazi Germany, yet almost immediately after the German defeat the British electorate voted him out of power and brought in a Labour government. In contrast, the informal power of the "core" leader has, by definition, no term limit. There have been no informal mechanisms to change the "core" short of a political upheaval. More importantly, the capacity or the will to do so could nowhere be found.

The case of Hua Guofeng stands in sharp contrast to Mao and Deng. It brings out the fragility of formal authority not backed by informal power. Hua held the formal positions of Chairman of the Central Committee, Premier of the State Council, and Chairman of the Party's Military Commission after the arrest of the Gang of Four in 1976. But he was not able to offer effective solutions to China's pressing problems and he was not able to build up sufficient informal power to hold onto his formal positions. He could not withstand Deng's challenge after the latter was rehabilitated and acquired the formal position of Vice-Chairman of the Central Committee and of the Party's Military Commission in 1977, which gave his informal power formal channels of expression. Hua was obliged to relinquish his formal positions as supreme leader one after another. By 1982, he was only an ordinary member of the Central Committee. An above-average politician, Hua must be given credit for his acceptance of the inevitable without causing serious political disruption, thus setting a good precedent.

The cases of both Mao and Deng point to a serious dilemma in politics among the elite. The leader holding the highest formal authority must have unchallengeable informal power to retain these positions and to emerge as the "core". The system could not maintain its continuity, nor its integrity and effectiveness, without "the core", as Deng himself suggested. But once there was a "core" combining informal power and formal authority, there was no way to remove him even if he committed disastrous mistakes, as in the case of Mao. Hence the fate of China depended on the wisdom of one man.

Deng from 1978 onwards held supreme informal power, which overshadowed his formal authority. He was wise enough to retire finally in fact as well as in form. Whether or not he should have stepped down before 1989 (in 1986 a sweeping reshuffle of the leadership was in process)[135] is a good question for speculation. Deng's program of economic development did lead to dramatic success, yet this achievement has been accompanied by many urgent problems that still need to be resolved: corruption, the rise of officials using political power to acquire economic power, the huge floating population of millions, large ruptures in the safety net, the confusion in ideology, and the fundamental problem of where to draw a line between public and private when there is an expanding private sphere. Jiang Zemin has needed to show that he can solve these momentous problems to become the "core" in fact as well as in name and to keep the system running. But once the "core", could he be removed without a serious political upheaval if he commits serious errors? This is the crucial and pressing problem confronting political reform in China. The answer is, obviously, to transform the political institution itself into the "core", replacing an individual "core" leader. The Chinese seem dimly to have begun to realize this. More and more frequently, when the Chinese use the term "core", they slip in after it the phrase "of the collective leadership". This is the first step in turning the "core" into an institution as distinguished from the "core" as a person.

The first decisive step must be to reverse the relations between informal and formal politics and between informal and formal relationships, making the former serve the latter without corrupting it. The merit of Dittmer's reorientation is that it can form the basis for this type of analysis. It suggests that the power of the "core" must be formalized and institutionalized, and informal power must be used to supplement formal power but not overshadow or supersede it. The "core" must be made responsible, in fact as well as in theory.

The relationship of responsibility and control between the "core" on the one hand and the Standing Committee, the Politburo, the Central Committee, the Party Congress, and the rank and file of the Party must be mutual rather than one-sided. In a perceptive moment, Deng Xiaoping warned against over-concentration of power: "concentration under the slogan of strengthening the monistic leadership of the Party, inappropriately and without analysis places all power in the Party Committee. This power is frequently concentrated in the hands of a few secretaries, particularly the first secretary, who takes command, making the final decision in everything. Hence, the monistic leadership of the Party frequently

---

[135]   According to Chen Yizi, it was planned that Hu Yaobang would take charge of the Central Military Commission and also become President of the country, leaving the position of Party General Secretary to Zhao Ziyang. See Hamrin and Zhao, *Decision-Making in Deng's China*, p. 141. Unfortunately, Chen does not tell us what position was planned for Deng after the reshuffle. At that time, Deng was Chairman of the Central Military Commission. Did the reshuffle imply that Deng would step down or that Hu would assume the actual responsibility, leaving Deng a figurehead? The rumour at that time was that the plan for the reshuffle was a factor in Hu's loss of favour with Deng in the summer of 1986 and that it paved the way for the downfall of Hu in early 1987.

becomes the leadership of the individual.[136] This advice must also be applied to the concentration of power in the "core" leader.

The procedures to replace the "core" must be formalized and regularized when the "core" proves unable to solve the pressing problems confronting China. All this is more easily said than done. It depends on two preconditions. The first is a system of objective structural constraints. In the relationships within the Party and among strong political forces in society, this constraint can take the form of a stalemate between two polarized political forces, so that neither side can win all and neither side fears losing all, and both sides realize their interdependence. Within the Party, the same relationship obtains between the various political action groups and networks or factions. The second "contingently necessary condition" is a change in the perception of the nature of political power from monistic to pluralistic, abandoning the notion that supreme political power is one and indivisible and its marginal utility is always increasing. The two "contingently necessary conditions" in combination become the sufficient condition that makes possible the abandonment of the game of win all or lose all and replaces it with dialogue, negotiations, bargaining and compromise. The agreements reached should be self-enforcing. Alternatively, the other powerful forces in society that are not directly involved in the contestation could serve as a balance between the contestants and as guarantors to the settlements. The Chinese will have a long and difficult journey ahead of them, full of pitfalls and twists and turns. They will also be confronted with numerous outside influences that cannot affect the final outcome but could make the road more hazardous and the costs greater.

All of the methodological, theoretical and reformist ideas underlying this chapter are nothing more than the A, B, Cs of Political Science 201. What I am trying to say is that in endeavouring to build a model or theory, we should not be tempted to make a leap to X, Y, Z under the influence of popular political writings and media reports on elite Party politics. I am advocating a return to basics in the social sciences, that we cross-fertilize the social sciences with Chinese history, and that we move back and forth between concepts and data in the realization that social science theory will help us to understand China but should not be mechanically applied. Chinese history is so complex that it provides many hard tests for theories, models and general propositions based on Western cases. In turn, the Chinese experience might form the basis for new general propositions enriching the theories and models that have been built on the Western experience.

---

[136]   *Deng Xiaoping wenxuan, 1975–1982* [Selected Works of Deng Xiaoping 1975–1982] (Beijing: Renmin Chubanshe, 1983), pp. 288–9.

FIVE

Factionalism in Chinese Politics from a New Institutionalist Perspective*

Andrew J. Nathan and Kellee S. Tsai

For more than a quarter of a century scholars have found the factionalism model a useful starting point for analysing how Chinese elite politics work. The notion of clientelist connections upon which the model is built has also found acceptance and served as the core of a wide range of research.[1] But Lowell Dittmer and other scholars have found various aspects of the model problematic.[2] We agree with much of what the critics have said, but not with Dittmer's proposed solution.

---

*   We wish to thank Steven Solnick, Jonathan Unger and two anonymous reviewers for their comments.

[1]   Examples include Joseph Bosco, "Taiwan Factions: *Guanxi*, Patronage, and the State in Local Politics", *Ethnology*, Vol. 31, No. 2 (April 1992), pp. 157–83; Bruce Jacobs, "A Preliminary Model of Particularistic Ties in Chinese Political Alliances: *Kan-ch'ing* and *Kuan-hsi* in a Rural Taiwanese Township", *The China Quarterly*, No. 78 (June 1979); Jean Oi, "Communism and Clientelism: Rural Politics", *World Politics*, Vol. 37, No. 2 (January 1985), pp. 238–66; Jean Oi, *State and Peasant in Contemporary China: The Political Economy of Village Government* (Berkeley: University of California Press, 1989); Tang Tsou, "Prolegomenon to the Study of Informal Groups in CCP Politics", *The China Quarterly*, No. 65 (January 1976), pp. 98–114; Tang Tsou, *The Cultural Revolution and Post-Mao Reform: A Historical Perspective* (Chicago: University of Chicago Press, 1986); Andrew Walder, *Communist Neo-Traditionalism, Work, and Authority in Chinese Industry* (Berkeley: University of California Press, 1986); and David L. Wank, *Commodifying Communism: Business, Trust, and Politics in a Chinese City* (Cambridge: University of Cambridge Press, 1999).

[2]   Lowell Dittmer, "Bases of Power in Chinese Politics: A Theory and an Analysis of the Fall of the Gang of Four", *World Politics*, Vol. 31, No. 1 (October 1978), pp. 26–60, p. 39, n. 26; Lowell Dittmer, "Patterns of Elite Strife and Succession in Chinese Politics", *The China Quarterly*, No. 123 (September 1990), pp. 405–30; Lowell Dittmer and Yu-shan Wu, "The Modernization of Factionalism in Chinese Politics", *World Politics*, Vol. 47 (July 1995), pp. 467–94; Avery Goldstein, *From Bandwagon to Balance-of-Power Politics* (Stanford: Stanford University Press, 1991); Harry Harding, "Competing Models of the Chinese Communist Policy Process: Toward a Sorting and Evaluation", *Issues & Studies*,

In our view, many of the factionalism model's problems derive from the fact that it did not succeed in distinguishing between cultural and structural (or institutional) variables in the explanation of political behaviour. The model was intended as a structural argument: one about how factional groups' institutional patterns affect their patterns of behaviour.[3] Factions as structures were said to have certain attributes regardless of the culture in which they operate. The argument claimed to identify patterns of behaviour that would be true of factions in any cultural setting. It thus resonated with what later came to be called "new institutionalist" theory,[4] which explains patterns of political behaviour by reference to opportunities and constraints presented to actors by institutions.

Vol. 20, No. 2 (1984), pp. 13–36; Jing Huang, *Factionalism in Chinese Communist Politics* (Cambridge: Cambridge University Press, 2000); Kenneth Lieberthal and Michel Oksenberg, *Policy Making in China: Leaders, Structures and Processes* (Princeton: Princeton University Press, 1988); and Tang Tsou, "Prolegomenon to the Study of Informal Groups", and *The Cultural Revolution and Post-Mao Reform*.

[3]   As stated in the original article, "the model deals only with what might broadly be called organizational constraints on political behaviour, and not with the other sets of constraints—such as ideological and cultural—which provide additional 'rules of the game'". Andrew J. Nathan, "A Factionalism Model for CCP Politics", *The China Quarterly*, No. 53 (January-March 1973), p. 36. Many readers seem to have interpreted the model as essentially a cultural argument—for example, Dittmer and Wu, "The Modernization of Factionalism", p. 472. Others, such as He Baogang, view the factionalism model as incorporating "both the cultural and institutional approaches". He Baogang, "A Methodological Critique of Lucian Pye's Approach to Political Culture", *Issues & Studies*, Vol. 28, No. 3 (March 1992), p. 107. This misunderstanding must be blamed on the failure of the original article to distinguish clearly between the two types of arguments.

[4]   "New institutionalism" is a diffuse collection of literature, including contributions from economics, political science, political economy, organization theory and sociology. In an effort to distinguish among new institutionalist debates, Hall and Taylor identified three new institutionalisms: historical institutionalism, rational choice institutionalism, and sociological institutionalism. Peter Hall and Rosemary Taylor, "Political Science and the Three New Institutionalisms", *Political Studies*, Vol. 44, No. 5 (December 1996), pp. 936–57. Also see Thráinn Eggertsson, *Economic Behavior and Institutions* (Cambridge: Cambridge University Press, 1990); Ellen M. Immergut, "The Theoretical Core of the New Institutionalism", *Politics and Society*, Vol. 26, No. 1 (1998), pp. 5–34; Thomas Koelble, "The New Institutionalism in Political Science and Sociology", *Comparative Politics*, Vol. 27 (January 1995), pp. 231–43; Gary Miller, "Rational Choice and Dysfunctional Institutionalism", *Governance*, Vol. 13, No. 4 (October 2000), pp. 475–99; Walter W. Powell and Paul J. DiMaggio (eds), *The New Institutionalism in Organizational Analysis* (Chicago: University of Chicago Press, 1991), pp. 1–38; Karol Soltan and Virginia Haufler (eds), *Institutions and Social Order* (Ann Arbor: University of Michigan Press, 1998); and Sven Steinmo, Kathleen Thelen and Frank Longstreth (eds), *Structuring Politics: Historical Institutionalism in Comparative Analysis* (Cambridge: Cambridge University Press, 1992), pp. 1–32.

Over the years many readers have remained unpersuaded by the structural claims of the argument. If Chinese factional behaviour is structurally determined, they ask, why does the same behaviour not appear more fully in other systems that are similarly factionalized, say Italy? Why don't other systems where clientelist connections play a major role also become factional, say Massachusetts? Why do Chinese politicians behave in many of the ways that the theory describes even when they are functioning not in factions but in the paramount leader's court,[5] in a bureaucratic "fragmented authoritarianism",[6] or in "informal groups"[7] that do not fit the strict definition of factions? Why is it that even though the Chinese style of politics remains fairly constant, major shifts occur in ideology and in policy directions contrary to the predictions of the theory?[8] And why does China have such a system in the first place? To many readers, the theory seemed to put more explanatory burden on structure than structure could bear.

Culture was available to share the explanatory burden. Culturalists argued that the behaviour manifested in the factionalist pattern was cultural in genesis. It occurred throughout Chinese history and in all sorts of Chinese arenas, whether or not factions were the dominant form of organization at the given time and place, and (by implication) not in other cultural systems even when dominated by factions.[9] But this reading had problems of its own. If factionalism is a cultural phenomenon, why does so much of the same behaviour occur in other cultures, say in the US Congress? And why does the theory apply only to the elite level of the Chinese system? The culturalist argument also runs into problems of proof and of the emic-etic distinction.[10] Are Chinese politics substantially different in practice from other systems, or chiefly in self-image? Perhaps Chinese culture is not as distinctive as many Chinese claim. Perhaps it is theoretically fallacious to restate a

---

[5]   Representative versions of the Mao-in-command model include Philip Bridgham, "Mao's Cultural Revolution", series in *The China Quarterly*, No. 29 (January 1967), No. 34 (April 1968), No. 41 (January 1970); Michel Oksenberg, "Mao's Policy Commitments, 1921–1976", *Problems of Communism*, Vol. 25, No. 6 (November-December 1976), pp. 1–26; and Frederick Teiwes, *Politics at Mao's Court: Gao Gang and Party Factionalism in the Early 1950s* (Armonk: M. E. Sharpe, 1990).

[6]   Kenneth Lieberthal, *Governing China: From Revolution through Reform* (New York: W.W. Norton & Co., 1995), esp. pp. 82, 169–70, 180.

[7]   Tang Tsou, "Prolegomenon to the Study of Informal Groups".

[8]   See, for example, Parris Chang, *Power and Policy in China*, 2nd ed. (University Park: Pennsylvania State University Press, 1978); "Chinese Politics: Deng's Turbulent Quest", *Problems of Communism*, Vol. 30, No. 1 (January-February 1981), pp. 1–21.

[9]   Lucian Pye, *The Dynamics of Chinese Politics* (Cambridge, Mass.: Oelgeschlager, Gunn & Hain, 1981).

[10] This problem is discussed with respect to the importance of personal connections in politics in Andrew J. Nathan, "Is Chinese Culture Distinctive?—A Review Article", *The Journal of Asian Studies*, Vol. 52, No. 4 (November 1993), pp. 923–36.

Chinese self-stereotype in the guise of a social science finding about the differences among cultures.

In short, many scholars agreed that things often happened in China the way the factionalism model described, but they felt uncomfortable explaining these patterns in terms of either structure or culture. This quandary relates more broadly to the traditional polarization of cultural and structural approaches in China studies: the respective independent variables are presented as mutually exclusive, yet they are hard to distinguish. And neither cultural nor structural arguments alone seem to carry sufficient explanatory power.[11] We will refer to this long-standing issue as the culture/structure problem.

This essay re-examines the relationship between culture and structure by recasting the factionalism model in new institutionalist terms. First, we will demonstrate how the culture/structure problem confronted by the factionalism model derives in part from the model's origins in several disciplines; and how the tension between culture and structure as competing explanations continues to trouble the new institutionalist school of thought. After clarifying the respective roles of culture and structure in the factionalism model, we will respond to Dittmer's critique of the model. The third section of the chapter presents a new institutionalist restatement of the factionalism model and sketches the more general theory of which it serves as an application. Finally, we explore some broader implications of our approach.

Factionalism and the Culture/Structure Problem

The factionalism model was not persuasive as a purely structural theory because it incorporated an ontological confusion between structure and culture that was present in the sources in political anthropology, organization theory and social psychology that were used to construct the model. The same problem has cropped up in much of the recent work on new institutionalism, which draws on many of the same sources.

Throughout the social sciences (although less so in anthropology), structure tends to be conceptualized as patterns of incentives outside actors' heads, and culture as attitudes, values and beliefs inside actors' heads. From an actor's point of view, structure is a situation (or part of it) and culture a set of attitudes (or some of them) that he or she brings to the situation. Structure in this sense is thought to impose the exogenous discipline of means-ends rationality on actors,[12]

---

[11]   See Bruce Dickson, "What Explains Chinese Political Behavior? The Debate over Structure and Culture (Review Article)", *Comparative Politics*, Vol. 25, No. 1 (October 1992), pp. 103–18; and He Baogang, "A Methodological Critique".

[12]   That is, given certain ends, the actor is constrained in the choice of means by structurally defined positive and negative incentives.

while culture is the source of values that are not determined by structure and are in this sense non- (or pre-) rational.[13]

Like the factionalism model, most variants of new institutionalism[14] intend to be arguments about the behavioural consequences of structures—that is, how institutions *structure* outcomes.[15] Structural explanations based on institutional constraints are seen as being rigorous and theoretically appealing due to their relative transposability across cultures. In contrast, cultural explanations appear to be limited to specific cases and often seem unfalsifiable.[16] Most new institutionalists thus avoid using the term "culture" in their analyses.

Nonetheless, the culture/structure problem persists. At one extreme, political-economy approaches within the new institutionalism posit functionalist and rationalist explanations for the existence of institutions and treat culture as epiphenomenal. But in more dynamic approaches, especially historical

[13] For further analysis of the relationship between culture and non-rationality as these ideas are construed in modern social science, see Andrew J. Nathan, "Universalism: A Particularistic Account", in Lynda S. Bell, Andrew J. Nathan and Ilan Peleg (eds), *Negotiating Culture and Human Rights* (New York: Columbia University Press, 2001), pp. 349–68.

[14] The exception is sociological institutionalism, which works more directly with cultural variables. The following discussion draws from Kellee S. Tsai, "New Institutionalism, Culture, and Ideology: The Search for a Theoretical Relationship", unpublished manuscript, Columbia University, November 1994.

[15] For clarity, we will adopt the core new institutionalist position and vernacular that institutions "structure" opportunities and outcomes, and to avoid confusion we will refer to what has traditionally been termed "structural" explanations in social science as "institutional". For potential explanations of why phenomena associated with "structure" came to be replaced with "institutions", and the accompanying use of "structure" as a verb rather than a noun in social science discourse, see Powell and DiMaggio (eds), *The New Institutionalism*, pp. 1–40; cf. Charles Camic, "*Structure* After 50 Years: The Anatomy of a Charter", *American Journal of Sociology*, Vol. 95, No. 1 (July 1989), pp. 38–107. Ronald Jepperson, "Institutions, Institutional Effects, and Institutionalism", in Powell and DiMaggio, *The New Institutionalism*, traces the relationship among "institutions", "institutional effects", and "institutionalization". For now-classic articulations of constructivism and structuration theory, see Peter Berger and Thomas Luckmann, *The Social Construction of Reality* (New York: Doubleday, 1966) and Anthony Giddens, *Central Problems in Social Theory* (Berkeley: University of California Press, 1979), respectively.

[16] The perceived disadvantages of cultural explanations in political science derive in part from the political culture research agenda. For a convenient compilation of the debate over political culture, see Gabriel Almond and Sidney Verba, *The Civic Culture Revisited* (Newbury Park: Sage Publications, 1989). In addition, see David Elkins and Richard Simeon, "A Cause in Search of its Effect, or What Does Political Culture Explain?", *Comparative Politics*, Vol. 11, No. 2 (January 1979), pp. 127–45.

institutionalism, "softer" variables[17] such as norms, beliefs and symbols often slip into explanations for institutional emergence and change. Cultural variables enter the argument in the guise of "historical and contextual factors" either when theorists realize that the norms embedded in institutions do not conform with those expected under a "hard" rationality assumption, or when they encounter difficulties in accounting for variation among cases. Like earlier behaviouralist analyses,[18] such institutional approaches produce tautological arguments due to their conflation of culture and structure. For example, Robert Putnam's *Making Democracy Work*, which employs both historical institutionalist and behaviouralist arguments, associates certain institutions (social structures) with political outcomes. He then traces the institutions inductively back to a particular culture and associates the culture with institutional results.[19] It is difficult to identify culture and structure as distinct independent variables because they are *defined* as a mutually reinforcing pair.

The factionalism model, like new institutionalist frameworks, was intended to be a theory about the "rules of the game", conceived not as cultural givens, but as consequences of structure.[20] But in a new institutionalist perspective, it is difficult to treat these rules *a priori* as either structurally or culturally generated because rules are themselves institutions, and institutions embody, in their phenomenal existence, both structure and culture.[21] Although certain technological, ecological

---

[17]   Robert Bates is often quoted as recommending the incorporation of "soft" phenomena into the behavioural assumptions of game theory modeling; see "Contra Contractarianism: Some Reflections on the New Institutionalism", *Politics and Society*, Vol. 16, Nos 2–3 (1988), pp. 387–401.

[18]   The classic example is Gabriel Almond and Sidney Verba, *The Civic Culture: Political Attitudes and Democracy in Five Nations* (Princeton: Princeton University Press, 1963).

[19]   Robert D. Putnam, *Making Democracy Work: Civic Traditions in Modern Italy* (Princeton: Princeton University Press, 1993). Putnam concludes that the institutional viability of democracy hinges upon the degree of civic community, as measured by Tocquevillian networks of civic engagement, which derive from social capital (norms of reciprocity, trust). Social capital and the density of associational life are traced back to critical junctures in medieval Italy. For other examples, see Douglass North, *Institutions, Institutional Change, and Economic Performance* (Cambridge: Cambridge University Press, 1990); and Steinmo, Thelen and Longstreth, *Structuring Politics*.

[20]   Since Dittmer writes in Chapter One that Frederick Teiwes focuses on the "rules of the game" rather than factions or informal groups, it is worth pointing out that the original factionalism model treats the "rules of the game" as a consequence of structure, while for Teiwes they represent an independent variable.

[21]   For example, Ann Swidler views culture as a "'tool kit' of symbols, stories, rituals, and worldviews", from which people construct "strategies of action". Yet strategies of action are evocative of institutions as they represent "persistent ways of ordering action through time" (p. 253). Ann Swidler, "Culture in Action: Symbols and Strategies", *American Sociological Review*, Vol. 51, No. 1 (April 1986), pp. 273–86.

and geographic realities may create incentive structures that are exogenous to culture, in *political life* most structures are created by actors who are also the bearers of culture.[22] That is, political institutions represent products of human interaction, which itself is culturally conditioned. Certainly this is the case with the scenarios described by the factionalism model. In these situations, structures (such as the rules of the game) are partly derivative of culture, if only because participants are able to understand these rules and accept them as legitimate; and culture in turn is shaped partly by socialization to existing patterns of incentives— that is, to structures. Hence, structure and culture are not only socially constructed but also mutually constitutive in the Geertzian sense.[23] Most of the criticisms of the factionalism model flow from this failure to clarify the relationship between culture and structure, a failure widely shared in the new institutionalist literature.[24]

We propose to address this problem by sharpening the conception of factions as institutions. While recognizing that human interaction defines both culture and structure, we contend that once created, institutions become an "objective" reality to actors. This "institutionalization" of structure has been well articulated by Peter Berger and Thomas Luckmann:

> Institutions ... by the very fact of their existence, control human conduct by setting up predefined patterns of conduct, which channel it in one direction as against the many other directions that would theoretically be possible. *It is important to stress that this*

---

[22]   In this sense the culture/structure problem is closely related to the agent-structure problem. As pointed out by Anthony Giddens, the agent-structure problem "emerges from two uncontentious truths about social life": i) human agency is the only moving force behind the actions, events and outcomes of the social world; and ii) human agency can only be realized in concrete historical circumstances that condition the possibilities for action and influence its course. Anthony Giddens, *The Constitution of Society* (Berkeley: University of California Press, 1984); cf. Roy Bhaskar, *The Possibility of Naturalism* (Atlantic Highlands, NJ: Humanistic Press, 1979), esp. Ch. 2.

[23]   Clifford Geertz, *The Interpretation of Cultures* (New York: Basic Books, 1973), esp. pp. 87–125. Berger and Luckmann's phenomonological approach has inspired much of the work in sociological institutionalism. Garfinkel's ethnomethodology—that is, how everyday interaction creates practical meaning in social life—has also been influential and resonates with Giddens' structuration theory. See, for example, Jepperson, "Institutions, Institutional Effects", and Lynne G. Zucker, "The Role of Institutionalization in Cultural Persistence", in Powell and DiMaggio, *The New Institutionalism*, pp. 83–107. Bordieu's notion of the *habitus*, "which is constituted in practice and is always oriented towards practical functions", is also increasingly employed in sociological institutionalism. Pierre Bordieu, *The Logic of Practice* (Stanford: Stanford University Press, 1980), esp. pp. 52–65.

[24]   Koelble, "The New Institutionalism in Political Science and Sociology".

controlling character is inherent in institutionalization as such, prior to or apart from any mechanisms of sanctions specifically set up to support an institution.[25]

In other words, once institutions are established, actors manoeuvre within their boundaries. The factionalism model sought to specify how strategies of action are available or limited for actors located in the particular institutions defined as factions. The third part of this chapter presents a reconceptualization of factions as institutions based on this approach. But first we review Dittmer's proposed solution to the culture/structure problem in the study of factionalism.

Response to Dittmer

In contrast to the approach we propose, Dittmer suggests that the problems in factionalism theory be resolved by rendering it more clearly a theory about culture. Following Tang Tsou and Lucian Pye, he argues that Chinese political culture gives a particularly important place to informal relationships and involves informal relationships of a culturally distinctive type. There is thus a distinctive style of elite Chinese informal politics that becomes the appropriate subject for theoretical effort. We will present three objections to this approach.

First, Dittmer's attempted distinction between two kinds of politics, formal and informal, is problematic. Social and political structures, processes, institutions and relationships are almost always both formal and informal.[26] Procedures or norms can sometimes be described as either exclusively formal or exclusively informal, but the situation is different with structures and processes: formal and informal aspects almost always co-exist. It may be useful to distinguish analytically between the formal and informal aspects of, say, what goes on at a Politburo Standing Committee meeting or in the National People's

---

[25]   Berger and Luckmann, *The Social Construction of Reality*, p. 55; emphasis added.

[26]   In their definitions of institutions, historical institutionalists generally include both formal and informal rules, which in turn, constrain behaviour. See, for example, North, *Institutions, Institutional Change*, p. 20. Eggertsson offers an equally general definition in *Economic Behavior and Institutions*: "Institutions (are) sets of rules governing interpersonal relations" (p. 70). Sociological institutionalists suggest that the formal structure of organizations reflect the (informal) myths of the broader institutional environment. For example, see John W. Meyer and Brian Rowan, "Institutionalized Organizations: Formal Structure as Myth and Ceremony", in Powell and DiMaggio, *The New Institutionalism*. The isomorphism between formal organizations and their informal environments was also acknowledged earlier in Chester Bernard's classic discussion of cooperative behaviour in formal organizations. Chester Bernard, *The Functions of the Executive* (Cambridge, Mass.: Harvard University Press, [1938] 1971), esp. pp. 114–23. Defining informal organization as "unconscious processes of society" and formal organization as "conscious processes" (p. 116), Bernard wrote, "the attitudes, institutions, (and) customs of informal society affect and are partly expressed through formal organization. They are interdependent aspects of the same phenomena—a society is structured by formal organizations, formal organizations are vitalized and conditioned by informal organization" (p. 120).

Congress legislative process.[27] But this is not the same as describing the entire process as wholly or predominantly formal or informal. Still less can it make sense to say of the West—as Dittmer does—that "formal politics is clearly dominant", or of China at the highest levels that "informal politics prevails" (p.19).[28] Indeed, Dittmer's claim to be able to make such distinctions is undermined when he acknowledges (as he must) that "the relationship between formal and informal politics is fluid and ambiguous" (p. 17).

We agree with Dittmer and a colleague when they wrote in a *World Politics* essay that factions should be defined "exclusively in terms of their structure".[29] But this goal is realized neither in their *World Politics* essay nor in Dittmer's contribution to this book. Rather, both of his discussions of informal politics are cast in historical and cultural terms—and, quite literally, in Chinese terms (for example, *shili* as informal power and *quanli* as formal power).

Second, trying to frame the formal-informal distinction in terms of the *purposes of action* raises operational difficulties. To the extent that we know anyone's purposes in relationships, we know them to be valued as both value-rational and purpose-rational, at once as ends in themselves and as a means to other ends. At one extreme, even marriage and parenting are not devoid of what Dittmer calls "other ends" (p.12); at the other extreme, colleagueship, partnership, or organizational participation do not prosper without intrinsic as well as extrinsic satisfactions.[30] We do not object to all efforts to classify intentions or motives but

---

[27] For example, Kenneth Lieberthal and Michel Oksenberg's study of the government energy bureaucracy in China reveals that the top leadership is "not defined only by formal position", but rather, membership in the top group derives from a "combination of intangible attributes: one's standing with the preeminent leader of the country, the respect and influence one has with one's colleagues, the network of personal ties one commands in the country at large, and the attractiveness and seeming pertinence of one's ideas and vision". Lieberthal and Oksenberg, *Policy Making in China*, p. 35.

[28] Even if we accept this unlikely premise, the distinction appears hard to apply. When Dittmer concludes in Chapter One of this volume that politics in China is becoming more formal, does it follow that Chinese politics is becoming culturally less Chinese and more Western? But then, in a *World Politics* essay that Dittmer co-authored, the authors contend that "the realm of informal politics actually expanded during reform" (p. 480). The malleability and contradictory implications of "informal politics" in both essays call into question its theoretical utility.

[29] Dittmer and Wu, "The Modernization of Factionalism in Chinese Politics", p. 479.

[30] See, for example, Gary Becker, *The Economic Approach to Behavior* (Chicago: University of Chicago Press, 1976); and Gary Becker, *A Treatise on the Family* (Cambridge, Mass.: Harvard University Press, 1981); Peter Blau, *Exchange and Power in Social Life* (New York: John Wiley and Sons, 1964); Gary Miller, *Managerial Dilemmas* (New York: Cambridge University Press, 1982); Mancur Olson, *The Logic of Collective Action* (Cambridge, Mass.: Harvard University Press, 1965); and James Q. Wilson, *Political Organizations* (New York: Basic Books, 1973).

specifically to the attempt to do so on the basis of the value-rational versus purpose-rational distinction. Later we will suggest a concept, "bases for association", that may sound similar to "purposes of action", but does not have the operational problems of Dittmer's proposal.

The mix of value-rational and purpose-rational motives is especially marked in politics, where actions have to be at once selfish and public-minded in order to have any effect. Weber, by whom Dittmer is otherwise influenced, explained this at the outset of the well-known essay "Politics as a Vocation":

> [P]olitics as a vocation . . . offers first of all a sense of power. Even in positions which are, formally speaking, modest, the professional politician can feel himself elevated above the everyday level by the sense of exercising influence over men, of having a share in power over their lives, but above all by the sense of having his finger on the pulse of historically important events. But the question which he has to face is this: through which personal qualities can he hope to do justice to this power . . . and so to the responsibility it lays on him?[31]

Politics is the realm of power. A politician achieves his or her purposes (whether these are to realize a personal or a general interest) by getting and using power. Power is always in the first instance an immediate advantage to oneself or one's family, group or organization, even if it is intended ultimately to be used as an instrument to influence policy in the general interest.[32] Power, like money, is a resource or capability that is not marked by the final purpose for which it is to be used.

Thus, to distinguish between types of political action by referring to their purpose founders on the fact that political action always has the achievement or maintenance of power as at least one of its purposes. If informal politics is the search for power, as Dittmer suggests (pp. 14–15), then all politics is informal. Dittmer never cites a relationship in Chinese politics that he thinks was purely formal (purpose-rational), and he mentions policy (purposive) consequences, which arise from all the relationships that he cites, as being chiefly value-rational. Dittmer and his colleague were thus correct when they declared in their *World Politics* essay that "defining informal politics in general, and factionalism in particular, is a conceptual dead end in terms of identifying actors' purposes".[33] But this insight challenges his effort in Chapter One to use differences of purpose as the benchmarks of formal and informal politics.

---

[31]   Max Weber, "Politics as Vocation" (1919), in W. G. Runciman (ed.), *Weber: Selections in Translation* (Cambridge: Cambridge University Press, 1994), p. 212.

[32]   For example, see the brief but revealing discussion of the private-public tension in the US Congress in Paul Quirk, "Deregulation and the Politics of Ideas in Congress", and Steven Kelman, "Congress and Public Spirit: A Commentary", in Jane Mansbridge (ed.), *Beyond Self-Interest* (Chicago: University of Chicago Press, 1990), pp. 183–206.

[33]   Dittmer and Wu, "The Modernization of Factionalism in Chinese Politics", pp. 478–9.

Third, Dittmer's approach commits the methodological fallacy of using systems rather than variables as predictors in social theory. If comparative social theory consisted of theories of particular systems, there would be as many theories of politics as there are cultural systems. Such an approach might represent an advance in hermeneutic studies, but not in the social-science tradition to which Dittmer and we seek to contribute. As one of us has argued elsewhere, the attempt to explain Chinese behaviour as a unique Chinese pattern ultimately defeats the purpose of comparative studies, because causal propositions in theories of particular systems are tautological and untestable.[34] Although it may seem paradoxical, a cultural argument needs to be specified as part of a cross-culturally general theory to be useful in a progressive research program. As David Elkins and Richard Simeon write, "The use of culture for explanation . . . must always be comparative".[35]

While we suggest an institutional rather than a cultural approach in this essay, we recognize that cultural explanations can be valid for certain purposes. But they need to state how particular cultural attributes or syndromes affect particular behavioural attributes across systems. In other words, as Adam Przeworski and Henry Teune put it, "The goal of comparative research is to substitute the names of variables for the names of social systems".[36] Dittmer's approach does the opposite: it names a system rather than variables as its predictor.

A New Institutionalist Restatement

In order to resolve the problems in the factionalism model, we propose to take seriously the institutionalist logic of the original model. Although we accept that culture and structure are mutually constituted, we contend that once they take shape as everyday, taken-for-granted reality, institutions provide an objective basis for substantially structuring behaviour. As Robert Grafstein, a sociological institutionalist, explains, "members work within their institutions and not on them because to step outside the institutional structure is to step into a social void".[37] While institutions have historical roots, they can be treated as if they were relatively autonomous at a given point in time in the ways they affect the choices of individuals acting in social situations. For heuristic purposes, one can outline the theoretical relationships in the following schematic sequence:

[34]   Nathan, "Is Chinese Culture Distinctive"?

[35]   Elkins and Simeon, "A Cause in Search of its Effect", p. 131.

[36]   Adam Przeworski and Henry Teune, The Logic of Comparative Social Inquiry (Malabar: Krieger Publishing Company, 1982), p. 8.

[37]   Robert Grafstein, Institutional Realism: Social and Political Constraints on Rational Actors (New Haven: Yale University Press, 1992), p. 100.

Human Interaction ⇒ Culture + Structure ⇒ **Institutional Form**
(Groups/Organizations) ⇒ **Behaviour**

Rather than indicating causation, the arrows refer to the constitutive priority among the labels. Hence, the string could be read backwards: behaviour is structured by the institutional form of groups and organizations, which are constituted by culture and structure, which in turn represent products of human interaction. A reaction to this formulation might be that, in reality, a feedback loop exists between structured "behaviour" and "human interaction" on the one hand, and "culture" and "structure" on the other. Point taken. However, the question of what causes what is different from the question of analytical priority. To ask about the consequences of factions' existence is not to claim that factions—their existence, structure, prevalence, or patterns of functioning—are uncaused or unexplainable. It is only to say that factions have consequences as well as causes. To utilize the explanatory logic of institutions, a focus on institutions is necessary.[38]

Let us illustrate this explanatory logic briefly by restating the original theory more explicitly in terms of how two institutional attributes of factions create incentives and disincentives for certain kinds of behaviour by their members, with further consequences at the group and system levels.[39] Factions are based on *exchange*[40] and operate through *noded* communications: that is, communications are transmitted through a network of two-person links, but are disproportionately routed through certain individuals, who thus stand at the foci or nodes of the network.[41] Groups with this communications pattern are likely to have unclear membership boundaries. Yet they are internally differentiated, since

---

[38] Therefore, the issue of institutional emergence, while interesting, is beyond the scope of the present analysis, as in the original factionalism model.

[39] The argument is more fully stated, and more examples are given, in our article in *The China Journal*, No. 34 (July 1995), especially pp. 169–85.

[40] *Exchange*-based participation is motivated by the individual's pursuit of relatively tangible and immediate incentives, such as money, goods, office or protection. This includes both short-term, socially disvalued or neutrally valued exchanges such as pay-offs or log-rolling and relatively well-established, persistent, socially valued patterns of exchange such as "clientelism". See, e.g., Steffen Schmidt, James Scott, Carl Landé and Laura Guasti (eds), *Friends, Followers, and Factions: A Reader in Political Clientelism* (Berkeley: University of California Press, 1977).

[41] Etzioni, *A Comparative Analysis of Complex Organizations*, pp. 191–254; Adrian Mayer, "The Significance of Quasi-Groups in the Study of Complex Societies", in Michael Banton (ed.), *The Social Anthropology of Complex Societies* (London: Tavistock, 1966), p. 117; and Nathan, "A Factionalism Model for CCP Politics", pp. 40–1. Cf. Harrison White, *Identity and Control: A Structural Theory of Social Action* (Princeton: Princeton University Press, 1992), pp. 84–93.

the persons standing at the communications nodes have greater power and are perceived as leaders.

Because of their self-regarding motives for participation, faction members are unwilling to risk violence on behalf of factional goals. The personal nature of communications permits flexibility and endurance in tactical politics. Although the members seek particularistic gains in personal power, position and wealth, because of their intimate understanding of leaders' strategies they tolerate indirect tactics that bear little obvious relationship to their goals. Group actions are often cloaked in ideological garb, but ideology is flexible and does not restrict factional alliances or policy positions.[42]

Factions are as concerned to protect what they have as to gain more, so they often use defensive strategies. But periodically they initiate offensives to try to take office and power from rival groups. Factional systems are characterized by shifting alliances dictated by the defensive strategy. While the level of violence is low, the level of ideological disputation, rumour and personal character assassination is high. A faction continues in existence as long as its leader remains active and the net flow of rewards continues.[43] After the leader's retirement, the faction usually dissolves or splits along the vertical cleavage lines of the previous sub-factions.

As long as they deliver benefits for participating members, political systems dominated by factions tend to be stable. Factions rise and fall in size and influence, but the system as a whole tends to persist rather than to evolve into something else. By defending their positions of power against one another, factions prevent the rise of dominant leaders who might supersede the factional system as a whole. The resulting balance of power may be considered systemic. In other words, would-be hegemons (certain factional leaders) are thwarted from achieving pre-eminence in the system.

Some critics of the factionalism model have noted that Mao's apparent pre-eminence seems to violate this last prediction of the model. We believe the original essay was correct when it suggested that Mao was less dominant than he seemed. During most of his rule he was checked by the factions of other top leaders, and during the Cultural Revolution he tried unsuccessfully to mobilize forces outside the factional system to break it down. We think Deng, too, was less dominant inside top Party councils than he was made to appear to the general

---

[42]   This point resonates with the expectations of neo-realism in international relations theory, and for similar reasons. See Kenneth Waltz, *Theory of International Politics* (Reading: Addison-Wesley, 1979); Stephen Walt, *The Origins of Alliances* (Ithaca: Cornell University Press, 1988); and Avery Goldstein's adaptation of neo-realism to the Chinese domestic political context in *From Bandwagon to Balance-of-Power Politics.*

[43]   The model rests on an assumption of subjective expected-utility calculations by the actors.

Figure 1: Summary of Theoretical Relationships of Factions

I. CLASSIFIERS (institutional attributes)	II. CONSEQUENCES AT THE GROUP LEVEL
1. Basis of association—exchange • material, self-regarding, instrumental and immediate goals • goods are mostly private, not public	*Organizational capabilities* 3. Not willing to take risks 4. Willing to pursue intermediate goals 5. Unstable in group membership 6. Not likely to survive from one generation to the next; likely to dissolve 7. Not very resistant to repression 8. High degree of flexibility 9. Capable of maintaining secrecy
2. Pattern of coordinative communication—noded • high tightness, authoritativeness, and secrecy • low level of differentiation	*Strategies and tactics* 10. Avoid violence due to their self-regarding nature 11. Shift ideology to meet tactical needs 12. High level of bargaining, negotiating and alliance behaviour
	III. CONSEQUENCES AT THE SYSTEM LEVEL
	13. Conflict patterns: low level of violence; high level of alliance behaviour, and shifting ideological articulation 14. Tendency towards systemic balance of power 15. Tendency towards systemic persistence

public.[44] And the dynamics of factionalism have become even more apparent under Jiang Zemin.[45]

---

[44] Relevant evidence on this point has come to light in Zhang Liang (compiler) and Andrew J. Nathan and Perry Link (eds), *The Tiananmen Papers* (New York: Public Affairs, 2001). The minutes of the Elders' meetings in the spring of 1989 show that Deng Xiaoping made key decisions on the basis of a consensus formed first between him and Chen Yun and Li Xiannian, and then broadened to include the other five Elders.

The factional system from time to time issues decisions that all the factions have agreed are necessary to resolve some crisis, but these consensuses rapidly break down and give rise to fresh cycles of recrimination and alliance-shifting. Figure 1 summarizes the theoretical relationships derived from the institutional features of factions.

A Rethink

Dittmer's attempt to resolve problems in the factionalism model has provided us with an opportunity to refine the original approach. We agree that the factionalism model had a variety of problems. Most of them flowed from its failure to distinguish clearly between cultural and structural factors in the explanation of organized political behaviour. We propose to resolve the problems in the model by moving in the opposite direction from the one Dittmer suggests, by accentuating its institutional rather than its cultural possibilities.

Since culture and structure are mutually constituted, institutions can be said to have cultures. A given political action, say an episode of factional maneuvering, is for the actors at once a decision adopted from within a set of attitudes and a choice taken with an eye to an institutionalized situation. "Bases for association" are at once attributes of organizations and value commitments that motivate individual action. But culture and structure are analytically distinguishable. At a given moment, institutions confront their participants in the form of incentives and disincentives, possibilities and impossibilities, and prudential and normative rules. These influence behaviour in addition to, apart from, and in many respects more than, the concurrent influences of culture. We agree more generally with Elkins and Simeon that "Explanations based on national cultures can be persuasive only after we have ruled out some structural and institutional explanations".[46]

---

[45]   For some particularly vivid evidence, see Zong Hairen, *Zhu Rongji zai 1999* [Zhu Rongji in 1999] (New York: Mingjing Chubanshe, 2001). An English translation of the book is scheduled to be published in the January-February and March-April 2002 issues of *Chinese Law and Government*, with an introduction by Andrew J. Nathan.

[46]   Elkins and Simeon, "A Cause in Search", p. 130. By structural explanations, they mean those pertaining to the statistical distribution of various categories of persons among the population—that is, what are usually called composition effects. King, Keohane and Verba make a similar argument, suggesting that explanations for policy outcomes based on material interests should be ruled out first in order to establish the causal importance of ideas. Gary King, Robert O. Keohane and Sidney Verba, *Designing Social Inquiry: Scientific Inference in Qualitative Research* (Princeton: Princeton University Press, 1994), pp. 191–3.

SIX

Reflections on Elite Informal Politics

Lowell Dittmer

Informal politics, all of our distinguished contributors agree, has been an extremely important factor in understanding Chinese politics, particularly at the elite level. And yet, owing to a peculiar form of cultural inferiority complex, the explicit study of informal politics has been unduly neglected; that is to say, biographers pay attention to it, students of power politics cannot but pay attention to it, but very few have forthrightly acknowledged its existence and undertaken to show how it functions and how it informs our understanding of Chinese politics as a whole. This is in large part because, I think, most Chinese regard the "stuff" of informal politics—factional intrigues, succession conspiracies and so forth—as somewhat distasteful, even embarrassing. Not to study it, not to construct theoretical frameworks to explain how it works, is a way of pretending that it does not exist. Many Western Sinologists, in a spirit of cultural empathy, join in a tacit denial of culturally uncomfortable political realities. Yet the informal dimension does exist, and its impact on the Chinese political system can be ignored only at the risk of misunderstanding what Chinese politics is all about. Although each of the foregoing chapters presents a somewhat different conception of the nature and dynamics of informal politics, all six of the authors concur in forsaking that "three monkeys" stance of culturally correct oblivion.

There is a consensus among all six of us that beneath the phenomenological surface of Chinese elite politics there is a pattern underlying the pattern: what Andrew Nathan and Kellee Tsai, following the structural linguists, call its "deep structure". There is disagreement about its importance, ranging from Teiwes's inclination to minimize its scope to Pye's proclivity to maximize it. There is also disagreement about its conceptual bounds, its essential characteristics, its nomenclature, and much else—but there is a consensus that it exists. Its existence is inferred from political phenomena that defy explanation purely in terms of formal structures. Deng Xiaoping's persisting power even after his resignation from all formal offices is one clear-cut example. Another is the amazing set of coups in which putative retirees purged two Party General Secretaries from positions of formal superordination in the late 1980s. These political gyrations cannot be explained by reference to an organization chart or to any obvious political calculus.

To study such phenomena is not easy. Only during the occasional outbursts of polemics, most notably in the Cultural Revolution, do we get more than a glimpse of the inner workings and underlying tensions of politics within the leadership. Formal documents normally make no mention of them (except between the lines, or retrospectively). How do those interested in understanding the subtext of Chinese elite politics then figure out what is going on? Journalists in Hong Kong and Taiwan, culturally sensitized to the subtle meanings of Aesopian signals and well plugged into Beijing's gossip networks, are sometimes able to see beneath the placid surface—though like journalists everywhere, they sometimes sensationalize its significance. Both Mao and Deng were reported to be on the brink of death so often during their later years that such news was widely discounted (though we now know that both men indeed were periodically afflicted with serious ailments). There is also a black market for an ephemeral, quasi-clandestine literature of political exposé in China's metropolitan centres.[1] This literature varies widely in credibility, ranging from outright political pornography to well-informed conjecture, some of which is based on interviews or personal experience.

There are two methodologically legitimate ways of coping with the wide range in the quality of information on elite politics. The purist way is to eschew whole categories of information—the Hong Kong press, say—as unverifiable hearsay, and to rely exclusively on primary documents. This expedient, as advocated for example by Frederick Teiwes, ensures that if there is to be speculation it will be solely that of the analyst, based on verified sources. The second solution is to use these sources judiciously, cross-checking them against already authenticated sources as well as against one's sense of contextual plausibility. My own inclination is to opt for the second route, for two reasons. First, there is no way to avoid the burden of judgment in the review of sources, for even primary sources range widely in authenticity. This is almost necessarily the case with regard to a regime that systematically hides or manipulates information in order to enhance its legitimacy and to socialize the population along preconceived normative lines. This official tactic skews both the official and (indirectly) unofficial sources.[2] Second, unfortunately no single category of information about the Chinese leadership is either completely incredible or completely credible, and so a lot of chaff must be threshed to glean the wheat.

---

[1]   E.g., cf. Yuan Huizhang, *Zhao Ziyang zui hou de jihui* [Zhao Ziyang's Last Chance] (Hong Kong: Mingjing Chubanshe, 1998); Fang Wen, *Tian nü* (Heaven's Wrath) (Beijing: Yuanfang Chubanshe, 1997), to take just two random examples (both purchased in Beijing).

[2]   For example, the authenticity of *The Tiananmen Papers* (Andrew J. Nathan and Perry Link (eds), New York: Public Affairs Press, 2001) is now broadly accepted by the community of China scholars, but questions have been raised in view of the provenance of the papers as a leak through an anonymous Chinese supporter of the reform faction. See my review in *China Quarterly*, summer 2001.

The scandal-mongering Hong Kong and overseas Chinese exposés (which are often derived from mainland sources that cannot be published there) also contain, along with unverifiable hearsay, perceptive insights not otherwise available; and given the customary dearth of information about the power-political dimension in the official media any intelligent discussion is welcome.

Aside from sources, an important distinction among us has to do with the role of theory. The approaches employed in this book can roughly be categorized as deductive vs. inductive. Andrew Nathan's approach, both here and in his pathbreaking 1973 article on factionalism, has been *a priori*, tending to move from the universal to the particular (though Tang Tsou may be correct in tracing the theoretical assumptions ultimately back to Nathan's empirical work on Beijing factionalism in the 1920s). Frederick Teiwes and the rest of us have been more inclined to proceed *a posteriori*, first accumulating empirical episodes, then constructing hypotheses and then finally generalizations. This appears to be part of what Nathan has in mind when he contrasts his "positivistic" analysis to my allegedly "hermeneutic" interpretation: the former is constructed deductively or "nomothetically". A deductive approach to theory construction, supplemented by interdisciplinary cross-fertilization, does indeed offer the prospect of bold leaps through essentially tautological elaboration from first premises rather than gradual, disjointed incrementalism. This is part of what made Nathan's 1973 article so compelling. The danger in such deductive leaps is of course that they may be premature and mistaken, as several have argued with regard to specific aspects of Nathan's 1973 model. Thus the relation between deduction and induction is a dialectic, in which abstract models are confronted with empirical research findings.

Nathan's current model in the pages of this book is ostensibly based on "new institutionalist" methodological premises. New institutionalism, as I understand it, has made a major contribution to organization theory by providing an economic rationale for the emergence of large-scale organizations in a free market context, namely in order to eliminate free riders and reduce "transaction costs" and other frictions. These organizations in turn define the "rules of the game" and structure the rewards and penalties within which individual actors make strategic choices. Whether transaction costs help us to understand the formation of factions and other informal organizations under the peculiar circumstances prevailing in the Chinese political environment remains to be seen, but it is a fascinating idea. One danger that it poses, however, is that of conflating systemic function and historically efficient cause: if we may assume that preliminary factional slatemaking lowers the transaction costs involved in convening a Party Congress, does that explain why it was done? That might be viewing Chinese politics a bit too simply. A second complication is that the theory calls for empirical evidence for confirmation or falsification (one of Nathan's criteria for nomothetic analysis) that is likely to be unavailable in the context of Chinese elite politics. (Why Rao Shushi took up with Gao Gang is likely to have had little to do with cutting transaction costs.) Third, in its focus on rational choice explanatory models, new institutionalists tend to downplay historical or cultural factors.[3] Perhaps the most promising venue for new institutionalism, with its implicit neoclassical normative premises, would be among political/business groups with immediate market access during the post-Mao reform era—for example, the use of a web of connections (*guanxiwang*) by private or collective firms to cut their transaction costs, e.g., by building a network of suppliers or customers, or by evading special tax assessments.

Whether the behaviour of faction members conforms reliably to the structural requirements of Nathan's factional model will require further empirical testing. Initial observations suggest that, paradoxically, linkage to external political markets is often a factor inducing behaviour that would have to be considered "irrational" from the elite perspective (*vide* the cases of Hu Yaobang and Zhao Ziyang, who could not resist the opportunity for grandstanding). The factional structural constraints at local levels may be yet another story. Indeed, the whole question of the relationship between informal politics at elite and at subaltern levels remains virgin theoretical territory.

At this point, new institutionalism has not yet produced a new set of hypotheses about the formation or operating dynamics of Chinese factions. The goal so far seems to be rather to use general theory to ban the spectre of Chinese exceptionalism, under the apparent assumption that any resort to cultural explanation implies cultural uniqueness.[4] Unfortunately, this reflects a rather widespread misunderstanding of the role and validity of political cultural analysis. Certainly China has a unique culture of ancient provenance, of which it is on the whole proud, and it hardly seems far-fetched to assume that (as in all countries)

---

[3]   This is often pointed out by "old" or historical institutionalists, who tend to look for crucial events precipitating institutional change, as in the concept of path dependency. See Paul Pierson, "Increasing Returns, Path Dependence, and the Study of Politics", *American Political Science Review*, Vol. 94, No. 2 (June 2000); Amitav Acharya, "Realism, Institutionalism, and the Asian Economic Crisis", *Contemporary Southeast Asia*, Vol. 21, No. 1 (April 1999); John Groenewegen, Frans Kerstholt and Ad Negelkerke, "On Integrating New and Old Institutionalism", *Journal of Economic Issues*, Vol. 29, No. 2 (June 1995); Arthur Stinchcombe, "On the Virtues of the Old Institutionalism", *Annual Review of Sociology*, Vol. 23 (Annual 1997), pp. 1–19, inter alia.

[4]   Nathan's concern with this question is reflected in his "Is Chinese Culture Distinctive? A Review Article", *Journal of Asian Studies*, Vol. 51, No. 4 (November 1993), pp. 923–37. My own position on this issue is that to the extent we are interested in understanding how various aspects of Chinese political culture function, we may to that end formulate hypotheses about those aspects that are in principle universally applicable but are likely in fact to be tested only in China. Whether the scientific "knowledge" thereby generated is applicable to other cultures beyond China is not necessarily our concern: *ars longa, vita brevis*.

culture will have an impact on politics. Although any nation's culture is no doubt a unique ensemble of beliefs, values and attitudes, its discrete parts are hardly unique but can be causally analysed and compared just like any other set of social science data.[5] As Nathan Leites explained in an early but still relevant analysis, to cite some cultural pattern in explanation of a given political event is not to say that culture is the sole cause, that the pattern is universal to the culture, that there are no differences among subgroups in the culture, or that there are no similarities to subgroups (such as classes, or elite factions) in other cultures.[6] In other words, if we are interested in explaining Chinese leadership behaviour through reference to certain alleged cultural patterns of organization, that does not absolve us of the need to collect evidence or to articulate theories of how cause and effect fit together, or otherwise place us beyond the scientific pale. Culture is perhaps not the *terminus ad quem* of scientific analysis (and runs the perennial risk of over-generalization), but I would argue that it takes us a step closer to the "real world", with all its *non sequiturs*, than structure.

If we define the universe or field with which we are concerned empirically, there is considerable consensus. China is run by an elite corps of some 200 people commonly referred to as the "centre". At the centre of the centre is a supreme or paramount leader, now (following Deng Xiaoping's coinage) termed a "core". In Deng's day, the core shared authority with a group of esteemed senior veterans, and delegated policy implementation and other weighty responsibilities to a slightly less senior group of cadres known as the "first front", who sat in the Party Central Committee, the Party Secretariat, the Politburo and the State Council. The relationships within the combined elite are governed by the rules of "democratic centralism", which mediate a delicate balance between collegiality and hierarchy. When these "normative rules"[7] are flouted, organizational sanctions may be imposed, ranging from criticism and self-criticism to purge, eviction from the Party or even imprisonment.

We can all agree on this basic empirical structure; it is when we try to account for the occasional deviations from the formal structures and normative rules that the situation becomes more complex. Nathan's (and Pye's) conceptual innovation explicates the construct of "factions". But while Nathan's conceptualization of the faction suggests that it supplements formal organization (factions extend themselves

---

5   See Lowell Dittmer, "The Analysis of Chinese Political Culture", in Amy Wilson et al. (eds), *Methodological Issues in Chinese Studies* (New York: Praeger, 1983), pp. 51–69; also "The Comparative Analysis of Political Culture", *Amerikastudien*, Vol. 27 (1982).

6   Elizabeth Wirth Marvick (ed.), *Psychopolitical Analysis: Selected Writings of Nathan Leites* (New York: John Wiley, 1977), pp. 31–47.

7   Frederick Teiwes, *Leadership, Legitimacy and Conflict in China* (Armonk: M. E. Sharpe, 1984).

along the formal hierarchy like roses along a "trellis"),[8] Pye takes a more extreme position in his chapter, that the personal nexus is "very nearly the sum total of Chinese politics" and that formal behaviour is a mendacious façade that nobody takes too seriously. Thus he sees little value in the distinction. Teiwes's chapter provides a valuable corrective to such a dismissal, demonstrating that the game has actually been played with greater concern (though hardly religious fidelity—after all, this is politics) for the formal structures and official norms than one might imagine. Indeed, if Pye stands at one end of the spectrum concerning the empirical relevance of norms and rules, Teiwes is at the other, tending to minimize the rift between Deng and Hu Yaobang or Chen Yun in particular. Tang Tsou, by contrast, hews to the centre in his critique of "rampant factionalism", defining informal politics in terms of its relation to formal politics. In his contribution to this book, Tsou goes on to elaborate on the various forms of formal and informal groupings (both of which he now terms "political action groups") and their complex reciprocal dynamics.

Figure 1:   Characterizations of Informal Politics

Comprehensiveness

		Complete	Partial
Homogeneity	Uniform	Pye	Nathan
	Segmentary	Tsou	Teiwes Dittmer

In sum, while we all agree on the empirical field of analysis, there are still a number of significant distinctions which will require further empirical analysis to settle. One dimension is comprehensiveness: is Chinese politics almost completely informal, or only partially so and partially formal? That is, does our analytical framework comprehend the entire political system or only a part of it? The other dimension is what might be called internal homogeneity: is the informal domain, whatever its scope, relatively uniform (e.g., entailing pervasive

---

8   Nathan's position is, however, ambiguous: while the trellis metaphor would suggest a formal/informal distinction, Nathan and Tsai take exception to that distinction in their essay in this book and reject the whole category of informal politics, for reasons still unclear to me. Their characterization of factions as "structures" is also difficult to reconcile with Nathan's metaphor of a vine intertwining the formal structures.

vertical patron-client factionalism) or segmentary (i.e., including horizontal as well as vertical networks, tightly bounded and loosely bounded frames, as well as various mixed types of informal relationships)? Table 1 encapsulates where each of the contributors appear to stand with regard to these two issues:

A second issue involves the behavioural substance of informal politics. What do informal groups do, and how does their behaviour differ from that of more formal groupings? There seems to be a general consensus that informal politics is a consequence of the functional inadequacies of formal politics (for instance, the refusal to make any provision for ideological or policy differences, as a result of which disagreement must take clandestine form) plus the personal, role-transcendant needs of bureaucratic actors (such as the need for security of tenure). Defining informal politics solely in terms of formal politics reduces the concept to a residual variable: informal is all that formal is not. My own conceptualization distinguishes between formal and informal in terms of the logic of the "relationships" (*guanxi*) of which they are constructed: formal groups consist of "purpose-rational" relations, typically recruited from current bureaucratic subordinates and colleagues, while informal groups consist of "value-rational" relations, recruited from primordial associates and cronies. This "value" has nothing to do with morality (indeed factional connections are usually held in moral opprobrium in China). Rather, the term means that a relationship has a value transcending the immediate political objectives at stake. What is meant by "rational" is simply that there is a coherent political calculus between means and ends, though there are different forms of rationality.[9] The logic of that calculus is none too precise, as Pye points out, noting that "the particularistic basis of a relationship does not in itself provide a clear clue for predicting the purposes for which the relationship might be directed" (p. 46).[10] For example, the Cultural Revolution showed us that Hunanese revolutionaries with "red area" backgrounds are not necessarily Maoist radicals, and the Lin Biao incident in 1971 demonstrated that not all Fourth Army veterans were willing to go down with Lin Biao (though they probably all came under suspicion).[11] But rather than inferring that an informal relationship is simply indeterminate, one might say that it is flexible and strategic. A given veteran cadre may well have been born in

---

[9]   There are so many ways of using the word "rational" that its use begs a lot of questions. In addition to Max Weber, see Paul Diesing, *Reason in Society: Five Types of Decisions and Their Social Conditions* (Urbana: University of Illinois Press, 1962); and Robert Nozick, *The Nature of Rationality* (Princeton: Princeton University Press, 1993), *inter alia*.

[10]   This point is also thoroughly demonstrated in Pye, *The Dynamics of Chinese Politics* (Cambridge, Mass.: Oelgeschlager, Gunn & Hain, 1981), pp. 77–96, 117–27, *et passim*.

[11]   For a monumental recent study of central elite factional politics from the Long March period through the end of the Cultural Revolution that relies heavily on the importance of early ties cultivated in the revolutionary base areas, see Jing Huang, *Factionalism in Chinese Communist Politics* (New York: Cambridge University Press, 2000).

Shanghai, studied a year or two in France, had a prominent role in the Nanchang Uprising, helped organize students and workers against Japanese occupation forces near Beijing during the war, after which he participated in the abortive negotiations with the KMT toward forming a coalition government in Chongqing. Each experience could be expected to provide him with a different network of associates in what would later become conflicting factions.

What then can be said of the relationship between the informal/formal dimension and elite political behaviour? There is no simple relationship between a factional linkage or set of such linkages and a determinate pattern of political behaviour or preferences. There is, however, a relationship between the concatenation of associations accumulated in the course of a career and one's political base. The necessary but not sufficient condition for a value-rational relationship is the presence of one of six or eight conceivable primordial ties or bonding experiences, while the sufficient condition is a current political need and use for that relationship. There is also a conditionality between type of base and the political uses to which it can be put: due to the different levels of commitment of their constituencies, formal bases may be used for mundane disputes over "non-antagonistic" bureaucratic turf or policy issues,[12] while only informal groups can be mobilized for "antagonistic" conflicts in which one's career or life stands at risk. Membership in the two different types of relationships and types of bases is not, however, mutually exclusive but frequently interpenetrating, as patrons appoint clients to formal positions or as work colleagues become committed friends. In sketching the sociometric diagram of a given political actor's interpersonal network and trying to figure out from this his or her menu of feasible options, one can infer that some relations can only be informal, that some are almost surely purely formal, and that many are likely to be both, or some sort of hybrid that might be utilized one way or the other depending on the situation and personal needs of the participants. Although the nature of the relationship is in such cases inherently ambiguous, there are usually empirical clues available: previous associations in a career trajectory can be compiled and reviewed, networking options gauged and compared.

---

[12]   This has been the subject of insightful analyses of the energy policy community by Oksenberg and Lieberthal, health care by Lampton, the pre-Great Leap heavy industry coalition vs. the financial group by Bachman, in commercial policy by Solinger, and so forth. Cf. Kenneth Lieberthal and Michel Oksenberg, *Policy Making in China: Leaders, Structures, and Processes* (Princeton: Princeton University Press, 1988); David M. Lampton, *The Politics of Medicine in China: The Policy Process, 1949–1977* (Boulder: Westview Press, 1977); David Bachman, *Bureaucracy, Economy, and Leadership in China: The Institutional Origins of the Great Leap Forward* (New York: Cambridge University Press, 1991); Dorothy Solinger, *Chinese Business Under Socialism: The Politics of Domestic Commerce in Contemporary China* (Berkeley: University of California Press, 1984); and David M. Lampton (ed.), *Policy Implementation in Post-Mao China* (Berkeley: University of California Press, 1987).

A third basis for the formation and cohesion of factions that has been historically important, though it has fallen into relative desuetude in recent years, is ideological commitment. Tsou testified to the importance of ideology in orienting factional behaviour in his critique of Nathan. An ideological engagement is similar to (and might empirically overlap) an informal patron-client tie in terms of its long-term time horizon and orientation to "value" transcending the political issue at stake, but it is comparable to formal relationships in enjoying official sanction. Following the Sovietologists, we may refer to ideologically driven elite groups as tendency groups.[13] In practice, tendency groups might be expected to function most like personal factions, albeit with at least two important differences. First, tendency groups may be intensely motivated but more fractious and difficult to lead than either formally or informally coordinated ones, as the experience of mass factionalism during the Cultural Revolution (or for that matter the European Reformation) made plain. Second, as Nathan notes and Tsou confirms, personal factions cannot outlive their patron, but a dedicated tendency group has the wherewithal to survive personnel vicissitudes. Just as Mao's ideological "line" survived his personal death under Hua Guofeng's auspices, despite its unpopularity and the arrest of its most committed and articulate paladins, the survival of Zhou Enlai's "line" made possible the resurrection of Deng Xiaoping from his second political graveyard. Ideology was clearly less powerful and coherent during the Deng than during the Mao era, but it cannot be completely discounted. Thus despite the personal animus between Hu Yaobang and Zhao Ziyang, the demotion of Hu resulted in Zhao's inheritance of Hu's informal following or "tail" (*weiba*), based presumably on shared ideological affinity.

All things considered, it may be said that relations among top leaders are what the Chinese call "complicated" (*fuza*). I find it useful to dichotomize them into hierarchical and collegial categories. Collegiality (as in "collective leadership") is the norm, whereas in actual practice hierarchical deference is prevalent, even informally (as in Peng Dehuai's obsequious letter to Mao at Lushan, which Mao deemed a *casus belli*; or Hu Jintao's January 2001 disquisition on Jiang Zemin's ideological innovations). It is worth thinking about the nature of the interaction between normative and actual dimensions. The normative dimension is adhered to in public ceremonies in order to enhance leadership legitimacy and to promote more general adherence to the norms, of course, but it is presumably also invoked to govern the internal dynamics within the group. For example, it seems to ensure certain minimal rights to all within the elite circle (such as the right to a certain deference, or the right to vote). Secondly, this norm is invoked as a deterrent against excessive abuses of hierarchical

---

[13]   Cf. Franklyn Griffiths, "A Tendency Analysis of Soviet Policy-Making", in H. Gordon Skilling and Franklyn Griffiths (eds), *Interest Groups in Soviet Politics* (Princeton: Princeton University Press, 1971), pp. 335–79.

advantage, such as the supreme leader's unwarranted accusations or purge of his colleagues.

Contrariwise, there is a functional and causal interdependence between factional splits and rigid hierarchy, as Tsou points out: the invocation of discipline reinforces leadership. In terms of dynamics, the "supreme leader" or "core" is at the hub of the communications net (at least under the last two dominant leaders), and uses his (until now, a male) centrality to initiate most policy initiatives. Given the official taboo against "factionalism" most of the relationships tend to be bilateral ones between the "core" and various other leading figures. The currently preferred form of functional subdivisions seem to have been into various "leading groups"—the Foreign Policy Leading Small Group, the Taiwan Policy Leading Small Group, and so forth. But the obsession with control and with preventing adverse combinations makes such subdivisions risky to their membership, as was apparent from the fate of the first front in the 1960s. Jiang Zemin has avoided this possibility by serving as a member (actually, serving as leader) of all leading small groups—a rather labour-intensive solution. The "core's" centrality is obviously a major structural advantage, but he (or she) must also know how to "use people" with both charm and prudence to retain leverage.[14] The anecdotal evidence concerning Mao's relations with Deng Xiaoping, Lin Biao and Peng Zhen, or Deng's relations with Wang Zhen, Hu Yaobang and Deng Liqun, is telling: the leader uses the assignment of responsibilities as both a reward and a test, and the follower also has a range of reciprocal options (agreeing, deferring, joking, flattering) to choose from in the ongoing "game".

Still among the most delicate but inevitable questions for the Party leadership is how to handle intra-elite disagreement. Amid what seems to be strong pressure for unanimity, the normatively correct way is for the person who is in a minority position, assuming he or she is a subordinate, to exact whatever price he or she can negotiate and then change one's mind. This is what Wang Zhen apparently did after Deng delegated him to tour the Special Economic Zones as a way of encouraging him to reconsider his opposition to them. If the dissident cannot be persuaded, he should at least remain silent: this was Chen Yun's wonted tactic,

---

[14]   Teiwes, whose discussion of the role of the "core" has been most illuminating, faults me for inconsistency, depicting Deng on the one hand as a supreme leader whom no one can openly challenge and on the other as having to contend with various "strong rivals". Yet both statements are true. In the subtle game of wits and power among senior officials, the core leader is quite frequently presented with indirect challenges that leave the challenger free to back down, more rarely with blunt challenges to which the core leader must respond (and that may require disciplinary measures). As Teiwes himself notes in his chapter, "there are many examples, in the classic manner of court politics, of different leaders and groups using Deng's views to push their particular perspectives, seeking to persuade him of their positions in order to pre-empt collective decisions, or of the leader's intervention ending a contentious debate where significant interests were engaged".

for example, after visiting the same Special Economic Zones (Chen Yun's longest period of strategic silence was of course during the Cultural Revolution, enabling him to survive virtually unscathed). It is also possible to be in a minority even if one is Supreme Leader, and Mao himself resorted to this posture (with bitter resentment) more than once. However, a Supreme Leader has more options: one can manifest one's true views to one's support group, including *via* commentator articles in flagship media; one can make sarcastic speeches to various forums; one can absent oneself from key meetings; one can launch a discussion group.

If the issue is a matter of "principle", a dissident may feel impelled to speak out, to convene meetings, to mobilize one's political base, and to otherwise gird for combat, resulting in the notorious "struggle between two lines". Tang Tsou has perhaps done most to illuminate this type of confrontation in his penetrating analysis of the "game to win all or to lose all". Do the dynamics of elite interactions and disagreements inexorably culminate in such a zero-sum confrontation? I think surely it is fair to say that Chinese political actors at the pinnacle have what in American politics is referred to as a healthy instinct to "go for the jugular", i.e., *ceteris paribus*, a disputant would prefer any dispute to be resolved with clear-cut victory. Yet in CCP theoretical thinking about inner-Party struggle there has long been a distinction between antagonistic and nonantagonistic contradictions, and one naturally assumes that both are realistically possible resolutions of disagreement. The former are often considered watershed events in Chinese politics, not only because of the heavy personnel turnover but because of the shift in policy "line" that often attends them, and the emergence of bold new leadership. Whereas one can think of many instances in which a nonantagonistic contradiction deteriorates into antagonism, I can think of none in which an acknowledged antagonistic contradiction is successfully alleviated into a nonantagonistic one. But the nonantagonistic option should not be left out of the equation simply because the distinction between the two is empirically blurred or because it may in some cases become antagonistic.[15] Although the former are more dramatic and consequential, the latter may represent the salvation of Chinese politics, for example when the politically victorious position is objectively mistaken, or when the two sides in a disagreement are evenly matched, or both fulfil some objective functional need. Whether these two types of contradictions have the systematic differences I have ascribed to them in terms of origins, political bases, strategic options, and conflict scenarios will require additional study.

One of the most interesting questions to have been raised in this book has to do with the impact of the reform era on informal patterns that were initially defined in a Maoist political context. While I think we all agree that there is sufficient continuity to ensure the framework's continuing relevance, there have

---

[15]   Cf. Dittmer, "Bases of Power in Chinese Politics", *World Politics*, Vol. 31, No. 1 (October 1978), pp. 26–61.

also been significant changes. In the remainder of this chapter I shall focus on the changes from Mao to Deng, taking the post-Deng changes more fully into account in my later chapter. In terms of continuity, the basic pattern of "court politics" persisted, lubricated by consultations and professions of esteem, despite Deng Xiaoping's slightly less prepossessing revolutionary credentials (*zige*). The "core" role remained pivotal, with a hub-and-spoke communications pattern and the core's predominating influence over other members of the inner circle. On the "code of civility" and other normative rules of the game, there are differences of judgment. Teiwes and Tsou view these as having been substantially restored, while Pye seriously doubts that they ever existed. In my own view, there was certainly greater tolerance shown under Deng for ideological disagreement at the elite level, not to mention considerable freedom to vent (economic) policy ideas, though I think the Hu Yaobang and Zhao Ziyang cases both demonstrated that any challenge to the informal elite hierarchy (or indeed to social "stability") would be firmly suppressed. Meanwhile, the advent and rapid spread of the market and its so-called ethic fostered a greater hiatus between the ideological and normative code that still governed life at the top and the dog-eat-dog mass public than at any time since the early 1950s. (Barring corruption, the direct impact on the elite was essentially confined to their entrepreneurial wives and offspring.)

Which brings us, of course, to areas of discontinuity between the Maoist and Dengist eras. Teiwes concurs with Parris Chang that the "core" grew weaker,[16] and he plausibly extrapolates a continuing decline into the future. Indeed he is on record with the prognostication that the role of "supreme" or "paramount" leader could not survive Deng. It does seem to be true that despite Deng Xiaoping's generally successful economic policy choices and amazing dexterity in manipulating the bureaucratic levers of power, Deng's less illustrious revolutionary achievements, his scrupulous avoidance of the trappings of a personality cult, his apparent indifference to the use of ideology as a visionary guideline to the future, his generally more consultative approach to leadership, and the Tiananmen tragedy all considerably diminished his charismatic candlepower relative to Mao Zedong. (All the same, it should be borne in mind that Mao's public support underwent greater cyclical variation than appears in mythologizing retrospect, and his exaggerated complaints of having been ignored by colleagues cannot be entirely discounted.) Should the post-Mao trend toward charismatic extinction continue, a weaker core would enable the leadership to more closely approximate the Party norm of "collective leadership", which is likely to be a less decisive one.

Second, the relationship between the first and second fronts has changed. As Teiwes notes, while Mao was basically the sole standing member of the second

16   Parris Chang, *Power and Policy in China* (Dubuque, Iowa: Kendall/Hunt, 1990, 3rd ed.), pp. 243–70.

front, during the Deng era the second front of elderly Party "immortals" became virtually a shadow Politburo Standing Committee. Yet the functions of the two fronts do seem to have been retained, relegating the first front to policy implementation and routine administration while reserving for the second front the task of charting the nation's policy "line", together with the prerogative of reasserting hands-on control during national emergencies (as defined by members of the second front). While one might anticipate that these interventions would complicate the situation due to the number of veterans of nearly equal status, in the most important cases (viz., 1987 and 1989) they seem to have re-entered the scene *en bloc*, in effect giving Deng a trump card. Yet the essentially informal basis of their power (plus Deng's gradual divestiture of all formal positions and his much slower relinquishment of informal influence) contributed to an even sharper distinction between formal and informal power than during the Maoist era, when Mao remained chair of both the Party Central Committee and its Central Military Commission. (After the elimination of the Central Advisory Committee of octegenarian leaders at the 14th Party Congress in October 1992, and their subsequent attrition through death, this generational overhang in the form of a "second front" has now all but disappeared, and informal politics reverted to the less salient role it played in the 1950s, before Mao's "retirement".)

Third, there has been a general slackening of ideological discipline, as Pye has emphasized. This occurred for a number of reasons: the revived "code of civility" and enhanced elite deference noted above, the essentially complete elimination of top-down mass campaigns aimed at monitoring elite deviance, and the elaborately masked (but nonetheless inescapable) "contradiction" between Marxist ideology and such reform policies as marketization and privatization. The impact of this third change has been to facilitate the proliferation of an informal political economy of a pragmatic and sometimes corrupt form, particularly at the provincial and local levels, in the name of rapid economic growth. Although this new political economy is still loosely linked to the formal political network through patron-client ties, the Party leadership is clearly worried about losing control of the situation. I have suggested elsewhere that ideological decay also stimulated informal politics at the highest leadership levels by making it less dangerous— redefining policy as an area in which one may legitimately form opinion groups or even enduring bureaucratic interest groups.[17]

Fourth, as Tsou has also noted, the informal sector became increasingly differentiated. Although vertically organized patron-client networks were still important, even indispensable, the devolution of authority that accompanied reform has permitted vertical segmentation to be breached and more horizontally structured interest groups to form. This was, for instance, visible in the demands by provincial leaders for greater discretion to control local investment funds in

---

[17]   Lowell Dittmer and Yu-shan Wu, "The Modernization of Factionalism in Chinese Politics", *World Politics*, Vol. 47, No. 4 (July 1995), pp. 467–94.

the course of formulating draft revisions for the Eighth Five-Year Plan (1991-95), or in the proliferation of trade associations and other "non-governmental organizations" to promote their specific sectoral interests.[18] Above all, it implies the proliferation of mixed, quasi-autonomous, public-private, vertical-horizontal groupings, as one set of relationships leads to another (after all, a key function of a "connection" is to introduce other connections).[19]

Finally, the apparatus has become more "formalized", in the sense of having more frequent and more regularly scheduled meetings, debating legislation before approving it, holding more meaningful elections, and otherwise taking itself more seriously, in hopes of realizing some of its constitutionally vested powers.[20] This is not the place to discuss the prospects of this form of revitalized institutionalism, but insofar as it is permitted to develop (and its progress has been very slow and subject to political interruption) it might represent, if not necessarily "democratization", a countervailing trend to some of the informal excesses noted above.

Nathan has acutely pointed out that I have (in different publications) both characterized the trend toward greater informal politics as rampant and confidently predicted its demise. Which is it? Fair enough: My answer is that the predominant trend during the reform era has permitted various forms of informal politics to flourish as never before. This is by no means an unequivocally negative phenomenon, having contributed at the grassroots level to the growth of "civil society" and to the booming pace of economic growth in the small business sector. At the same time, marketization and privatization and an opening to the outside world in what is still essentially a legal vacuum have contributed to the largest wave of corruption since the late 1940s. But even though the elite were not able to insulate themselves from these developments, the proliferation of informal politics at these empyrean levels has been less affected by the socio-economic reforms below. At the top, the growth of informalism is primarily attributable to other factors: the slackening of ideological discipline, the difficulties of institutionalizing "retirement" in a culture still deeply imbued with respect for the older generation, and Deng Xiaoping's apparent personal indifference to formal arrangements when confronted with more immediately pressing issues (or when given the opportunity to trade formal for informal power). Again, this was not necessarily a completely adverse development, but

---

[18]   See Susan H. Whiting, "The Politics of NGO Development in China", *Voluntas*, Vol. 2, No. 2 (November 1991), pp. 16–48.

[19]   Peter M. Blau, Danching Ruan and Monika Ardelt, "Interpersonal Choice and Networks in China", *Social Forces*, Vol. 69, No. 4 (June 1991), pp. 1037–63.

[20]   See Murray Scot Tanner, "The Erosion of Communist Control Over Lawmaking in China", *The China Quarterly*, No. 138 (June 1994), pp. 381–404; and Kevin J. O'Brien, *Reform Without Liberalization: China's National People's Congress and the Politics of Institutional Change* (New York: Cambridge University Press, 1990).

Janus-faced. Informal politics has the potential to facilitate reform by providing policy short-cuts and uninstitutionalized halfway houses for new experimental programs. At the same time, it leaves open a window of opportunity in the event of an emergency for a charismatic "man on horseback" to seize the reins and "stabilize" the situation. The overall impact is to make politics more flexible and responsive but less predictable.

My statements regarding rationalization and formalization are essentially predictive rather than positive, and must therefore be taken with all due caution. Even if the current trends from which they are extrapolated continue, which is by no means certain in a country whose progress has been characterized by frequent breakthroughs and reversals, they are so mixed and ambiguous in direction that there is plenty of room for honest differences of opinion in assessing them. Informal politics may confidently be expected to continue, but it may with any luck take a form more functionally compatible with the formal structures in which it is nested (or the trellis along which it creeps) than has hitherto been the case.

II

The Nature of Politics

Under Jiang

SEVEN

China's Political System: Challenges of the
Twenty-First Century

Michel Oksenberg

China at the beginning of a new century still confronts the challenge it faced a hundred years ago: can its leaders, drawing effectively upon the talents and wisdom of its diverse people, forge a durable political system that is not plagued by costly social and political instability?

The Current Chinese Political System

China's current system defies encapsulation in a single short phrase. Such previous depictions as "totalitarianism", a "Leninist party state", "fragmented authoritarianism", "soft authoritarianism" or "bureaucratic pluralism" miss the complexity of China's state structure today.[1] The system is perhaps best conceived as an eclectic set of three types of institutions:

---

[1]   On "totalitarianism," see Tang Tsou, *The Cultural Revolution and Post-Mao Reforms: A Historical Perspective* (Chicago: University of Chicago Press, 1986). Analyses of China as a Leninist state include Bruce Dickson, *Democratization in China and Taiwan: The Adaptability of Leninist Parties* (New York: Oxford University Press, 1997); and Barrett McCormick, *Political Reform in Post-Mao China: Democracy and Bureaucracy in a Leninist State* (Berkeley: University of California Press, 1990). "Fragmented authoritarianism" is developed and analyzed in Kenneth Lieberthal and Michel Oksenberg, *Policy Making in China: Leaders, Structures, and Processes* (Princeton: Princeton University Press, 1988) and in Kenneth Lieberthal and David Lampton (eds), *Bureaucracy, Politics and Decision Making in Post-Mao China* (Berkeley: University of California Press, 1992). On "soft authoritarianism," see Edwin A. Winckler, "Institutionalization and Participation on Taiwan: From Hard to Soft Authoritarianism?", *The China Quarterly*, No. 99 (September 1984), pp. 481–99. The "bureaucratic pluralism" framework is discussed in H. Gordon Skilling, "Interest Groups and Communist Politics Revisited," *World Politics*, Vol. 36 (October 1983), pp. 1–27. For an interest group approach to Chinese politics, see Victor Falkenheim (ed.), *Citizens and Groups in Contemporary China* (Ann Arbor: The University of Michigan Center for Chinese Studies, 1987).

1) The core apparatus, primarily but not entirely Leninist or Soviet in origin, consisting of a fused Chinese Communist Party, government and army at the national, provincial, prefectural, county and township levels;

2) Linkage or intermediary institutions largely created in the past twenty years to manipulate, control, isolate and exploit the outside world; and

3) The legal, semi-legal and illegal organizations and associations that are arising in the social and economic space created by a market economy and the state's retreat from total control over society and culture.

The Core State Apparatus

Principal Structural Features

The core apparatus is itself in the midst of considerable change, but it still reflects its Soviet or Leninist origins. Its principal attributes include these features:

1) Enormous power resides in the pre-eminent leader and the Standing Committee and Politburo of the Party Central Committee (roughly twenty to thirty people) who basically are not accountable to any other agency or to any judicial restraints.

2) The Party committees and their Organization Departments at each level control appointments and dismissals of key officials from the Party, government and state-owned enterprises at their own level and one level below (the nomenklatura system).

3) The military apparatus is commanded by the Party Central Military Commission, which reports to the Party Standing Committee. The Party Central Military Commission commands the armed services, through the General Staff of the army, navy, air force and rocket forces, the Logistics Department and the Political Department. Civilian control over the chain of command is weak.

4) The law-enforcement apparatus at each level of the hierarchy—the state security, public security, procuracy and judicial agencies—remains under the coordinated control of the Party political-legal committee at that level.

5) The ownership of the means of production largely belongs to state bureaucracies and state-owned enterprises. Even though the private sector now accounts for an increasing percentage of total production and even though individual savings constitute a substantial portion of bank deposits, a significant portion of the country's wealth still is in the possession of the state.

Ideology

Ideology, by which I mean a set of explicitly held beliefs that guide action, remains a key ingredient of the system. The ideology of the political elite is no longer limited to Marxism-Leninism-Mao Zedong Thought, but most leaders remain committed to state ownership of the core means of production and distrust the capitalist or bourgeois class. These beliefs affect and constrain public policy. During the post-Mao era, the ideological premises have been extended to involve an unquestioned and explicit commitment to modernization, industrialization and urbanization and include self-conscious nationalistic themes infused with Confucian rhetoric.

The vision of modernity is embodied in the urban and regional plans (*chengshi guihua*) produced by the various architectural design institutes and provided to local governments around the country, a vision enriched by karaoke and television. This vision of modernity is enforced in the criteria for evaluating the performance of localities and local officials and for judging progress toward being classified as a "comparatively well off" (*xiaokang*) township, village or household. Embedded in the exuberant embrace of economic growth are unquestioned assumptions that material progress will produce a happier, more stable and more just society, that social stability (obtained if necessary through suppressing those who would challenge the system) is a prerequisite for economic growth, and that material progress and social stability must precede such other desirable objectives as democratization or environmental protection.

A Mobilization System

There still lurks a Great Leap mentality in China, and the persistence of a mobilizational apparatus facilitates its implementation. Campaigns are no longer called *yundong*; Deng Xiaoping proclaimed their end. But mobilization (*dongyuan*), as it is now labelled, still occurs (although reduced in scope, intensity and number), as illustrated by the "strike hard" campaigns against corruption, Jiang Zemin's "three emphases" (*san jiang*) and the attacks against the Falungong sect. Designating a specific objective as a central or important task, creating a headquarters or a small group to coordinate the fulfillment of the objective, disseminating slogans and wall posters to publicize the effort, and setting quantitative targets to measure success are still part of the system.

The mobilization system includes several transmission organizations under the control of the Party that are intended to strengthen the leaders' reach into specific sectors of society, such as the official trade union, the Communist Youth League and the Women's Federation. These organizations still attempt to galvanize support for state policies and serve as a recruitment ground for Party membership and the officialdom.

Some Qualifications

This portrayal of the core elements of the Chinese state needs immediate qualification and refinement. First of all, the core system is not entirely Leninist-Soviet in origin. Some aspects—such as the mobilization system, the nature of Party–army relations and the fusion of Party and government—can be traced to Yan'an and the guerrilla past. Other parts of the bureaucracy reflect a deeper imperial heritage, such as the revenue system, the method of classifying documents and the influence of Chinese cosmology. Yet other parts of the institutional arrangements derive from the Republican Kuomintang era, such as the Chinese People's Political Consultative Conference, the Party's United Front policy and the location of the State Copyright Administration inside the State Press and Publications Administration. Some other agencies continue to bear the imprint of their Western, especially American, origins such as the Ministry of Public Health and the Ministry of Education. Nowhere are the diverse institutional origins of the core state apparatus more evident than in the state structures that implement policies concerning the ethnic minorities. These organizations are an amalgam of Soviet, Republican and imperial practices. In short, the contemporary Chinese state never was simply a replica of a Leninist-Soviet system; from its founding, it has been a mixture of diverse institutions over which the Party achieved an overwhelmingly dominant position and into which it inserted itself to varying degrees at varying times.

Second and most important, this core apparatus has been undergoing considerable change. Important initiatives during the past twenty years include:

- considerable administrative decentralization in personnel management and financial systems, although some reversal of these measures has occurred since the mid-1990s;

- the creation of mechanisms to circumvent restrictions on property rights and state ownership of the means of production;

- the formation of quasi-autonomous or government-approved non-governmental organizations;

- a gradual spread of the rule of law through the promulgation of laws (*falü*) and regulations (*guiding*) in place of the unvetted personal edicts of rulers;

- the gradual introduction of a civil-service system and a major effort to improve the quality of the officialdom (to be younger, better educated and more professional);

- the professionalization of the military through reducing its size, improving its equipment and training, and altering its doctrine and missions;

- an increased reliance upon monetary and fiscal instruments for regulating the economy and decreased importance of the planning (*jihua*) agencies and mechanisms;

- the transformation of the banking system through the creation of commercial banks (previously specialized development banks) and a central reserve bank;

- the indigenization of local elites at the county level and above in areas which until the early 1980s were dominated by officials from the regions in north China where the Red Army had recruited personnel prior to its advance into the southern and southwestern regions of the country;

- greater transparency of a previously opaque system;

- a reduction in the strength of the propaganda apparatus (for example, through the expansion and commercialization of a substantial portion of the cultural market);

- some diminution in the dominance of the public-security apparatus and an enhancement of the judiciary within the political-legal system;

- the invigoration of the parliaments or assemblies at each level of the hierarchy;

- the introduction of fair and competitive elections of village assemblies and village chiefs;

- an altered policy process that involves more consultation with the affected agencies and some solicitation of expert advice; and

- a reduction in the grip that the state-sector work unit (*danwei*) has over its employees through its provision of services and its control over career mobility; the unit provides fewer services today and employees enjoy greater mobility.

This is an impressive list of governmental changes, but all of them are proceeding slowly and encountering difficulties and resistance. These considerable adjustments mean that the conventional wisdom in the West about the reform era—that China has had economic reform without political reform—is inaccurate. However, the changes have not yet brought about a systemic transformation; to repeat, at its core it is still a Soviet-Leninist state.

It is notable, too, that although the core state apparatus exhibits many shared characteristics throughout the country, especially with respect to the formal structure of the Party, there are subtle regional differences with respect, for example, to the dominance of the Party and its fusion with the government, the role of the military, the extent of ideological uniformity and the vibrancy of the mobilization system. Such factors as the presence of an ethnic minority population, the level of economic development, the history of the locale (a revolutionary base area, for example), the extent of a foreign presence and the preferences of local leaders also have an effect upon the local state's structures and functions and the extent of reform.

Linkage Organizations

Since 1978 China's leaders have created numerous organizations to channel the outside world's activities within the mainland. These "linkage", "intermediary" or "window" institutions include the four original special economic zones at Shenzhen, Zhuhai, Shantou and Xiamen; the economic development zones of many cities (the best known of which is Shanghai's Pudong); joint ventures with foreign companies; agencies especially designed for foreign cooperation (such as the China National Off-Shore Oil Company [CNOOC]); the international trust and investment corporations (of which the best known is the China International Trust and Investment Corporation [CITIC]); listings on the newly established

Shenzhen and Shanghai stock exchanges in which foreigners are able to invest (the "B" shares); and various agencies within ministries that facilitate cooperation with foreign counterpart agencies (such as divisions within the People's Bank and the Ministries of Finance and Foreign Trade to deal with the International Monetary Fund, the World Bank and the World Trade Organization). Moreover, such organizations as the Bank of China, the China Travel Service, the civil aviation industry and the Foreign Employment Services Corporation (which supplies staff to foreign employers) have expanded rapidly to accommodate the foreign presence.

Another set of organizations has been expanded or created to deal with Taiwan and the presence of Taiwanese corporations and passport holders on the mainland. Some of these are nested within the Party's United Front Department and others lie within the Ministry of Foreign Affairs and economic agencies. The number of overseas Chinese has also grown enormously, with some of these exchanges with overseas Chinese falling within the domain of the Overseas Chinese Commission and travel agencies aimed at ethnic Chinese in other countries.

Finally, Hong Kong and Macau are now part of the People's Republic as Special Administrative Regions (SARs), and several organizations have been created on both sides to implement Hong Kong's Basic Law and the "one country, two systems" policy. The Ministry of Foreign Affairs and the People's Liberation Army now have an official presence in the two former colonies, and the Chinese Communist Party, as before 1997, maintains an underground apparatus that has as its external face the New China News Agency. Even more important are the tight web of economic linkages between the two SARs and the mainland. The Bank of China, CITIC, the China Overseas Shipping Company and the state-owned tourist agencies are among the most noticeable of such organizations. Equally noteworthy, many provinces and even counties—legally unable to open offices in Hong Kong—have created trading companies or other devices to circumvent the law, and these subsidiaries have offices in SARs to pursue their regional government's interests there.[2]

To varying degrees, China's linkage or intermediary organizations are not well integrated into the core Party-state apparatus. They have been structured as intervening institutions so that the core will not be contaminated by the outside world. Initially designed to keep the non-mainland world at arms length, they now perform a filtering function. The core party-state apparatus uses these window

---

[2]   Yun-wing Sung, "The Role of Hong Kong in China's Export Drive", *The Australian Journal of Chinese Affairs*, No. 15 (January 1986), p. 98. Thousands of Hong Kong firms are also active in the mainland, operating factories, developing real estate and building, owning and/or operating transportation and communication systems. The intertwining has resulted in many thousands of PRC citizens working for mainland firms in Hong Kong, and tens of thousands of Hong Kong citizens residing and working throughout the mainland. And none of this movement is under the tight control of either government.

organizations to monitor, exploit, manipulate and extract resources from the outside world.

It is interesting to speculate about the inspirations for these institutions. Some, as already noted, existed before the 1978 opening to the outside world. Others, such as the SEZs, owe their inspiration to Taiwan. Yet others, such as CNOOC, were designed through studying the ways that other countries handled similar issues. One wonders, however, whether the rapidity with which these intermediary agencies have proliferated is also owing to imperial China's traditional ways of handling barbarians who wished to reside within the realm. As John Fairbank noted in his explanation of the origins of the treaty ports in the 1800s, China had a long tradition of creating zones within the empire where foreigners, whom the rulers considered unable to reach the high cultural level necessary to adhere to the Confucian norms of the state, were able to govern themselves. The Qing dynasty, as with its predecessors, had its own version of "one country, two systems". The core system was rooted in Confucian norms, which the Chinese were expected to obey. A second set of arrangements for the imperial system's benefit enabled barbarians to reside within the realm under constrained self-rule.

Organizations in Society and the Economy

During the past twenty years, the core state has retreated from its once totalitarian penetration of the economy and society. A proto-market economy now exists, and prices reflect supply and demand, albeit imperfectly. Yet capital still is allocated through non-market forces; and local governments still intervene extensively in the economy. As a result it is not entirely accurate to assert that China now has a full-fledged market economy. Nonetheless, the 1990s has witnessed an explosion of individual entrepreneurs (*getihu*) and privately owned enterprises (*siying qiye*); and a much freer labour market has developed, in which an estimated one hundred million migrants are "temporarily" residing in Chinese cities or other rural areas.[3] Yet these migrants retain their rural household registry (*nongcun hukou*) and have not been incorporated into the area where they currently live.

The state has also retreated from its previous intensive control of society and culture. Traditional marriage, death and family rituals have been revived—or at least a contemporary facsimile of what is recalled as the traditional rituals, combined with a heavy dose of "modernity" ritual. A youth culture now exists in the big cities. And a new and prosperous middle class now has disposable income

---

[3]   Samuel P. S. Ho, "Rural Non-Agricultural Development in Post-Reform China: Growth, Development Patterns, and Issues", *Pacific Affairs*, Vol. 68, No. 3 (Autumn 1995), pp. 360–91; Linda Wong, "China's Urban Migrants—The Public Policy Challenge," *Pacific Affairs*, Vol. 67, No. 3 (Autumn 1994), pp. 335–55. The delineation between city and countryside is a very complicated and arcane matter. It is an administrative and bureaucratic distinction that is increasingly useless for analytical purposes.

that enables them to nurture communities where, within limits, they can act upon their values.

The result is a proliferation of legal, semi-legal and illegal organizations inhabiting the economic and social space that the state's withdrawal has created. It would be wrong to conceive of these as the emergence of a "civil society". The differences between the Chinese and the Eastern European conditions are too great to apply a term arising from the Czechoslovakian, Hungarian and Polish experiences of the 1970s and 1980s. But an important development is occurring, manifested in the reappearance of secret societies and criminal gangs; in the formation of government-approved interest groups such as those of environmental protection activists, associations of retired cadres and private entrepreneurs; in the resurgence of state-licensed, state-tolerated and illegal religious organizations (including ones that are Buddhist, Catholic and Protestant); the proliferation of professional associations that have their own journals and annual national and provincial conventions; the expansion of groups based on hobbies and shared cultural and literary interests; and the reappearance in some urban areas of organizations of migrants who hail from the same region (*tongxiang hui*) that are intended to protect their members and give them a voice.

The spread of the Falungong sect in 1999 is perhaps the most dramatic example of developments in this sphere, but it is by no means the only one. Americans and Western Europeans have watched with interest whenever organizations with Western values have been formed, such as illegal trade unions, the underground Christian churches and democratic political parties. Westerners are playing a role in fostering these associations. However, the linkages being established between mainland Han Buddhists, overseas Chinese, Japanese and Korean Buddhists, and even Tibetan Buddhists are possibly more significant. Traditionally, Chinese and Tibetan Buddhists had little to do with each other, but overseas Buddhists are financing the rebuilding and expansion of both Chinese and Tibetan Buddhist temples, and Han are apparently exhibiting increasing interest in Tibetan Buddhism. Those organizations with genuine indigenous roots enriched by a Chinese modernity—secret societies, *tongxiang hui*, Buddhism, lineage associations and professional associations   (which echo a long tradition of guilds)—are likely to spread more rapidly, have greater appeal and prove more difficult for the core state apparatus to control, precisely because they cannot be dismissed as creatures of the outside world.

Factors Producing Change

In the 1980s, in a series of writings, David Lampton, Kenneth Lieberthal and I coined the phrase "fragmented authoritarianism" to capture the nature of the Chinese system.[4] Many others helped us to elaborate this model. However, as the

---

[4]   Lieberthal and Oksenberg, *Policy Making in China*, and Lieberthal and Lampton (eds), *Bureaucracy, Politics and Decision Making in Post-Mao China*.

above portrayal of the current Chinese system suggests, "fragmented authoritarianism" no longer adequately captures the essence of the system. That model accurately depicted the core state apparatus for that period of time, but as the writings of Harry Harding, Susan Shirk, Barry Naughton and Gordon White, among others, recognized, an intellectually satisfying depiction had to capture the forces producing change in the system.[5] "Fragmented authoritarianism" offered a detailed but static description of how the core state apparatus worked in the mid- to late 1980s and, to a considerable extent, still works. As a static model, however, it did not anticipate the changes of the 1990s. Moreover, as the diverse writings of Elizabeth Perry, Vivienne Shue, Tianjian Shi, Merle Goldman and others have demonstrated, the revitalization of Chinese society requires us to include state–society interactions in any comprehensive model of the Chinese system.[6]

In short, one cannot rest content with a description of the system. We must ask: what has prompted the system to evolve from that of the 1980s to that of the late 1990s? Four interrelated factors have been at work: idiosyncratic ad hoc responses of the top leaders to the series of structural challenges that they have faced; the consequences of opening China to the outside world; the emergence of a proto-market economy; and the transformation of telecommunications and transportation that is sweeping China. These powerful factors are generating an evolution of the system, but in an incoherent and uncoordinated fashion. Increasingly, the system has a disjointed, byzantine quality to it. The leaders appear to lack an overarching vision of the nation's political future that guides their incremental responses to the institutional challenges that confront them. They do have a vague vision of a Chinese modernity concretized, as noted earlier, in the grand architectural designs of Shanghai's Pudong district, the rebuilt Chang'an and Wangfujing boulevards in Beijing, and the urban construction plans of county towns. Without a vision of China's political future, the leaders are incapable of molding or guiding the nation's political trajectory. They are the

---

[5]   Susan Shirk, *How China Opened its Door: The Political Success of the PRC's Foreign Trade and Investment Reforms* (Washington, DC: Brookings Institution, 1994), especially Chapter 3; see also Harry Harding, "Comments", in Shirk, pp. 92–9; Barry Naughton, *Growing Out of the Plan: Chinese Economic Reform, 1978–1993* (New York: Cambridge University Press, 1995); and Gordon White, *Riding the Tiger: The Politics of Economic Reform in Post-Mao China* (Stanford: Stanford University Press, 1993).

[6]   Elizabeth J. Perry and Mark Selden (eds), *Chinese Society: Change, Conflict, and Resistance* (New York: Routledge, 2000); Vivienne Shue, *The Reach of the State: Sketches of the Chinese Body Politic* (Stanford: Stanford University Press, 1988); Vivienne Shue and Marc Blecher, *Tethered Deer: Government and Economy in a Chinese County* (Stanford: Stanford University Press, 1996); Tianjian Shi, *Political Participation in Beijing* (Cambridge, MA: Harvard University Press, 1997); and Merle Goldman, *Sowing the Seeds of Democracy in China: Political Reform in the Deng Xiaoping Era* (Cambridge, MA: Harvard University Press, 1994).

captives of the three forces that their earlier decisions unleashed: the opening of China to the outside world, the spread of a market economy and the transformation of telecommunications and transportation.

The Institutional Challenges Ahead

This brief sketch of the Chinese political system and of the factors pushing its evolution pinpoints the challenges that China's leaders and people face in the years ahead. Some of these challenges are endemic to any Leninist system. Others arise from the structural changes that have occurred since 1978. And yet others necessitate managing and channelling the forces that are propelling the system in new directions—lest they overwhelm both the leaders and the led.

The Vulnerabilities of the Core Leninist System

Succession

As in many other authoritarian arrangements, Leninist systems have no institutionalized and orderly procedures for selecting the successor to their paramount leader. In many respects, this is the Achilles heel of the system. There is nothing in a Leninist system short of a coup to prevent the pre-eminent leader from remaining in power after his mental and physical capabilities have eroded. As the leader ages, the personal rivalries that he may have fostered in order to remain in power intensify and unbridled struggles among potential successors erupt, fed by personal ambition and fear. Those who have risen with aging members of the leadership—including their wives and children—worry about their own fate after their chieftain passes from the scene and often prevail upon him to remain in office so that they can use the remaining time to enhance their own wealth and power. The paramount leader's courtiers often foster a cult of personality to enhance their own stature within the bureaucratic system. Particularly in authoritarian systems, many leaders fall to the temptation to indulge their own whims and those of their subordinates. It is a rare leader who is able to keep himself in perspective in that heady environment and avoid a touch of megalomania. Deng Xiaoping was unusual in his recognition of the problem. He set a precedent in avoiding a cult of personality and of slowly withdrawing from power.

As the new century dawns, the leaders of China face this age-old dilemma. The 1999 ceremonies in Beijing at the 50th anniversary of the founding of the People's Republic provided ample reminders of the danger. The gathering of the top leaders to review the parade from atop the Gate of Heavenly Peace harkened back to Stalin-era and Brezhnev-led celebrations in Moscow's Red Square and to the Maoist era of the 1950s and the 1960s. As if to underscore the situation, the portrait of Jiang Zemin followed those of Mao and Deng during the parade. The top four leaders—Jiang Zemin, Li Peng, Zhu Rongji and Li Ruihuan—are all over 70 years of age. When and how will their successors be selected? Do the current set of leaders command sufficient respect and authority to be able to anoint their successors and to make their selection stick after they pass from the scene? Even Deng faced severe opposition in the arrangement he made in the

1980s with Hu Yaobang and Zhao Ziyang; in fact, in 1986 and 1987, other Party elders put great pressure on him to overturn the arrangement. He and the other elders retained enough legitimacy within the Central Committee to impose another set of successors after the June 1989 Tiananmen debacle, installing a collective leadership of people then in their early sixties, with Jiang as the first among equals. Since then, Jiang has increasingly sought to distinguish and separate himself from the other Standing Committee leaders.

At the 14th Party Congress in 1992, an agreement was apparently reached to institutionalize succession procedures. Central to the rules was the notion of term limits—no more than two terms or 10 years in office. But will all of the rulers adhere to that agreement as their terms in office expire? Will Jiang be willing to step down at the 16th Party Congress in 2002? If not, will others also seek to remain in office and resist any effort for them to retire? Could the leaders divide over succession issues, as occurred in 1964–66, 1969–71, 1973–76, 1978–81 and 1986–89?

In these instances, bureaucrats and the populace quickly detected signs of a divided leadership at the top. In a complicated fashion, factionalism at the top on these previous occasions became linked to and exacerbated societal cleavages. Can such a sequence be avoided in the years immediately ahead? The evidence thus far is murky. Some signs point to an effort by Jiang to arrange for an orderly succession, possibly centring on Vice-President Hu Jintao. But other signs point to opposition to Jiang's effort to mastermind the succession process. Some observers also discern the initial stages of a Jiang Zemin cult of personality and a desire by Jiang to remain an active political force beyond 2002. The Chinese system is clearly entering an important stage in its evolution, as the current aging leaders who have piloted the nation during the past decade enter the final phase of their long careers.

The Role of the Party

In line with Marxist-Leninist ideology, the Chinese Communist Party long claimed to be the vanguard of the proletariat, and the leaders of the Party continue to assert a responsibility to discern and defend the interests of the working class. The Party was structured to carry out a revolutionary wage-class struggle, run a state-controlled economic system and mobilize the population in pursuit of socialism. It unabashedly enforces a dictatorship. However, the revolution is over, the leaders have proclaimed an end to class struggle, the state is abandoning its command of the economy, and the pursuit of socialism has yielded way to the pursuit of economic growth.

To recite the ideology that defines the Party's purpose, in short, is to recall its irrelevance. Since 1989 the leaders and their house intellectuals have not undertaken a serious effort to redefine the role of the Party in a market economy and increasingly diverse society. The Party and its leaders justify their right to rule on three pragmatic grounds: they have protected the sovereignty and territorial integrity of the country, they have maintained China's unity and domestic stability, and they have achieved rapid economic growth and a higher standard of living for the overwhelming majority of their people. But even these justifications are under challenge. Involvement in the international economy arguably intrudes on aspects of Chinese sovereignty. Taiwan's de facto independence challenges China's unity. Rising crime, social disorder and corruption call into question the Party's ability to maintain stability. And economic growth is slowing, with growing numbers of urban unemployed. In reality, as Jiang Zemin has explicitly acknowledged, the Party is an increasingly corrupt organization that dispenses patronage through the posts that it controls and the access to power and resources that these posts provide. It persists in using old methods to solve new problems. This is a sure prescription for obsolescence.

The Party is not in imminent danger of collapse, but the 1980s and 1990s have witnessed a severe erosion in the efficacy of its ideological appeals, a weakening of its authority over other institutions and an atrophying of its core apparatus. Yet, as noted earlier, the Party remains the most important organization in China. Through its control of key personnel appointments, its coercive capabilities, its eroding propaganda apparatus, its manipulation of patriotic and nationalistic appeals, and its command of the government and the People's Liberation Army, it provides the glue that holds the country together. The mainland's unity would be imperiled without the continued existence of the Party. By design, it has no substitute.

In short, China's leaders and people face a dilemma that is likely to intensify in the early decades of the 21st century. On the one hand, the Party is indispensable; on the other hand, it needs to reform if it is to remain attuned to the new conditions. Thus far, with the exception of 1984–88, when Hu Yaobang and Zhao Ziyang acted with Deng Xiaoping's encouragement, China's leaders have been reluctant to embark upon a genuine reform of the Party. Several factors explain their reluctance: deep and potentially polarizing differences among the leaders about the ultimate objectives, means and urgency of Party reform; fear that the results would lead to the same disaster as Mikhail Gorbachev's efforts to transform the Communist Party of the Soviet Union (CPSU); concern that the foreign powers and Taiwan would seek to use loosened Party control over the political system as an opportunity to overthrow it completely; a desire of the leaders to focus on what they know and have shown they can do best—economic development; and few overt indications that the populace demands a reform of the Party.

In essence, the leaders face five alternatives, each of which has attendant risks:

- to persist as the dominant, mobilizational institution of a fused Party-government-military apparatus, with the risk of decay, irrelevance and political and social instability;

- to return to totalitarian rule and class struggle, risking economic stagnation, international isolation and domestic resistance;

- to change into a highly nationalistic and externally assertive party, which would necessitate greater reliance on the support of the military, thereby risking a coalition against China and an exposure of Chinese weakness in the international arena;

- to transform the Party into an instrument explicitly responsible for guiding China's gradual political evolution into some form of democracy, with the risk of social disorder and debilitating splits among the leaders during the difficult and protracted transition; or

- to postpone such choices, with the risk of purposelessness, drift and inconsistent ad hoc responses to problems as they arise.

These strategic options involve concrete questions. For example, should the Party actively recruit and welcome into its midst members of the new entrepreneurial class, especially wealthy owners of private enterprises? Thus far the Party has been quite ambivalent on this issue. The remaining ideologues in the Party are reluctant to embrace the new classes. They attribute the CPSU's abandonment of socialism and the collapse of the Soviet Union to the Party's loss of identity as a vanguard of the proletariat. But if China's Communist Party does not recruit energetically from among China's new classes, a bifurcation of political and economic elites will occur.

The relationship between the Party and the government presents another huge dilemma for the leaders. In a sense, the fusion of the Party and the government places excessive burdens on the Party committees at each level of the hierarchy. The Party is so immersed in the day-to-day details of running the country that all grievances get directed against it. In 1987 the 13th Party Congress raised the slogan of separating the Party from the government (*dangzheng fenkai*). This would have entailed abolishing the Party committees within each government agency and abandoning the nomenklatura system. The Party would have to redefine its role as setting the broad parameters for the nation's development. It would need to seek to include and reconcile the diverse interests in society rather than enforcing the interests of a single sector as articulated by the leaders. Although Deng Xiaoping continued to say after the Tiananmen debacle that all the formulations (*tifa*) of the 13th Party Congress remained valid, in fact the resolution to separate the Party from the government (*dangzheng fenkai tifa*) was not raised again during either the 14th or 15th Party Congresses of 1992 and 1997. But, without a separation of Party and government, can the rule of law be established when judges remain subordinate to Party committees? Can administrative decentralization be effective when its main result is to strengthen the authority of local Party committees over the local agents of central government?

Vulnerabilities of the Linkage Organizations

The proliferation of linkage organizations and of laws and regulations dealing with them have created a hodgepodge of agencies with ill-defined, competing and overlapping jurisdictions. The jumble is more complex than the participants—be they foreigners or Chinese officials—can handle. First of all, many of the laws and regulations are secret; foreigners are unable to inform themselves of the regulatory environment that they are expected to obey. Second, many of the laws and regulations are contradictory. Even worse, there is no supreme body short of the Party Standing Committee and the State Council that has the authority to reconcile the differences. Third, different foreign organizations are expected to adhere to different regulatory regimes. The size of foreign investment is a critical factor; investments of different magnitudes must be approved by different levels of the system, with the largest investments requiring approval at the highest levels. Furthermore, some early joint ventures are exempted from subsequently enacted regulations. Taiwan firms are treated differently from firms of other origins. The regulatory regimes within China's "Special Economic Zones" obviously differ from those in other areas of China, and various localities establish their own arrangements within the industrial parks they have established. As the default of the Guangdong International Trust and Investment Corporation revealed, the financial backing that such organizations enjoy is unclear.

In addition, the foreign presence has outgrown the vague vision that guided the formation of the window organizations. Despite their complexity, the linkage organizations have been more successful than even the most optimistic projections for them. However, instead of serving primarily as channels of control and manipulation, to a considerable extent they have also become channels through which foreigners can penetrate to the core of the system. They inadvertently serve as Trojan horses through which the outside world can influence the core state apparatus.

Several factors produce this effect. First, the linkage organizations develop shared interests with their foreign partners. Indeed, the Chinese within the window organizations deliberately use the foreigners as a conduit to higher levels in China, since frequently foreigners have better access and influence in Beijing than the lower-ranking Chinese do. Second, since the Chinese in the linkage organizations frequently hold extended and close associations with foreigners, their values and aspirations often change as a result. Third, the linkage organizations, while handicapped in some respects, enjoy privileges in China that are denied to domestic institutions. For example, while joint ventures do not automatically enjoy the same access to the domestic market as their indigenous competitors (for example, in establishing service networks), they are subject to more favourable tax laws. As a result, some indigenous firms create subsidiaries in Hong Kong that then create joint ventures on the mainland. Such firms are treated as foreign rather than as local and therefore enjoy the tax breaks accorded to foreign investors. The result is the partial transformation of a domestic firm into a foreign one.

Fourth, many intermediary organizations have established a presence abroad not in order to invest their profits within the mainland as a foreign firm but in order to invest in Hong Kong or abroad, to improve access to foreign markets and to obtain capital in Hong Kong and foreign financial markets. Examples include CITIC, CNOOC and the Bank of China. This requires abiding by foreign laws and regulations, thereby affecting operations within China such as accounting procedures, financial practices, management practices and communication procedures and technologies. The portions of the core state apparatus with which these agencies deal, such as the Ministries of Finance and Foreign Trade, the People's Bank and the state petroleum industry, must then adjust their practices. The dynamics that have been unleashed are the inescapable consequences of China's entry into the global economy.

Institutional Vulnerabilities in the Economic and Societal Spheres

As noted earlier, as the core state apparatus has retreated from its total penetration and control of the economy and society, various legal, semi-legal and illegal formal organizations and informal associations have emerged. An underground economy of uncertain size exists outside the current reach of the state. People, communications, material goods and capital cross China's borders beyond state control. Tens of millions of recent urban migrants are not incorporated into the state structures. And, as seen when the Falungong sect used e-mail, fax and cellular phones to mobilize thousands of its faithful for a demonstration outside Zhongnanhai, the new telecommunications and information technologies enable non-state actors to undertake activities that the state presently can not easily monitor and control.

The leaders' instinct is to suppress the illegal organizations, but there are limits to their capacity to do so. One constraint is that local officials might not comply with the directives to crack down on these organizations. In the case of the Falungong, some members of the military and the public-security forces and their family members are Falungong practitioners. Criminal gangs that deal in narcotics and entrepreneurs in private enterprises that pirate intellectual property use bribery to secure the protection of local officials. In yet other cases, local officials may simply prefer to tolerate and not report violations of laws restricting certain organized activities in the knowledge that local officials are evaluated, in part, on their record in maintaining social order; an increase in reported crimes—even if solved—may prompt a negative rating in this category.

Repression is not the only response, however. Through various reforms the leaders are attempting to extend the reach of the central state so as to incorporate and give voice to potentially discontented elements in society. These measures include improving methods of tax collection (on the one side to alleviate the burden of local taxes on the peasantry and on the other to reduce the magnitude of the underground economy); expanding government activities at the township level; opening up channels through which aggrieved citizens can address complaints and seek remedies for state malfeasance; increasing the transparency of Party and government procedures; and, as mentioned above, promoting elections of village government leaders, strengthening parliamentary bodies and showing greater state tolerance for approved non-governmental organizations.

While these measures are not trivial, they seem inadequate to the challenge at hand. Will the state be able to meet the yearnings of the populace to participate in the political decisions that affect their lives? Will the populace enjoy adequate means to articulate their interests? Will the state be able to regulate markets effectively, keep crime and corruption within bounds and meet expectations for the provision of social services? The answer to these questions are presently unclear. Any solutions might require the extension of the state into the space its prior retreat has created, but in a fashion that responds to popular demands rather than suppressing and controlling them.

An additional challenge that the leaders face is to regulate the interactions among sectors of an increasingly eclectic polity: between the core apparatus and the organizations and associations in the economy and society; between the core apparatus and the linkage organizations; and between the linkage organizations and the economic and social associations. (These interactions are among the most interesting and ill-understood developments in contemporary Chinese politics.) Thus far, the leaders have been slow in addressing these complex issues, with the result that the interactions mostly occur outside a regulatory framework.

Conclusion: Responding to the Forces Producing Institutional Change

This analysis prompts more questions than answers as one speculates about the future of the Chinese political system. How imperative is it for the leaders to remedy the various vulnerabilities of the current system? Can the system persist in the long term even though it increasingly lacks coherence? Do the leaders and the led require a vision or design to guide their institutional responses to the forces propelling them in new directions?

It may indeed be possible for China's leaders to cross the river stone by stone, to use one of their favourite metaphors, not only in the economic realm (where the metaphor was first applied) but in the political realm as well. After all, many political systems have muddled forward, with their leaders making pragmatic and incremental institutional adjustments in order to resolve problems as they arise. But we are inclined to believe that the forces buffeting the Chinese system are of such magnitude that incremental and ad hoc responses are not adequate. Rather, an underlying consensus must be forged as to the ultimate political objectives and the strategy for getting there. Otherwise, there is a danger that the centrifugal forces acting upon China could ultimately prevail. The lessons of the Soviet Union and Indonesia stand as stark warnings about the fate of authoritarian political systems whose leaders postpone the challenge of coherent political reform on the assumption that a heavy reliance on a coercive apparatus will enable them to avoid difficult choices.

EIGHT

Jiang Zemin's Style of Rule: Go for Stability, Monopolize Power and Settle for Limited Effectiveness

Lucian W. Pye

It is a peculiarity of political systems that usually it is easy to characterize past systems but hard to generalize about current ones. The international system during the Cold War can now be easily described, but we have trouble explaining post-Cold War world politics. So it is with China: the essence of Mao's China was clearly the sovereignty of ideology, Deng's China is captured by the concepts of pragmatism, reform and opening, but it is not easy to find the right few words to characterize elite politics in Jiang Zemin's China. There are too many contradictory trends, and it is hard to tell which will be the historically decisive ones and which ephemeral.

As a start, however, we can certainly say that political stability has been the overriding objective of Jiang Zemin's leadership circle. Their guiding principle is the belief that preserving the Party's monopoly on power is in China's highest national interest; and needless to say, they also agree that preserving the Party's domination is also in their own best personal interest. Jiang Zemin was selected the nation's leader in the heat of the Tiananmen crisis when the Party elders thought that chaos was about to take over and everything the revolution stood for would end in anarchy. Jiang's marching orders were to bring order to the country.

Operationally this emphasis upon stability has meant that the leaders want governing to be a normal, routine matter—nothing dramatic or extreme. They want government to be just the practice of management, not of politics, for that would involve contending over values. In contrast to the constant drama and excitement over new departures that characterized the Mao and Deng eras, public affairs under Jiang has become a prosaic, almost colorless activity.

This quality of dullness seems to match Jiang's public persona, a technocrat who, on becoming the Party chief just after Tiananmen, was scornfully called the

"Flowerpot" because of his "penchant for standing around and looking pleasantly idle".[1] Chinese political gossip has been filled with deprecating jokes about Jiang's presumed limited abilities. The truth, however, is that as a private person Jiang Zemin is remarkably lively and talented for a Communist cadre: he speaks excellent Russian and workable English, German and Romanian—he likes to quote from Shakespeare and Goethe. He grew up in a scholar's household, surrounded by books, paintings and music; he plays the piano and enjoys listening to Mozart and Beethoven.[2] Culturally, he is probably the most sophisticated of all of China's Communist leaders.

In a peculiar way, this contradiction between Jiang the public man and Jiang the private man parallels the contradiction between the dullness of official politics under Jiang and the lively pockets of activity in the private sectors of the Chinese economy and even more dramatically in some intellectual spheres, especially in China's think tanks and arts and cultural communities. Urban China abounds with activities that seem to contradict the repressive spirit of official politics.

The leadership's overriding concern for stability and for holding onto power has inhibited bold initiatives. The prosaic goal of just managing a government would seem easy enough to achieve, especially when coupled with a willingness to use repressive means. China has all the essential institutions of a modern government, and there is no shortage of technocrats to staff the various offices. Moreover, the Chinese public is strongly supportive of stability, for as we all know a key feature of the Chinese political culture is a deep-seated fear of *luan* or chaos. Governing on automatic pilot therefore should be easy.

Yet, it turns out that effective, routine government has in fact been surprisingly difficult to achieve. The elaborate and well-defined structures that make up the Chinese state and Party bureaucracies fail somehow to provide the leadership with the necessary tools for maintaining Beijing's control in all fields. Throughout the maze of offices, all staffed with reasonably skilled personnel, there seems to be a huge gap between policy and performance, between purpose and accomplishment, and between intentions and results. In some areas state policies are effectively enforced, but in many fields the leadership's will does not command.

It is, of course, true that Mao was constantly frustrated by his inability to make the state and Party bureaucracies operate according to his wishes, and under Deng the lack of coordination in what was manifestly an authoritarian system led Kenneth Lieberthal, Michel Oksenberg and David Lampton to characterize China

[1]   Bruce Gilley, "Jiang Zemin: The Great Autopilot", *International Herald Tribune*, 27 September 2000.

[2]   Lee Kuan Yew, *From Third World to First: The Singapore Story: 1965–2000* (New York: HarperCollins, 2000), pp. 63–7.

as having a "fragmented authoritarian" government.[3] The offices, bureaus and departments that Deng's leadership circle controlled were supposedly quite prepared to make decisions on command, but in practice the various *xitongs* or hierarchies of command often failed to work together to produce coordinated rule.

In an effort to gain better coordination in policy implementation the central authorities increasingly came to employ informal bureaucratic arrangements by creating special leadership small groups (*lingdao xiaozu*). These task force arrangements were generally formed by seconding officials from the separate bureaucratic hierarchies that might have some responsibilities for the problem that needed addressing. Some of the leadership small groups were temporarily formed to manage a crisis problem, but others deal with enduring problems, as for example, the National Security Small Leadership Group (*anquan lingdao xiaozu*) and the Taiwan Affairs Leading Group. Different problem areas have thus had their special leadership small groups, but coordination has remained a continuing problem. Indeed, in some respects the proliferation of leadership groups has only added to the bureaucratic confusion and thus further weakened the authority of the Centre.

Under Jiang Zemin the erosion of authority has become considerably more serious. People occupying what the formal organizational charts designate as the pinnacles of power can issue stern orders, but the responses are often surprisingly limited. Those who are supposed to have high authority cannot always command the actions of those who ultimately implement state policies. Much actual authority in China now seems to operate in violation of the laws of hierarchy in that the devolution of power to the lower levels of the bureaucracy and to local officials has made them the organs of effective power. At times, and in certain areas, the will of the centre can prevail, but not always; hence power is "fragmented" and governing is erratic.

This process of devolution was started under Deng Xiaoping, and it was initially greeted as a healthy development because the system he inherited was overly centralized, with too much power in the hands of his predecessor, the fabled Helmsman. With Jiang Zemin, however, power has flowed downward and out from Beijing to such an extent that the centre has increasingly less control over the initiatives of local authorities, even in such critical areas as tax collection.

Under both Mao and Deng, there were ongoing debates and factional divisions because the decisions at the centre were sovereign commands. With Mao the stakes in the factional clashes were extremely high, often life and death matters.[4] Under Deng's rule the tensions in elite relations were significantly

---

[3] Kenneth Lieberthal and David M. Lampton (eds), *Bureaucracy, Politics and Decision Making in Post-Mao China* (Berkeley: University of California Press, 1992).

[4] For a detailed analysis of factional politics under Mao, see Jing Huang, *Factionalism in Chinese Communist Politics*, (New York: Cambridge University Press, 2000).

reduced, and losers did not always suffer any severe punishment. The topmost officials were, however, still operating in terms of their factional alignments, which continued to define how power was distributed within the elite.

Under Jiang the standards of civility have been raised even further. But more importantly, there has been a significant change in the structure of the factions. Instead of factions being defined by the personal relationships among the top leaders, the devolution of power to the localities has shifted the alignments so that the figures at the centre are associated with different geographical locations. We now have the Shanghai or the Sichuan or other provincial cliques. Under Mao and Deng, those at the capital had command of the resources that were used to consolidate the different factions. With Jiang those who are closer to the ground level are the ones who hold command over resources, and thus geography counts.

The informal *guanxi* ties that hold the factions together, however, do not necessarily follow the bureaucratic lines of authority, as they will often jump from one *xitong* to another, thereby exaggerating the "fragmented" character of politics. Even when the linkages are institutionally clear, the supposed "clients" down the line will often ignore the wishes of their "patrons" because the powers of the centre are so manifestly limited. In contrast, under Mao the intense bonding within the factions meant that a few cryptic code words would be enough to galvanize all the members into concerted action. This shift in the structure of the factional bases of informal politics has exposed the limits of Beijing's authority over the entire country. Those who occupy the topmost positions can continue to pretend that they are all powerful, but increasingly they have to hold back on issuing demands and orders for fear of exposing their own impotence. Those at the lower levels who now find that they command effective power are content to leave undisturbed the pretensions of their honoured superiors at the centre.

What has happened is that China has reverted to its great tradition of government by feigned compliance. Imperial China possessed impressive bureaucratic structures for governing, but in practice the emperor never had the total power he pretended to have as the Son of Heaven. He and his ministers could issue their imperial decrees, and all below would pretend to tremble and obey, but, at the operating level, local authorities would do what made sense. No overt challenges needed to be made, for everyone simply hailed the greatness of the emperor and pretended to be in compliance, and thereby stability was ensured.

That system worked well over the centuries, but it will not do today. With modernization, China's economy and society have become more complex, with ever greater functional specialization and social differentiation creating an ever-richer diversity of interests. The traditional Chinese social order was relatively simple and could be held together by the bonding spirit of Confucianism. Social gradations existed, but they were easily legitimized by the moral authority of Confucian orthodoxy. Now, however, the advancement of specialization in modern China has resulted in the emergence of increasing numbers of strong and competing special interests.

In this critical realm of interest formation, social change has outstripped changes in political attitudes. The political instincts of the elite are still those appropriate to a traditional and highly homogeneous society. The leaders still feel that by stating what they view as best for China, they have articulated the interests of everyone. They do not know what to make of the emergence of such a diverse range of special interests. As we observed in an earlier chapter, historically in China any assertion of private interest was seen as dishonourable and inherently immoral. To articulate one's own interests openly was seen as a display of crass selfishness.

Today, the elite still believe that once they have defined the collective good, everyone should suppress their different interests and accept what the leaders have judged to be for the good of the whole country. Jiang Zemin's main contribution to the Party's ideological thought, the Three Representations, holds that the Party should "represent" the interests of the "whole people". Thus, the leadership continues to ignore the reality that coastal China has significantly different interests from interior China, that urban interests are not those of the countryside, and that economic progress is producing an increasing division of interests. The leadership decided, for example, that it would be a good thing for China to join the World Trade Organization, for membership would give the country dignity and status in the eyes of the world, but they have been slowly forced to face the fact that membership will, in the short run, produce a host of losers who could become troublesome opposition elements.[5]

The persistence of traditional cultural attitudes about the treatment of private interests, when combined with the devolution of power to the localities, has contributed to the shocking spread of corruption under Jiang. Traditionally, the Chinese imperial system operated under the principle that the law-making processes of government were the sole preserve of the elite—the emperor and his ministers. As the wisest people in the realm, they should be totally free to design policies and laws. If elements of society had any problems with the resulting laws, they should seek redress at the law-enforcement level. Rules should not be so rigid as to cause undue difficulties, and interests could come to the enforcing magistrates and seek a special dispensation on the grounds that while they agreed that the emperor's rules were wise and just, maybe in their own particular case an exception might be made. And to compensate the official for his trouble, there was often a "small gift".

In contrast, in modern societies the legitimate realm for the political play of interest groups is precisely the law-making process—the belief that if the law damages one's interest, one should seek to change the law. Under the rule of law there is an absolute taboo against tampering with the law-enforcement process, for to do so is by definition corruption. The current Chinese leadership is happy to preserve the traditional Chinese view that it is taboo to try to influence the law-making authority, for that is the domain that they are most anxious to preserve for

---

[5]   For a general analysis of the implications of China's membership in the WTO, see the special issue of *The China Quarterly*, No. 167, September 2001, and in particular Joseph Fewsmith's contribution, "The Political and Social Implications of China's Accession to the WTO", pp. 573–91.

themselves. In the less differentiated, more simply structured traditional Chinese society there were not enough variations of interests to overload the pressures applied to the law-enforcement processes. But with the emerging, modern Chinese socioeconomic system, the pressures seeking exceptions has grown exponentially, and so has the feeling that corruption is running rampant.

The persistence of other traditional Chinese attitudes toward authority has also greatly weakened the capabilities of the central bureaucracy. The current leadership still operates with the notion that authority should be able to issue orders and expect nothing less than docile obedience. Modern governance, however, requires authority figures to engage in all manner of entreating, appealing, soliciting and imploring in order to win over others. In the Chinese tradition, such beggar-like behaviour was seen as inconsistent with the dignity associated with authority. China did not have a tradition of chivalry, of gallant knights winning fair ladies, and thus there is no basis for honouring the arts of courting and beseeching. Hence cajoling and winning over others has been seen as inconsistent with the requirements of dignity that lie at the heart of the Chinese notion of authority.

In a government with limited capabilities and limited ambitions beyond maintaining stability and encouraging the economy to grow, relations among the topmost figures have been more tranquil than at any time in the history of the PRC. Jiang has been able to preserve elite consensus by speaking in general terms in support of the economic reforms and, when necessary, mouthing a bit of leftist rhetoric to pacify those with lingering memories of revolutionary glory. The leaders are aware that there is a need for some political reforms, but no-one in the inner circle has wanted to rock the boat by calling for the degree of radical political reform that would shake up the system, and probably benefit the country, but might also bring an end to Communism. To a man, the leaders agree that Gorbachev had been foolish, and that they would never allow what happened to the Soviet Union to happen in China. They deeply believed that Milosevic in Yugoslavia was their soul-mate who knew how to hold firmly onto power, so when he recently crashed they must have felt shocked. The elite are more than ever committed to the proposition that they must hang together or they will hang separately.

None of Jiang's peers had the stature to challenge him. Zhu Rongji, the recognized economic specialist, was given thankless tasks in pushing the transition from central planning to a market economy, and with the inevitable difficulties, his reputation became a bit tarnished. But good soldier that he is, he loyally works on, content with his assigned role. Li Peng, supposedly Jiang's nemesis, is enough of a realist to know that, even if he might wish it, there is no turning back the clock to more ideologically focused politics. So he seems content with his role of heading the National People's Congress. Under Mao and also under Deng, leaders in the position of Zhu Rongji and Li Peng would have had to seek security by covertly building or strengthening a factional base. With Jiang, concerns about personal security can be taken care of by performing well one's assigned responsibilities.

Moreover, the fragmented character of the governing structure also means that it is hard for anyone to build up a power base strong enough to challenge Jiang. In 2002 Jiang is due to bow out as president, and probably hopes to play the role that Deng created of "listening to government from behind the curtain". As of now it appears unlikely that there will be a fight over the succession, for the putative top spot is not all that attractive. Jiang will therefore probably be replaced by Vice President Hu Jintao, a colourless figure whose advantage is that he is 16 years Jiang's junior. Official leadership will not go to anyone of Jiang's generation because he has proclaimed that the consensus of the leadership is that there should be no-one in the Politburo over 70, unless he is "indispensable".

In contrast to Jiang's cautious and placid approach to governing, developments in the Chinese economy and society are turning increasingly tense and indeed potentially explosive. Rural unrest has been rising at an alarming rate as peasants rebel at paying the fees and taxes that the local authorities keep raising.[6] Graft at the local level has also hurt Beijing, as the siphoning off of tax revenues is depleting the national treasury. The well-known problems with the state-owned enterprises and the state banking system continue to resist solution. The list of problems is much longer, but the concluding point is that everyone is aware that the country's troubles could be a lot worse, and thus Jiang is seen as something of a hero for staving off the easily imagined worst-case scenarios.

As China's problems accumulate and intensify, the leaders will naturally tend to have differing views as to what should be done. In contrast, however, to Mao's time and even Deng's, when policy "debates" drew the lines of combat between the factions, now under Jiang's more restrained governing style there is less likelihood of disruptive clashes, as the leaders are more inclined to defer to each other's areas of competence and responsibilities. They have learned to live and let live over differences about policy issues. Under Mao policy debates provided the pretext for factional struggles, and thus it was usually the symbolism and not the content of the policy issues that counted. Under Jiang the substance of the policy issues matter, but since there are no easy solutions, the participants are less inclined to become passionate about alternatives. The overriding concern for stability and for holding onto power will probably be enough to hold in check any drift toward disruptive clashes. It is significant that even Jiang's 2001 proposal that entrepreneurs and thus capitalists be admitted to Party membership, a direct violation of the tradition of the Party representing the proletariat, did not produce much of a reaction from the Leftist remnants in the Party who once were the

---

6   Thomas P. Bernstein and Xiaobo Lu, "Taxation without Representation: Peasants, the Central and Local States in Reform China", *The China Quarterly*, No. 163 (September 2000), pp. 742–63. The government admitted that the total number of peasant and worker demonstrations in China in 1999 was about 100,000, and the figure for subsequent years would be higher. For an analysis of the role of protest in modern Chinese political history see Elizabeth J. Perry, *Challenging the Mandate of Heaven: Social Protest and State Power in China* (Armonk: M. E. Sharpe, 2001).

guardians of correct ideology. (The fact that the Party already has some 10,000 entrepreneurs who joined when they were working in state enterprises or the government no doubt blurred the issue.)

Jiang Zemin's ultimate place in history will of course depend on the outcome of China's groping transition from totalitarianism. It is likely that he will be able to muddle through the remainder of his time in office, counting on the Chinese tolerance for approximate solutions, for *chabuduo* outcomes. More importantly, the hundred years of turmoil the Chinese people have had to live through, from the collapse of the Qing through the decades of Mao's erratic and violent rule, has left the national psyche somewhat traumatized.[7] Consequently, the Chinese public is now highly risk averse, and thus psychologically unprepared to engage in the confusion and clashes that would probably accompany any national debate over what should be a new basis for national identity and state legitimacy. The mood of the country is thus consistent with going slow over any grand political issues.

However, even if Jiang Zemin escapes disaster on his watch, there will be many who in time will hold him accountable for not having boldly pushed through the political reforms that would have given China a new basis of legitimacy to replace the discredited ideology of Marxism-Leninism-Mao Zedong Thought.[8] Thus, while Jiang's style of governing has in general matched the national mood, and has provided a popularly welcomed period of political stability, history may ultimately render a more critical judgment of his role, by holding him accountable for not having taken the risk to undertake the needed political reforms.

Yet, to be fair, Jiang has been caught in a predicament. He has been a prisoner of the fact that his legitimacy as China's leader stemmed directly from the suppression following the Tiananmen massacre, and thus, even had he wished to, he has not been in a good position to champion significant political reforms. Jiang's hypersensitivity about regime legitimacy was manifested in the way in which he personally took the lead in incriminating and suppressing the Falungong. More than a dozen years of relatively tranquil rule has not relieved his anxieties about the stability of the Party's rule.

---

[7]   Lucian W. Pye, "Traumatized Political Cultures: The Aftereffects of Totalitarianism in China and Russia", *Japanese Journal of Political Science*, Vol. 1, No. 1 (2000), pp. 113–28.

[8]   The appearance in early 2001 of the Tiananmen Papers, which exposed the leadership's decision-making during the crisis, provided evidence of a leak by elements in the Chinese leadership who would like to see significant political reform.

NINE

The Changing Form and Dynamics
of Power Politics

Lowell Dittmer

Although the pace and drama of political change at the pinnacle of the Chinese political system have gradually faded, the "centre", consisting at its core of the half dozen or so Han Chinese males who constitute the Politburo Standing Committee, remains the pivotal actor in Chinese politics, the "principal" of which all other organs are "agents". Despite the modification of nomenklatura rules, the advent of local rural multiple-candidate elections, and other facets of decentralization and devolution that have coincided with the reforms, the central Party-state has taken care to preserve its leading role. This is particularly so since Tiananmen and the collapse of European communism, which provided what the elite considered an object lesson in the dangers of excessive, precipitate liberalization.

China's central leadership sees itself in a threatened but commanding position, an elite for itself as well as in itself. Reform would continue, but it would be guided by different priorities: the central state apparatus, under the leadership of the Communist Party, must be strengthened, not weakened, by reform. As a consequence, the Central Committee, in a resolution of September 1994, declared that all state organs must subordinate themselves to the leadership of the Communist Party. The result has been that the differentiation between Party and state (*dang zheng fenkai*), which Deng engineered in the 1980s, has been replaced again by a reassertion of Party-state integration (*dang zheng yitihua*). Despite important structural reforms in the National People's Congress, all key leadership positions remain under the sway of the Party. Powers over civilian and military personnel appointments and periodic rotations of officials have enabled the Centre to check the autonomy of regional organs. While the Party's future is by no means assured, the vigorous organizational reassertion of the "leading role of the Party" stands guard against the nightmare scenario unveiled at Tiananmen and locks in the continued relevance—indeed, dominance—of the central Party elite up through its "fourth generation" leaders.

My purpose in this chapter is to reconsider those areas that have conventionally comprised the most important components of central power politics, and to ask whether and in what ways their structure and function have changed. The chapter examines the form and function of the central political arena, the functional distribution of power, the apparent demise of informal politics and its displacement by more formal arrangements, the perenially tense issue of leadership succession, and the role of mass publics.

The Central Political Arena

Let us begin by constructing a model of leadership policy making and dispute resolution in the Party. During the Maoist era, informal small groups within the elite pursued their preferences through a tactically flexible Realpolitik, without much regard for constitutionally ordered formal political arrangements except as a matter of window dressing. Using policies and ideological lines as a rationale, the true goal of factional maneuvering was the maximization of power. This was realized through periodic sweeping purges of factional opponents, beginning at the top and ricocheting through the hierarchy, creating vacancies for appointing one's own protegés. Although opinion is divided among experts about whether the systemic goal of this incessant power struggle was equilibration of a factional balance of power or rather a game to win or lose all, there is agreement that the struggle was incessant albeit spasmodic in its intensity.

Elite conflict often involved mobilizing an influential constituency that might selectively express or withhold its support. Which constituencies and groups of leaders were influential varied according to circumstances: the PLA's power tended to wax during national security crises such as the Sino-Soviet border dispute or the various Taiwan Strait embroilments, whereas the ministries might be expected to have greater leverage during severe economic setbacks such as the "three bad years" of 1960–62. As the national economy has made its transition from central planning to the "socialist market", the influence of the State Planning Commission (now called the Commission on Economic Planning and Development) and the heavy industrial and energy industries closely linked with it have waned, while that of the State Economic and Trade Commission and the Ministry of Foreign Economic Relations and Trade (and their bureaucratic dependencies) has increased.

The question of who had power was also complicated, as we observed in Chapter 1, by the fact that power came in two disparate forms: "authority" (*quanli*), based on the political leverage inherent in one's formal rank and post in the Party, state and military hierarchies; and political influence (*shili*), made up of the personal relationships (*guanxi*) that a political actor accumulates in the course of a career. Whereas the exercise of these two forms of power is to some extent fungible and even mutually complementary, Chinese Communist politics was considered distinctive in the degree to which the locus of power in the formal and informal realms sometimes diverged. This has remained the case for a considerable time after Mao's death. Thus Deng Xiaoping could re-emerge from political oblivion after having been purged in 1976 to mount a successful challenge to the new leader, Hua Guofeng, even though Hua monopolized supreme formal power in the Party, state and military hierarchies. Deng subsequently could also assemble an ad hoc collection of cronies from the margins of official power to unseat two heirs apparent, Hu Yaobang and Zhao Ziyang, who formally outranked him.

If this description approximates the political situation in former times, to what extent has it gradually been rationalized during the era of reform and opening up? We can subdivide this question into three issues: the role of ideology, the existence of distinct and discrepant formal and informal realms, and the dynamics of factional struggle.

It is often alleged that leadership has become less "ideological" in the post-Mao era. That is correct but somewhat misleading. Certainly it is true, as the left wing of the Party leadership has indicated most clearly, that the "broad masses" have become less responsive to the leadership's ideological guidelines, having been afflicted since the advent of reform policies with a "crisis of faith". At the same time, the Party-state attaches undiminished importance to its Caesaro-Papist monopoly over politically relevant information, endowing itself with the right to tell everyone what to do to be in step with historically correct socio-economic development and firmly to silence anyone who says otherwise. It may be useful to distinguish here between the decline, "death" or "extinction" of ideology as forecast by Daniel Bell, Francis Fukuyama or Ken Jowitt, and what Tang Tsou has referred to in this book (and elsewhere) as the "deradicalization" of ideology. Starting very early in the reform program, virtually all of the radical hallmarks of Maoist ideology—the cult of personality, class struggle as the "key link", revolutionary "politics in command", and the priority at crucial historical junctures of the ideological superstructure over the socioeconomic base, as well as radical transformations of "relations of production" through the collectivization of agriculture, the nationalization of industry and the repudiation of markets and almost all private property or interests—were refuted or strongly qualified. Thus the version of Marxism-Leninism-Mao Zedong Thought that emerged from the watershed Sixth Plenum of the 11th Party Congress in June 1981 after nearly two years of controversial retooling had been made far more compatible with the functional requisites of industrial modernization than the Maoism of the Great Leap and Cultural Revolution. It had been rendered comparable in this respect to the belief systems of other successful late-industrializing countries (e.g., Kemalism in Turkey, Taiwan's Three People's Principles). In the mid-1990s even marketization became part of the official ideology.[1]

But the leadership has made clear that deradicalization does not imply completely abandoning the use of ideology as a political tool in fashioning central policy, as indicated by its consistent enforcement of Deng's "Four Cardinal Principles", by the 1989–91 campaign against "peaceful evolution", and most recently by the attempt to cultivate "Jiang Zemin theory" via his "three emphases" and "three representations" campaigns. Nor has the use of ideology disappeared as a factional rallying call in high-level policy debates, as in the 1978 campaign in support of "practice as the sole criterion of truth" and against "whateverism", the 1981 campaign in support of a "socialist spiritual civilization" and against "spiritual pollution" and "bourgeois humanism", the 1991–92 inner-Party quest to define and defend the essence of socialism against the wave of "peaceful evolution" felt to have

---

[1]   See, for example, Stephen B. Herschler, *The Sources of State Power in Communist China: Ideology and Organization in a Socialist Market Economy*, PhD dissertation, Political Science Department, University of Chicago, 2000.

subverted socialism in Eastern Europe and the Soviet Union. The tenaciously successful careers of Hu Qiaomu and Deng Liqun testify to the abiding utility of ideological symbol-manipulation skills in building a factional base. The political use of ideology has been more discrete than during the Maoist era, in the sense that the losing faction is no longer publicly exposed and linked to the repudiated ideological position, as was Liu Shaoqi in 1969 or Lin Biao in 1973–74. But this represents not the displacement of ideological absolutism by cognitive pluralism (the "correct" position is still unequivocally affirmed) so much as an increase in intra-elite political civility (about which more below).

A distinction between formal and informal realms is normal and universal, but it is the degree of the hiatus, and the political incompatibility between the two, that has characteristically distinguished elite CCP politics. Although the discrepancy is as old as that of the CCP as an organized group,[2] since Liberation in 1949 it has been given formal sanction, as in the permission granted to elite "opinion groups" to "retain their opinions" in the aftermath of contrary elite decisions, or the functional distinction between the first and second "fronts" of the leadership (the first front being concerned with mundane managerial problems, the second front with long-term ideological issues). Having thus been granted organizational license, informal loyalty groups (latent factions) would quietly form, discuss and coordinate their positions on the issues of the day, bursting into public prominence as manifest factions or conflict groups only during periods of crisis when the leadership's line suddenly became vulnerable.

Thus elite policymaking and dispute resolution are both more institutionalized and less transparent than in the Maoist period, but purges continue to occur and all available clues indicate that informal policy groups ("factions") continue to function, though they no longer call each other names in public. It has sometimes been said that the tendency to create such informal groups has diminished in the reform era as a consequence of the institutionalization of formal bureaucratic arrangements, and there is perhaps some truth in this observation. Yet at the same time the formation and utilization of informal groups has been emancipated by reform. There has certainly been an institutionalization of formal leadership arrangements in the post-Mao era, as indicated by the proliferation of rules and legal codes, the greater frequency and regularity of formal meetings (which now proceed almost like clockwork), and the greater security of cadre tenure. Whether this has entailed a reduction of informal group activity it is really hard to say, because institutionalization has also entailed a plugging of "leaks" and a decline in transparency. But any reduction of informal group activity seems doubtful. At least we know that serious elite disagreements continue to erupt, and that they are still resolved through purges (i.e., zero-sum fights) with approximately the same frequency.

---

2   For example, the charismatic Li Lisan never held the position of Secretary General, though he was clearly the dominant Party leader from 1928 to 1930. Xiang Zhongfa officially held the post.

This is clear from a crude comparison of the Maoist and the post-Mao eras, both of which are now of about the same duration. During the Maoist era the major purges were of the Gao Gang-Rao Shushi group in the early 1950s, Peng Dehuai's grouping in the late 1950s, the Liu Shaoqi-Deng Xiaoping "bourgeois reactionary line" during the Cultural Revolution, and the Lin Biao clique in 1970–71. During the post-Mao era, the major purges were of the Gang of Four in 1976 (followed by their public trial in 1980), the removal of Hua Guofeng and the "small gang of four" in the early 1980s, the demotion of Hu Yaobang in January 1987, the purge of Zhao Ziyang and Hu Qili in 1989, the purge of the "Yang family clique" in 1992, the arrest of Chen Xitong and the reorganization of the Beijing municipal Party committee in 1995, and the "involuntary retirement" of Qiao Shi in 1997.

It should be noted that purges still typically sweep up clusters of leaders, though the size of the cluster has diminished appreciably since the sweeping purges of the Cultural Revolution decade or the 1957 anti-Rightist movement. Despite the greater frequency and regularity of formal meetings, a consensus to purge a leading member is still first generated informally and then given an official stamp of approval in more formal meetings: thus the decision to demote Hu Yaobang was reached by an ad hoc work conference in January 1987 and not properly formalized until the 13th Party Congress many months later. Although Zhao Ziyang's fall was more promptly formalized by a Central Committee plenum in late July 1989 (partly in response to criticisms of the constitutional irregularity of Hu's demotion),[3] we now know that Zhao had been removed from the corridors of power and placed under house arrest by informal but authoritative decree about a month earlier. Continued reliance on informal decision-making behind the veneer of formally institutionalized proceedings, plus curtailment of the phase of public criticism that previously legitimized purges and provided an ideological rationale (however implausible), have made the purge mechanism even less transparent than during the Maoist era, when mass movements occasionally penetrated the public-private barrier that normally kept information about inner-Party splits hidden from view. Elite policy-making and dispute resolution today are both more institutionalized and less transparent, but purges

---

[3]   The resolution to accept Hu Yaobang's resignation was made at an enlarged meeting of the Politburo convened by Deng Xiaoping on 16 January 1987, comprising, in addition to the 18 members and two alternate members of the Politburo, four members of the Secretariat, 17 members of the Central Advisory Committee, two members of the Central Discipline Inspection Committeee and "other comrades". Bo Yibo, a nonmember of the Politburo, presented the summary of complaints. From the perspective of constitutional law, the meeting was problematic with regard to the following points: (1) according to Section 3, Article 21 of the Party Constitution, the Secretary General should convene the Politburo, not Deng Xiaoping, at that time still a Politburo member but holding no leadership position within it. (2) According to Section 3, Article 20, the Secretary General should be elected (or deposed) only by a plenary session of the entire Central Committee. See Zhongmei Yang, *Hu Yaobang: A Chinese Biography* (Armonk, NY: M. E. Sharpe, 1988), pp. 156–7.

continue to occur and all the available clues indicate that informal policy groups continue to function, though they no longer call each other names in public.

What about this has changed and what has remained the same? There are at least two key differences. First, the emphasis on institutionalization has entailed greater security of cadre tenure, entailing a reduction of negative sanctions against factional intrigue. Most post-Mao purge victims have been spared the public humiliation that many officials apparently used to dread as much as incarceration. Thus, whereas an elite faction during the Maoist era coalesced to enhance its members' mutual security or personal power, the reduction of sanctions has permitted factions to coalesce in support of shared policy interests as well. In this sense the mobilization of informal elite policy groups has been emancipated, though the groups being mobilized may be becoming more openly policy oriented and less "factional". This is not to say that the old bases for factional ties (*guanxihu*) no longer exist. Hu Yaobang's group was based on an "old school tie" dating back to Hu's leadership of the Chinese Communist Youth League before the Cultural Revolution; Chen Yun's more conservative grouping coalesced around control of the State Planning Commission and the Central Committee's Propaganda Department; and Jiang Zemin's "mainstream faction" was built during his long tenure in Shanghai. There is apparently a loose grouping, led by Hu Jintao, sharing engineering credentials from Qinghua University, while Chen Xitong's *Beijing bang*, no less an "independent kingdom" than Peng Zhen's municipal Party committee in the 1960s, allegedly coalesced in support of corrupt personal interests.

Second, although elite purges have not declined in number, they have declined in intensity. Since the arrest of the Gang of Four in 1976, there have not been any sweeping purges in which a pattern of contagion is established and pursued on the basis of an imputed "line" of shared ideological dissent and conspiratorial association. And, with a few problematic exceptions, purges no longer culminate in the death or physical incarceration of the target (as in the cases of Gao Gang and Rao Shushi, Liu Shaoqi, and Lin Biao).[4] What accounts for this apparent abatement of intensity? Purges during the Maoist era sometimes partook of a self-consciously demonstrative use of violence in order to establish public markers of what was wrong and what was right, as a result of which a purge would typically be followed by mass criticism movements and struggles against pre-set quotas of "capitalist roaders" and other "enemies of the people". That means the struggles were deliberately escalated to a Beijing Opera level of emotional intensity. (Thus during the Cultural Revolution the idea was purveyed that a targeted person should be

---

[4]   The exceptions include the Gang of Four, all of whom were incarcerated and all but one of whom (Yao Wenyuan) subsequently died in prison; Beijing Mayor Chen Xitong, who was jailed on corruption charges arising from the Shougang scandal, and his deputy mayor Wang Baosen, who committed suicide before he could be apprehended. These cases differ from the cases of Gao-Rao or Liu Shaoqi in that the victims were sanctioned on criminal rather than political charges. To what extent their criminal indictments were influenced by political considerations is a relevant issue that cannot be dealt with in this brief compass.

thought of as a rat crossing a street.) Such mass movements were in principle discontinued during the early reform era. Elite purges have in practice as well become less polemicized and more tightly contained, losing at once their socially disruptive character and their dramatistic, pedagogical utility. In fact, the ouster of Yang Shangkun and of Qiao Shi was given no official explanation other than retirement.

Although the death of Mao thus marked an important watershed in elite Party politics, the real heyday of informal politics, in a sense, was not the Maoist but the Deng Xiaoping era. Mao certainly had his "favourites", who owed their political preeminence purely to the favour of the Chairman. But the organization of politically signifiicant small groups during the Maoist era was oriented around ideological "lines", not around personal charisma. Sometimes, as during the early years of the Cultural Revolution, this resulted in vertical coalitions of elites and mass constituencies with transregional ideological linkages having little factional coherence based on either geographic links or primordial associations. (To be sure, the two were not necessarily mutually exclusive: for example, Jiang Qing was after all Mao's wife, Chen Boda, his former secretary, Kang Sheng and Jiang Qing both stemmed from the same village in Shandong, and so forth. The "Gang of Four" coalesced informally, even conspiratorially, initially as favourites without portfolio, after June 1966 as members of a "small group" with power based on their links to Mao, not their official positions. But in principle ideology overrode considerations of personal loyalty, as illustrated by the way Mao ruthlessly decimated the old Hunan gang.)

The Deng regime, on the other hand, having repudiated ideological polarization in favour of pragmatism, bureaucratic rationalization and reform, paradoxically found itself obliged to rely on ad hoc, informal expedients to achieve reformist results. This began with Deng Xiaoping himself, who remained true to his word and never laid claim to the highest of Party or state posts, preferring to amass informal power even as he divested himself of formal positions, with the result that he was able to manipulate the Tiananmen crackdown without even having a seat in the Politburo. The policy of leadership rejuvenation initiated by Deng and Hu in 1984–85 resulted in the wholesale retirement of senior cadres who possessed great informal power to nominally impotent "advisory" positions, from which Deng could, however, recall them in cases of perceived emergency. The famous "sitting committee" of retired oligarchs thus provided the quorum to decide upon the purges of Hu Yaobang and Zhao Ziyang and the suppression of the 1986 and 1989 mass protest movements.[5]

---

[5]   According to *The Tiananmen Papers*, the decision to forcibly disband the protests proceeded in two stages: the decision to invoke martial law on May 20, and the decision to "clear" the Square on the night of 3-4 June. When the Politburo Standing Committee stalemated on 17 May over Deng's proposal to invoke martial law (Li Peng and Yao Yilin in favour, Zhao Ziyang and Hu Qili opposed, Qiao Shi abstained) the issue was submitted to Deng, in accord with a secret inner-Party resolution. At this point Deng and the elders joined the Politburo Standing

Only during the era of Jiang Zemin, it would seem, did the formalization of politics truly begin to come into its own. This was partly attributable to the demise of the senior revolutionary veterans who practised footloose informal power: Deng Yingchao and Hu Qiaomu died in 1992, Wang Zhen and Li Xiannian in 1993, Chen Yun in 1995, and Deng Xiaoping in 1997. Even before then, the institutional base of this consultative elite, the Central Advisory Committee, was rather surprisingly eliminated on schedule at the 14th Party Congress in 1992. The reforms instituted during Deng Xiaoping's tenure, such as term limits and pre-mortem retirement, also kicked in, resulting for example in the 1992 retirement of Wan Li and Bo Yibo and the rotation of Li Peng from his premiership to a less powerful National People's Congress chairmanship. The introduction of the principle of term limits also provided a pretext for the elimination of Qiao Shi in 1997 and for the scheduled retirement of Jiang Zemin, Li Peng, Zhu Rongji, et al., at the 16th Party Congress in 2002. The institutional innovation of retirement, unheard of among CCP elites before 1985, has taken effect with such speed and efficacy that in contrast to the unsinkable Deng Xiaoping after his second purge in 1976, Yang Shangkun, Yang Baibing, Wan Li, Qiao Shi, Liu Huaqing and Zhang Zhen seem to have vanished into political oblivion without a trace.

Finally, Jiang Zemin himself has felt no compunction (and has shown great stamina) in accruing all available executive positions for himself, thereby eliminating any possible discrepancy between formal and informal power based upon false modesty. The informal realm has become weakened to the extent that even though Jiang Zemin has long been known to be interested in assuming Deng Xiaoping's role of senior political ventriloquist upon Jiang's announced retirement in 2002 and 2003 from his major positions atop the Party and state, it is not clear that he will succeed in doing so.[6] Formal power having become such an apparent political powerhouse, we turn now to a closer consideration of its distribution.

The Distribution of Power

At the pinnacle of political power today we find a coterie of several dozen men, each of whom can be expected to have a portfolio providing access to at least one formal hierarchical apparatus and a wide-ranging informal base (though not as broad or deep

---

Committee to form a super-majority, which decided to blame Zhao and Hu for the failure of martial law and (on 27 May) to replace Zhao with Jiang Zemin. The order for the PLA to clear the Square was arranged by Deng and Yang Shangkun, as chair and vice chair respectively of the Central Military Commission. All these decisions were ratified post hoc by a Central Committee Plenum in June.

[6] According to the rule devised to facilitate the retirement of Qiao Shi at the 15th Party Congress, Jiang Zemin must step down as Party General Secretary at the 16th Party Congress in around October 2002. He must step down from the state presidency at the 1st Session of the 10th National People's Congress in March 2003, according to the State Constitution (Arts. 60, 61, 79, 93). His term as chair of the Party's Central Military Commission elapses simultaneously, but there is as of now no legal retirement regulation governing Party positions.

as their predecessors in previous leadership generations). In the course of overseeing their various responsibilities and servicing their constituencies, these men may see their interests diverge on any number of policy issues.

Members are distinguished subtly but quite precisely in the distribution of their ranks and power, as frequently indicated by the sequential listing of their names in communiqués and press reports (although ranking may sometimes be disguised by listing them in order of brush strokes), the seating arrangements in group photographs or portraits, in public meetings or on the Tiananmen reviewing stand, and the order in which they walk down the street in a public procession. Because these niceties are so fastidiously observed, they are categorized as "protocol evidence", on the basis of which not only rank order but alignment on key policy issues may be inferred (based on who attends meetings convened to launch a new policy initiative, who stands next to whom, and so forth).[7]

Members of the Politburo are formally deemed equal in keeping with the norm of "collective leadership". They hold equal voting rights within the Politburo, although according to available accounts most sessions do not culminate in a formal vote. In terms of actual power they are unequal, more or less, depending on age and experience, depth and breadth of their career backgrounds, the relative stature of their contributions and the functional needs of the political system at a particular stage. Inequality is assured not only by the unequal distribution of such attributes but also by their recruitment pattern to the leadership elite. This is cooptive and permits individual incumbents to vouch for new recruits, who are then expected to remain beholden to them. Inequality during recruitment may be exacerbated by the leadership's distribution of portfolios and perquisites of office, which is an enormous discretionary power. In particular, the chair may completely undercut an opponent by denying him a portfolio or discouraging his attendance at meetings, as was the case with Hu Yaobang from January 1987 until the spring of 1989, when he suffered a heart attack while attending his last Politburo meeting.[8]

Except in a clear case of an "antagonistic contradiction", such extreme tactics are now eschewed. The chair's normal political strategy is to distribute political

---

[7]   Protocol evidence is hardly definitive. Thus a leader's absence from an official event may imply death or serious illness, temporary loss of favour, purge or even the voluntary withholding of support for the event being sponsored, as in the case of the disappearance of Deng Xiaoping supporters between February and 8 April 1976, when Deng was being publicly criticized for his alleged "reversal of just verdicts", or the lower profile of the radicals between 9 and 20 April 1976, when Deng was permitted to retain his Party membership.

[8]   Hu Yaobang reportedly attended no central meetings at all from his deposal in January 1987 until the meeting on education at which he collapsed fatally in April 1989. Pang Pang, *The Death of Hu Yaobang* (Honolulu: University of Hawaii, Center for Chinese Studies, 1989), trans. Si Ren. During the Cultural Revolution, major purge victims were excluded from the flow of official documents, and Liu Shaoqi's telephone line was even cut in January 1967. Although it is unclear how many such strictures are still imposed on, say, Zhao Ziyang since 1989, certainly the security forces still play an important role in isolating any designated target.

resources and perquisites fairly even-handedly, in keeping with the functional division of labour and the norms of collective leadership. But he is apt to form offsetting coalitions with weaker or more supportive members, playing balance-of-power politics to prevent anyone from accumulating sufficient power to challenge him. Thus Mao in the last decade of his life formed a coalition with the weaker but personally loyal Gang of Four against the more senior members of his leadership team—Zhou Enlai, Ye Jianying and Deng Xiaoping.[9] Deng's reliance on the relatively weak and junior Hu Yaobang and Zhao Ziyang can be perceived in the same light, as can Jiang's acceptance of the most junior member of the Standing Committee, Hu Jintao, as his heir apparent, followed in the fall of 2000 by an attempt to promote the personally loyal Zeng Qinghong to counterbalance him.

It has been suggested that in the course of generational transition there has been a shift from a monolithic to a more collegial distribution of power. A safer inference at this point, it seems to me, would be that the distribution of power varies cyclically in the course of succession, typically beginning with a relatively equal distribution of power at the outset but tending over time toward a more hierarchically skewed distribution as the paramount leader eliminates rivals and accumulates hegemonial status. Thus Deng Xiaoping began by sharing power with Ye Jianying, Li Xiannian, Chen Yun and Bo Yibo, but in the course of the 1980s succeeded in monopolizing power to the extent that he was able to coordinate the Tiananmen crackdown almost autocratically once Zhao Ziyang and Hu Qili had been swept aside. Jiang Zemin in the early 1990s was considered a somewhat lacklustre member of a third-generation cohort that included Chen Xitong, Qiao Shi, Li Peng and Zhu Rongji, but by the end of the 1990s the second generation had died or been retired (viz., Bo Yibo, Wan Li, Liu Huaqing and Zhang Zhen), and Jiang had reduced his own cohort to three (Jiang, Li and Zhu), among whom relations are said to be "complicated".

All other things being equal, one would expect alignments to be closely correlated with the seniority-skewed distribution of power, and this indeed seems normally to be the case. But under exceptional circumstances, a member of the younger generation may split with his patron over a decision that is damaging to his own political base. These disagreements are particularly explosive because of the "face" involved. This was true of Zhao Ziyang in the early spring of 1989, when the elders were pressuring him to crack down on the intellectuals who had signed three petitions in support of the release of "political prisoners" and were also pressuring Zhao to curb Shanghai's *World Economic Herald* (which was supporting the dissident intellectuals). Zhao personally opposed the Shanghai Party's handling of

---

[9]   Mao's shifts became ever more mercurial as he saw his own death approach, and quotations revealing his disenchantment with the Gang were found and published posthumously. Though these citations are credible, statements indicating his disenchantment with the moderates could no doubt also be found. In any event, it is hard to see how the Gang could have survived without Mao's support, in view of the swiftness of their political demise as soon as he left the stage. It is quite conceivable, I think, that he was disillusioned with both the left and the moderates, perhaps even consciously playing them off against each other.

the *Herald* issue, but was overruled by Deng and the Party elders. Two months later, Zhao exacerbated the split among the political elite by opposing the suppression of the student protesters in Tiananmen Square, who reciprocated by aiming their barbs at Li Peng and Deng Xiaoping.

Separately, there may be several separate patron-client networks within the Politburo, giving rise to distinct factional interests. During the period culminating in the Tiananmen crackdown, for example, there were three power centres: the Deng Office (*Deng ban*), the Joint Office of the State Council and the Central Military Commission (*lian shu ban*), and the Party Centre. The Deng Office, operated by Secretary Wang Ruilin, was where the final decision to crack down was made. During this critical period, the Joint Office, coordinated by Yang Shangkun and Li Peng, functioned as an information hub and as an executive arm for Deng and the back-stage veterans. The Party Centre under Zhao Ziyang and Hu Qili coordinated negotiations with the students, but became virtually powerless after the decision to impose martial law was announced on 19 May. These three power centres did not share all the information they received from their respective sources. The Deng Office, for instance, cut off contacts with the Party Centre after 15 May, while the Joint Office leaders tried to manipulate decision-making by skewing their reports to the back-stage elders.

Since the 15th Party Congress, at least three distinct hierarchical networks have emerged, emanating from Jiang Zemin, Li Peng and Zhu Rongji. This troika seems to have an essentially cooperative relationship with no basic ideological cleavages, but they do have different policy priorities and predispositions and have reportedly quietly disagreed internally over such issues as how to handle the Falungong.

Central meetings are where the informal and formal powers contest their interests and sort out policy lines. All sorts of meetings are held by the Party elite, some of them according to more or less fixed schedules (these were frequently thrown into disarray by the storm and stress of the Maoist era), some named after the place they were held (the Lushan conference, or the annual summer meetings held at the Beidaihe resort), some distinguished by the number of attendees and some referred to merely as "working meetings" or "Party life" meetings. Although held for different purposes, they all provide a means—really the sole legitimate means—for mobilizing constituencies and sorting out policy decisions. The rules of procedure for such meetings appear to be rather flexible, but the chair can usually control the outcome by holding preparatory meetings, setting the agenda, choosing the participants (sometimes packing the meeting with non-members in an "expanded" session) and the speakers, and deciding whether to call the question.[10] A meeting's outcome is normally quite predictable, as we may adduce from Mao's outrage on those rare occasions when it was not, such as the July-August 1959 Lushan plenum when Peng Dehuai submitted his modest criticisms of the Great Leap, or the 2nd

---

[10]   Kenneth Lieberthal and Bruce Dickson, *A Research Guide to Central Party and Government Meetings in China, 1949–1986* (revised and expanded edition) (Armonk, NY: M. E. Sharpe, 1989).

Plenum of the 9th Party Congress in 1970 when Lin Biao unexpectedly nominated Mao to the position of chief of state after the latter had disclaimed any interest in the post.

Meetings are normally predictable not only because such elaborate pains are taken to prepare for them, but also because if any hint of dissensus should become evident in the course of these preparations, the meeting is typically postponed—as was the 9th Party Congress due to the 1966–68 upheaval (thus allowing the 8th Congress to sit for 13 years), or the scheduled 4th NPC because Lin Biao's unanticipated chief-of-state proposal derailed preparations (allowing the 3rd NPC to sit for ten years). Such lengthy delays in the convening of constitutionally mandated meetings (once every four years) may be interpreted as a sign of difficulty in ironing out preliminary consensus, just as the deferred adjournment of a meeting (usually scheduled to last a week to ten days) signals the eruption at it of unexpected disagreement (neither of which will ever be publicly admitted). The reform era has been characterized by much tighter discipline in the scheduling of meetings, closing this window of interpretation of their issue agenda. The last concerted analysis of central meetings was made by Lieberthal and Dickson, still based largely on materials made public by Red Guards during the Cultural Revolution.[11] Since that time the number and venue of central meetings has proliferated, but although their actions are catalogued in yearbooks and other reference books and the memorial literature may provide some information on content there has not been a concerted analysis of this important dimension of elite politics since 1989.

Conflict

On those relatively rare occasions when senior leaders have basic, irreconcilable disagreements, these are resolved through "inner party struggle", a process commended in the canonical literature as a way of mobilizing mass support for new policy agendas. Although conflict does have positive attributes, it is also notoriously disruptive and a high stakes gamble with devastating penalties for losers. Such confrontations may vary in length from a few months to several years, but nevertheless tend to undergo a certain process. During the Maoist era, this typically consisted of three stages: factional polarization accompanied by open debate; the resolution of the issue; and the political removal and possible destruction of the defeated opponents.

1. The first stage is one of open but usually Aesopian debate, in which the issues remain somewhat confused and the identities of the main protagonists remain masked. This was true even during the savage polemics of the Cultural Revolution, when Liu and Deng were referred to as only the "top Party person in authority taking the capitalist road", and the "No. 2" Party person in authority taking the capitalist road. The June 1959 confrontation at Lushan between Mao and Peng Dehuai was preceded by at least half a year of tolerance of public criticisms of the more radical

---

[11]   Ibid.

Leap programs.[12] In the post-Mao era, the arrest of the Gang of Four was preceded by a period of 18 months of uninterrupted public polemics. The political demise of Hua Guofeng and his retinue was preceded by the "criterion of truth" campaign and by Democracy Wall, the only known instance of spontaneous grassroots mobilization that Deng unequivocally endorsed. The summer of 1986 was one of unprecedented intellectual openness launched by the 30th anniversary of the "double hundred" (let a hundred flowers bloom, let a hundred schools of thought contend), the 20th anniversary of the publication of the "May 16 Circular" (which inaugurated the Cultural Revolution), and the 10th anniversary of the end of the Cultural Revolution. The public debate ultimately culminated in the student protest movement that helped to precipitate Hu Yaobang's demotion. The Tiananmen crackdown of course climaxed the most broadly based instance of mass "blooming" since the 1966–68 Cultural Revolution.

2. A "settling of accounts", or resolution of the issue, takes place at a meeting or series of central meetings, always culminating in a Central Committee Plenum or even a Party Congress. But the first meeting is pivotal: the July 1959 Lushan Plenum that resolved the "contradiction" between Mao and Peng Dehuai, the 11th Plenum of the 8th Central Committee that formally launched the Cultural Revolution, the Third Plenum of the 11th Central Committee in December 1978 when Deng Xiaoping's ascendancy was confirmed, the January 1987 Party Life conference that decided (with dubious legality) upon the demotion of Hu Yaobang, the 4th Plenum of the 13th Central Committee that resolved to dismiss Zhao Ziyang, the 1st Plenum of the 14th Central Committee that decided upon the removal of the Yang family clique, and so forth. These meetings are high-stakes encounters in which the usual rules of parliamentary procedure are often disregarded—thus the winning side often packs the house with informal supporters in an "expanded" session. Prior to the formal meeting, a "special investigation committee" may be named to sift through relevant documentary material (in Hu's case, this consisted of Bo Yibo and Zhao Ziyang; in Zhao's case, it consisted of Yang Shangkun, Li Peng and Qiao Shi). Depending on the attitude of the accused and other relevant circumstances, verdicts may range, in ascending order of severity, from forced retirement, to an ouster from all Party and government posts, to eviction from the Party, to a trial with criminal charges. In some cases (e.g., Gao Gang and Rao Shushi, Lin Biao, the Gang of Four), death or imprisonment may be the ultimate outcome, but this is usually not part of the formal sentence nor a welcome development from the leadership's perspective (e.g., Liu Shaoqi's death was not even officially acknowledged until nearly a decade later).

3. Resolution is followed by the removal and in the most extreme cases the political destruction of the target. The latter option may include three sub-phases: the imposition of military curfew, dispersal of the target's political base, and public degradation ceremonies. The military may be called in to surround and place the

---

[12] See *The Case of Peng Teh-huai 1959-1968* (Hong Kong: Union Research Institute, 1968); also Teiwes, *Politics and Purges*, pp. 384–411.

target under house arrest even during the initial phase of open debate, as was the case during the Cultural Revolution, when Liu and Deng were placed under house arrest in early 1967.[13] This pattern of troop movement and military intimidation was also clear in the case of the arrest of the Gang of Four.[14] No evidence of military intimidation against Hua Guofeng has been found, but in the January 1987 demotion of Hu Yaobang, Deng announced a full military alert, and Peng Zhen surrounded Beijing with the people's armed police that he commanded.[15] In Zhao Ziyang's case the PLA of course became more extensively involved than at any time since the Cultural Revolution, and their movements in May-June 1989 have been fully documented.[16] Although generally assumed to be mobilized primarily for crowd control, it is clear that their marshalling on 20 May must have been highly intimidating to Zhao's supporters within the political elite, underscoring the elimination of any further consideration of the peaceful resolution option he had come to stand for.

Disarming the target's power base must proceed with considerable delicacy, usually using divide and conquer tactics, buying off those who can be bought and purging those who cannot. Lin Biao's power base was particularly formidable,[17] and Mao moved against him with all the deliberation of a military campaign.[18] Similarly, Deng began to maneuver against Hua quite soon after Hua had approved Deng's second comeback. After the dismissal of Wu De and Chen Xilian and their replacement by Deng supporters, Deng proceeded to reduce further the number of

---

[13] These may include a shift of the Beijing Garrison Commander or Military Region Commander, transfer of officers or troops associated with the target out of the capital, replacement of the public security minister and vice-ministers, and the transfer of loyal troops into the capital arena. See Michael Pillsbury, "Patterns of Chinese Power Struggles: Three Models", unpublished paper prepared for the University Seminar on Modern China, Columbia University, New York, March 27, 1974.

[14] There may have been fears that the target might mobilize military counterforce: Mao Yuanxin allegedly attempted to mobilize 10,000 troops in the Shenyang Military Region based on his position as political commissar, and there were apparently unsuccessful intrigues to arm Shanghai's urban militia. See Andres D. Onate, "Hua Kuo-feng and the Arrest of the 'Gang of Four'", *China Quarterly*, No. 75 (September 1978), pp. 540–66.

[15] Yang, *Hu Yaobang*, pp. 156–8.

[16] See for example Harlan Jencks, "China's Military After the Beijing Massacre", *Air Force Magazine*, November 1989.

[17] Lin's Fourth Field Army loyalty group dominated five provinces, held a strong position in two, a weaker position in six others, whereas 14 provinces were under the control of his opponents and two under the domain of the Cultural Revolution left. (Juergen Domes, *China After the Cultural Revolution*, pp. 130–1.)

[18] "Summary of Chairman Mao's Talks to Responsible Local Comrades During His Tour of Inspection" (Mid-August to September 12, 1971), in Michael Kau, *The Lin Piao Affair: Power Politics and Military Coup* (White Plains, NY: International Arts and Sciences Press, 1975), p. 62.

Hua's men on the Politburo Standing Committee from seven to three to two while increasing the number of his own supporters from seven to 13 or 14.[19]

Public degradation ceremonies are designed to prepare public opinion for the invocation of severe sanctions against a once-honoured leader, and to discredit a slate of unwanted policies by associating them with the target. The polemics are no longer Aesopian but quite explicit, and "black material" discrediting the target may be researched and published. The Cultural Revolution critique of Liu Shaoqi, in the most notorious case of this type of public destruction, became explicit after the 12th Plenum of the Eighth Party Congress in the autumn of 1968, some two years after his fall. The criticism of Lin Biao did not become explicit until some ten months after Lin's death in the September 13 Incident of 1971.

After the public trial of the Gang of Four, the central leadership has tended to omit the phase of public degradation. Hua Guofeng retained a token seat on the Central Committee. Hu Yaobang remained an inactive member of the Politburo until his death. Even the unrepentant Zhao Ziyang was not subjected to public polemics, trial or eviction from the Party, and he has subsequently been seen on Beijing's golf course. Only Chen Xitong, the corrupt Beijing Party secretary, remains in prison, his case aggravated by a criminal indictment. The price, however, is that these targets remain live symbols of the crises that laid them low: thus Hu Yaobang's political reputation was salvaged and could be put to political use in the spring of 1989 by critics of the leadership; and letters allegedly written by Zhao Ziyang endorsing a reversal of verdicts on Tiananmen appeared in public during the 15th Party Congress and on various other occasions.

A purge nonetheless is still normally followed by some policy backlashes: the early post-Mao purges of the Gang of Four and then Hua Guofeng were followed by a rightist tilt, and the later purges of Hu Yaobang and Zhao Ziyang by a lurch toward reaffirmation of Maoist values. Yet with the exception of Chen Xitong, who has become a vehicle for anti-corruption rhetoric, policy backlash seems to have vanished from the Jiang Zemin era purges, perhaps because they involved no mass mobilization on behalf of some policy object lesson. Jiang thus felt quite free to coopt Qiao Shi's reform constituency and policies upon Qiao's forced retirement.

Succession

Succession is both important and problematic in all Communist Party states.[20] China has had only two realized successions, yet six of the PRC's major elite splits (Mao vs. Liu, Mao vs. Lin, Hua vs. Deng, Deng vs. Hu, Deng vs. Zhao and Jiang vs. Qiao Shi) have at least implicitly involved succession arrangements. In most other

---

[19]   Jurgen Domes, *Government and Politics of the PRC: A Time of Transition* (Boulder: Westview, 1985), p. 163, as cited in Schattschneider, p. 124.

[20]   See Myron Rush's classic analysis in *Political Succession in the USSR* (New York: Columbia University Press, 1965), and *How Communist States Change Their Rulers* (Ithaca: Cornell University Press, 1974).

Communist systems the typical pattern is one of postmortem succession, in which the incumbents defer clear succession arrangements during their lifetimes, as in the successions to Stalin or Brezhnev. In such circumstances, the incumbent does not make premortem arrangements out of fear that the heir apparent might seek to succeed him pre-emptively, as occurred in the cases of Ulbricht in East Germany, Khrushchev in the Soviet Union or Gheorghiu-Dej in Romania. The Chinese in contrast are distinctive in the strength of their attachment to premortem succession arrangements. One consequence is that in China the period of susceptibility to succession disputes lasts throughout the incumbent's tenure.

Although succession is apt to precipitate a relatively raw form of power struggle, concerned only with who rules, not how or what for, the implications are apt to be profound and long-lasting in terms of policies as well as power. There are at least two schools of thought about its implications: one is that succession incapacitates the system (the "succession crisis" school), and the second is that succession renews and invigorates the system. The scenario of a succession crisis implicitly assumes an unresolved postmortem succession, with the system paralyzed by indecision, rift and deadlock, as every major issue presupposes an answer to the moot question: who decides? Having just emerged from one oppressive incubus, the surviving members of the Politburo are not eager to throw themselves beneath another, and the leadership finds itself torn between fear of renewed tyranny and the need for strong leadership. Until such a leader emerges, decisions can be arrived at only through a process of circuitous and time-consuming consultation and compromise known as "collective leadership". While the leadership under these circumstances becomes at least temporarily more consultative, even pluralistic, the system tends to stagnate.[21]

Valerie Bunce and, with some important qualifications, Philip Roeder, argue in contrast that succession crises stimulate political innovation rather than paralyzing the system's capacity, as young and more imaginative successors seek to consolidate a new regime with policies designed to attract a politically significant constituency.[22] Thus succession in socialist countries is an opportunity for change analogous to electoral turnover in bourgeois democratic systems.

There are certain similarities between these two succession theories—both agree that succession tends to be followed by a return to strong personal rule—but for Bunce a strongman poses the danger of stagnation (as the competitive impetus for innovation is removed), while for Myron Rush (and Roeder, departing from Bunce)

---

[21]   Rush, *Political Succession in the USSR*.

[22]   See Valerie Bunce, *Do New Leaders Make a Difference? Succession and Public Policy Under Capitalism and Socialism* (Princeton: Princeton University Press, 1981); and Philip G. Roeder, "Do New Soviet Leaders Really Make a Difference? Rethinking the 'Succession Connection'", *American Political Science Review*, Vol. 79 (1985), pp. 958–76. Roeder argues in contradistinction to Bunce that the innovative capacity of a new leader tends to be low, with the result that early years tend to be focused around consolidation, and reform is postponed until afterward.

the new monocratic leadership may be expected to proceed with whatever innovations were introduced to mobilize support in the winner's grasp for supreme power. In the Chinese case, only two of the six struggles that involved succession have been postmortem (Hua vs. Deng, 1976-81, and Jiang vs. Qiao, 1997). In these contests, the evidence appears to bear out Bunce most clearly in the first instance, for no sooner had Deng gained dominance than a series of boldly innovative programs and central endorsements for locally initiated experiments began to issue from the new leadership. In short, Deng did not consolidate his power before proceeding, but utilized reform as a way of consolidating his power. The case of the Jiang-Qiao split is more ambiguous, but it appears that Jiang moved to coopt Qiao's support for political reform rhetorically before pushing him out of the Politburo at the First Plenum of the 15th Central Committee. After pushing Qiao out, however, Jiang failed to follow through with much political reform, reportedly because he considered the socioeconomic situation too delicate.

The more typical Chinese pattern is a premortem succession crisis. What distinguishes a premortem crisis from a mere power struggle is that the incumbent has already manifested his intention to pass the torch, anoint an heir apparent and invest the latter with plenary powers. The incumbent then steps into the wings to think about more profound matters, always ready to reappear if needed, as in a monarchical regency. This arrangement often takes the form of two leadership "fronts", the first led by the regent, who looks after routine affairs, the second by the incumbent, who allows himself to be "kicked upstairs" to deal with long-range planning issues (and sometimes to nurse fragile health).

The first regency was established by Mao Zedong in the late 1950s, setting the stage for a premortem succession crisis that was to last for the next decade and a half. Deng made analogous arrangements with first Hu Yaobang and then Zhao Ziyang. The recurrent pattern for both Mao and Deng was for the incumbent to designate an heir, grow disillusioned with him over time as various inadequacies became manifest (among them a failure to consult with the incumbent), and then in a climactic episode to become sharply disappointed with some initiative undertaken by the heir and on that basis to kick him out and find a new favourite. Deng Xiaoping became disillusioned first with Hu Yaobang and then Zhao Ziyang, yet Deng redeemed the pattern somewhat by facilitating the smooth succession of Jiang Zemin (who was not his personal choice) without further equivocation. And Jiang in turn has indicated his interest in maintaining the same pattern, signaling his intention to step down to make way for the fourth-generation leadership at the 16th Party Congress in 2002 (along with all but two of his Politburo Standing Committee colleagues). Yet Jiang has also warned that the Taiwan issue will require the experienced hand of revolutionary veterans, suggesting his own interest in retaining the chairmanship of the Central Military Commission until that issue is resolved. While the basic dynamic is dyadic, other players may also play a role: any rival contender for power will find both the pretext and opportunity to climb aboard the regent's bandwagon, or to help sour the relationship between the incumbent and heir apparent in hopes of arranging another regency.

In contrast to postmortem succession, the systemic implications of this Don Juan pattern of premortem succession arrangements conformed to the Rush model during the Mao and Deng eras. There were conflicts of interest not only between the heir apparent and other potential successors, as in a postmortem succession, but also between the incumbent and his designated successor. The resultant pattern is one of stagnation in policymaking, in which innovation is inhibited and becomes difficult to institutionalize. The incumbent's innovations are tolerated but not vigorously implemented as those of a "lame duck", while innovation on the part of the heir apparent tends to arouse the suspicions of the incumbent. The graduated succession by Jiang Zemin avoided this dilemma in that Jiang simply avoided policy innovation during his regency, thereby avoiding the fate of Liu Shaoqi or Lin Biao—a pattern Hu Jintao thus far seems eager to emulate. Thus there has been some institutional learning, the successor having learned the value of forbearance, the incumbent the need to avoid costly course reversals. The transition has become smoother, stabler and less innovative. But perhaps the major lesson to date of the Chinese experience of successions has been the omnipresence and extreme sensitivity of the issue.

Mass Mobilization

Mass mobilization has played some role in at least four of the past six elite splits, those involving Mao vs. Liu, Hua vs. Deng, Deng vs. Hu and Deng vs. Zhao. The role played by the masses has generally been that of a dependent variable, in which the winning party seeks *post hoc* popular legitimation for personnel shifts and policy innovations. Yet mass involvement may also function as an independent variable, polarizing cleavages that might otherwise have remained latent by bringing the always delicate issue of "face" into play. One prominent pattern during the Maoist era, in addition, was for activists aligned to the Gang of Four to use the mass movement as a "free ride" to elite careers.

The major distinguishing feature of mass mobilization since the Cultural Revolution is that the initiative seems to have irretrievably slipped from elite control, responding to changes and opportunities in the socioeconomic environment rather than to elite policy initiatives. During the 1980s, it became possible to correlate mobilization with the economic cycle, augmented by incendiary incidents (creating a "cause" to rally around) and the presence of political entrepreneurs and symbolically appropriate holidays or anniversaries when mass activity is officially sanctioned. The Tiananmen protests of 1989, for instance, erupted during an economic downturn and were sparked off by Hu Yaobang's untimely death, galvanized by charismatic student speakers such as Wuerkaixi and Chai Ling, and escalated into a massive demonstration on the anniversary of the May Fourth Movement. Although such movements no longer provide a route for upward mobility, they still have an impact on elite incumbents, which may vary with the power and skill of the elites involved: Deng was able to exploit mass protests at the Third Plenum in December 1978, but neither Hu Yaobang nor Zhao Ziyang was able to do so in the autumn of 1986 and the spring of 1989, respectively.

A mass protest could occur either during a boom or a bust. If it occurred during a boom, there was less likelihood of a crackdown, because booms were typically periods of ascendancy for the "reform" faction, which disliked crackdowns on young reform supporters (moreover, a crackdown tended to have a chilling spillover effect on the economy). But the boom could trigger a countercyclical application of fiscal austerity that precipitated a hard landing, which might in turn trigger mass protest. Busts were conducive to renewed assertiveness by the more orthodox wing of the leadership, and any protest at this point was likely to precipitate a crackdown, as well as political trouble for any sympathetic elite reformers. Thus both the December 1986 and June 1989 crackdowns occurred during economic downturns precipitated by the use of countercyclical instruments to impose fiscal and monetary austerity. Thus GDP growth in 1986 was only 8.1 per cent, after growth rates of 14.7 per cent and 12.8 per cent in 1984 and 1985, respectively; GDP growth in 1989 was only 4 per cent, after growth rates of 10.9 per cent and 11 per cent in 1987 and 1988. Consumer Price Index fluctuations followed the same pattern.

Since Deng's last hurrah in 1992, China has been characterized by mass political apathy and economic stability. On the economic side, Zhu Rongji's 1993-94 financial reform seems not only to have achieved a "soft landing" but to have tamed China's business cycle, leaving in its wake a basically stable but deflationary economy with a gradually declining but still high rate of economic growth. The major concern accordingly shifted from a search for countercyclical tools to efforts to reduce industrial overcapacity and to compete for foreign investment via continuing industrial and financial reforms. On the political side, the sanguinary Tiananmen crackdown of 1989 seems to have had a lasting deterrent effect on nationwide mass movements, as the Chinese populace turned its attention exclusively to economic activities. The leadership, with its focus on "stability above all" (*wending ya dao yiqie*), in the context of growing social unrest, seemed essentially content with this depoliticization, though there has been some concern about mass indifference to politics (note Jiang's call to "emphasize politics").

Yet over time, this social contract has begun to fray. By the turn of the millennium, renascent unauthorized mobilizational activity had taken three forms. First, beginning in the late 1990s a meditational sect with a transendental Weltanschauung, the Falungong (or Falun Dafa), led by exiled charismatic leader Li Hongzhi, has been successful in mobilizing millions of followers to practice its exercise regimen, for which it claims supernatural efficacy. Although the sect (or "cult", in the regime's parlance) disclaims any political agenda, its adherents for a disconcertingly long period defied suppression with tenacious zeal.

Second, there has been an increasing incidence of urban and rural portest movements, whose agendas are localized, without any overarching ideological appeals, and often concerned with increasing bureaucratic corruption and social inequality. Finally, since permitting the publication in 1996 of *China Can Say No*,[23] which became a best-seller and was followed by a host of imitators, the government has sought to identify its own agenda with the upsurge of nationalism that such publications tapped. This was expressed, for example, in the anti-American demonstrations that followed the May 1999 bombing of the Chinese embassy in Belgrade. Such demonstrations, whose ferocity revealed unsuspected underlying

---

[23]   Song Qiang, Zhang Zangzang and Qiao Bian, *Zhongguo keyi shuo bu* [China Can Say No] (Beijing: Zhongguo Gongshang Chubanshe, 1996).

emotional tensions, have been carefully curtailed since then by the government. This indicates an elite awareness that xenophobic nationalism could quickly turn against the leadership on charges that the government does not respond to foreign provocation strongly enough. (This has been a current pattern among nationalistic demonstrators since the May Fourth Incident of 1919.) In sum, the initial post-Tiananmen civil quiescence has given way to renewed demonstrations of diverse types, under the pressure of growing social dislocations unleashed by increasingly painful economic reforms. The leadership thus far has been able to contain these unauthorized movements with a mixture of repression and controlled nationalistic catharsis and by maintaining a firm united front.

Conclusion

Certain recurrent patterns have become discernible that help us to understand the nature of the elite power game in China. One is that, now and perhaps for the foreseeable future, it is still men and not laws or ideas that govern China, and that their interpersonal behaviour tends to follow certain general rules. Thus it is possible to depict the overall warp and woof of elite politics and to clarify the choices and penalties at hand, even though we may not necessarily be able to predict which options the political actors will choose. If this conception is correct, it behooves us to focus on those institutional nodes where the pattern is most scrambled. One area of special sensitivity is clearly that of leadership succession. The Chinese preference for premortem arrangements, though designed to minimize uncertainty, makes succession more explosive by forcing the transition when all of the principals still have multiple live options. The issue of mass involvement has been so sensitive that in the post-Mao era the masses have been effectively excluded from elite decision-making and personnel transitions, despite a tradition of populism. Even so, the spectre of the "masses" continues to haunt elite political discussions.

China has matured and some observers have posited that the political system has made the transition from "strongman leadership" toward functionally integrated team efforts, from charismatic ideology toward technocracy, from ideological impulse toward rational calculation, from mass mobilization to stable institutions, all in accord with the Parsonian pattern variables. Although there are tendencies in this direction, signals are still mixed. Informed Beijing observers note that Jiang has exhibited no interest in ceding his strongman prerogatives, and beginning from a position as first among equals has taken every opportunity to strengthen his own position and diminish that of his rivals. The cumulative pattern has been impressive, as Jiang has triumphed over Yang Shangkun, Chen Xitong and Qiao Shi. As noted, these ousters have been more discreetly handled than under Mao, as the leadership has lost confidence in its ability to mobilize the masses without risking economic instability and scaring off flight capital. Thus the Jiang-Qiao showdown was no game to win all or lose all, in the sense that Qiao Shi obtained some concessions for playing by the rules. Even though Li Peng vetoed Qiao's choice of reformer Tian Jiyun as his replacement, Tian was permitted to remain vice-chair of the National People's Congress and a full Politburo member; and Qiao's protegé Wei Jianxing remained chair of the Central Disciplinary Inspection Committee, overriding Jiang's preference for Shanghai Party Secretary Huang Ju. With the exceptions of Zhao

Ziyang and Chen Xitong, all of the top purge victims have received the benefit of honourable retirement rather than ideological vilification or prison sentences.

Predictions of the advent of "collective leadership" following the demise of the charismatic generation of revolutionary veterans similarly seem to have been overstated. Although Jiang Zemin no doubt lacks the stature of Mao or Deng, that is like comparing Kennedy to Lincoln. His predecessors' charismatic brilliance is irrelevant to Jiang's bid to establish hierarchical supremacy over his own generation, at which he seems to have largely succeeded. Jiang's focus during his regency was on retaining his ascendancy, a process in which a high-profile policy resumé was a risk, even a liability. Since redefining political succession, Jiang has gone on to firmly establish his personal power, where his touch has been quite masterful, whatever the fate of his policy innovations. Many of the policies that observers have questioned on their merits, such as whipping up nationalism against the US, or leading a campaign against cults, have (thus far) been unqualified successes in enhancing Jiang's personal stature. The Jiang coalition has also succeeded in formulating and implementing an impressive series of reforms, including some, such as financial and tax reforms, that consistently eluded his revered predecessor.

The other side of the coin is that Jiang's leadership position depends upon the acquiescence of his colleagues. It is noteworthy that Jiang's nomination of trusted advisor Zeng Qinghong to full Politburo membership at the Fifth Plenum of the 15th Central Committee in October 2000 was reportedly rejected by the Politburo Standing Committee by a vote of five to two.[24] This is not necessarily to say that elite pluralism has usurped the role of *primus inter pares* in the Politburo. Zeng may be a special case, whose promotion was opposed for other reasons, including those having to do with Zeng himself. In general, the 15th Central Committee was able to maintain unity on most basic ideological and policy issues. But each vote must be carefully elicited by a *quid pro quo* tailored to members' particular interests, and Politburocrats are apt to resist naked power plays. Thus the dialectic between hierarchy and collegiality remains unresolved, a matter of constant negotiation and political tradeoffs.

It can also be said that the Party leadership as a whole is weaker than during the Mao or Deng eras, due to the attenuation of ideology as a guide to correct political action, the various unintended consequences of reform such as growing economic and social inequality, budget deficits, corruption, the decentralization of power and the advent of the market as an alternative source of political resources.[25] The Jiang regime has been intent upon correcting this decline in the role of ideology and in the effectiveness of central power since the early 1990s, but has found the effort difficult. For one thing, the necessary but much lamented post-Mao ideological

---

[24]   Willy Lam, "Not All the President's Men", *South China Morning Post*, 25 October 2000.

[25]   See He Qinglian, *Xiandaihua di xianjing: dang dai zhongguo di jingji shehui wenti* [Pitfalls of Modernization: Contemporary China's Socioeconomic Problems] (Beijing: Contemporay China Pub., 1997).

deradicalization has entailed a diffraction of Manichaean political morality into a spectrum suffused by grays, no longer permitting new and dramatic ideologically based policy initiatives.

In this more stable and bureaucratically permissive context, elite groups may combine in pursuit of policies that enhance their bureaucratic or economic interests, no longer impelled by the need, for their own security, to focus so exclusively on personal connections. And a convergence of factional interests with broader economic and even class interests in society is increasingly discernible, as illustrated by loosely coordinated responses to the gyrations of the economic cycle. The residual reform bloc, relying implicitly on the intellectuals and the young and the entrepreneurial for mass support, has tended to support fiscal and monetary stimulus, intellectual openness, and the decentralization or devolution of power to the grass roots; while the "leftist", more orthodox bloc, in support of fiscal and monetary austerity, centralization, greater distributive equity, and intellectual repression, relies upon beneficiaries of the socialist status quo—probably leaving the urban middle class split. While these are only latent tendencies at present, it is possible to envisage a gradual institutionalization of factional loyalty around different policy lines and social preferences, perhaps even leading eventually to a multiparty system. But China still has a long way to go to reach that stage.

TEN

Normal Politics with Chinese Characteristics *

Frederick C. Teiwes

"All politics is broken-field running".
—Chas Freeman[1]

"I tell you one thing, I've fought 100 battles already, I have seen a lot".
—Jiang Zemin[2]

In my chapter on elite politics under Mao and Deng (Chapter Three), I have argued that the post-Mao period saw an evolution toward "normal politics". This transition has gathered apace in the past half decade, in no small measure due to the passing of Deng Xiaoping, but more fundamentally to the quickening of the enormous changes in the polity and society that his policies have produced. Yet distinctive, and disconcerting, Chinese characteristics remain.

To elaborate on the earlier discuscussion in this volume, "normal politics" most fundamentally means that political leaders at the apex of an at least partially institutionalized system are beset with an enormous range of issues and pressures, without any dogmatic ideological compass to guide them. It means that leaders perform the function of aggregating diverse interests into a coherent, or not so coherent, program to satisfy various constituencies in order to maintain a policy thrust or to build support for an individual or a leadership group. Unanticipated problems are the stuff of normal politics, whether it be policies that fail to

* Discussions with and/or comments on a draft of this chapter by Chris Buckley, Joseph Fewsmith, David Goodman and Warren Sun are gratefully acknowledged, as is the support of the Australian Research Council.

[1] "Broken-field running" is a term in American football referring to a player dodging and weaving to avoid tacklers. The comment was made during an interview with Chas Freeman, formerly Director of Chinese Affairs at the US Department of State and more recently Co-chair of the US–China Policy Council.

[2] Jiang's outburst to Hong Kong reporters when questioned on his government's support for the reappointment of Hong Kong's chief executive, Tung Chee-hwa, 27 October 2000.

produce expected outcomes (often forcing a retreat from the desired objective), or more disorienting political challenges that require truly improvised broken-field running (one thinks of the Monica Lewinsky affair and the Belgrade bombing). It is a world of opponents, whether to specific policies or, usually in exceptional circumstances, to the leadership of a system's ranking individual. Leaders fight hundreds if not thousands of battles of various types, and the currency of power is results, or the perceived ability to achieve results.

The issue here, and one paradox of my earlier chapter, is not the existence of a strong leader who almost invariably gets his or her way—such leaders are largely compatible with normal politics. In democratic systems one thinks of Margaret Thatcher, in half-dictatorial systems one thinks of Lee Kuan Yew, and the reference point for us here is Deng Xiaoping. The exceptional case, of course, was Mao Zedong, the master of "abnormal politics". Despite some broken-field running in both the "good Mao" days of promoting Party unity and coherent policy, and in the weird and destructive period of his later years, the defining feature of Mao's rule was his ability—through fear, belief and loyalty—to get leaders, institutions and the populace to carry out, or at least accept, courses of action inimical to personal, group and national interests.

In contrast, although Deng never lost any battle that he undertook in the post-Mao period, he did aggregate interests, seek non-ideological results and zig and zag according to pressures and unanticipated developments. Certain instances, notably the "southern tour" of 1992, where a retired Deng bypassed the central leadership to go to the "masses" to advocate a deepening of reform, strained the notion of normal politics, but overall he skillfully used the enormous advantages that history and ability gave him to guide the system in the "normalizing" direction that he sought. He never dominated the system as Mao had, but whereas the Chairman's abnormal politics produced such severe damage that Mao's deepest wishes were quickly overturned after his death, Deng's strategic management left a legacy of results which, their deep contradictions notwithstanding, Jiang Zemin could only build upon.

In considering the elite politics of the Jiang era, it is necessary to examine the historical background shaping both the actions of Party leaders and the perceptions of outside observers, and I shall therefore review the salient trends from the Mao period onward. It is also necessary to reiterate the difficulty and tentativeness of the exercise. Simply put, to a very large extent current elite politics takes place in a black box, making key developments opaque to the outside observer and conclusions speculative. Nevertheless, some patterns are worth exploring.

"A Game to Win All", or the Pursuit of "Stability and Unity"?

In Chapter Four, Tang Tsou offers a powerful image of elite Party politics as a "game to win all", a model of contending forces at the apex of the system periodically engaging in political struggles where the outcome led one side to totally vanquish its opponents. Tsou's model is both subtle and complex, and often frustratingly elusive. Despite the life and death tone of a "game to win all", Tsou's bottom line appears to be a less drastic loss of political influence, never to be regained—at least in a major way—during an individual's lifetime. While finding this game deeply rooted in the violent history of 20th century China and the Party's own revolutionary traditions, Tsou was not a determinist, and at different periods, particularly in the mid-1980s, he held out hope that the game could be transcended as a more institutionalized polity developed. Overall, however, Tsou's model posits that repeated struggles to the finish between irreconcilable forces have been inherent in the Communist system.[3]

While Tsou's emphasis on such integral parts of Party tradition as upholding a correct line, vigilance against deviant ideologies and the obligation of obedience to a supreme or "core" leader correctly identifies factors conducive to harsh inner-Party struggle, Mao's legacy was more complex. Although his success as a revolutionary leader owed much to his ability to mobilize his forces against external enemies, it was also based on a program of Party unity and eliminating the excessive factional struggles that had previously weakened the Party. This is not to ignore the continuing importance of a "struggle culture", but it does assert that unity was a key factor in revolutionary success, consciously pursued by Mao well into the PRC period, and deeply valued by other leaders. The fact that Mao's ideological and perverse personal concerns drove him to undermine that unity from the late 1950s onward, with particularly vicious politics taking hold during the Cultural Revolution, only made Party unity even more precious to the elite, and this was the first order of business after Mao's death and the elimination of the "Gang of Four" in what truly was a "game to win all".

Contrary to conventional wisdom, the basic thrust of the immediate post-Mao period was to restore stability and unity within the elite rather than to begin a new power struggle. Unity demanded the return of Deng Xiaoping to the leadership, a matter fundamentally settled by the end of 1976 with Hua Guofeng's active support. Deng's pre-eminence within the post-Mao leadership, based on revolutionary status and obvious talent, emerged very quickly and was not contested. The events that undermined Hua's standing were not designed by Deng: in some cases such as the "criterion of truth" debate, the prime mover (Hu Yaobang) was friendly to Hua; in others—for example, the overambitious economic program of 1978—Deng was equally culpable but politically invulnerable. Moreover, throughout the period, even when, probably in mid-1979, he decided that Hua would eventually have to go, Deng placed great emphasis on Party unity. The politics was complex, but it was not polarized. As

---

[3]   The model is used by Joseph Fewsmith, one of Tsou's former students, in the chapter Fewsmith has written for this book. Fewsmith's "Introduction" to his *Elite Politics in Contemporary China* (Armonk: M. E. Sharpe, 2001) provides a discerning discussion of Tsou's overall construct.

Deng Liqun recently recalled, "The contradiction and struggle did not form into two opposing armies; that wasn't the situation then".[4]

The removal of Hua from the Party'chairmanship meant Deng's leadership was completely unambiguous, even if Hu Yaobang and then Zhao Ziyang formally held the number one position. Stability and unity remained a preoccupation of the leadership throughout the 1980s, but a preoccupation that coexisted with multiplying differences of opinion over the course of reform. Much of this was normal politics, as different interests brought pressure to bear on the presumptive number one who, like his colleagues, was expected to produce results or otherwise be removed. More than anything else, it was the failures of Hu and Zhao as politicians which explained their demise. As argued in my earlier chapter, Hu alienated some of the most important inner-Party constituencies. In Tsou's terms, he was too much of a partisan to play the centrist role of "struggling on two fronts" against the right and left that was required to overcome the tendency toward "games to win all". In the words of one of Hu's Politburo colleagues, his essential shortcoming was an inability "to unite the Party".[5]

In Zhao's case, ultimate failure coincided with deep divisions at the top over how to deal with the Tiananmen demonstrations of 1989.[6] The net effect was to emphasize once again the crucial importance of stability and unity. It is hardly surprising that, in the face of an unprecedented challenge to the regime, sharp differences emerged within the leadership over the appropriate response to the student occupation of Tiananmen. Whether this initially amounted to a "Party split", as later officially claimed, may be a different matter, even if Zhao's subsequent refusal to endorse martial law can legitimately be so characterized.

---

[4]   *Deng Liqun guoshi jiangtan, disance* [Deng Liqun's Speeches and Talks on National History, Vol. III] (Beijing: Zhonghua Renmin Gongheguo Shigao Bianweihui, 2000), p. 358. The conclusions in this paragraph are based on research for a projected multi-volume study, co-authored with Warren Sun, and tentatively titled *Cultural Revolution, Restoration and Reform in China: The Politics of Transition, 1972–1982*. Chris Buckley has made a major contribution to this project.

[5]   See Tang Tsou, *The Cultural Revolution and Post-Mao Reforms: A Historical Perspective* (Chicago: University of Chicago Press, 1986), Ch. 7. The Politburo member's observation, which was originally made *well before* Hu came under heavy pressure in 1986, was related by an oral source who heard it first hand.

[6]   Zhao's position had already been weakened in 1988 due to the backlash against his expansionist economic policies that contributed to runaway inflation. Although Joseph Fewsmith, in "Elite Politics", in Merle Goldman and Roderick MacFarquhar (eds), *The Paradox of China's Post-Mao Reforms* (Cambridge: Harvard University Press, 1999), p. 64, interprets Zhao's policy initiatives as due to fear of losing power, which led him to risk everything in a new "game to win all", the degree to which a conflict over economic policy reflected a wider leadership polarization is far from clear.

Although Li Peng had taken a hard line toward the students at the outset, and eventually became Deng's mouthpiece for martial law, it is unclear to what extent he obstructed Zhao's conciliatory approach toward the demonstrators after 4 May; indeed, as matters rapidly came to a head on 17 May, Zhao spoke *for the entire Politburo Standing Committee* in offering concessions to the students, and Li, however awkwardly, met with a student delegation on the 18th. Li's action may have been play acting as Deng was literally mobilizing the troops. But if student concessions had been made then or earlier, an outcome of a peaceful settlement and a strengthened position for Zhao was within the realm of possibility. Deng, I presume, was interested in a successful result that preserved the Party's power, even if this involved some concessions. Dare one say it, but perhaps those most guided by the tradition of "winning all" were the young students who, even in the reform era, were fully familiar with the images and rhetoric of heroic revolutionary struggle.[7]

Tiananmen relates to the issue of Party unity in another sense—how the events were interpreted by the elite. While I believe that Andrew Walder's argument that political instability arises when elite conflicts "are revealed outside the circle of top leaders" is misleading *when applied to the events of spring 1989*,[8] this was precisely the lesson absorbed by Party leaders during and after the

---

[7]   The above is to a large degree based on Tang Tsou, "The Tiananmen Tragedy: The State-Society Relationship, Choices, and Mechanisms in Historical Perspective", in Brantly Womack (ed.), *Contemporary Chinese Politics in Historical Perspective* (Cambridge: Cambridge University Press, 1991), especially pp. 303 ff. The influence of revolutionary propaganda on the students was vividly captured in Richard Gordon and Carma Hinton's superb documentary, *The Gate of Heavenly Peace* (1995), in a sequence where a student "security officer" deploys his "forces" in a carbon copy manner to the portrayal of a Communist officer in a civil war film.

The Tiananmen Papers, compiled by Zhang Liang, edited by Andrew J. Nathan and Perry Link (New York: Public Affairs, 2001), strengthens my interpretation of elite politics as falling short of a "game to win all" before 17 May 1989. It must be noted, however, that there are major questions concerning the authenticity of the *Papers*. While these cannot be resolved at present, the following can be said. In broad terms, the picture that this collection of documents presents is credible, in large part because it confirms what was already known. Many of the bureaucratic documents, which were fairly widely available, are clearly genuine. However, the crucial documents purporting to convey the content of high-level meetings and personal conversations of Deng, Zhao, Yang Shangkun and Jiang Zemin are suspicious. They may indeed represent the gist of what occurred at the exchanges depicted, but they are not credible as verbatim records. Whether they were edited and polished by official organs, or fabricated by the Chinese compiler on the basis of widely held understandings within Party circles, is uncertain.

[8]   See Andrew G. Walder, "Does China Face an Unstable Future? On the Political Impact of Rapid Growth", in Maurice Brosseau, Kuan Hsin-chi and Y.Y. Kueh (eds), *China Review 1997* (Hong Kong: The Chinese University Press, 1997). I do not quarrel with Walder's typically insightful overview that places politics above sociology as a determinant of political instability. Nor do I question that the elite differences which became apparent after

crisis. Believing that internal divisions had caused the situation to get out of hand, they concluded that leadership unity had to be rebuilt. In terms of traditional Party norms, the renewed importance attached to unity can be seen in the remarkable leniency shown in the immediate aftermath of the Tiananmen crackdown to the "losers" among the political elite, in a game assertedly involving "counterrevolutionary turmoil" and a "Party split". But more fundamentally, as the Jiang Zemin era unfolded, there has been a determination to avoid disruptive elite dissention. Stability and unity once again was a dominant objective, but now with a chastening warning of what might eventuate if differences were not contained. To put the lesson another way, "we all hang together or we hang separately".

While the 1990s clearly witnessed the conflicts of normal politics, with Jiang and his colleagues fighting more than a hundred battles, there was no real evidence of struggles over the status of the notionally supreme leader, Jiang, as the "core", or indeed over the position of his putative successor. The three cases generally regarded as examples of "power struggle"—the Yang brothers in 1992, Chen Xitong in 1995 and Qiao Shi in 1997—all come up short. The first case, involving President Yang Shangkun and his half brother, Yang Baibing, the head of the army's political department, was the most important, not only because Jiang's position was not fully consolidated and Deng Xiaoping's "southern tour" at the start of the year amounted to a rebuke of Jiang's stewardship, but also because the case seemingly did involve a significant challenge. But while much remains unclear, the challenge apparently did not threaten Jiang's status as Party leader. According to well-connected oral sources, the affair was a result of Yang Baibing's attempt to freeze Jiang out of military affairs on the grounds he was a novice. It was, they reported, settled when Jiang appealed to Deng on the basis that he could not function in his position as chair of the Party's Central Military Commission under such circumstances, and Deng intervened decisively on his behalf. If true, this indicates another political skill of Jiang's apart from his well-known centrism—a willingness to act boldly when significant matters are at issue.[9] In the event, the affair was settled by Yang Baibing's dismissal from his

---

4 May 1989 made settling the Tiananmen crisis much more difficult. I do believe, however, that political instability had arrived with the student movement's unprecedented challenge to the Party by late April, and it would have been difficult, although not impossible, for even a unified leadership to bring the situation to a satisfactory conclusion.

[9]   Other explanations of this affair by interviewees in China suggest that Jiang's position as Party leader was not at issue. One version, focusing on military issues, pictures the matter as an intramural PLA dispute, with other military factions winning Deng's support for their objections to Yang Baibing's one-sided promotion of his own followers. While there is no reference to Jiang's involvement, this account also indicates weakness in his authority *vis-à-vis* the military prior to Deng's action. Cf. Joseph Fewsmith, "Reaction, Resurgence, and Succession: Chinese Politics since Tiananmen", in Roderick MacFarquhar (ed.), *The Politics of China, Second Edition: The Eras of Mao and Deng* (New York: Cambridge University Press, 1997), pp. 507–8. Another interview account does not involve military matters, but

military post (but not the Politburo) and Yang Shangkun's retirement with less influence than a long-time supporter of Deng could have anticipated.

In comparison, the Chen Xitong and Qiao Shi cases involved even less of a threat to Jiang, and were dealt with relatively easily. Chen Xitong was removed from his position on the Politburo and as Beijing municipal Party chief on corruption charges, finally winding up as a convicted felon. A man with a conservative reputation because of his prominent role in the 1989 crackdown but someone who had spoken out for reform measures on various occasions, Chen, as some sources suggest, may have had a low regard for Jiang, but there is little to indicate major differences or any effort to launch a "game" directed at Jiang. Chen's quite spectacular corruption may simply have given Jiang the opportunity to get rid of an annoyance while winning some points with a public fed up with official corruption. In the event, Jiang handled the case with sensitivity in order to avoid charges of factional bias, apparently gained the acquiescence of Li Peng in the removal of Li's 1989 ally, and acted well within formal procedures. Even if Chen wound up losing almost everything, there is no indication of a hard-fought "game" leading to his demise.[10]

As for Qiao Shi, despite persistent efforts of outside analysts to paint him as Jiang's "rival", there is again little persuasive evidence to suggest that Qiao imagined he could challenge Jiang after the latter was named the "core" of the so-called third-generation leadership in 1989. This is not to claim that there were no differences or tensions between the two—as in collective settings elsewhere, clashing egos and policies could coexist as long as restraint was observed. Apart from questions of evidence, the context did not seem right for an attempt to oust Jiang. The window of opportunity would have been more open in 1992, given Deng's dissatisfaction with the slow pace of reform, and indeed this has been suggested in some accounts linking Qiao to the Yang brothers.[11] This, however, would have been an exceptionally bold and dangerous move in a situation where stability and unity were arguably the regime's top goal, and where the only man with the clout to upset the apple cart—Deng—had made a substantial investment in Jiang. In short, making a move was a recipe for "losing all", while sitting tight guaranteed another comfortable term on the Politburo Standing Committee.

---

instead focuses on Deng's personal disenchantment with Yang Shangkun. According to this version, Deng was angry with Yang for leaking information concerning his "southern tour", and this was his main motivation in acting against the brothers later in the year. I am indebted to Warren Sun for notifying me of this latter explanation.

[10] See You Ji, "Jiang Zemin: In Quest of Post-Deng Supremacy", in Maurice Brosseau, Suzanne Pepper and Tsang Shu-ki (eds), *China Review 1996* (Hong Kong: The Chinese University Press, 1996), pp. 14–17; and Joseph Fewsmith, "Institution Building and Democratization in China", in Howard Handelman and Mark Tessler (eds), *Democracy and Its Limits: Lessons from Asia, Latin America, and the Middle East* (Notre Dame: University of Notre Dame Press, 1999), pp. 100–1.

[11] See Fewsmith, "Institution Building", p. 100.

Whatever the problems between Jiang and Qiao five years later, there was no one among the leadership who would have encouraged the 73-year-old Qiao to make a bid for the top job. Again using existing, if loosely defined, procedures, Jiang apparently maneuvered Qiao into retirement. Moreover, as Joseph Fewsmith has observed, Jiang then moved toward the policy positions Qiao had advocated, a phenomenon quite different from the ritual denunciation of losers of "games to win all". The indications are that Qiao did not appreciate the outcome, but it was more a golden handshake than the result of a no-holds-barred struggle.[12]

The above analysis, while in line with my argument that few if any true "games to win all" took place in the PRC apart from the Cultural Revolution, also demonstrates a long-term post-Mao trend toward less "struggle" for ultimate or penultimate power. At the same time, normal politics involves Party leaders in unending battles over specific policies and interests, and the "core" leader has fewer resources than his heroic predecessors did. Such a paradoxical conclusion is at odds with many of the attempts to decipher who is doing what to whom within the black box and with broader assessments that see nothing but trouble at the top. Such assessments anticipate "a state of chronic succession crisis" that would be "very costly, entailing potential instability, conflicts, and breakdowns".[13] Such gloomy predictions, much like Tsou's basic construct, point to a low degree of political institutionalization as the cause. This appears not to be the case today. In addition to the long-established tradition valuing Party unity and the costly lessons of the Cultural Revolution and Tiananmen, it is precisely a creeping institutionalization at the centre of the system that is behind the decline in observable struggles for the top positions.

Institutionalizing the "Core", Pluralizing the "Factions"

Institutionalization of the affairs of the political elite has been a key trend of the post-Mao period. After a brief period of simply restoring the institutions of the pre-Cultural Revolution period, attention turned to more fundamental questions. With Deng Xiaoping taking the lead, a serious analysis of past disasters led to the conclusion that the lack of effective institutions and of checks on arbitrary authority had helped bring about these disasters, and measures were undertaken

---

[12]   See *ibid.*, pp. 100, 101–2; and Fewsmith, "Introduction", n. 33. For a summary of varying Hong Kong accounts of the manoeuvers allegedly surrounding Qiao's retirement, see Richard Baum, "Jiang Takes Command: The Fifteenth National Party Congress and Beyond", in Hung-mao Tien and Yun-han Chu (eds), *China under Jiang Zemin* (London: Lynne Rienner Publishers, 2000), pp. 23–5.

[13]   Andrew J. Nathan and Robert S. Ross, *The Great Wall and the Empty Fortress: China's Search for Security* (New York: W.W. Norton, 1997), p. 136; and Peter Nan-shong Lee, "The Informal Politics of Leadership Succession in Post-Mao China", in Lowell Dittmer, Haruhiro Fukui and Peter N.S. Lee (eds), *Informal Politics in East Asia* (Cambridge: Cambridge University Press, 2000), p. 182.

to introduce various procedures and limits concerning the exercise of power. The results have been considerable: Party and state bodies meet regularly according to constitutional schedules; the role and significance of the National People's Congress has expanded; retirement systems to eliminate life-long tenure have been introduced; a personnel policy emphasizing youth and education, while not strictly institutionalized, serves to enhance the rotation and diversification of power; and term limits, including the so far observed constitutionally mandated two-term limit for the premier, are clear manifestations of regular procedures. Of course, institutionalization does not guarantee the attenuation of conflict, and under conditions of normal politics it may intensify divisions in some circumstances,[14] but overall it forces more power sharing, consultation and consensus building.

The problem is that there are definite limits to the institutionalization of political power, especially as one ascends to the apex. I would, however, take a somewhat different view from that of Fewsmith and others that "politics at the top remains uninstitutionalized, and outcomes are based on who has more power".[15] The first point is that, while true to a degree, this applies to highly institutionalized systems as well—for example, Hillary Clinton's informal but influential role during the first Clinton administration. Second, and crucially, there has been a clear trend toward institutionalization at the Party's top during the reform era (with the limits on this very much linked to the person and interests of Deng Xiaoping until the latter half of the 1990s). And finally, while Jiang Zemin's pre-eminence is due to a substantial degree to his political skills, it is fundamentally based on the authority of his office, together with the leadership's commitment to stability and unity. These points can be illustrated by an examination of the limits to institutionalization during the reform era.

Limits to institutionalization were inevitable in the process of generational transition. Only Deng and his generation had the prestige based on revolutionary achievements to exercise decisive authority at a time of profound change. Deng was explicit that his generation would control the leadership transition even as he and the other elders retreated to the "second front". He noted that the selection of successors "is a comparatively easy (question) to solve while veteran comrades are still around".[16] Deng's ultimate personal authority was not only reflected in various statements by Hu Yaobang and Zhao Ziyang, but crucially in the secret resolution of the 13th Party Congress in 1987 to refer all important matters to him for final decision, a resolution which, together with Deng's post as head of the Central Military Commission, provided quasi-legal authority for his decision to

---

[14]   The accession of Li Peng to the premiership in 1988 on the reform principle of separating the Party and government in fact deepened the struggle over economic policy.

[15]   Fewsmith, "Institution Building", p. 99.

[16]   *Selected Works of Deng Xiaoping, Vol. II (1975–1982)* (Beijing: Foreign Languages Press, 1984), p. 199.

crush the student movement in 1989. Subsequently, when Deng promised not to interfere in the affairs of Jiang's new leadership, he included the proviso that his withdrawal would take effect "once the new leading group has established its prestige".[17] He accordingly continued to influence the make-up of the Central Military Commission. Deng not only installed his former subordinate Liu Huaqing as its vice chair at the point that he formally retired from the chairmanship of the body in November 1989, he also arranged for another loyal follower, septuagenarian Zhang Zhen, to take over as another vice chair in 1992. More famously, Deng spectacularly interfered in the political scene through his 1992 "southern tour", an intervention that Chen Yun reportedly considered an unseemly violation of retirement in contrast to his own behaviour. Be that as it may, in the twilight zone of quasi-legality, Deng's suppression of the democracy movement in 1989 arguably had more formal institutional justification than his revitalization of reform in 1992.

But what of the position of the new leader, the "core", Jiang Zemin? The concept of the "core" only emerged during the crisis of spring 1989, and was clearly designed by Deng and other Party elders to provide greater authority to Jiang as the new successor than had ever been given to Hu Yaobang and Zhao Ziyang, both of whom laboured under the notion of "collective successors". While collective leadership was still to be maintained, "core" status became Jiang's most precious political asset, linking him symbolically to the stability of the system and providing a basis for amassing additional institutional powers. Of course, Jiang, like Hu and Zhao before him, had been selected by an electorate of veteran revolutionaries, in the new General Secretary's case seemingly consisting basically of Deng, Chen Yun and Li Xiannian.[18] More broadly, given that the emphasis on stability has meant that Politburo members have regularly been re-elected (save for having passed the retirement age, or having become embroiled in a political crisis as in 1989, or steeped in corruption as in the Chen Xitong case), today the top Party leadership as a whole still bears Deng's stamp.[19]

---

[17] *Selected Works of Deng Xiaoping, Vol. III (1982–1992)* (Beijing: Foreign Languages Press, 1994), p. 292.

[18] Deng spoke of consulting with Chen and Li when he announced Jiang's elevation to an undoubtedly surprised Li Peng and Yao Yilin; *Selected Works of Deng (1982–1992)*, p. 288. According to a normally well-informed source, it was actually Chen Yun who nominated Jiang, but clearly the final decision was Deng's.

[19] Two-thirds of the Politburo elected in 1997 had initially been chosen in earlier years when Deng was making the final decisions. According to one unconfirmed source, at the 15th Congress Jiang found himself pleading for the re-election of unpopular Politburo members Ding Guan'gen and Li Tieying not only on the stability principle, but because they had been placed there with Deng's assent. Of special importance is that Hu Jintao's elevation to the Standing Committee, and thus as potential "core" of the "fourth generation", occurred at the 14th Congress in 1992; see below, note 24.

Nevertheless, even while Deng lived, the system of leadership selection was already evolving in a direction of managed institutionalism.

This system is based on what might be called a set of fuzzy principles. Of course, some of the principles are unknown to outsiders. Who has a say in selecting the successor to the "core" or the members of the collective leadership? It is undoubtedly managed by a few at the top, although subject to election at Party congresses, but the process remains obscure. How much power does the "core" have relative to the collective—presumably it is closer to a Westminster cabinet system than a US presidential system, but how much do we really know? Within the collective, are the institutions as hierarchically organized as they seem on paper, or does the inner leadership group have great flexibility? Specifically, does the Politburo Standing Committee meet regularly to make decisions, or is Jiang easily able to assign issues to different arenas to maximize his goals? How does a top leader campaign for promotion—what is acceptable in a system where the norms have always rejected the seeking of factional advantage? These matters of procedure are as deeply ensconced in the black box as questions of who is doing what to whom. But there are some fuzzy principles that can be examined.

Current operating principles relate to age, qualifications and tenure. While no absolute rule has apparently been laid down, since the 13th Party Congress in 1987 an age criterion of sorts has been enforced. By the time of the 14th Party Congress in 1992, leaders in their seventies were routinely retiring from the Politburo (with the exception of military figures): both Yao Yilin and Song Ping left the Standing Committee on that occasion. As we have seen, retirement was one explanation for the exit of Qiao Shi at the 15th Congress in 1997, and military representatives now observed the age principle.[20] Indeed, unverified Hong Kong reports claim there was spirited discussion at the Beidaihe meetings preceding the Congress over a formal retirement system for Politburo members, setting an age limit of 70, along with related proposals to limit the number of terms that could be served: for example, two for the General Secretary.[21] The apparent fact that there has been no formal decision along these lines indicates the limits to institutionalization, as does the 15th Congress's exception in retaining the 71-year-old Jiang as the "core", but regular practices that shape behaviour do appear to be emerging.

The exception in Jiang's case, I would argue, had less to do with the office than the political situation. As the "core", and a "core" only marginally older than his senior peers, Jiang was crucial to the system at that juncture less because of

---

[20] The new PLA representatives, Zhang Wannian and Chi Haotian, were 69 and 68 respectively—thus within the age limit but still 6–7 to 15–16 years older than other newly elected Politburo members.

[21] *Sing Tao Jih Pao* (Sing Tao Daily), 15 September 1997, in Foreign Broadcast Information Service-China-97-258; and *Cheng Ming* (Contention), 1 September 1997, in *ibid.*-97-268. As for Jiang's state position as PRC president, a constitutional two-term limit does exist, and presumably will be honoured as the corresponding limit for premier has been.

his skills than because competition (not necessarily "struggle") to obtain the succession would have been deemed a threat to stability. But certainly there is the expectation that Jiang will gracefully step down when the 16th Congress convenes in 2002, and he has indicated that he will do so, although there is some ambiguity about whether he plans to stay on as the chair of the Central Military Commission. Whether he attempts such a maneuver, and whether it is accepted, will say much about the apparent trend of institutionalization.[22]

If the 15th Congress is any indication, a system is in place to bring younger, better educated leaders into the Politburo who can serve three or four terms and become the basis of future "generations" of leadership. Military figures aside, all of the newly elected Politburo members ranged between 53 and 62 years of age and held professional credentials. As Li Cheng has noted, nepotism and favouritism may play a pivotal role in the choice of individuals for the Politburo and other influential posts, but wide administrative experience and other "objective" criteria are also essential.[23]

Moreover, it is quite clear that a successor, the "core" of the "fourth generation", has been chosen and already granted the institutional positions to facilitate the transition. Hu Jintao, who had been positioned for the role by his elevation to the Standing Committee in 1992 when Deng was still ultimately calling the shots,[24] was all but treated as a "core in waiting" in the official biography issued at the 15th Congress. The following year he was made vice-president with the right of automatic succession should anything happen to Jiang, and in 1999 he was named vice-chair of the Central Military Commission. Given the age structure of the Standing Committee, there is little chance for anyone else

---

[22]   While there has been much speculation on this point, according to an 8 March 2001 *Asia Times* online report, the Party organization chief and Jiang Zemin's long-time associate, Zeng Qinghong, said such an outcome was "not likely" during an inspection tour in Shenzhen. On several subsequent occasions, Jiang himself sidestepped questions about his future.

[23]   Li Cheng, "China in 1999: Seeking Common Ground at a Time of Tension and Conflict", *Asian Survey*, Vol. 40, No. 1 (January/February 2000), pp. 116–7.

[24]   In addition to Deng's undoubted approval of Hu Jintao's 1992 promotion, unconfirmed reports published outside the PRC claim that Deng dictated a succession plan stipulating Hu's elevation to the top post. A plausible account in Yang Zhongmei, *Hu Jintao— Zhonggong kua shiji jiebanren* [Hu Jintao—The CCP's Successor for the New Century] (Taibei: Shibao Chubanshe, 1999), pp. 160–4, falls sort of this, but still indicates Deng's crucial role in positioning Hu for the eventual succession. According to Yang, on the eve of the 14th Congress Jiang Zemin, Qiao Shi and Song Ping (the latter two having been Hu's enthusiastic patrons) approached Deng with a draft list of candidates for the new Standing Committee based on Deng's earlier instruction to include figures considerably younger than the existing members. When Hu's name was mentioned, Deng reportedly responded with "Hu Jintao is a fine person", an interjection that settled the matter.

on that body to aspire to be the "core" and to mount an effective challenge.[25] Aged 59 in 2002, Hu Jintao will be poised for two terms as "core".[26] The real succession issue at the next Congress, I suggest, will be the selection of a "core in waiting" for the "fifth generation", or possibly the selection of several prospective candidates, with the definitive choice left to the 17th Congress in 2007.

Can this managed institutionalism work? In terms of leadership stability at the apex it has worked since Tiananmen, and it has enabled the political leadership to avoid "games to win all" in choosing the "core" and his successor.[27] Managed succession elsewhere, moreover, provides a notable precedent with broad similarities to the Chinese case. In Mexico the presidential succession was determined by the sitting president choosing his successor from members of his cabinet after consultation with an array of ruling-party and government leaders during the final third of a mandated single six-year term. This regularized transfer of ultimate power prevailed for 65 years, without disruptive political struggles.[28] We should not assume a similar longevity in the Chinese case, where serious questions can be raised about the Party's staying power. But it does indicate the possibility of an elite sustaining regularized replacements of leadership over a substantial period.

Institutional management of the succession issue and stable leadership arrangements do not obviate the hundreds of battles to be fought in normal politics. For Jiang Zemin and his colleagues, these battles are first and foremost shaped by the vast agenda of issues that have to be dealt with by a results-

---

[25]   Jiang, Li Peng and Zhu Rongji, who will all be well past 70, can be expected to retire, while Li Ruihuan's position appears anomalous. Although likely to be re-elected, as he will only be aged 68 in 2002, Li's power can be regarded as suspect given the relative insignificance of his main organization, the Chinese People's Political Consultative Conference. The newly appointed Standing Committee members in 1997, Wei Jianxing and Li Lanqing, will be 71 and 70 years old respectively when the 16th Congress meets. Standing Committee membership, presumably, is a requirement for elevation to "core" status, at least short of a major crisis.

[26]   Hu will be two months short of his 70th birthday when the 18th Congress is scheduled to meet in 2012, and thus under current practice still eligible for another term. If the process of insitutionalization is further embedded, however, a two-term limit will most likely then be in place.

[27]   Cf. Frederick C. Teiwes, "The Problematic Quest for Stability: Reflections on Succession, Institutionalization, Governability, and Legitimacy in Post-Deng China", in Tien and Chu, *China under Jiang*, pp. 77–8.

[28]   See Roderick Ai Camp, *Politics in Mexico* (New York: Oxford University Press, 1993), Ch. 5.

oriented rather than a "Party-line"-oriented leadership.[29] These issues include the need to sustain economic growth while at the same time dealing with the dislocations caused by the growth strategy; the effort to sustain viable central government institutions in the context of decentralization where the incentives for lower-level obedience have diminished; a complex and rapidly changing sociopolitical environment where, unlike in the 1980s, substantial groups of "losers" are emerging in society; a recognition of the need for the state to retreat from traditional responsibilities and facilitate the emergence from within society of quasi-autonomous groups to assume the discarded functions; the challenge of globalization and the threats it poses for domestic interests; and a more pluralistic intellectual environment with the Party subject to criticism from the right, the left, and nationalist sentiments. These and many other challenges form an agenda that would threaten to overwhelm any political elite, and certainly are guaranteed to generate serious disputes within the political class. Perhaps most striking are the signs of nervousness—a lack of confidence in the capacity of the system to sustain the unavoidable shocks. As Joseph Fewsmith correctly observed a few years ago, "There was no sense a decade ago (in the mid-1980s) that too much reform might bring down the whole system; today, there seems to be a fear that even the current amount of reform presents a danger to political stability. The loss of ideological legitimacy and political self-confidence is palpable".[30]

In this context, the utility of the concept of "factionalism" is limited. This is not to deny the existence, indeed the significance, of factions in the patron–client sense. As Tang Tsou has observed in the pages of this book, "Everyone has 'his own men or women', their *banzi*" (p. 138), but he went on to detail a whole array of other "political action groups" (bureaucratic interest groups, groups based on ideological affinities, opinion groupings on specific issues, groups shaped by all sorts of informal ties, situational groups) that are often more significant for political outcomes. As Chinese politics becomes ever more interest-based in response to the vast agenda, personal loyalty groups can play an important role as issues are fought out, but only as part of a much larger and complex whole. This can be better understood by examining long-term trends in the roles of factions and other interests.

The PRC under Mao can essentially be divided between the period before 1958 when the Chairman listened to interests within the system and sought results that took those interests into account, even when the general direction was driven by "Party-line" considerations, and the subsequent "later Mao" period when he simply overrode interests, or compromised with them because of the dire state of the nation and/or because he had no clear idea of what to do. In the earlier

---

[29]   An excellent recent overview of these issues is Joseph Fewsmith, "Historical Echoes and Chinese Politics: Can China Leave the Twentieth Century Behind?", in Tyrene White (ed.), *China Briefing 2000: The Continuing Transformation* (Armonk: M.E. Sharpe, 2000).

[30]   Joseph Fewsmith, "Chinese Politics on the Eve of the 15th Party Congress", in Brosseau, Kuan and Kueh, *China Review 1997*, p. 12.

period, interests were largely expressed by the established Party leadership and the various official institutions charged with economic development or with responsibility for various sections of society. Also important was one form of "faction"—the "mountaintops" (*shantou*) or constituencies from pre-1949 revolutionary organizations. Despite ambivalence among the top Party leadership about the existence of these groups, they were regarded as legitimate and formed the basis for staffing official organizations. The name of the game in this regard was to unify the mountaintops, a game Mao usually played well. As a result, the mountaintops in most cases were not divisive, but instead played an important role in informal elite communication where factions overlapped formal organizations.[31]

In the latter period, in both the Great Leap Forward and Cultural Revolution, Mao designed courses of action profoundly inimical to institutional interests. Under such circumstances, the institutional actors either attempted to carry out the Chairman's program, as in the Great Leap, or many of them simply collapsed during the Cultural Revolution. As for the mountaintops, they were drawn into the vortex of Cultural Revolution factionalism as the chaotic conditions of the period led leaders to turn toward their historical connections for survival. Subsequently, as a "game to win all" with the radical "Gang of Four" unfolded, the various mountaintops formed a tacit alliance against the radicals, who lacked this older generation's pre-1949 revolutionary credentials. This alliance of mountaintops became explicit following Mao's death, and Deng's ascension to power was partly based on it.

Under Deng, there was a return to the "traditional" roles of both institutional interests and the mountaintops of the pre-Great Leap period—but with significant differences. In the new circumstances, powerful economic institutions argued both for their own interests and for what they believed would produce the best results for the nation, but the long-term trend toward marketization eroded their historic functions. The mountaintops again became a potent channel of intra-elite communication, particularly for Party elders on the "second front". But with the exception of the military, these mountaintops were rapidly fading as binding ties among those on the "first front", whose credentials were increasingly based on post-1949 bureaucratic careers.

The main factor that limited the fading of the mountaintops and the assertion of institutional interests was Deng himself. Deng turned to the mountaintops to bolster his political sway, while a key aspect of the 1980s and early 1990s was his capability to override institutions. Yan Jiaqi's observation, noted in my earlier chapter, that Deng had to be obeyed as long as his demands were reasonable

---

[31]   The exception was the 1953–54 Gao Gang affair where Mao's dissatisfaction with Liu Shaoqi led Gao to whip up various *shantou* against Liu. Mao, however, soon recovered his bearings and again played the game of balanced moutaintop representation in the organs of power. See Frederick C. Teiwes, *Politics at Mao's Court: Gao Gang and Party Factionalism in the Early 1950s* (Armonk: M.E. Sharpe, 1990), Chs. 4–5.

indicated such a capability. The qualifier is a significant distinction from Mao, but Deng's capacity to push his aims against considered advice was starkly, if briefly, seen in the disastrous price reform of 1988.[32] As for mountaintops, in the PLA where ties to senior officers during the revolutionary struggle remained potent, Deng assured support not only through strategic Central Military Commission appointments, but also through the appointment of command officers heavily weighted to his own Second Field Army.

But, as everyone knows, Jiang Zemin is no Deng. He cannot override institutions with harebrained schemes, although he can fight battles to amass sufficient leadership support to overcome substantial institutional opposition, as in the decision to join the WTO. He can place personal loyalists in some key positions, but his so-called Shanghai clique[33] is much smaller and less prestigious than the mountaintops of the revolution. Jiang may have the last word in approving PLA appointments, as You Ji notes in Chapter Twelve of this book; but as You Ji also notes, Jiang's approval is based on institutional recommendations, and the beneficiaries feel nothing like the debt their predecessors felt to their leaders on the battlefield.

Jiang's lack of revolutionary prestige notwithstanding, a more fundamental cause for such changes involves the great shifts in China's polity and society in the 1990s. As society has become markedly more diversified, politics has followed suit. Factions in the traditional sense are a relatively small part of the equation, which now includes broader public opinion.[34] The forces having an input into political outcomes are far more pluralistic than ever before, even as the centre struggles to manage them within a framework of normal politics. The situation has been succinctly captured in the observation of Li Cheng: "No faction, no institution, no region, and no individual can really dominate power".[35]

The Benefits and Perils of Normal Politics with Chinese Characteristics

In the final appraisal, a leadership will be measured by its successes and failures in dealing with the manifold problems of the nation in its care, rather than by

---

[32] See Cheng Xiaonong, "Decision and Miscarriage: Radical Price Reform in the Summer of 1988", in Carol Lee Hamrin and Suisheng Zhao (eds), *Decision-Making in Deng's China: Perspectives from Insiders* (Armonk: M.E. Sharpe, 1995).

[33] There is even a question concerning the degree to which Jiang himself was responsible for the promotion of various members of this "clique". Politburo members Wu Bangguo and Huang Ju were reportedly favourites of both Deng Xiaoping and Chen Yun. See You Ji, "Jiang Zemin", p. 28.

[34] For a discussion of the influence of public opinion on foreign policy, see Joseph Fewsmith and Stanley Rosen, "The Domestic Context of Chinese Foreign Policy: Does 'Public Opinion' Matter?", in David M. Lampton (ed.), *The Making of Chinese Foreign and Security Policy* (Stanford: Stanford University Press, 2001).

[35] Li Cheng, "China in 1999", p. 117.

whether it manages to contain intra-elite conflict. To put it another way, avoiding "games to win all" does not guarantee satisfactory outcomes. Success is particularly difficult to achieve in today's China because of the fragility of the regime's legitimacy—a fragility due to an official ideology few believe in, the inability of the leadership to curb rampant corruption, and the fact that a legitimacy based on economic performance is inherently vulnerable.[36]

Fundamental transitions always place political systems under great strain, often involving violent suppression. China is currently undergoing at least three such transitions—from a traditional agrarian society to a modern society, from a state-socialist economy to a market economy, and from a Leninist political system to something else. Given the potential for disorder, the principle of containing leadership disputes in order to avoid undermining political stability is taken seriously in China, not just for the comfort of the elite, but for the benefit of the larger society. It is the populace's fear of chaos, its own wish for stability, that is arguably the regime's greatest resource, and the governing elite will not lightly jeopardize this. Another feature of current normal politics that is to some degree encouraging is the emergence of an educated technocratic elite. Whether this elite is truly "more tolerant of criticism ... more willing to admit problems, and more enterprising in allocating resources"[37] in all circumstances remains to be seen, but it does seem that on various issues there is a resort to more "scientific methods", consultation with affected groups, objective analysis before decisions are taken, and careful monitoring and consultation during implementation.

These features of China's normal politics can be looked at differently, however. Technocratic decisions do not equal good decisions, despite claims that "bureaucratic insulation" produces effective economic reform.[38] In a state-socialist context, the dominance of engineers in the 15th Party Politburo presents an unsettling, if somewhat misleading, similarity to a Soviet leadership dominated by engineers during the Brezhnev period that presided over an "era of stagnation".[39] Perhaps the main problem with bureaucratic insulation is that it

---

[36]   See Teiwes, "Problematic Quest", pp. 84–8; and Guoguang Wu, "Legitimacy Crisis, Political Economy, and the Fifteenth Party Congress", in Andrew J. Nathan, Zhaohui Hong and Steven R. Smith (eds), *Dilemmas of Reform in Jiang Zemin's China* (London: Lynne Rienner Publishers, 1999).

[37]   Li Cheng, "China in 1999", p. 114.

[38]   A case in point is the Mexican experience where insulated technocratic rule exacerbated the financial crisis of the 1980s and 1990s. See Denise Dresser, "Mexico: The Decline of Dominant-Party Rule", in Jorge I. Dominguez and Abraham F. Lowenthal (eds), *Constructing Democratic Governance: Latin America and the Caribbean in the 1990s* (Baltimore: The Johns Hopkins University Press, 1996), p. 169.

[39]   See Teiwes, "Problematic Quest", pp. 83, 94 n.59. The CCP's "fourth generation", however, is more diverse, including more economic/financial experts and lawyers. See the detailed

keeps policymakers out of touch with society, feeding the pervasive sense of "them and us", although it has to be said the Party is very sensitive to the public's moods. In Zhu Rongji's words, "We know the score. ... We are not morons".[40]

But the situation can be viewed from yet another angle. The emphasis on stability and unity—especially personnel stability at the top, which was also a feature of the Brezhnev leadership—may produce lowest common denominator politics, a muddling-through approach, full of zigs and zags whenever issues become too divisive, and even, in the eyes of some observers, something approaching immobilism. The concern of the governing elites about stability and unity in leadership politics arguably merges with worries about challenges to stability and unity in society, resulting in a fear of a social backlash and loss of control if reform measures are carried through to the end. Is this the current record?

Muddling through is a feature of present policy in China, as in all normal politics, but it hardly equates with immobilism so far as economic policy is concerned. While the leadership probably felt it had no choice, the implementation of state-owned enterprise reform, with its resultant unemployment, and the decisive steps to join the WTO despite huge potential social problems, demonstrates a regime willing to take more risks in the economic sphere than seemed likely even a few years ago. It is in the political sphere that something akin to immobilism exits. Although think tanks with links to top leaders study European social democracy, whenever a whiff of a threat arises the instinct has been to tighten up or crack down. What is most striking on the ground is the variation, even incoherence, in the attitudes of officials concerning large and small matters alike. A colleague who recently returned from China reported a conversation with a high-ranking provincial official who spoke of the need for competitive elections. Yet in the same place, at the same time, a local publisher backed out of a non-controversial book project largely on the basis that a foreigner was involved.

Chinese characteristics born of links to an increasingly irrelevant past as much as a reluctance to carry out meaningful political reform prevent a truly normal politics. Further examples abound: Party "liberals" dredging up old mistakes in the style of the Cultural Revolution to attack their enemies; Hua Guofeng re-elected to the Central Committee despite the norm concerning retirement, simply because Deng had originally endorsed Hua's arrangement; Jiang seeking ideological legitimacy by expounding the "three representations"; and provincial leaders clambering to endorse the leader's effort as if it were a 1950s campaign, while the population reacts with incomprehension and derision. It is hard (although not impossible) to imagine a Chinese leadership in the

---

study by Cheng Li (Li Cheng), "Jiang Zemin's Successors: The Rise of the Fourth Generation of Leaders in the PRC", *The China Quarterly*, No. 161 (March 2000).

[40] Cited in Joseph Fewsmith, "China in 1998: Tacking to Stay the Course", *Asian Survey*, Vol. 39, No. 1 (January/February 1999), p. 113.

foreseeable future taking the initiative to break with such practices. More likely is a leadership ignoring such contradictions while trying to stick to its course and keeping to the fuzzy guidelines of stability and unity in its internal politics. It will be a few yards at a time, with more than a few broken-field runs along the way.

ELEVEN

The Evolving Shape of Elite Politics*

Joseph Fewsmith

Chinese politics during the late 1990s and first years of the twenty-first century are substantially different from what they were in the years prior to Tiananmen. Four factors in particular have been important in propelling substantial political change in China over the past decade: generational change within the top leadership, economic development and differentiation, the shadow of Tiananmen, and the different domestic and international political environments that have emerged during the post-Tiananmen and post-Cold War period. These factors have evolved more or less simultaneously and have interacted with one another, so the following discussion is not intended to imply prioritization or causality.

First, during the 1990s the actuarial tables finally caught up with the revolutionary generation that had dominated politics for half a century. Former president Li Xiannian, Jiang's closest political supporter, died in June 1992. Not long after, Hu Qiaomu, Mao Zedong's former secretary and the Chinese Communist Party's most authoritative ideologue, passed away. Chen Yun, the conservative economic specialist, died in April 1995; and Deng Xiaoping, the "paramount leader", finally succumbed in February 1997. Although Deng liked to refer to himself as the "core" of the "second generation" of leadership, so as to differentiate and distance himself from Mao, he and his colleagues were clearly part of the first generation, the revolutionary generation who had undertaken the Long March and led the revolution to victory. As these dominant leaders of the revolutionary generation passed from the scene, a few of their generational cohort—Wan Li, Song Ping, Deng Liqun, Liu Huaqing, and so on—have lived on into the new millennium and influenced politics from time to time, but their interventions have been episodic and of declining importance (an exception perhaps being during the crisis following the bombing of the Chinese embassy in Belgrade). The revolutionary generation no longer dominates the political scene.

*   The author would like to thank John Frankenstein and the other members of Columbia University's East Asia Institute for their thoughtful comments at a Modern China seminar.

The passing of the revolutionary generation necessarily freed the new leadership (the Jiang Zemin generation) from the constraints imposed by "old men's politics" (*laoren zhengzhi*) even as it forced leaders like Jiang to look for new political alignments now that the leaders who had promoted him to the post of Party general secretary were gone. It also forced him to begin to think about what sort of political institutions he wanted to bequeath to the next generation and to articulate a new set of ideals that would mark his political legacy (see below). Thinking about one's place in history is not always a bad thing to do.

The 15th Party Congress in 1997 is usually taken as the symbolic turning point when power passed from the revolutionary generation to the first group of leaders who had won their promotions through their bureaucratic service rather than by force of arms (though the Fourth Plenary Session of the 14th Central Committee in September 1994 marked an important substantive transition). This new generation of leaders was technically trained, and that background has influenced its approach to decision-making.[1] Technocrats are problem solvers by training, not ideologues; they focus on "problems", not "isms". This transition, of course, was neither absolute nor unencumbered by ties to interests. In particular, Li Peng, premier for most of the 1990s, emerged as the champion of bureaucratic interests and of the remnants of the old planned economy and, as the adopted son of Zhou Enlai, had the closest ties with the revolutionary generation. Nevertheless, the change was real. The new generation is more interested in managing the enormously difficult problems China faces than in carrying on the ideological battles of its predecessors. Denunciations of "bourgeois liberalization" emerge from time to time, but these are increasingly superficial and ineffective.

Most importantly, as the first non-revolutionary generation of leaders, Jiang Zemin and his colleagues necessarily have had to seek legitimacy in something other than their contributions to the revolution. This means that they have had to turn increasingly to procedural legitimacy. At the leadership level this has meant, with some exceptions, enforcing norms of retirement and term limits in office.[2] As technocratic problem solvers in an increasingly complex environment, the leadership has turned naturally to expertise and institutions to forge policies and consensus. The decision-making process has thus been enlarged to include additional actors and, to an extent, institutionalized. This trend has allowed the National People's Congress (NPC) and its specialized committees to play a more important role.[3] Although China has not developed a Western-style tripartite government with checks and balances, institutions do play a greater constraining

---

[1]   Cheng Li, *China's Leaders: The New Generation* (Lanham: Rowman and Littlefield, 2001).

[2]   Melanie Manion, *Retirement of Revolutionary Cadres in China: Public Policies, Social Norms, Private Interests* (Princeton: Princeton University Press, 1993).

[3]   Murray Scot Tanner, *The Politics of Lawmaking in China: Institutions, Processes, and Democratic Prospects* (Oxford: Oxford University Press, 1999).

role than they did in the past. It has also led to a greater emphasis on the role of law, a theme touted loudly by the 15th Party Congress and re-emphasized at the Fifth Plenary Session of the 15th Central Committee in October 2000.[4] If the implementation of law remains uneven, it is better than before and at least accompanied by greater recognition of the need for law.[5]

If generational change is one factor that has affected the conduct of politics, then the expansion and diversification of the economy is another. The economy has grown significantly in the past decade. There have been ups and downs, including significant economic difficulties, but the economy is now more than twice the size it was in 1989, at the time of Tiananmen. More important from a political perspective, the structure of the economy has changed greatly. The private economy has grown rapidly. The TVE (township and village enterprise) sector has been largely privatized over the past decade, but its role in job creation has stagnated in recent years after two decades of rapid growth. The state enterprises have done poorly. And foreign trade has continued to grow. Today, China's economy conforms more closely to the country's comparative advantage (that is, it has developed labour-intensive industries and taken advantage of international export markets), and the country has worked hard to develop high-tech/information industries. In short, there are a far greater number of economic interests at work in turn-of-the-century China than there were just one decade ago.

This diversification of economic interests does not mean that all of the economic news has been good. The ongoing economic reforms have seen the emergence of winners and losers. State-enterprise and urban collective workers who have been laid off—some 39 million between 1996 and the end of 2000—are the economic reforms' most obvious losers,[6] but those who live in the country's interior, particularly the agricultural poor, have also suffered, at least in relative and sometimes in absolute terms.[7]

These trends have had three obvious impacts. First, the government faces more demands from more diverse interests than ever before. To a greater extent

---

[4]   "Communiqué of the Fifth Plenary Session of the Fifteenth Central Committee of the Communist Party of China", Xinhua, 11 October 2000.

[5]   Stanley Lubman, *Bird in a Cage: Legal Reform in China After Mao* (Stanford: Stanford University Press, 1999).

[6]   State Statistical Yearbooks for these years, as calculated in Joseph Fewsmith, "The Political and Social Implications of China's Accession to the WTO", *The China Quarterly*, No. 167 (September 2001), p. 579. On the difficulties of calculating the number of layoffs, see Dorothy J. Solinger, "Why We Cannot Count the Number of 'Unemployed'", *The China Quarterly*, No. 167 (September 2001), pp. 671–88.

[7]   Wang Shaoguang and Hu Angang, *The Political Economy of Uneven Development: The Case of China* (Armonk: M. E. Sharpe, 1999); and Thomas Bernstein and Xiaobo Lu, "Taxation Without Representation: Peasants, the Central and Local States in Reform China", *The China Quarterly*, No. 163 (September 2000), pp. 742–63.

than in the past, it must take these interests into account. In general, it has done so by expanding the role of "intermediate" associations, although one hesitates to use the term because of its connection with the far more independent and voluntarist groups that exist in Western democracies. Chinese associations are clearly more corporatist in structure than their Western counterparts but, as their numbers have grown and their interests diverged, some of them have moved away from the narrow "transmission belt" function they had in Maoist China to take on a role of articulating, at least to some degree, societal interests. As Anita Chan and Jonathan Unger put it, some associations have moved along a continuum from "state corporatism" toward "societal corporatism".[8] In short, the growth and diversification of societal interests has forced the state to seek a new accommodation with society. It remains premature to speak of a public sphere, but the state has clearly yielded the monopoly it once held on the expression of societal interest.

Second, as large numbers of workers and farmers have suffered relatively or absolutely from reform, they have taken direct action through strikes, demonstrations and violence to press their demands. In 1993, Wan Li, then head of the NPC, spoke emotionally about peasants saying they wanted another Cheng Sheng or Wu Guang, legendary leaders of the ancient peasant rebellion that led to the fall of the Qin.[9] According to Thomas Bernstein and Xiaobo Lu, half a million people participated in the wave of rural riots that took place in May and June 1997.[10] Lu Xueyi, the former head of the Sociology Institute at the Chinese Academy of Social Sciences (CASS), reports that there has been a major increase in the number of petitions, both individual and collective, since 1997, and notes that some areas have even started classes to teach people how to draw up petitions.[11] The *China Investigation Report, 2000–2001*, which was written by the Organization Departments of various provinces and edited by the central Organization Department, confirms that there are increasing numbers of demonstrations or riots, that they are better organized in the past, and that thousands—and sometimes tens of thousands—of people participate. Whereas in the past, most participants had been farmers and retired workers, now laid-off

---

8   Jonathan Unger and Anita Chan, "Corporatism in China: A Developmental State in an East Asian Context", in Barrett L. McCormick and Jonathan Unger (eds), *China After Socialism: In the Footsteps of Eastern Europe or East Asia?* (Armonk: M. E. Sharpe, 1996).

9   Lu Yu-sha, "Wan Li Delivers Speech Expressing Worry about Peasant Rebellion", *Dangdai*, 15 April 1993, FBIS, No. 72, p. 43, cited in Thomas P. Bernstein and Xiaobo Lu, "Taxation Without Representation", p. 753.

10 Ibid., p. 754.

11 Lu Xueyi, "Zhongguo nongcun zhuangkuang ji cunzai wenti de yuanyin" (The Situation in China's Countryside and the Cause of Existing Problems), in Ru Xin, Lu Xueyi and Dan Tianlun (eds), *2001 nian: Zhongguo shehui xingshi fenxi yu yuce* [2001: Analysis and Predictions of the Situation in China's Society] (Beijing: Shehui Kexue Wenxian Chubanshe, 2001), p. 159.

workers, small tradespeople (*getihu*), demobilized soldiers, technicians and even cadres are reported to be joining in.[12]

The government can and does suppress these actions, sometimes violently, but it must also take them into account. As Zhu Rongji put it, if the government uses violence and it misfires, it may well beget rebellion.[13] The sources of complaint must be addressed. Indeed, the very publication of the *China Investigation Report* suggests that the Party is acknowledging the size and importance of such problems. There is no longer a feasible option of suppressing protests by labeling their participants as "counterrevolutionaries".

Third, the very rapid increase in income inequalities, both intraregional and interregional, has raised the issue of social justice in a new and potent way especially since such inequalities are widely believed to result in part from the abuse of political power. Zheng Yongnian cogently argues that in the 1980s demands for social justice were expressed largely in broad ideological terms, but in the 1990s demands for social justice were expressed in more specific, concrete terms. Whereas ideological demands, especially those rooted in the minds of a relatively small group of intellectuals, can be relatively easily dismissed through campaigns against spiritual pollution and bourgeois liberalization, those that are rooted in the interests and demands of millions of workers and farmers are not so easily put aside.[14]

The third factor that has influenced the conduct of politics in recent years is the impact of the Tiananmen demonstrations and crackdown. The Tiananmen protests affected Chinese politics because they forced the leadership to place a higher premium on political and social stability. In the 1980s the Party (or at least the reform leadership) had tried to carry out two separations: separating enterprises from the government on the one hand and the Party from the government on the other. These moves weakened its political dominance. The leadership has thus placed a new premium on stability ("stability overrides everything" [*wending yadao yiqie*], in Deng Xiaoping's famous phrase).[15]

The urge for political stability was not limited to political hard-liners. Even reform-minded intellectuals began to rethink the reform process. In the 1980s political choices were largely perceived to be between "conservatism" and "reform". The Tiananmen crackdown and particularly the break-up of the Soviet Union added a third and unpleasant choice: social, political and economic

---

12   Zhonggong zhongyang zuzhibu ketizu (ed.), *Zhongguo diaocha baogao, 2000–2001: xinxingshi xia renmin neibu maodun yanjiu* [China Investigation Report, 2000–2001: Research on Contradictions among the People under the New Circumstances], Beijing: Zhongyang Bianyi Chubanshe, 2001), pp. 285–6.

13   Cited in Zheng Yongnian, *Jiang Zhu zhixia de Zhongguo* [China under Jiang and Zhu] (Hong Kong: Pacific Century Press, 2000), p. 9.

14   Ibid.

15   Ibid., p. 5.

collapse. Although a number of democracy activists retained their desire for rapid political change, the majority of intellectuals tempered their previous enthusiasm for rapid political change.[16] At the same time, a minority of them focused on the "injustices" associated with the introduction of capitalism in China, which had resulted, as many saw it, in the inequalities and social inequities mentioned above. While the demands for political reform conceived in terms of separating Party and state, developing a multiparty system and expanding electoral democracy declined, the demand for what might be called social or economic democracy—social equality and social justice—increased.[17]

As a result, the Party has proceeded very cautiously with regards to political reform, focusing instead on the separation of enterprises and government. This was the thrust of the 15th Party Congress report, and the decision to pursue World Trade Organization membership clearly reinforced this direction. The focus on social stability on the one hand and enterprise reform on the other has not "unified" the Party (indeed, there have been some notable clashes over the years), but it has kept disputes within reasonable bounds. Perhaps more importantly from the Party's point of view, it has (so far) prevented any large-scale social upheaval that would divide the Party and bring about another leadership crisis. The downside is that as the new millennium gets under way, the social pressures are again mounting, both from those who have benefited from reform and especially from those who have not, suggesting that the task of political reform is again forcing itself onto the agenda.[18]

Finally, the international political environment has changed. As just noted, the break-up of the Soviet Union and the end of socialism in Eastern Europe has led many Chinese intellectuals to rethink China's economic and political reforms. The result of Russia's "shock therapy" was not, as they saw it, prosperity and social peace, but rather economic and political decline combined with social disorder, corruption and crime. Some began to perceive of reform as a far more complex, time-consuming and incremental process than they had imagined only a few years before, while others went further and began to question the legitimacy of neo-liberal economics, political democracy, the international capitalist order and other forms of Western cultural "hegemony".[19] While China's intellectuals

---

[16]   Li Ping, *Zhongguo xiayibu zenyang zuo*? [How Should China Take the Next Step?] (Hong Kong: Mirror Books, 1998).

[17]   Cheng Li, "Promises and Pitfalls of Reform: New Thinking in Post-Deng China", in Tyrenne White (ed.), *China Briefing 2000: The Continuing Transformation* (Armonk: M. E. Sharpe, 2000), pp. 123–58.

[18]   Joseph Fewsmith, "Is Political Reform Ahead?—Beijing Confronts Problems Facing Society—and The CCP", *China Leadership Monitor*, No. 1 (Winter 2001), at <www.chinaleadershipmonitor.org>.

[19]   Joseph Fewsmith, *China Since Tiananmen: The Politics of Transition* (Cambridge: Cambridge University Press, 2001).

did not necessarily cozy up to the government (albeit some did), they did moderate their opinions, and this gave the government more leeway to reject Western models of economic and political reform and provided it with a more relaxed environment in which to carry out incremental reform.

At the same time, relations with the United States became considerably more tense, and sometimes hostile. The triumphalism of some in the United States and their harsh criticism of China stimulated nationalism among many Chinese. More than any other single event, the opposition of the United States in 1993 to Beijing's bid to host the 2000 Olympics convinced many Chinese that the United States did not simply oppose the Chinese government but were opposed more generally to the rise of China as a nation, thwarting what many Chinese people believed to be China's natural right to resume great power status. These perceptions led people who had been enthusiastic admirers of the United States only a few years before to reject the American economic and political model as something that China should adopt,[20] which reduced domestic demands for democratic reform.

In short, generational transformation of the leadership, the growth and diversification of societal interests, and changes in the domestic and international political context have strengthened the role of political norms, diminished the role of ideology, enhanced institutions and begun to forge a new state-society relationship and a new sense of nationalism.

To argue that there have been significant changes in the composition of the elite, in the relationship between the state and society, and in the conduct of politics is not to say that there are not important continuities. As Michel Oksenberg points out in his chapter, much of the core structure of the old Leninist system remains intact. Indeed, much of what makes the present era distinctive is the particular ways in which the trends identified above have combined with the legacies of the Dengist (and, before that, Maoist) order.

One continuity lies in the role of ideology. To say that ideology plays a diminished role in the present era is not to say that it plays no role, a mistake frequently made. Although we normally think of ideology as defining the Party's identity or mission, ideology is most closely identified with leadership. It is impossible to think of Mao Zedong without Mao Zedong Thought or Deng Xiaoping without "reform and opening up" (now known as "Deng Xiaoping Theory"). The supreme leader inevitably has put his stamp on the ideology, to define a "line" that is both personal and organizational. This is how a leader in the PRC defines his leadership, and it is why the ideological portfolio is always the ultimate responsibility of the leader. Ideology is thus a potent resource of leadership. A leader defines what is particular to his leadership, distinguishing his leadership and his era from that of his predecessor.

---

[20]   This trend is most clearly exemplified by the popularity of the book by Song Qiang, Zhang Zangzang and Qiao Bian, *Zhongguo keyi shuo bu* [China Can Say No] (Beijing: Zhonghua Gongshang Lianhe Chubanshe, 1996).

Jiang has faced difficulty in the ideological sphere through the 1990s. This was perhaps, as the critics charge, because Jiang lacks a strong vision of the future. But if Jiang has lacked vision (at least up until his promotion of the "Three Representations"—see below), the difficulty has not been entirely personal. It is also generational; people with technocratic backgrounds, as noted, have taken over the Party leadership. While the strength of technocrats lies in their ability to fix problems, their weakness lies in an inability to articulate a vision.

This lack of vision, however, is not just because Jiang and the broader leadership are technocratic but also because of the combination of domestic and international problems they face. As many Chinese put it, Mao's task was to centralize political leadership to instill unity in China, while Deng's task was to decentralize it in order to enliven the economy. Jiang, in contrast, has the more technically difficult task of separating the political system from the economy in ways that maintain a sufficiently strong state without stifling the economy. Internationally, Jiang must join the world without giving up the Party's domestic legitimacy, and every time he moves to engage the world more deeply, conservatives at home allege (correctly) that he is moving yet further away from Marxism-Leninism. These are not tasks that stir the blood. Given the ideological and historical bonds within which the leadership operates, Jiang spent most of his time in office dealing with these tasks rather stealthily (which rarely deceives domestic critics and even more rarely gains plaudits abroad), thereby undermining his ability to lay out a vision.

Beginning in 2000, Jiang's efforts to be identified with a vision took a "great leap forward". In February of that year, Jiang articulated his concept of the "Three Representations" (that the Party represents the broad mass of the population, advanced culture and the most advanced forces of production—this latter item meaning profitable, modern enterprises). The campaign began to gather steam after Jiang reiterated his ideas in May 2000.[21]

On 1 July 2001, the 80th anniversary of the Party's founding, Jiang gave a long speech in which he called for drawing Party membership from all sectors of society, including private entrepreneurs, for re-evaluating the Marxist theory on labour and labour value, and for expanding democracy by increasing its scope within the Party. Although highly controversial within the Party, especially among the Old Guard, these ideas, set within Jiang's framework of the Three Representations, were endorsed by the 6th Plenary Session of the 15th Central Committee in September 2001. Although the content of the ideas and their implications will no doubt become more apparent during and after the 16th Party Congress, scheduled for fall 2002, we can perhaps draw some tentative

---

[21] *Shenru xuexi "sange daibiao"; quanmian luoshi "sange daibiao"* [Deeply Study and Comprehensively Implement the "Three Representations"] (Beijing: Xuexi Chubanshe, 2000).

conclusions about what these ideological innovations tell us about the state of PRC politics in the era of Jiang Zemin.

First, Jiang's determination to establish an ideological system of his own underscores the continuing importance of formal ideology to the political system, even if the content of that ideological system is transformed and adulturated. Perhaps Jiang's determination in this regard is, as some critics say, because of Jiang's vanity and efforts to build a cult of personality. But it is also because ideology remains a source of legitimacy, and even as Jiang retires from the post of general secretary he seems determined to retain his influence over the system. One of his levers of control is his ability to define the ideological framework. In other words, he will have considerable influence over future policy decisions because only he will have the ability to determine if policy is, or is not, in accordance with the "Three Representations". There is clearly a continuity in this regard with Mao Zedong and Deng Xiaoping (as well as earlier leaders such as Sun Yat-sen and Chiang Kai-shek).

To say that ideology remains important to the exercise of personal authority and the overall political system is not, however, to say that its role in the system remains the same. Jiang's Three Representations do not constitute a mobilizing ideology along the lines of Mao Zedong Thought. Nevertheless, Jiang's proclamation does play a specific purpose. Deng inaugurated the Party's turn from an "exclusionary" orientation to an "inclusionary" one, but Jiang's Three Representations go way beyond Deng's reconciliation with society, by trying to incorporate the rapidly proliferating societal forces under an ever broader ideological umbrella.[22] This ideological evolution parallels other efforts to incorporate societal forces, such as bringing them under the auspices of corporatist organizations and by reserving political positions for non-Party people. The Three Representations can also provide a broad rubric under which the rationalization and institutionalization of the state can continue; indeed, it can accelerate this process because recruitment can be based even more on meritocratic criteria now that references to class can be dropped.

Jiang's Three Representations, as amplified by his 1 July 2000 speech and the 6th Plenum's "Decision on Strengthening and Improving the Construction of Party Style", mark a much more frontal assault on Marxist ideology than has been launched in China in some years.[23] In the plenum's insistence that Marxism is a methodology for understanding the world rather than a set of conclusions, Jiang's doctrine harkens back to Hu Yaobang's famous speech on the centennial of Marx's death. In that speech, Hu depicted Marx as a humble scientist forging

---

[22]   The terms exclusionary and inclusionary are borrowed from Kenneth Jowitt, "Inclusion and Mobilization in European Leninist Regimes", *World Politics*, Vol. 28, No. 1 (October 1975), pp. 69–96.

[23]   For a more detailed discussion of Jiang's speech, see Joseph Fewsmith, "Rethinking the Role of the CCP: Party Commentators on Jiang Zemin's July 1 Speech", *China Leadership Monitor*, No. 2 (Spring 2002), at <www.chinaleadershipmonitor.org>.

an epistemological weapon rather than as a political ideologue who had arrived at set truths.[24] Similarly, the 6th Plenum depicts Marxism as an open-ended system that can be employed to explore an evolving reality; Marxism is the enemy of dogmatism.

Jiang, however, went beyond Hu or other reformers of the 1980s by declaring class struggle dead (that seems to be the import of his call to admit private entrepreneurs [capitalists] into the Party). Indeed, the Party has laboured under the yoke of a contradiction throughout the reform era: namely the removal of class labels, the rehabilitation of the millions wronged in the Anti-Rightist Movement and Cultural Revolution, and the shift in Party focus from class struggle as the "key link" to economic modernization (contained in the Third Plenum resolution of 1978) on the one hand, and the assertion that class struggle continued to exist and "under certain conditions could become worse" contained in the history resolution of 1981.[25] Deng's assertion of the Four Cardinal Principles had been an awkward way of dealing with this contradiction that remained at the centre of Party doctrine. Jiang's call to admit capitalists into the Party appears to move the Party a significant step toward wiping out the last vestige of class struggle in Party doctrine, though references in the media to the continued relevance of the Four Cardinal Principles (inserted perhaps to protect Jiang's left flank) qualify this conclusion.

It is not only in allowing capitalists into the Party that Jiang breaks with Marxist tradition but also in his call to re-evaluate the Marxist theory on labour and labour value. In his 1 July speech, Jiang did not elaborate on this notion, but it is at least as important as his call to allow capitalists into the Party. After all, it is Marx's view of the labour theory of value that underlies the concepts of surplus value and exploitation. *If* wages are determined, as they are said to be by neo-classical economics, by supply and demand, there can be no *exploitation*. Writing the notion of exploitation out of Party doctrine might make good economics and is certainly consistent with admitting capitalists into the Party, but it leaves precious little justification for a Communist Party, thus pointing to the Party's ever-weakening legitimacy even as it moves to "revitalize" its ideology.

Moreover, Jiang's 1 July speech opened the door—albeit not widely—to political reform by calling for inner-Party reform as a way of furthering democratic reform (*Tongguo fazhan dangnei minzhu, jiji tuidong renmin minzhu de fazhan*). This suggests that one should not anticipate any democratic opening any time soon, but it is nevertheless important that the Party recognizes that greater democracy within the Party is a necessary part of political reform.

---

24   Hu Yaobang, "The Radiance of the Great Truth of Marxism Lights Our Way Forward", Xinhua, 13 March 1983, trans. Foreign Broadcast Information Service (FBIS), *Daily Report*, 14 March 1983, pp. K1–16.

25   "Resolution on Certain Questions in the History of Our Party Since the Founding of the People's Republic of China", Xinhua, 30 June 1981, in FBIS, *Daily Report*, 1 July 1981, pp. K1–38.

Although there is room to be skeptical about how much democratic reform there will be in the near future, it is worth noting that this stress on inner-Party democracy parallels the argument developed by Pan Yue, deputy head of the State Commission on Economic Structural Reform. In a report that has not been published but has been circulated on the Internet, Pan argued that the Party needed to carry out political reform in order to bolster its legitimacy, but for at least the present such reforms should be limited to strengthening procedural legitimacy within the Party.[26]

Jiang's efforts to revise Party ideology and to rebuild the Party underscore both the continuities and the differences in the China of the early twenty-first century and only a decade ago. On the one hand, the sorts of changes in state-society relations outlined above and discussed widely in Chinese publications in recent years have made an impact on Party ideology. The Party no longer feels that it should not respond positively to societal change. In this sense, the 1990s, when the Party did try to "hang tough" in the face of change (at least in ideological terms) are over. This reflects the passing of the old guard, the rise of a more pragmatic leadership and the impact of the enormous socio-economic changes that have taken place over the past decade. On the other hand, one still finds ideology central to the Party's definition of itself and to the establishment of a leader's legitimacy. Perhaps even more to the point, at the very time that Chinese society appears to be pluralizing and that Party doctrine itself is recognizing that diversity, there is no sign that political power is evolving from individual leaders to institutions. Indeed, in revising Party ideology—which should be welcomed as a tentative first step— Jiang is nevertheless using ideology in time-honoured fashion to reinforce his authority at the very time that he is presumably leaving the political stage. Perhaps he is merely, as some say, securing his place in history. But the probability that he is working to secure his post-retirement power through ideology seems large.

This change in Party ideology, which no doubt will be ratified and expanded upon at the 16th Party Congress, is not insignificant. As Tang Tsou puts it in his chapter, in order to break with the tradition of elite politics as a struggle to win all, the Party must adopt a theory of class accommodation to replace inherited notions of class struggle. Even more important, as Tsou notes, is an "explicit and total repudiation of the thesis that conflicts within the Party are a reflection of class struggle in the society at large". It appears that Jiang Zemin's 1 July speech accomplishes the former, and the discussion of political reform authored by Pan Yue, while not yet formal Party doctrine, shows that people near the top of the system are thinking about moving in the latter direction as well.

If ideology is one component of leadership, it plays a diminished role that must be supplemented, as argued above, by more formal authority—norms, laws and institutions. However, because formal authority remains weak, leadership is also enhanced by informal authority, particularly personalistic ties. As

---

[26]   This document is untitled, but is dated 23 January 2001.

revolutionary legitimacy declines, as ideology loses its power to persuade, much less mobilize, and as Party discipline declines, there appears to be an increase in the importance of personal power and personal ties, all the while that institutions (such as the NPC) and procedures (such as rules governing retirement) grow in importance. This is not to say that the system has become factional (although no doubt factions exist), because factional arrangements continue to be constrained by the force of norms that de-legitimize their existence as well as by formal institutions which, however weak, do exert force. Nevertheless, given the unreliability of other sources of power, personalistic ties and patron–client relations do appear to be more important than before.

Neither the changed and weakened role of ideology, the diversification of ideology and the limited dispersion and personalization of political power, nor the greater weight of formal rules and procedures suggest any fundamental change in what Tang Tsou identified in the pages of this book (and elsewhere) as the central characteristic of 20th-century Chinese politics: namely the assumption that political power is "monistic, unified and indivisible". Indeed, Jiang Zemin's efforts to reshape ideology, put his own stamp on it, and secure his own authority through the promotion of protégés provide evidence that unified political power remains important. Not having the revolutionary legitimacy of his predecessors and facing a more complex and diversified socioeconomic environment and the institutional resources of his colleagues makes Jiang's effort to consolidate and retain that type of power more difficult. But even though unified political power (the "core") is more difficult to attain, it is still the game of elite politics.

Although I agree with much of what Frederick Teiwes has written in his contributions to this book, the concept of "normal politics" does not capture my understanding of the dynamic of contemporary Chinese elite politics. It is certainly the case that in today's China, leadership politics are at least partially institutionalized and that there is no dogmatic ideological compass to guide the leadership. But questions remain as to whether norms of compromise have been internalized and whether the means for distributing power have been institutionalized.

Conceiving of power as monistic and indivisible is different than simply having (to quote from Teiwes's second chapter) a "strong leader who almost invariably gets his or her way". The former implies both a cultural framework and a personalistic system that would be fundamentally altered if the core leader were removed.[27] In China, these characteristics are combined with a formal ideological system (however attenuated) and a Leninist party organization, thus clearly distinguishing the Chinese system from the sort of personalistic rule that

---

[27]   I am using the term "cultural framework" along the lines that Clifford Geertz has outlined. See Clifford Geertz, *The Interpretation of Cultures: Selected Essays* (New York: Basic Books, 1973); and Joel Migdal, *State In Society: Studying How States and Societies Transform and Constitute One Another* (Cambridge: Cambridge University Press, 2001), pp. 236–41.

prevails in sultanistic regimes.[28] The notion of a Party "line" remains relevant, as Jiang's recent efforts to define his own line in ideological terms demonstrates, and continues to be central to defining power. Any efforts by others in the Party to alter the Party line are often implicit given Party strictures against factionalism, and are inevitably seen to be efforts to challenge the monistic and indivisible power of the core leader and thus threaten to trigger a game to win all. The term "game to win all", in my understanding, implies much more than one leader being replaced by another; it means a re-orientation of Party policy ("line") and has implications for cadres up and down the hierarchy. An example of such a struggle was the conservative effort in the years immediately following Tiananmen to redefine the Party line in a way that would weaken and indeed almost marginalize Deng Xiaoping (thus provoking his famous Southern Journey [*nanxun*]). Other examples were the circulation of various 10,000-character manifestos in the 1995–97 period that challenged Jiang's ability to define his own "line", and the assault launched by conservatives following the Belgrade bombing that threatened Zhu Rongji directly and Jiang indirectly.[29] It should also be noted that while Tsou's notion of power as "monistic and indivisible" affected the conduct of politics on a regular basis, he referred to "games to win all" as being "triggered" in periods of crisis. This leads to an empirical difficulty, given that during non-crisis periods there is no reason that a game to win all should be observable. Thus, it is difficult to know whether politics are really becoming "normal" in Teiwes's sense of the word or whether Chinese politics are merely in a trough between games to win all. Although I would agree with Teiwes and others that changes in Chinese society and generational changes seem to be constraining politics within certain limits, I remain cautious about assertions that the era of "winning all, losing all" is over. After all, there were clear aspects of this sort of political game being played out during the Tiananmen crisis,[30] as well as less definitively in the years since, and the sort of political culture that underpins such political struggle is unlikely to have changed so rapidly.

If China moves, as Teiwes suggests, toward the sort of compact that underlay Mexican politics for so many years, namely that a leader can stay in power for only a specified number of years and then selects another leader to pass power to, then perhaps we could assert that the conduct of elite politics has changed definitively. We will have to see how the retirement of Jiang Zemin plays out, and perhaps even whether his successor follows a similar pattern. Then we could

---

[28]   Houchang E. Chehabi and Juan J. Linz (eds), *Sultanistic Regimes* (Baltimore: Johns Hopkins University Press, 1998).

[29]   These are discussed in Joseph Fewsmith, *China Since Tiananmen: The Politics of Transition* (Cambridge: Cambridge University Press, 2001).

[30]   Tang Tsou, "The Tragedy of Tiananmen: The State-Society Relationship, Choices, and Mechanisms in Historical Perspective", in Brantly Womack (ed.), *Contemporary Chinese Politics in Historical Perspective* (Cambridge: Cambridge University Press, 1991), pp. 265–327.

say with confidence that "life-long tenure" has been ended for all political leaders and the game of elite politics has been fundamentally altered.

For the moment, all we can say is that Jiang's apparent agreement to step down as general secretary at the 16th Party Congress poses a sort of challenge that the system has never faced before: namely, the transition in power from one leader to another while the first remains alive and well.[31] The problem, of course, is Jiang's apparent disinclination to give up power when he retires. This natural human impulse is also conditioned by the system: if Jiang were to give up all political power, the interests of those who have risen with his assistance would be adversely affected—so they support, and perhaps press, Jiang's efforts to retain effective political power. Jiang's situation is made more difficult by the fact that the person in line to succeed him as general secretary—Hu Jintao—cannot be counted as a Jiang loyalist. The details of this story need not detain us here; suffice it to say that Jiang seems to believe the only way he can continue to exercise effective power after the 16th Party Congress is by consolidating his ideological vision and promoting people personally loyal to him.

The situation makes an informative contrast with the time in 1987 when Deng Xiaoping gave up his position on the Politburo Standing Committee at the 13th Party Congress. That congress passed a secret resolution to refer major questions to Deng as "helmsman". Whether this resolution was demanded by Deng in exchange for his retirement or whether it was more of an accolade given by the Central Committee in recognition of Deng's stature and service is not altogether clear, but surely the resolution marked some sort of need for a (secret) retention of formal authority to legitimize Deng's status (and presumably to entitle him to the flow of documents that normally go to Politburo Standing Committee members). Jiang, whose prestige and authority are palpably less than those of Deng, has little hope of securing a similar Party resolution, suggesting ironically that any hope he has of retaining authority following the 16th Party Congress rests on the prior appointment of political loyalists. Thus, one is confronted by the contradictory spectacle of a system in which the increased role of norms and rules necessitates Jiang's retirement, thereby creating a situation in which he must attempt to maintain his influence through informal politics.

This contradictory mixture of formal and informal authority is hardly limited to Jiang. It characterizes the political resources of other top leaders as well.

---

[31] This situation is different from Mao's cultivation of Liu Shaoqi and Lin Biao or Deng's grooming of Hu Yaobang and Zhao Ziyang. In these instances, the younger leaders may have been installed as successors while the supreme leader was still alive, but they were not expected to take over until after the leader's death. Jiang, of course, took over while Deng was still alive, but there was never a question as to who held the ultimate authority (as Deng demonstrated emphatically through his southern tour). In Jiang's own case, it is expected that he will be stepping down as general secretary, and another leader, presumably Hu Jintao, will take over. The question is the relationship between the new general secretary and Jiang (who may retain his position as chair of the Central Military Commission, but may not exercise the authority of a leader like Deng).

Jiang's apparent desire to promote Zeng Qinghong at the 5th Plenary Session of the 15th Central Committee in September 2000 was reportedly thwarted by other leaders. Their very ability to resist Jiang's preferred arrangements hinged on the same increase in institutional authority (the formal authority that goes with being vice-president of the PRC, head of the National People's Congress, premier, and so on) and the same pursuit of personal interest (how would Zeng's appointment affect the political and perhaps personal fortunes of any given leader?) that Jiang's authority rests on. The arguments surrounding Zeng's failed promotion, like most of the differences of opinion among the elite these days, seem rooted more in bureaucratic and individual interest than in ideological concerns (the Party "line"). The rise of a technocratic elite means a withering away of the great ideological disputes associated with the revolutionary generation, but the decline of "isms" has exposed a contestation of individual self-interest.[32]

This situation sheds light on the "monistic, unified and indivisible" nature of political power because it suggests that the current contest in Beijing is about whether or not Jiang Zemin will retain his core status. That such a contest can be joined in the first place reflects the growing role of formal norms, the weakening of ideology (hence, Jiang's efforts to reinforce it), the diffusion and personalization of political power, the weakening of Party discipline, as well as widespread disappointment within the Party regarding Jiang's political leadership. Although Jiang may yet lose this contest, the rules of politics in China still give an enormous advantage to the incumbent.

The picture of Chinese politics laid out above suggests that important changes in state-society relations, in the role of ideology, in the impact of norms and institutions and in the broader political atmosphere have not so much changed the fundamentals of Chinese politics and the rules of the game, as conditioned their exercise. Post-Tiananmen, it is now more difficult to engage in a winner-take-all contest for political power in a situation in which the likely outcome is not that one side will win but that all will lose. It is also more difficult to trigger such a contest if the problems to be solved are considered both more discrete and more amenable to technocratic solution. Similarly, to the extent that promotion and retirement are governed by norms and institutions, political conflict is likely to be more circumscribed.

Such a picture is cautiously optimistic (if one assumes gradual institutionalization and evolution to be both possible and good), but it also calls attention to the continued possibility of rupture. Ideology may have weakened, but it has not died. New social divisions have emerged as regional and class differences have widened and issues of social justice have been thrust to the fore. Corruption and the personalization of power have given advantages to special interests at the expense of laws and institutions. And globalization in the form of

---

[32]   An exception to this generalization was the strong reaction of conservatives following the U.S. bombing of the Chinese embassy. But even in this instance, bureaucratic and individual interests were visible as well.

the WTO injects potentially new and disruptive forces into society and politics. Some combination of such forces and issues could trigger a new struggle to win all or lose all, in which case much of the progress made in the past two decades would be lost.

TWELVE

The Supreme Leader and the Military

You Ji

When Jiang Zemin was appointed as Party general secretary in 1989 few analysts believed that he was likely to establish full authority over the People's Liberation Army (PLA), given his total lack of experience with the armed forces. More than a decade later, Jiang is the most powerful political figure in China owing in part to his congenial relations with the military. Indeed, the PLA can be considered Jiang's primary power base, and he has made use of its support to consolidate his position within the Party.

Jiang's interaction with the PLA has brought a new dimension to the study of China's elite politics. Some fundamental questions can be asked. Has his success with the PLA been based on his own personal endeavours or has it more generally been due to the institutionalization of elite politics? Does Jiang's example provide any clues that would enable us to divine his successor's future relationship with the PLA?[1]

I would like to argue that Jiang has been accepted by the PLA for seven reasons: first, he has astutely gone along with the transition in China's post-Deng civil-military relations; second, he has taken advantage of his institutional authority more adeptly than his Politburo colleagues have; third, he has skillfully managed his personal relations with the top military brass; fourth, he has convinced the PLA that the military's interests are best served with him in charge; fifth, the rise of professionalism in the PLA, as reflected by a reduction of stress

---

[1]   Jiang's designated successor, Vice-President Hu Jintao, serves as deputy head of the Central Military Commission under Jiang. Hu's appointment to this position in 1998 indicated that the grooming of Hu to succeed Jiang was well under way. According to Beijing sources, Hu has attended all Central Military Commission meetings but has normally kept silent. In 1998 he took charge of the mission to delink the military's commercial concerns with the PLA and won general praise from Jiang and the top commanders. However, is Hu really Jiang's preferred choice? He was groomed for the successor's position before Jiang's return to Beijing in 1989. If Hu's accession eventuates without Jiang's support, he would be the first successor not anointed by the nation's leader.

on ideology, a new defense strategy and a new officer corps, has reduced the room for the military to interfere with civilian leaders' policy-making process; sixth, the military reform program under Jiang has produced positive results that strengthen his legitimacy in running the armed forces: and seventh, Jiang has demonstrated a high level of competence in handling the discord between the civilians and the generals regarding the thorny issues of national reunification. In short, Jiang's success with the PLA involves factors of institutionalization of civilian control, coalition building, personal skills and tangible commitment.

Institutionalizing Civilian Control in Jiang's Hands

When Jiang assumed the office of commander-in-chief, China's civil-military relations were moving beyond the stage of personal control over the PLA by Party strongmen. By personal control, I mean the ability of a political leader to impose his own preferences without any prior consultation with the generals. Mao unilaterally used the PLA to launch the Cultural Revolution, causing the military to become politicized and fragmented. Deng was also a master of personal control, imposing his will whenever he deemed that overriding authority was needed to push forward a controversial reform. In 1992 he permitted Yang Baibing, the head of the PLA's General Political Department and younger brother of Yang Shangkun, the Deputy Chair of the Central Military Commission (CMC), to speak about the PLA's mission of *"baojia huhang"* (protect the emperor and guard his inspection tour): that is, to protect Deng's way of reform.[2] This was the most serious example of PLA interference in domestic politics during the reform era, in that it exerted tremendous pressure on the first-line leadership represented by Jiang. Using Yang Baibing's support, Deng dictated his own opinion to the Party leadership in a way not too different from Mao's involvement of the PLA in factional Party infighting in 1966.

The danger to the country's political stability of such personal control over the PLA is obvious. Deng realized that he would be the last person in the Party capable of exercising such control and that if he did not address this problem, effective civilian control over the PLA after his death would be difficult. Deng accordingly sought to strengthen civilian authority over the PLA in his last years. In 1992 Deng dismissed the Yang brothers, despite the fact they were among his best personal friends, because they might have formed a second power centre and challenged Jiang. More importantly, he tried to enhance the institutional authority of the chairmanship of the CMC. This civilian position, which is held by the Party general secretary, has the final say on all military matters, including personnel, legal, commercial and cultural issues, and control of the nuclear button. Deng also promoted a number of professionally minded generals, such as Liu Huaqing

---

2   For more details see You Ji, "Jiang Zemin: In Quest of Post-Deng Supremacy", in Maurice Brosseau, Suzanne Pepper and Tsang Shu-ki (eds), *China Review* 1996 (Hong Kong: The Chinese University of Hong Kong Press, 1996), pp. 1–28.

and Zhang Zhen, to key posts in the military. These generals had no political ambitions nor any visible interest in ideological disputes. Finally, Deng endorsed the CMC's proposal to shift the PLA's national defense strategy from his own notion of "fighting a people's war under modern conditions" to "fighting a regional war under high-tech conditions", which helped to unify the strategic thinking of the armed forces.

Jiang has taken advantage of the institutional power and high level of autonomy that comes with the chairmanship of the CMC. In the Party's hierarchical chain, the CMC is under the Politburo. In actuality it largely operates beyond the Politburo's reach. This long-established practice can be traced back to Mao, who deliberately separated the state and the military under the formula of "*zhengzhiju yi zheng, junwei yi jun*" (the Politburo's realm is state affairs and the CMC's is military affairs). Deng maintained this division. The CMC reported its affairs only to him throughout the 1980s. So far not one corruption case concerning the military has been dealt with by the Party's Central Disciplinary Inspection Commission. The CMC has its own commission that operates independently from the Party's. This means that Jiang is able to punish a senior general without needing to discuss the matter with his Politburo colleagues.

The powerful authority of the CMC chair rests on a system of commander responsibility. While the Party's civilian activities are based on collective leadership, the chair of the CMC, in contrast, has unchallenged personal power in appointing top brass, overseeing troop deployments and approving budget allocations. For instance, promotions of senior officers above the divisional level are not valid until signed off by the CMC chair. So, too, the movement of troops is very strictly controlled. Without the seal of the CMC chair, the relocation of army units above a certain size can be blocked by the PLA's logistical departments, civilian transport systems and local governments.[3] These institutional mechanisms make it relatively easy for the CMC chair to assert personal authority and build up a following. Although today the PLA is very prudent in exercising its power to influence who should be the Party's leader, this has still given the incumbent leader an advantage.[4] The continued ascendancy of

---

[3]   Li Xuefeng (former Politburo member and Beijing's Party boss), "Xianwei renzhi de wenge fadong neiqing" (Insider's Information about How the Cultural Revolution was Launched), in Xiao Ke, Li Rui and Gong Yuzhi (eds), *Wo qinli guode zhengzhi yundong* [The Political Movements I Experienced], Beijing: Zhongyang Bianyi Chubanshe, 1998, p. 317. Although Li alluded to a case of three decades ago, the situation remains the same today.

[4]   There are rumours in Beijing that the military wishes Jiang to continue to occupy the CMC chair for some time beyond the 16th Party National Congress in 2002, on the grounds that the current domestic and international situation is too tough for a newcomer to handle. This was the view expressed by Zhu Chenghu, deputy director of the Institute for Strategic Studies of the PLA National Defense University in his speech to the Beijing Institute of Contemporary International Relations on 15 October 1999.

Jiang in the Party is due in part to the fact that he has been accepted by the PLA as undisputed CMC chair.

While the formula "*zhengzhiju yi zheng, junwei yi jun*" has allowed Jiang to exclude his civilian Politburo colleagues from overseeing military affairs, this has also occurred because of the growing institutionalization of civil-military relations. The Party and PLA leaders have established regulations governing interactions. Safeguards have been put in place to stop civilian and military leaders from involving themselves in areas that are not their responsibility. In the past such interference was the catalyst for the formation of Party factions and political-military alliances, but over the last decade there have been no signs of civilian leaders trying to penetrate the military in their own pursuit of power, or vice versa. With civilian leaders no longer able to order the military to intervene in Party politics, the PLA top command has had a high degree of autonomy to run its own affairs.

Both Party and military leaders cooperate to avoid becoming involved in any activity that would escalate intra-Party policy debates into factional strife. A series of informal codes of conduct have been implemented for consensus building, including extensive consultation, debates within Party/PLA forums, and decision-making that considers all affected interests. Efforts are made to stop disputes between civilian and military leaders from intensifying and getting out of control. Specifically, there is a stricter division of power in relation to policy formulation concerning civil and military matters. On issues of national security that involve both, the Politburo is the locus of decision-making, with key PLA leaders participating, and the relevant State Council departments have established closer channels of communication with the PLA on foreign and defense affairs. Jiang has been the major beneficiary of this institution building because, with other civilian leaders otherwise insulated from military affairs, he is the only person to bridge the two sectors as Party boss and commander-in-chief.

The Give and Take in Relations

Jiang has also won firm support from the PLA due to his extraordinary efforts to convince PLA soldiers that he is one of them. This has helped Jiang pass the invisible test imposed on him by the PLA in 1989 when he became commander-in-chief. As soon as he assumed office, he started making efforts to improve the living standards of the rank-and-file officers, who in gratitude supported Jiang. In his first five years as commander-in-chief, he increased the wages of officers and the troops three separate times. Under his detailed instruction, the 1995 reform of military housing allowed massive sales of cheap homes to retired senior officers and provided handsome living space to active officers at the regimental level and above.

Jiang's vigorous campaign to enlarge military spending was the first major step to win the PLA's support. His first speech to the CMC in late 1989 emphasized the equal importance of economic development and the modernization of the defense forces (a policy later called the "double emphasis").[5] Deng had inadvertently given Jiang an opening in this regard, since during Deng's decade of command over the PLA the military's interests had been suppressed for the sake of economic reform. Deng repeatedly ordered the military not to demand higher budget allocations, and could do so due to his huge personal authority over the armed forces. Nonetheless, critical voices were raised about this among some of the generals who were not in Deng's own Second Field Army and who had been sidelined.[6]

Jiang took a proactive approach to the PLA.[7] Although the military is never satisfied with the budget it receives each year, the double-digit annual growth of the military budget marks a distinction between Jiang's leadership and that of Deng and Zhao Ziyang in the 1980s. Jiang has avoided the vulnerability of Zhao, who had re-emphasized Deng's call for the PLA to show self-restraint (*jundui yao rennai*). In contrast, in 1991 when addressing the PLA conference on the Gulf War, Jiang pushed the "double emphasis" concept a step further by stating that the PLA should receive budgetary increases in line with the growth of the national economy.[8] This idea was incorporated into the National Defense Law in 1997. The last few years have seen the increase of the military budget *surpass* the growth in GDP by a large margin, with a rise of the military budget in 2001 of 17.8 per cent, double the GDP growth of 7.8 per cent.

The interaction between Jiang and the military has been one of give and take. Despite the positive interactions between Jiang and the top brass, one implicit reason for the PLA's acceptance of Jiang may be his relatively weak personal authority as compared to Mao and Deng. It is easy to give positive support, but the test of authority comes only when the two sides encounter sharp policy differences. While Jiang's predecessors could be confident of victory when such differences occurred, Jiang has always tried to avoid them. For the first time in many years, the PLA is free from the strongman control that has damaged its key

---

[5]   Wu Xiuyong and Lie Jingdong, "Jianchi xietiao fazhan shi Jiang Zemin guofang zhanlie lilun de zhongyao tese" (Upholding Coordinated Development is a Key Element of Jiang Zemin Theory), *Guofang daxue xuebao* [Journal of the PLA National Defense University], No. 5 (2000), p. 8.

[6]   See, for instance, Qian Diqian, "Production Must Serve Military Training", *Junshi jingjixue* [Military Economics], No. 2 (1989), p. 21. Qian was formerly vice-president of the PLA National Defence University. Some generals also expressed discontent about the fact that Deng had promoted his Second Field Army followers to key commanding posts in the PLA.

[7]   For instance, Jiang told top PLA officers at the 1995 armed forces conference on political affairs that he had always tried to convince the National People's Congress to agree to a larger military allocation in the annual state budget. However, he continued, it was difficult for him to press the matter if large numbers of cases of corruption involving the PLA were exposed. (Oral source from the PLA during my fieldwork trip to Beijing in January 1996.)

[8]   Wu Xiuyong and Liu Jingdong, "Jianchi xietiao fazhan", p. 8.

interests in the past. The PLA does not seek to have another Mao or Deng sitting over it again.

Political Skills and Coalition Building

Management skills have also been important in establishing Jiang's ascendancy among the military. As newly appointed commander-in-chief, his initial problem was that he lacked a power base in the military, but he overcame this obstacle by building relations with all the main groupings in the PLA. At the time there were three main factions: the generals of Deng's Second Field Army; the Yang brothers' entourage; and military elders who did not belong to the first two categories, represented by Yang Dezhi, Hong Xuezhi, Xiao Ke and Zhang Zhen. Jiang made an effort to coordinate all three groupings rather than being partial to a single one (although whenever Deng had made his position known as to whom to favour, Jiang supported Deng's preferences).

After the removal of Yang Baibang, the PLA's mainstream leadership was composed of Liu Huaqing and Zhang Zhen, the two new deputy chairs of the CMC, with whom Jiang enjoyed good working relations. Jiang's coalition with Liu and Zhang was crucial in consolidating his leadership over the PLA. He took advantage of the fact that the two men had respected Deng's choice of Jiang as his successor. We should not underestimate the constraining power of the tradition of *tegu* (entrusting close followers with the mission of protecting the successor) that can be brought to bear on the top generals. Certainly such an influence is a slippery concept to measure, as seen from the example of Hua Guofeng. However, these two most powerful generals in the PLA did faithfully uphold Deng's will at the crucial early stages of Jiang's accession.

After Liu and Zhang retired, Jiang's control of the PLA was made easier, as he only dealt with military leaders of his own generation. However, the give-and-take relationship remained as important as before. Because the PLA has increasingly acted as a corporate body with a high level of unity, the divide-and-rule method of Mao and Deng no longer worked. Jiang therefore needed to further consolidate good personal relations with the military's new leaders, Zhang Wannian and Chi Haotian. This did not present any problem for Jiang, as early on he had supported these men for the top positions.[9]

The secret of Jiang's successful relations with the top military leadership has been his adoption of a "reign but not rule" principle: that is, he gives only broad policy guidance instead of detailed instructions. When the top professional soldiers recommend some major policy adjustment, he sits down with them and works out the best policy acceptable to all the interests involved. This leadership

---

[9]   It has been widely rumoured in PLA headquarters that Zhang Wannian was criticized by PLA elders in 1996, the crucial period when his succession to Zhang Zhen was in the balance, for spending too much public money to build his own home, and that it was Jiang who covered up for him.

style is clearly reflected in his handling of appointments. Although Liu Huaqing and Zhang Zhen both had no political ambitions and formed no visible factions of their own, they did promote a number of senior officers they liked. Jiang seldom vetoed these promotions. Jiang believed it would be better to take over Liu's and Zhang's following when they retired than to create his own, as he knew few people in the PLA personally. Now most of the senior officers appointed by Liu and Zhang are loyal to Jiang. Among these are You Xigui, the director of the Central Security Bureau and commander of the 8341 troops; Xing Shizhong, president of the PLA National Defense University; and Shi Yunsheng, the commander-in-chief of the Navy.

Yet "reign but not rule" does not mean a hands-off approach. Jiang reserves the final say on the most important military matters. For instance, he entrusts to Zhang Wannian and Chi Haotian the task of candidate selection and ranking but retains control over the appointment process. Thus, for the most crucial high-level military posts, he examines a list of names presented to him by Zhang Wannian and Chi Haotian, conducts face-to-face interviews with the candidates and solicits opinions about them from their work units. Generals Guo Boxiong (the executive deputy chief of staff) and Xu Zehou (the executive deputy director of the General Political Department) were promoted in this manner in 1999 as the duo slated to succeed Zhang Wannian and Chi Haotian. Jiang has also tried to keep the military happy by promoting top officers to the status of three-star generals shortly before they retire. Most of the 60 lieutenant generals who became full generals during Jiang's term as CMC chair were promoted in this way. His benevolent rule over the PLA has won him general praise from the top officers, in contrast to his relatively lower rating among the public.

Jiang's success in becoming the unchallenged leader despite an initially weak position tells us much about China's elite politics. Whereas in the past the succession to the top leadership entailed several periods of showdowns, under Jiang it has been a quiet fight for acceptance. Jiang has made it less a zero-sum game and more a case of power sharing. What makes this possible is Jiang's consensual leadership style. For a leader without a solid power base, observance of traditional Party norms and prudential politics can be effective weapons in dealing with difficult personal interactions, as Frederick Teiwes pointed out in the first section of this book. As most of the other top leaders value unity and stability, this enlarges the space for the Party boss to operate within. Analysts used to have doubts about Jiang's fate as leader, in that he lacks charisma. Yet this has proved to be Jiang's chief asset in an era that emphasizes collective leadership, consensus and compromise.

Promoting "Objective Control" as a Means of Effective Control

The PLA has been a professional military all along, even though it has taken on many other missions that are regarded as non-military by a standard Western definition. For a long time the PLA could be referred to as a revolutionary professional army, similar to the nature of the Israeli armed forces. What has changed in the last two decades is that the notion of it being a revolutionary army is fading rapidly, while the signs of it being a full professional organization are ever more clear. This changing nature of the PLA has provided a useful foundation for Jiang to tighten his control over the armed forces. By promoting professionalism within the military, the propensity of the armed forces to interfere in domestic politics is reduced. The ideal form of objective control, as pointed out by Samuel Huntington, is that the military leaders obey the government not because they agree with its policies but because they feel it is their duty to obey and to fight successfully for whatever ends the government wishes them to pursue.[10] Civilian control over the military is also greatly enhanced if the latter is directed mainly towards external missions.[11] Certainly China's civil-military relations are still far from the reality of objective control. Yet Deng and Jiang have understood that objective control is the ultimate means of effective Party control over the military after the age of strongmen. This is more cost-effective than measures of divide-and-rule, give-and-take incentives and ideological indoctrination. The rationale is clear: when officers are obsessed with high-tech toys, they will become more indifferent to politics. Jiang's effort to turn the PLA into a high-tech army parallels his effort of tightening up control over the officer corps. This can be seen in the following aspects.

Changing the Ideological Foundation

One major characteristic of the Party–PLA relations before the Dengist reforms was the strong ideological tendency of the armed forces. Ideological control was an integral part of Party control over the PLA. Consequently the PLA became class-based and an ideological model for society. Since the 1980s, the ideological thrust in the PRC has gradually shifted towards nationalism.[12] This has had a profound impact on civil–military relations. First, ideology is seen as unhelpful to the modernization efforts of the PLA, since an ideologically inclined military rejects professionalism as the primary goal of the armed forces and is more likely to challenge civilian leadership. Second, it is easier for the Party and the PLA to find common ground in nationalism. When the PLA is no longer required to service the narrow purposes of the working class, it can embrace a wider definition of national interests and is thus more readily accepted by the population, which is now cynical about Communism. Third, when Party–military relations are guided by common national goals rather than ideological correctness, there is less need for the Party to indoctrinate the soldiers so forcefully. The

---

[10]   Samuel Huntington, *The Soldier and the State: The Theory and Politics of Civil–Military Relations* (Cambridge, Mass: Harvard University Press, 1957).

[11]   Muthiah Alagappa, "Military Professionalism: A Conceptual Perspective", in Muthiah Alagappa (ed.), *The Professionalism of Asian Armed Forces* (Honolulu: East-West Center Press, 2001), pp. 1–18.

[12]   See, for instance, Yongnian Zheng, *Discovering Chinese Nationalism in China* (Cambridge: Cambridge University Press, 1998).

servicemen pick up patriotism themselves. Bilateral relations between the Party and army thus become easier to maintain.

Externally, the reduction of ideology in the PLA has highlighted the new identity of the PLA as a guardian of national interests rather than a revolutionary tool. This can be seen from its support for the Party's decision to remove ideology as the guideline in conducting foreign relations. Since the founding of the PRC the PLA has been involved in nine wars. These wars can be roughly categorized into two groups: namely, wars fought for ideological reasons and wars fought for the protection of national sovereignty and territorial integrity. Most of the military action occurred in the 1950s and 1960s. In the 1990s no wars were recorded. This underscores two important facts. First, after China gave up treating other nations by an ideological yardstick, the chance of war was significantly reduced. Secondly, even though China has always adopted a non-negotiable approach towards sovereignty and territorial issues, it realized in the 1980s that as a responsible international player it should place a peaceful settlement of disputes above military threats, which are to be used only as a last resort in protecting national interests.[13] This is a chief reason why the existing disagreement between the generals and Jiang over foreign policy and the Taiwan issue has not unduly hampered Jiang's command over the military.

Dropping ideology as the foundation of foreign and defense policy serves the PLA well. It was battered in various wars fought along ideological lines. It paid a particularly heavy price in achieving a stalemate with the US in the Korean War. The shift away from ideology has given the PLA much needed space to tackle its major problem of backward equipment. Having rid itself of its identity as a revolutionary tool, it has had to construct a new, more narrow mission as the guardian of national interests. This mission is not necessarily more peaceful but it gives the PLA the drive to enhance its professional pursuits and organizational cohesion.

The New Defense Strategy and Jiang's Command of the Gun

One key measure to gauge a professional military is its defense strategy. Since 1949 the PLA several times has altered its defense strategy, and from following Mao's doctrine of people's war it has shifted today to the so-called Revolution in Military Affairs (RMA) as the guide for modernization. The RMA emphasizes the external missions of the armed forces, and the generals have been convinced more than ever before that winning a hi-tech war relies on superiority of hardware, sound tactics and a suitable force structure.[14] In 1992 the CMC put forward a new

---

[13]   Yao Yanjin and Liu Jixian, Deng Xiaoping xinshiqi junshi lilun yanjiu [Study of Deng Xiaoping's Military Theory in the New Era] (Beijing: PLA Academy of Military Science, 1994), pp. 71–6.

[14]   See the articles by PLA authors in Michael Pillsbury (ed.), Chinese Views of Future Warfare (Washington, D.C.: US National Defense University, 1997).

national defense strategy as a new guide for the PLA's modernization. For Jiang this has proved to be an effective way of enhancing his control over the military.

First of all, the new strategy filled a vacuum in China's national defense when it was first advocated. At the time it was Deng's "people's war under modern conditions" that was the official strategy. The strategy projected a sustained trench warfare against a Soviet land invasion. However, this strategy was out of touch with the changing world situation in which it became obvious that the USSR had no plan of invading China. For a long time China was without a grand defense strategy, although the PLA did put forward a number of strategic guidelines such as that of limited regional wars. Jiang ordered the PLA in 1991 to formulate a new grand strategy soon after the Gulf War, a strategy that could guide China's defense modernization in the new century. In so doing he demonstrated a level of political courage, as the new strategy had to revise Deng's "people's war under modern conditions" just two years after Deng had stepped down and while he was still alive. The new strategy also showed Jiang's grasp of the nature of the information age and its impact on military science. This contribution to the PLA's professionalism won him high approval from the top brass, which helped him consolidate his power as the new commander-in-chief.

Secondly, the new strategy provided a rallying point for the PLA to unify its strategic thinking. After 1949 the PLA had experienced several periods of disunity when it could not arrive at a consensus as to what its grand strategy should be. Mao's doctrine of people's war offered only broad guidelines for fighting a war. When it came to concrete strategies, disagreements emerged among senior commanders, such as those between Liu Bocheng, Peng Dehui and Lin Biao. Deng's strategy of "people's war under modern conditions" united the thinking of the PLA in the early 1980s. It was welcomed by the generals because they regarded a strategy of holding back the invaders in the border regions to be preferable to luring them into the heartland, as stipulated by Mao. But by the end of the 1980s the PLA became divided again in a search for a more suitable defense strategy. Jiang's new strategy mended the cracks. Moreover, the new strategy could serve as a new political banner for the factional-ridden PLA, following the serious rift between the Yang brothers and other more professionally minded generals like Liu Huaqing and Zhang Zhen. Jiang learned from Liu Huaqing's experience with the navy in the early 1980s. It was Liu's blue-water maritime strategy that united a divided naval leadership that had been scarred by the infighting of the Cultural Revolution. The new strategy entails a new set of criteria for officer promotion, war preparation and military reforms, and a decade after its introduction has resulted in a high level of unity in the PLA not seen since the early 1950s.

Thirdly, China's new national defense strategy sets the PLA on a path characterized more by external concerns.[15] This can seen from the following points:

1) The new strategy stresses the necessity of a forward defense, as it recognizes that in a high-tech war the enemy can launch a precision strike from a long distance.[16] While expanding defense depth may not stop the enemy's long-range attack, if the enemy can be effectively engaged at an outer defense line the PLA may cause greater losses to the enemy and secure precious early warnings.

2) The high-tech defense strategy is largely an offensive strategy reflecting the PLA's shifting emphasis towards the "active" versus the "defensive" side of war preparation. The PLA was quick to learn from the Gulf War that high-tech wars will not be fought along fixed defense lines. Trench warfare will be rare in future. Accordingly China's post-Cold War military guideline has changed from *yifang weizhu fangfan jiehe*, or "defense as the overall posture, offense as the supplement", to *linghuo fanying gong fang jiehe*, or "a flexible response based on a combination of offensive and defensive capabilities". Offense is now understood as capturing the nature of warfare today: the evolving hi-tech hardware is highly biased toward a fast offensive strike because technological innovation has increasingly blurred the boundaries between offensive and defensive weaponry. A digitalized battlefield, electronic soft kill, and pinpoint elimination of the enemy's key targets all indicate that the offensive side that seizes the initiative of the war has the best chance of success. The offensive posture and pre-emptive strikes are especially crucial for a weak military at the beginning of a high-tech war.[17]

3) The strategy's high-tech focus aims mainly at defense against the major military powers. At the same time the strategy is flexible in principle, catering to different scenarios, from major wars to small-scale border conflicts. This is a response to the country's changing security environment in the post-Cold War era. The new strategy is also forward-looking, as it is geared to preparation for action in the new century. So it prescribes measures for

[15] For a more detailed analysis of the PLA and RMA, see You Ji, "Revolution in Military Affairs and the Evolution of China's Strategic Thinking", *Contemporary Southeast Asia*, Vol. 21, No. 3 (December 1999), pp. 325–45.

[16] Guo Yongjun, "Fangkong zuozhan ying shuli quanquyu zhengti fangkong de sixian" (Air Defense Should be Guided by the Theory of Area and Integrated Defense), *Junshi xueshu* [Military Studies], No. 11 (1995), pp. 47–9.

[17] Shi Zhigang, "Jiji fangyu zhanlie sixiang zhai xinshiqi junshi douzheng de tixian" (The Application of an Active Defense Strategy in Military Preparations in the New Era), *Guofang daxue xuebao* [Journal of PLA National Defense University], August–September 1998, p. 100.

weapons programs, force organization, campaign tactics, and research priorities that do not aim at equipping the PLA just for the next few years but at the frontiers of high-tech breakthroughs some decades from now.[18]

China's new military strategy deepens the professionalization of the PLA and thus enlarges the foundation for the civilian leaders' objective control over it. High-tech "toys" and an externally-oriented mission pushes the PLA away from its political tradition. Jiang is effecting a shift that will significantly change the nature of Party–military relations.

Creating an Elite Officer Corps

Another key factor contributing to Jiang's control over the military is that he is now dealing with an officer corps composed of technocrats rather than revolutionaries. There are fewer than ten people in the PLA who joined the Party before the founding of the PRC, and they will all depart the scene in less than two years. Notably, in the armed forces Jiang's revolutionary credentials are better than all of the officers other than Generals Zhang Wannian and Chi Haotian. In a political culture that emphasizes seniority, this has been a strong plus for Jiang in chairing the CMC.

The majority of well-educated military technocrats have a grounding in scientific knowledge, not the spirit of radicalism. The result is that they are less likely to form factions along political and ideological lines. Their ties with civilian politicians are minimal. Such a new tendency can be seen most clearly at the lower levels in the PLA. 600,000 officers, or 90 per cent of the whole officer corps, have higher education qualifications, 20,000 officers have Masters degrees and over 4,000 officers have Doctoral degrees. This new organizational make-up of the PLA is a clear line of departure from its recent history.[19]

There are many other indicators of professionalization as a result of the changing of the guard. The PLA high command has substantially reformed military training and education. Officers need to go through an extended period of re-learning to meet the new requirements of warfare in the new era. They all are required to study new technology, to handle computers and to become familiar with the targeted enemy forces. Promotion is closely tied to their study efforts. One of the assessment criteria is the number and quality of their published material in academic journals and in internal policy debate. For instance, an indispensable rung on the ladder for promotion into senior posts is a period of intensive study in an advanced course for generals at the PLA National Defense

[18]   Tao Bojun, "Dangde sandai lingdao jiti yu keji qianjun" (The Party's Three Generation Leadership and Strengthening the Armed Forces through Technological Breakthroughs), *Zhongguo junshi kexue* [China Military Science], No. 3, 1997, pp. 65–73.

[19]   Wu Jianhua, "Wo jun zhonggaoji nianqin zhihui ganbu baiyang de kaocha yu jishi" (A Review of the Promotion of Young Senior Officers in our Army and its Lessons), *Guofang daxue xuebao* [Journal of the PLA National Defense University], No. 1, 2000, p. 51.

University.[20] It is said that Jiang as the CMC chair and/or his deputies read the graduation theses of the students in this class. Wang Zhuxun's promotion serves as a telling example of the emerging nature of the elite PLA officers corps. In the early 1990s he was commander of the 14th Group Army when he joined the class of generals. He wrote a graduation thesis entitled *The Strategic Path of Yunnan*, which argued that if a war erupted on China's coast, China's strategic path through the Pacific would be blocked. This would seriously affect China's economy because more than two-thirds of China's exports and imports took this route. He suggested that China should prepare to establish an alternative strategic path from Yunnan through Burma in order to reach the Indian Ocean. His thesis caught the attention of General Zhang Zhen, the third most senior military leader in China, who passed it on to Jiang with the remark that this was exactly the kind of personnel with broad strategic vision that we need for military modernization. Later Wang was promoted to become commander of a military region and president of the PLA Academy of Military Science. In fact, almost all of the current top officers have an impressive list of publications.

The Military Reforms

The rise of professionalism in the PLA also results from a series of far-reaching organizational reforms that the Chinese military has implemented since the 1980s. These include a major overhaul of the PLA's headquarters (changing it from three headquarters—the Departments of General Staff, Political Affairs and Logistics—to four headquarters, by adding a General Department of Equipment); a substantial reform of the logistical system (to create a united service supply system); a large-scale reduction of the force level by 1.5 million men, mainly from the ground force; and far-reaching restructuring efforts to the four services. The bulk of these reforms were conducted under Jiang's direct leadership.

All of the reforms are in pursuit of two guiding principles. The first is to effect two fundamental shifts in the PLA's mentality: the shift from an emphasis on manpower to hardware/software quality and a shift from a model of relying on inputs to one of maximizing outputs.[21] The second guiding principle is that all military modernization efforts should serve the goal of winning a war against powerful enemies. This requires the whole armed forces to learn how to fight high-tech warfare with particular opponents.[22] Related to this is a major force

[20]   This class admits students at the level of army commanders. Each year about 50 promising young major generals are enrolled in the course.

[21]   General Wang Ke (Director-General of the General Logistics Department), "Dali tuidong houqin gaige tigao junshi jingji xiaoyi" (Make a Big Effort to Push the Logistical Reform and Improve Military Economic Efficiency), *Zhongguo junshi kexue* [Chinese Military Science], No. 2, 2000, p. 10.

[22]   Fang Zhongxian, "Mianxiang xinshiji quanmian jiaqian he gaijing jundui sixiang zhengzhi jianshe" (Facing the New Century, Comprehensively Enhance and Improve the PLA's

redeployment to cater for the strategic shift in China's military security: namely, geographically the country's defense priority has shifted from the land borders of *sanbei* (north, northeast and northwest China) to coastal China; and politically, the preparation for war is being shifted from armed conflicts over regional territorial disputes to a high-tech RMA type of war of mass destruction.

As far as promoting military professionalism is concerned, two more reforms are crucial. The first is to establish a better division of labour between its various services. The Armed Police was created in the 1980s to handle the first-line domestic duties, to maintain law and order and social stability. Garrison forces will take care of the second line, to support the Armed Police when there are major social disturbances. The elite units (specialized services and group armies) are earmarked for dealing with external threats. This is to allow the combat troops more time for training and less need for involvement in domestic politics. The political significance of this reform involves a lesson the Party leadership learned in 1989: that is, elite troops should be saved from carrying out the dirty work of clearing the streets, as they were ordered to do during the Tiananmen protests, which so badly tarnished the PLA's image. Certainly, this new division of labour has contributed to professionalization of the PLA.

Another key reform was to delink the bulk of PLA business interests from its force structure in 1998. In the 1980s the PLA set up large numbers of firms. The purpose was to generate as much extrabudgetary income as possible to supplement the shortages in the military's allocated budget. The PLA had set up thousands of factories, firms, hotels and farms and become, as some people called it, a business army. This business expansion within the armed forces not only seriously undermined the professional efficiency of the PLA but also served as a hotbed for corruption. The reform to delink it was welcomed by the top generals and civilian leaders, who reached a consensus that if the PLA continued to engage in business China's military modernization would go nowhere. Because of this civilian/military joint effort, within half a year most of the businesses were removed from the PLA in one of the success stories of military reform in post-Mao China.

Jiang Zemin, the PLA and National Reunification

There is a lot of talk about discord between the civilian and military leaders regarding how to deal with the question of national reunification. The issue is where the country's priority lies: the continuation of Deng's political line of economics in command or an enhanced preparation for a possible war of national reunification. Clearly the civilian and military leaders have different vested interests in setting the course in either of these directions. This has posed a challenge to Jiang's command of the military from the very beginning. Jiang's consolidation of power within the Party leadership has so far proved that Jiang is

---

Political and Ideological Work), *Guofang daxue xuebao* [Journal of the PLA National Defense University], No. 2, 2000, p. 18.

capable of handling this challenge. While he has maintained Deng's policy line, the vested interests of the PLA have also been taken care of, although not completely to the satisfaction of the soldiers.

The Civilian Leaders' Peace Agenda and the PLA's Stance

The mainstream civilian leadership of Jiang and Zhu Rongji are more pro-Western than their predecessors and, perhaps, their successors. They were trained in Western-style universities in the 1940s. And they have both worked in economic management agencies, involving foreign trade. Their exposure to the West may have broadened their vision of the international system. This draws a sharp difference with their prospective successors, who will form the core of the fourth-generation leadership. The world outlook of these successors was shaped by the educational teachings of the 1950s and 1960s. The majority of them have been in charge of Party organization, propaganda and personnel management.

Jiang knows that China has the best chance in many centuries to fulfil the national goal of becoming rich and militarily powerful (fuqiang). The military threat to China on the ground is minimal, as there have been no prospects of a land invasion since the end of the Cold War. In Jiang's eyes China's foreign relations basically are in good shape,[23] while the country's domestic situation is fairly stable thanks to both political restrictions and economic growth.[24] In these circumstances, China's security should be enhanced through promoting a course of reconciliation with its potential rivals.[25] The only thing that may quickly torpedo the rise of China is an early war with Taiwan.

This is the reason why Jiang insists that China's foreign policy in the post-Cold War era should be non-confrontational towards the West. And the bottom line for this policy guideline is to handle the Western challenge cleverly in order to create a stable international environment for China's economic take-off. This policy of taoguang yanghui, namely taking a low profile foreign-policy stance in the world arena but quickening military modernization quietly, is one of the key strategies Deng had laid down for his successors when he retired in 1990.[26] Following this principle, Jiang seeks to take a long-term perspective in handling

23 See Jiang Zemin's speech to the PLA delegates to the 2001 annual session of the National People's Congress. Renmin ribao [People's Daily], 20 March 2001.

24 This situation has been analysed well by contributors to the book Is China Stable?, edited by David Shambaugh (Armonk: M. E. Sharpe, 2000).

25 Meng Xiangqing, "Jiang Zemin's anquanguan chetan" (An Initial Study of Jiang Zemin's Theory of Security), Waijiao xueyuan xuebao [Journal of the Foreign Affairs College], No. 2 (1999), pp. 38–42.

26 Qu Xing, "Shilun dong Ou jiupian he suliang jieti hou de Zhongguo duiwai zhengce" (China's Foreign Policy since the Radical Changes in Eastern Europe and the Disintegration of the USSR), Waijiao xueyuan xuebao [Journal of the Foreign Affairs College], No. 4 (1994), pp. 19–22.

acute conflicts with other major powers. Even if the quarrels involve matters of Chinese sovereignty (e.g., the West's weapons sales to Taiwan) Jiang may well make an initial harsh response (showing his resolve to PLA generals), but leave room to compromise for the sake of maintaining an overall relationship, again for economic reasons. The exception to this was his policy choice vis-à-vis the war over Kosovo, which had no immediate bearing on China's vital national interests. Beijing's unnecessarily critical position toward NATO cost China dearly in terms of its relations with the NATO powers, and especially with the US.[27]

Most of China's military personnel, and particularly the service commanders, see the matter differently. Their professional training is narrowly confined to combat situations. This tends to shape their mentality in terms of worst-case scenarios, dominated by a calculation of the balance of military capabilities with the enemy. Moreover, their early socialization in the PLA is marked by teachings that Taiwan presents the last unfulfilled mission of the PLA to liberate the whole country. The officers would regard it as an enormous loss of face if Taiwan were to declare independence and the PLA were unable to do anything about it.

The Taiwan issue has been the driving force for the PLA to step up war preparedness in recent years. Commitment to national reunification has convinced PLA officers that if need be, a war on this issue is worth fighting for. Such a stance wins substantial public support.[28] Institutionally the PLA enjoys a unique position in the policy-making process toward Taiwan. Mao decided in 1950 that the Taiwan issue should be handled by the Central Military Commission. The Party's Leadership Group on Taiwan Affairs has been the domain of the military as a result of Mao's decision and the continuity of this tradition. Jiang leads this powerful group due to the fact that he is the chair of the CMC. Other powerful members in the past were Yang Shangkun, Deng Xiaoping and Ye Jianying (as executive deputy chairs of the CMC). Despite the PLA's relatively low public profile concerning Taiwan policy alongside Jiang and a few other civilian leaders in the Leading Group, it actually enjoys a strong say on the matter, for without the military's consent no solution of the Taiwan problem can be found.

Consequently the PLA's position has had a decisive impact on how both sides in the Strait handle the dispute. An increasingly more nationalistic military will take the direction of the conflict away from a peaceful resolution, just as may happen in Taiwan if a ruling political party there presses ahead with an agenda of independence.

---

[27] Elsewhere I had made a detailed analysis of this exceptional case: see You Ji, "China's Perception on the Changing Security Situation in Asia and the Pacific", *China Studies*, Vol. 7 (March 2001), pp. 127–44.

[28] In a poll conducted by the magazine *Chinese Youth* immediately after Chen Shuibian's election victory, 95 per cent of those surveyed supported the option of war if Chen declared independence in Taiwan. Most of them had university qualifications. (*Zhongguo qingnian bao*, 25 March 2000.)

Consensus, Compromise and Debate

Taiwan is a headache to Jiang because he is the commander-in-chief and therefore should represent the PLA's vital interest. In the policy process, however, Jiang's heart is with the moderate economic managers. At times Jiang's non-confrontational approach toward the West and his hesitation in using a military threat against Taiwan has presented a problem for the military and the agencies dealing with national security matters.[29] But so far Jiang has struck a balance between the opposing views, as seen in the quite fluid range of policy options he has leaned toward, including periods of hardline outbursts, such as the missile firings in 1995–96 and the large-scale missile deployments close to the Strait since the end of the last decade. This is a reason why the PLA has not seriously challenged Jiang over his management of foreign affairs. However, the generally cooperative attitude of the PLA also reflects the fact that a broad foundation exists for the civilian and military leaders to formulate a consensus policy. Yet debate continues and may have serious implications in the future. Nonetheless, we can expect renewed consensus to prevail, for several reasons:

Sovereignty is non-negotiable

First of all, there is little room for major disagreements concerning matters of national security and reunification, and a common ground among civilian and military leaders is formulated on this basis.[30] This has three key components: 1) Beijing has more than one approach to achieve the goal of national reunification: peaceful means are most welcome but the use of force is not ruled out. Here the civilian and military leaders share a division of labour, one playing the "white face" and the other the "black face" as in Peking Opera. 2) There is agreement that if the situation in Taiwan takes a turn for the worse, the mainland's agenda in the next few decades should move from relying on peaceful inducements to military preparation, although peaceful reunification is a motto that should never be discarded. 3) If Taiwan declares independence, China should quickly switch to a war setting. As pointed out by Zhu Rongji, "there are things that China cannot swallow".[31] Jiang and his close associates are aware that, despite their concern for economic development and international reactions, in a showdown in the Taiwan

---

[29]   For instance, one senior researcher from the Ministry of State Security revealed at a seminar in Sydney in April 2000 that voices have been heard in Beijing criticizing Jiang's soft handling of Chen Shuibian's election as Taiwan's president. Some even indicated Jiang should resign.

[30]   You Ji, "Taiwan in the Political Calculations of the Chinese Leadership", *The China Journal*, No. 36 (July, 1996), pp. 117–25.

[31]   Zhu's speech to a news conference on 17 March 2000. He said in the news conference that the Chinese people would not be afraid to shed a lot of blood in safeguarding national territorial integrity.

Strait over this issue of independence other options would be largely foreclosed after years of popular education in nationalism.[32]

The Military takes a back seat to the Party

The second factor is that the PLA has become increasingly non-interventionist towards the Party's policy formulations in areas other than national defense. This makes civilian control over the armed forces easier, contrary to many analysts' predictions that the PLA would become more assertive in the post-Deng era.[33] Certainly, the PLA can still wield enormous political influence, especially at a time of succession, another round of which is around the corner. Yet the PLA chooses to use that influence more prudently and selectively, confining it largely to the realm of national defense. This does not fall outside the standard purview of military professionalism regarded as legitimate by Western countries.

For some time the civilian leaders have tried to prevent the PLA from holding hard-line attitudes on international politics. The military has not only followed the Party's wishes, but normally refrains from disagreeing with the civilian leaders even in areas of foreign policy related to national security issues. For instance, the military obeyed the Politburo's decision in 1991 that there should be a joint agency monitoring China's weapons sales in the international market. It took a pledge in 1993 not to use force to settle the South China Sea disputes when other claimants continued to occupy islets there. In 1995 it voiced support for Jiang's peace initiative toward Taiwan embodied in his 8-point declaration, which emphasized that "Chinese do not fight Chinese". The military did so despite the belief of its leadership that such an olive branch would not work. When its nuclear program for upgrading land and sea-based long-range nuclear missiles was at a crucial stage of development, it accepted the civilian leaders' decision that China should stop nuclear tests in 1997. Under the pressure of the Party it gave up its vast economic and commercial machine in 1998. Last but not least, after the spy-plane crash of 2001 the PLA ordered its combat units monitoring the spy activities of the US air force and navy in both the South and East China Seas to exercise maximum restraint toward the intruders, again

---

[32] For a good analysis of how the civilian leaders respond when backed into a corner by a crisis situation in Taiwan, see Thomas Christensen, "Posing Problems without Catching Up: China's Rise and Challenge for US Security Policy", *International Security*, Vol. 25, No. 4, 2001.

[33] See, e.g., Jeremy Paltiel, "PLA Allegiance on Parade: Civil-Military Relations in Transition", *The China Quarterly*, No. 143 (September 1995); David Shambaugh, "China's Post-Deng Military Leadership", in James Lilly and David Shambaugh (eds), *China's Military Faces the Future* (Armonk: M. E. Sharpe, 1999).

following the Politburo's decision.[34] All of this was not accomplished without a degree of disgruntlement. Yet the fact that the PLA has swallowed what is imposed upon it indicates that it is conscious of its subordinate position vis-à-vis the Party centre. Certainly the PLA's obedience is compensated elsewhere, such as receiving an ever increasing budget.

The time is not ripe for confrontation

The third factor in the PLA's acquiescence to Jiang's non-confrontational diplomacy lies in the current transitional difficulties it faces in its weapons research and development. Many of its new hi-tech weapons designs have just passed laboratory tests and several more years are needed for them to become deployable. Top PLA commanders know this is not a time to take action.[35] And the civilian leaders have successfully convinced PLA generals that if China has two more decades of peaceful development, both its comprehensive national strength and the PLA's high-tech inventory will decisively alter the balance of power between the mainland and Taiwan in the mainland's favour (even Taiwan recognises this).[36] To this end China's civilian leaders have obtained the agreement of PLA generals that a low-profile foreign policy is preferable to hawkish rhetoric. The PLA also knows that it would not benefit from a major war in the Taiwan Strait—that it would suffer a lot more casualties than it is willing to sustain.

Jiang shares the PLA's threat perception

Fundamentally, Jiang does not disagree with the PLA's perception of the external threat to China's vital national interests. Both Jiang and the military perceive an ultimate US intention to unseat the Communist government in China. They perceive an effort by Taiwan's mainstream elites to promote independence. They see how tough the challenge of globalization will be to China's economic standing in the world. Even Jiang no longer entertains any illusion that his Western friends are true friends.[37]

---

[34]   The US Secretary of State confirmed in Beijing that the Chinese military had stopped tailing US spy planes in the South and East China Seas. See the transcript of his speech to the news conference in Beijing during his first China visit as Secretary of State in July 2001.

[35]   You Ji, *The Armed Forces of China* (Sydney, London & New York: Allen & Unwin and I.B. Tauris, 1999), Chapter 3.

[36]   Speech of Taiwan's defense minister to the 1999 Asia-Pacific Security Forum Conference in Taipei, 17 December 1999.

[37]   In a news conference in Canberra during Jiang's state visit to Australia in September 1999 Jiang called Clinton his old friend. However, when he received the staff of the Chinese embassy and representatives of Chinese students during the evening of the same day, he

Nevertheless, disagreement arises when civilian and military leaders discuss how to handle these challenges. Many of the generals would like to see a firmer stance by Jiang against the "Western threat" and against Taiwan's independence than Jiang is willing to adopt. This has given rise to a quietly conducted debate among PRC leaders about the guidelines for China's post-Deng foreign policy in the new international climate. Especially in recent years, confronted by Bush's unilateralism and his depiction of China as a strategic competitor, Party and military leaders are engaged in a soul searching about whether a non-confrontational foreign policy works. After the Belgrade embassy bombing, Bush's open pledge to defend Taiwan and the spy plane collision, China's defense analysts suggest that it may not be up to Beijing as to whether it wants a confrontational policy or not. Many PLA officers feel a need to wage a counter-offensive to the growing US pressure and what are perceived to be intensified efforts of the Taiwan government to push toward independence.[38] In crisis situations such as the spy plane incident, the PLA wants to call for a tit-for-tat response to what it believes to be a deliberate US action to humiliate China. In contrast, Jiang and other civilian leaders consider more carefully before responding to the US, taking into account the current level of PLA modernization, the economic consequences, the international outcry, and all other consequences of a premature showdown with the US (and Taiwan).

The second point of debate is about national development priorities. Deng had revised Mao's assertion that war was inevitable, arguing that peace dominated the world system as of the 1980s, and 1990s, and he accordingly placed economics above national defense. As mentioned earlier, Deng set China's post-Mao policy as a formula of one centre (economics in command) and two basic points (reform and an open door). With the new international situation, defense planners see a need to adjust the formula inasmuch as it has slowed down the pace of military modernization. The military have sought to add to Deng's "one centre" (economics in command) another centre, namely safeguarding national sovereignty and territorial integrity, which would entail a major military build-up. They note that Deng once instructed the PLA's leaders that they should see the protection of national sovereignty and territorial integrity as the state's primary task.[39]

The Politburo's conference at Beidaihe in August 1995 put an end to the debate temporarily and upheld Deng's 28-character diplomatic principle, after

---

cited the example of the US bombing of the Chinese embassy in Yugoslavia as an example of how China's international enemies such as the US would not be at ease as China became stronger.

[38]   This was the central theme of China's defense-related media in the weeks after the American spy plane incident.

[39]   See, e.g., Peng Guangqian, Yao Youzhi and others, *Deng Xiaoping zhanlie sixianglun* [On Deng Xiaoping's Strategic Thoughts] (Beijing: the PLA Academy of Military Science Press, 1994), p. 109.

Jiang persuaded participants that it was not the right time for confrontation.[40] The Beidaihe conference in 1999, however, came to a new conclusion: that the bombing of the Chinese embassy exposed the bottom line of the West's policy toward China. A choice between peace and war was no longer in Beijing's hands. Jiang, as pointed out by senior PLA officers, decided to enhance the intensity of military preparation. He promised that the PLA would, as quickly as possible, acquire a capacity to win a high-tech war against a major military power.[41] Obviously this would dictate a substantial increase in the defense budget, reflected in a 17 per cent increase the following year. Although the Party's central task is still designated as promoting economic development, Jiang's position in handling the contradiction between economic construction and military modernization has tilted toward what the PLA has stood for all along. The PLA's request was difficult to deny. If the PLA is defeated in a major armed conflict due to the fact that Jiang places economic development above military modernization, the responsibility would be too heavy for him to survive politically. In November 1999 Jiang personally announced the Politburo's decision to accelerate military preparation at the Armed Forces Chiefs-of-Staff Conference.[42]

Although Jiang still believes that any security threat to China is largely long-term, the bombing of the Chinese embassy in Belgrade and the spy-plane incident of 2001 appear to have convinced Jiang of the need for the PLA to prepare for a worst-case scenario. He has begun to share the PLA's concern over its backward military arsenal. In dealing with "endless incidents" with the US in the first year of George W. Bush's administration, Jiang found it increasingly difficult for China to befriend the US. With a pro-independence political party in power in Taipei and Bush's new commitment to defending Taiwan, it seemed out of place for Jiang to reiterate that major wars can be avoided. The new assessment of the world order is more pessimistic than at any time since the beginning of the 1980s. The dominant view within the defense analysts' circles in Beijing is that a war may well erupt before the end of the second decade of the new century.[43] Jiang

---

[40] See You Ji, "Changing Leadership Consensus: the Domestic Context of War Games", in Suisheng Zhao (ed.), *Making Sense of the Crisis Across the Taiwan Strait* (London: Routledge, 1999), pp. 77–98.

[41] Peng Rixuan, Ying Lin and Li Tao, "Zhongguo jundui xiandaihua jianshe huigu yu zhanwang" (A Review and Forecast of the Chinese Military Modernization), *Guofang Daxue xuebou* [Journal of the PLA National Defense University], No. 5, 2000, p. 9.

[42] General Qian Guoliang (commander of the Shenyang Area of Military Command), "Quanmian luoshi 'silinbu jianshe gangyao', gao biaozhun zhuahao silingbu jiguan jianshe" (Comprehensively Implement the Guideline of Headquarters Construction, and Do a Good Job in Headquarters Construction), *Guofang daxue xuebau* [Journal of the PLA National Defense University], No. 6, 2000, p. 4.

[43] Yan Xuetong, "21 Shiji zhongguo jieqide guoji anquan huangjing" (The Security Environment for China's Rise in the 21st Century), *Guofang daxue xuebou* [Journal of the PLA National Defense University], No. 1, 1998.

has stated repeatedly that the negative new trends in international politics have imposed a great urgency in China's military and technological modernization.[44]

Yet it is interesting to note that, despite his supportive remarks for a quickened military build-up, Jiang has been reluctant to move China in a direction that may be interpreted by its neighbours as provocative. Whenever international events have damaged China's national interests, Jiang has stressed the hawkish side of national defense policy. However, whenever tensions eased, he has watered down his commitment to the PLA that war preparation would enjoy the same priority as economic development. And the same is true of Zhu Rongji. His very tough rhetoric at the news conference in April 2000 when he addressed the question of Taiwan's presidential election should not be taken at face value.

China's civilian and military leadership will be discussing how to react to Taiwan for a long time to come.[45] For instance, the PLA argues that it is now clear about the direction of Taiwan's next move. Peace is possible only when China tolerates Taiwan's independence. In this sense war is imposed upon China rather than China seeking it. Therefore, national reunification cannot be accomplished without a timetable.[46] Yet Jiang Zemin has not altogether given up the goal of peaceful reunification. And he sees the role of the military in resolving the Taiwan crisis more in the light of its deterrence effect rather than real use. To him a timetable is not yet an option, even though the 1999 *White Paper* threatens a war against Taiwan if it puts off negotiations indefinitely. Jiang may agree with the PLA that the prospects of war are visible but not that war is imminent. If China can secure a lengthy period of peace in which to ensure economic construction and military modernization, the trend toward war can be reversed. He believes the view that war is imminent is dangerous, as it will disrupt China's long-term strategic plans. An early war, given China's situation, would only make the enemy happy.[47]

---

[44] Ibid.

[45] In November 2000 a senior PLA researcher about China's Taiwan strategy told me that he had read all Jiang's speeches on the Taiwan problem in recent months and had found the speeches made to the PLA were tough in overture and emphasized military preparation but those made to civilians carried the message of hope for a peaceful solution. According to this officer, the moderate tone in public was meant to ease tensions when the military is not ready for a major conflict.

[46] Wu Xiuyong and Liu Jingdong, "Jianchi xietiao fazhan shi Jiang Zemin guofang zhanlie lilun de zhongyiao tese" (Upholding coordinated development is a key content of Jiang Zemin's national defense theory), *Guofang daxue xuebao* [Journal of the PLA National Defense University], No. 12, 1999, p. 12.

[47] Zhao Zuncai, "Congrong jiayu fuzai jiumian de chenggong shijian" (A Successful Case of Handling a Complicated Situation following NATO's Bombing of the Chinese Embassy), *Guofang daxue xuebao* [Journal of the PLA National Defence University], No. 9, 1999, pp. 30–3.

The question is: how long will the PLA continue to buy this argument if it does not receive a firm commitment from civilian leaders to address the problem of military backwardness? PLA generals need to consider that if a war erupts tomorrow, what weapons will they have available to fight it with? If incidents such as the embassy bombing and spy-plane clash occur regularly, the PLA, together with an increasingly nationalistic population, will put pressure on the civilian leaders to alter the Party's current foreign policy orientation, whose central thrust is cooperation with the industrialized nations.

While Jiang remains in command, though, it is likely that the Party will pursue a cooperative foreign policy with the West, unless Jiang himself is backed into a corner by the unpredictable changes in Sino-US relations. Bush's unilateralism presents a danger here. Eventually, it appears, national missile defense and theatre missile defense systems will be deployed; the US–Japan military alliance will be further strengthened to the point where Chinese defense leaders become very nervous; and Chen Shuibian and his successors in Taiwan are likely to enlarge the political distance between the island and the mainland. The PLA seems to have found a number of unlikely allies in the world who are helping it to present a justifiable case for quickened arms modernization. Already, the events of the last few years have seriously undermined Jiang's credibility. If these trends continue, China's civilian and military leaders would be forced to a cross-roads.

THIRTEEN

The Delayed Institutionalization of

Leadership Politics

Susan L. Shirk

The essays in this volume describe the institutionalization of Chinese leadership politics from the eras of Mao Zedong and Deng Xiaoping to the era of Jiang Zemin. The authors, while differing on many points, agree that during the first four decades of Party rule, informal status and relationships, much more than formal institutional roles and rules, shaped the behaviour of the top national leaders in China. In Lowell Dittmer's words, informal politics have been "historically dominant", with formal politics "no more than a facade" (p. 19). Only since the mid-1990s, under Jiang, have formal institutions become more important influences on the actual behaviour of politicians in Beijing. All of the authors, even Lucian Pye, who sees informal politics as "very nearly the sum total of Chinese politics" and as deeply rooted in Chinese political culture, observe the change toward institutionalization under Jiang.[1]

Of course, during the Mao and Deng periods formal institutions, while in the background, may have played a somewhat greater role in shaping informal behaviour than the authors recognize. For example, the authority of the Party Chairman—to call meetings, set the agenda and determine the participants of the meetings, control both internal and public communications, and approve key personnel appointments—helps explain why the distribution of actual power was highly skewed.

The formal authority of the Central Committee and the Party's Organization Department over personnel appointments (that is, authority over the nomenklatura), and the criteria for making these appointments, also were a very

---

[1] Pye notes that under Jiang, the decentralization of bureaucratic authority has caused so-called clients to ignore the wishes of their "patrons", and senior leaders now attain career security by performing their assigned responsibilities well instead of by building factional bases (pp. 212 and 214).

important feature of the institutional environment. This was the institutional context for clientelism and factionalism. Promotion and purge were based not on an objective meritocratic standard (such as examinations) but on subjective judgments about political loyalty and rectitude. "Virtuocracy"[2] gave senior leaders the latitude to promote their followers and provided lower-level officials with an incentive to seek out patrons.[3] The institutional arrangements of the centrally planned economy, moreover, amplified the patronage resources of senior leaders (and the dependence of clients on their patrons) and allowed no alternatives for ambition other than climbing the official ladder.

Much the same institutional landscape, and its associated behavioural consequences, were found in other Communist political systems. What is distinctive about China is how long it has taken to make consistent and effective the formal constraints on the behaviour of the top leaders. Written rules, such as those in the CCP Constitution, were flouted as often as they were followed. Decisions about who would fill top positions, while formally speaking the purview of the Central Committee, sometimes were made by a handful of leaders or by the pre-eminent leader alone. And many aspects of the system—for example, the size of powerful bodies such as the Central Committee, the Politburo and the Standing Committee—were not formally specified. According to Samuel Huntington's definition of institutionalization, as "the process by which organizations acquire value and stability",[4] or Tang Tsou's, "the process in which formal politics and formal relationships regularly prevail over informal politics and informal relationships" (p. 102), China is even today at a relatively low level of institutionalization. The upcoming succession in the top Party leadership in the autumn of 2002 will test just how institutionalized Chinese politics have become in the past half century.

One of the most interesting questions raised by the essays in this book is what accounts for the delayed and stunted institutionalization of the Chinese political system? Based on studies of the Soviet Union and Eastern Europe, scholars have observed that as Communist regimes mature and become focused on achieving economic goals, and as economic development causes their societies to modernize, their political systems become less dictatorial and more bureaucratic; more regularized and institutionalized; and more responsive to

---

[2]   Susan L. Shirk, *Competitive Comrades: Career Incentives and Student Strategies in China* (Berkeley: University of California Press, 1982).

[3]   As Lucian Pye writes, "Starting with admission into the ranks of the Party, which required the recommendations and personal vouching of two established members, career advancement and the accumulation of power depended upon the dynamics of acquaintanceships and of personal and professional relationships" (p. 42).

[4]   Samuel P. Huntington, *Political Order in Changing Societies* (New Haven: Yale University Press, 1968), p. 12.

social groups.[5] Chinese politics, while influenced by this modernization dynamic, have not followed the same evolutionary trend. Institutionalization has been retarded, uneven and reversible. Lucian Pye attributes China's difficulties in establishing a modern, institutionalized political system with the country's distinctive political culture. Certainly, in a comparison of countries with Leninist political systems, China stands out as particularly resistant to institutionalization, and many Chinese intellectuals themselves blame the persistence of personalistic, autocratic rule on their own culture.[6] Another contributing cause was the unique political dynamics within the small group that led a popular and successful revolution—creating the generation of leaders who can claim power and legitimacy as founders.

Mao vs. Institutionalization

After winning power in 1949, the CCP erected a set of political and economic institutions borrowed wholesale from the Soviet Union: parallel rule between Party and government bodies at all levels, with authority for administration delegated to the government but monitored intensively by Party groups; central control of the economy under the State Planning Commission and specialized economic ministries; and ultimate political authority held by the Party Central Committee but delegated to the Politburo, the Standing Committee of the Politburo and the Party Chairman or General Secretary.

With authority delegated to specialized organizations, an incipient bureaucratic politics began to emerge in the 1950s and 1960s. The chapters that discuss politics in the Mao Zedong era, while emphasizing its overwhelmingly informal nature, give hints of a trend of increasing formalization, by which they mean the expression of different policy views that appear to reflect the interests of different organizations within the Party, government and military. With the exception of Andrew Nathan and Kellee Tsai, the authors observe that groups within the elite consist not only of patron-client factions built on individual career interests but also of policy groups built on shared policy preferences.

Yet Mao Zedong did everything he could to obstruct this trend toward bureaucratic politics. He was highly suspicious of the central Party and government officials to whom authority had been delegated. He believed that they were robbing him of power and leading China in the wrong direction. To combat "bureaucratism", he ordered frequent rectification campaigns. Dissatisfied with the results of these campaigns, which themselves had became routinized, Mao launched the Cultural Revolution to demolish Party and

---

[5]   See the articles in Chalmers Johnson's classic volume, *Change in Communist Systems* (Stanford: Stanford University Press, 1970), particularly the chapter by Richard Lowenthal, "Development vs. Utopia in Communist Policy", pp. 33–116.

[6]   An important example is Zhengyuan Fu, *Autocratic Tradition and Chinese Politics* (Cambridge: Cambridge University Press, 1993).

government organizations and substitute a more authentic form of revolutionary politics.

Mao actively subverted the institutionalization of Chinese politics. He was able to do so, swimming against the tide of the modernization dynamic, because he held the unique role of father of the country—the supreme commander of the revolutionary army and the founder of the PRC. His dominant position in the Party hierarchy had been established in 1935 and was cemented by the miraculous victories against the Japanese and the Kuomintang achieved under his leadership. Few people ever dared to challenge Chairman Mao and most "bandwagoned" behind him.[7]

The Mixed Institutional Legacy of Deng Xiaoping

Mao's death in 1976 opened the way for the regularization and normalization of politics. Deng consolidated his leadership on a platform of political and economic reforms. He encouraged the criticisms of the political system expressed on the Democracy Wall in Beijing in December 1978 and held the most competitive local People's Congress elections to date under a new election law. An even more radical initiative was reversing the verdict on the Cultural Revolution and on Mao Zedong himself in his later years. In the "Resolution on Certain Questions in the History of Our Party Since the Founding of the People's Republic of China",[8] Deng's drafters offered a systematic critique of the disastrous consequences of the over-concentration of authority under Mao. Like Khrushchev's 20th CPSU Congress speech denouncing Stalin, it was intended to mark the end of personalistic dictatorship and the beginning of institutionalized governance.

In a very important 1980 speech, "On the Reform of the System of Party and State Leadership",[9] Deng spelled out more specifically the institutional changes needed to prevent abuses of political authority. The main problems he identified ("bureaucracy,[10] over-concentration of power, patriarchal methods, life tenure in leading posts and privileges of various kinds") are phenomena associated with a lack of institutionalization. He argued that fundamental changes were necessary to align China's governance with the priority task of economic modernization.

---

[7]   Avery Goldstein, *From Bandwagon to Balance-of-Power Politics: Structural Constraints and Politics in China, 1949–1978* (Stanford: Stanford University Press, 1991).

[8]   *Xinhua*, 30 June 1981, translated in FBIS, *Daily Report*, 1 July 1981.

[9]   *Selected Works of Deng Xiaoping (1975–1982)* (Beijing: Foreign Languages Press, 1984), pp. 302–25.

[10] What Deng meant by "bureaucracy" is the opposite of the usual Western definition that involves division of labour, hierarchy and rules: "Another cause of our bureaucracy is that for a long time we have had no strict administrative rules and regulations and no system of personal responsibility from top to bottom in the leading bodies of our Party and government organizations ... also lack strict and explicit terms of reference for each organization and post so that there are no rules to go by". Ibid, pp. 310–11.

Mao had stymied the modernization-institutionalization dynamic; Deng sounded like he was ready to accelerate it.

Under Deng a number of significant measures were introduced to enhance the institutionalization of political leadership. Party and government organs established regular schedules of meetings. An element of competition was introduced into the Party Congress' election of Central Committee members. A limit of two five-year terms was constitutionally mandated for the highest government and Party posts, as well as an age-70 mandatory retirement for top government and Party officials.[11] The National People's Congress began to exert its formal authority, debating and passing new legislation and interpolating ministry officials.

Yet Deng's legacy as an institutionalizer was mixed, starting from his own leadership authority, which was almost entirely disconnected from his formal institutional roles. In one important respect, Deng's regime was less institutionalized than Mao's: whereas Mao had held the supreme position of institutional power, the Chairmanship of the Chinese Communist Party, Deng never did. (When in 1980 the Politburo offered Deng the post of Party General Secretary, which had become the top Party position inasmuch as the post of Chairman had been abolished, he declined it, explaining that it should go to someone "young and vigorous".[12]) Deng served as Vice-Premier until 1980; held a seat on the Standing Committee of the Politburo until 1987; and served as Chair of the Central Military Commission until 1989. Someone else held the topmost formal position of Party General Secretary. But Deng exercised the authority of pre-eminent leader until he was physically incapacitated in the summer of 1994. Deng's authority, while blessed by a secret resolution of the 13th Party Congress in 1987 to have important political decisions referred to him,[13] was based largely on his informal status. As Dittmer observes, Deng promoted institutionalization only so far as it did not limit his own authority. Deng's motives were programmatic as well as self-serving, and the regime's low degree of institutionalization allowed him to take dramatic top-down initiatives like the 1978 market reform and opening.[14]

---

[11]   The age-70 retirement rule for Politburo Standing Committee members was introduced at the 15th Party Congress in 1997 as a way for Jiang Zemin to eliminate his rival, Qiao Shi. It is not a written rule, and an exception was made for General Secretary Jiang, who was 71. There may be a similar unwritten rule for retirement from the Central Military Commission at age 70.

[12]   Richard Baum, *Burying Mao: Chinese Politics in the Age of Deng Xiaoping* (Princeton: Princeton University Press, 1994), p. 117.

[13]   Baum (p. 218) states that important economic decisions were to be referred to Chen Yun. Teiwes disagrees, stating that there was no formal decision at the 13th Congress to require the referral of key decisions to Chen.

[14]   Dittmer notes (p. 36) that the flexibility of informal politics made possible Mao Zedong's reaching out to the United States in 1971 as well.

Deng's relationship to his senior colleagues was less dominant than Mao's had been. Whereas Mao had been on an elevated plane, Deng was more a "first among equals" with his comrades-in-arms from the revolutionary struggle. To accomplish his reform goals, he had to accommodate other powerful figures of the Long March generation, particularly Chen Yun.[15] To rejuvenate the leadership ranks and persuade his elderly peers to retire, he stepped down from the Politburo himself and offered the new retirees a golden parachute that allowed them to retain their influence in the policy process, as well as all their privileges in lifestyle. "Rule by elders" became a defining feature of the Deng Xiaoping regime. While the authority of the elders acquired a gloss of formality by the creation of the Central Advisory Commission in 1982, it primarily derived from their status as old revolutionaries. As Frederick Teiwes observes, "during the reform period, the ability of key figures to continue to exert a critical influence with few or no official posts ... indicates even less institutionalization of authority than earlier" (p. 62). His judgment on the Deng era hits the mark: "The policy process as a whole has become more consultative and systematic than previously but the fundamental obstacle to further institutionalization remained the authority of the retired leader and the older generation more broadly" (p. 89).

The remarkable longevity of this Long March generation—let us call it the "ginseng factor" in PRC political history—was an important reason why institutionalization did not keep pace with modernization in the two decades after Mao passed from the scene. Compare China's situation with the situation in Russia and Eastern Europe. Lenin died a few years after winning power, but Mao lived on for more than a quarter century. Stalin's purges wiped out almost the entire generation of revolutionaries in the Soviet Union and Eastern Europe,[16] but most Chinese revolutionaries survived the Cultural Revolution and were rehabilitated afterwards.

To enable the elders to participate in decision-making, the Politburo and Standing Committee continued to hold "expanded meetings".[17] From this position of power, the elders frequently frustrated the reform process. Although the elders did not all hold the same views on policy issues, most of them took a cautious approach to economic reform and were committed to preventing any leakage in the Communist Party's authority. The institutional separation of Party and government, envisioned by Deng in his 1980 speech ("It is time for us to distinguish between the responsibilities of the Party and those of the government

---

[15]   Teiwes notes that while a "'court politics' of accepting the leader's orders [and] pandering to his preferences" prevailed under Deng as under Mao, Deng was more amenable to persuasion by other leaders (p. 61).

[16]   Stephen White and Evan Mawdsley, *The Soviet Elite from Lenin to Gorbachev: The Central Committee and Its Members, 1917–1991* (Oxford: Oxford University Press, 2000).

[17]   Decisions taken at the summer meetings held at Beidaihe appear to be more "conservative" than regular Central Commission plenums because more of the elders are able to participate.

and to stop substituting the former for the latter")[18] and formally embedded in the Party Constitution in 1987, was never implemented and was revoked after 1989. The government's authority over the military failed to be established and the Party continued to control the Central Military Commission.[19]

The younger leaders who promoted market reform, Hu Yaobang and Zhao Ziyang, acting with Deng Xiaoping's support and anticipating that the formal authority of the Central Committee would finally be realized during the post-Mao era, tried to "play to the provinces", expanding the number of provincial officials in the Central Committee and using them as a counterweight to central officials.[20] But the reformist leaders also took care to maintain close communication with Deng and the elders, because the sharing of authority between the elders and the formal organs of the Party and government had been left in an ambiguous state.[21] Such gestures of deference were not enough to protect Hu and Zhao, Deng's chosen successors, from being ousted. In each case, the elders pressured Deng to act and used irregular procedures to get around the Central Committee.

The most dramatic manifestation of the elders' extra-institutional authority came during the pro-democracy student demonstrations of spring 1989. The "sitting committee" (i.e., the group of elders meeting in Deng Xiaoping's living room) made the crucial decision to impose martial law after the Standing Committee of the Politburo had held a split vote. This historic episode, widely publicized in *The Tiananmen Papers*,[22] could influence the debate over succession to the leadership at the 16th Party Congress in Fall 2002 (see below).

Institutionalization under Jiang Zemin

As many of the authors in Part Two of this volume observe, institutionalization has finally "come into its own" (Dittmer, p. 224) under Jiang, the first supreme leader who is not a member of the revolutionary generation. Almost all of the elders have died or been incapacitated by ill health.[23] Now that attrition has

---

18 "On the Reform of the System of Party and State Leadership", *Selected Works of Deng Xiaoping (1975–1982)*, p. 303.

19 There is a PRC Central Military Commission sign under the CCP Central Military Commission sign at the door, but there is only one actual body and its budget and actions are overseen by the Politburo, not the State Council.

20 Susan L. Shirk, *The Political Logic of Economic Reform in China* (Berkeley: University of California Press, 1993).

21 Teiwes quotes one of Zhao Ziyang's advisors as saying that Zhao paid a great deal of attention to the elders because "Those old folks need to be respected and what they fear most is to be ignored" (p. 85).

22 *The Tiananmen Papers*, compiled by Zhang Liang, edited by Andrew J. Nathan and Perry Link (New York: Public Affairs, 2001).

23 Song Ping, an exception, was still alive and attending meetings as of early 2002.

eliminated the "generational overhang" (Dittmer, p. 188), those who hold the top formal posts in the Party and the government exercise actual authority in the policy process and in personnel appointments. Jiang himself holds the top formal positions in the Party (General Secretary), the government (President) and the military (Chair of the Central Military Commission), as well as a seat on the Standing Committee of the Politburo. The position of President, in fact, has few constitutional powers and in the past has been purely ceremonial. Jiang, however, has exploited the international visibility of the presidency by frequent summit meetings at home and abroad, and thereby has been able to dominate foreign policy and enhance his domestic authority. He chairs both the Foreign Affairs and Taiwan Affairs leading small groups, as well as the new National Security Council. The second and third most powerful members of the Standing Committee of the Politburo hold the top government positions of Premier (Zhu Rongji) and Chair of the Standing Committee of the National People's Congress (Li Peng). Membership in the Central Committee is now determined by job-slot, with almost all provinces having two representatives.[24] These changes, along with the term limits, retirement rules and fixed terms of office, while not constituting a "systemic transformation" of the political system (Oksenberg, p. 197), help to regularize political competition.

Capitalizing on formal authority made sense for Jiang, who came to Beijing without the prestige or network of relationships of the founder generation. Having been selected as a compromise choice by the elders during the Tiananmen crisis in 1989, Jiang built up his authority on the basis of institutional roles and rules. As noted earlier, Jiang introduced the retirement-at-70 rule in 1997 to shunt Qiao Shi, his only potential rival, off the Politburo and its Standing Committee. Jiang has used the formal levers of power—especially the appointment powers of the Party General Secretary and Central Military Commission Chair—to consolidate his power much more effectively than observers had predicted. You Ji notes in regard to the military, however, that while Jiang used his formal authority as chairman of the CMC to appoint a new set of top officers, they are not "his people" in terms of personal loyalty (p. 280).

The 2002 Succession: A Test of Institutionalization

Will the Jiang-era trend toward institutionalization survive the transfer of power that is scheduled to occur in Fall 2002 at the 16th Party Congress? Institutionalization, as Samuel Huntington noted decades ago, can be reversed and followed by political decay. Organizational practices that are relatively new may not be able to adapt to changes in society caused by modernization. Rising political consciousness and popular demands for political participation can

---

[24]   The size of the Central Committee, Politburo and Politburo Standing Committee is still not fixed.

swamp an institutionalization process that is proceeding too slowly.[25] At the early stages of institutionalization, political actors also may design and redesign institutional arrangements to enhance their own power and influence.

According to the current rules, at the 16th Party Congress in 2002 Jiang Zemin, along with Li Peng, Zhu Rongji and other senior leaders who are over 70, should retire from the Party leadership and pass the mantle to the "Fourth Generation" of younger leaders.[26] At the 2003 National People's Congress Jiang, Li and Zhu, having served two terms in their government posts (as President, NPC Chair and Premier, respectively) should also hand these positions over to younger leaders. Jiang, like most leaders in most countries, believes in his own indispensability and appears reluctant to step down. When asked about his plans, he has refused to commit to retiring from all his posts, either because he has not decided what he wants to do or because he is trying to increase his leverage over other 16th Party Congress appointments. There is intense domestic and international speculation about Jiang's plans.

Jiang has three possible options:

1)   Keep all his positions (Party General Secretary, PRC President, member of the Standing Committee of the Politburo and Central Military Commission Chair).
2)   Retire from the positions of Party General Secretary, PRC President and Standing Committee member, but keep the position of Central Military Commission Chair and from that position try to exercise the role of pre-eminent leader on an informal basis just as Deng Xiaoping did.
3)   Retire from all his positions.

Jiang's choice, which will be known by the time this book is read, will help us understand the nature of the Chinese political system at the present stage of its evolution. His choice is a test of the degree of institutionalization of Chinese leadership politics, with option 1 representing the lowest degree of institutionalization, option 3 the highest, and option 2 in-between. The outcome will also enable us to infer what has been more responsible for retarding the institutionalization of leadership politics in China: persistent patterns in Chinese political culture or the time-bound influence of the founder generation?

Option 1: Keep all positions

If Jiang retains his positions in clear violation of the present rules on retirement and term limits, it will tell us that the top Chinese political organizations have not acquired any real stability or much institutionalization and that the political system remains autocratic and personalistic. If even Jiang, a leader without

---

[25]   Samuel P. Huntington, *Political Order in Changing Societies*, Ch. 1.

[26]   The only Standing Committee incumbents who will be under 70 in 2002 are Hu Jintao (59), the chosen successor, and Li Ruihuan (68).

previous national prestige or following, can perpetuate his personal power indefinitely in the context of an economy and society that is rapidly modernizing, it will be hard to find an explanation other than the remarkable persistence of Chinese political culture, particularly the search for authority and fear of chaos identified by Lucian Pye many years ago.[27]

Option 2: Retire from Party and government positions but keep the CMC Chair and try to retain authority on an informal basis, re-creating the "rule by elders"

Jiang has hinted that he may be leaning toward retiring from the General Secretary position and the PRC Presidency and membership in the Politburo Standing Committee. If he does, it will be a measure of the strength of elite support for term limits and retirement rules. Certainly Jiang would not give up Party and government power, especially the gratifications of presidential summitry, unless he had to. It will mean that the retirement rules for top Party and government posts have acquired an aura of permanence and value.

But will Jiang keep the chairmanship of the CMC and continue to rule from "behind the curtain"? The fact that Jiang has floated the possibility of his keeping the CMC post and that it seems plausible to people in China indicates that retirement from the PLA leadership body is less institutionalized than from the Party and government.

Jiang may be preparing to re-create the role of Deng Xiaoping, who called the shots informally from his living room, behind the institutional fig leaf of the CMC chair. Li Peng is rumoured to have threatened that if Jiang keeps the CMC position, he too will seek to take another position (e.g., the Presidency or the chair of the National People's Consultative Congress). In that case, even if Zhu Rongji personally prefers to retire, his reform-minded followers will urge him as well to take a leading post, such as the Presidency, to retain his influence over economic policy. All three men are active and apparently healthy septuagenarians. Even if Li Peng and Zhu Rongji are not personally ambitious, they have distinct policy objectives and are likely to want to maintain their influence if only to check one another. A new group of elders ruling from outside the Politburo would then be in the making.

Jiang, like Deng Xiaoping before him, has always appeared ambivalent toward the institutionalization of political leadership. He recognized that the new rules could be used as checks on his power and patronage. He hedged his bets by not putting in writing the retirement age for Party leaders or formally extending it to the CMC. And, unlike Deng, Jiang never pursued institutionalization in a self-conscious manner or claimed credit for it as a political reformer. As he sees forced retirement approaching, his enthusiasm for term limits and retirement rules is no doubt waning.

---

[27]   Lucian W. Pye, *The Spirit of Chinese Politics* (Cambridge: MIT Press, 1968).

Will the fourth generation of Party leaders allow the three-man oligarchy of Jiang, Li Peng and Zhu Rongji to reverse the trend toward institutionalization and perpetuate their power beyond retirement? The threesome may be banking on the deference of a Politburo and Standing Committee composed of a balanced set of their protégés. Acquiescence to the creation of a new group of influential elders would mean that Chinese politics at the top, even after the passing of the founder generation, are still highly personalistic and uninstitutionalized, as Joseph Fewsmith asserts in his chapter; that retirement and term-limit rules are followed in form but not in substance; and that informal authority can still trump formal authority. Such an outcome would also indicate that the sharing of power among factional networks is highly stable and congenial to Chinese political culture.

A variant on this option would be that Jiang retains the CMC Chair but that his efforts to play a Deng Xiaoping-type role as pre-eminent leader are frustrated by the younger leaders. The trend toward institutionalization may not have jelled firmly enough to prevent Jiang Zemin from retaining the chair of the Central Military Commission in 2002 (option 2), but just enough to limit his personal influence in that role.

A head-on confrontation with Jiang would be hard to pull off. Any coordinated action to challenge succession arrangements within a Communist Party always is difficult and risky, especially if no individual emerges as a focal point for the challenge. There is no sign that Hu Jintao, the consensus choice to succeed Jiang as Party General Secretary, is mobilizing an effort to block Jiang. (This may be the reason why a few people in China are quietly discussing the possibility of Li Ruihuan challenging Hu Jintao for the position of Party General Secretary. Li Ruihuan is the one Politburo Standing Committee member other than Hu who will not have to retire in 2002 and who straddles the third and fourth generations of leadership.) As of early 2002 rumours were circulating within China that Li Ruihuan had already announced his intention to retire as a way of pressuring Jiang to retire as well.[28]

If Jiang keeps his Central Military Commission position and attempts to re-create the Deng Xiaoping pattern of rule from behind the curtain, however, the new Politburo Standing Committee may try to establish norms that limit the meddling of Jiang and other retirees. At a minimum it is highly unlikely that they will pass a secret resolution to refer all major questions to Jiang, as the 13th Party Congress did for Deng when he stepped down from the Politburo in 1987. They might firm up rules about who may attend and vote at the meetings of formal bodies such as the Standing Committee and the full Politburo to prevent a continuation of the practice of "enlarged meetings", including the summer retreat at Beidaihe. The Standing Committee could redesign the flow of papers to allow elders to see documents only after, not before, Party formal bodies have made their decisions. (Another approach—opening up Party decision-making to greater transparency—would be viewed by most Politburo members, who are afraid of

---

[28]   *Kai Fang* (Hong Kong), 1 January 2002; FBIS, 1 January 2002.

their own society, as too radical and risky a departure from past practice.)[29]

Option 3: Retire from all positions

My own prediction is that any effort to restore personalistic rule will be contested, and that in the end Jiang will be forced to retire from all his positions. This outcome will indicate that the longevity of the Long March generation of leaders was responsible for the persistence of personalistic rule in China; once they were no longer in the way, transformations in the economy and society have produced a belated institutionalization in Chinese leadership politics. If middle-aged and younger officials succeed in preventing Jiang and his colleagues from hanging on to power and there is a complete transition, it will indicate that this institutionalization is already well rooted in political life.

Indeed, the debate over institutional issues within the top reaches of the Communist Party has already begun. The Fourth Generation is signaling its determination to stick to the rules and to force Jiang Zemin and the rest of his cohort to retire. Members of the Politburo and Central Committee have already shown a willingness to stand up to Jiang Zemin. They reportedly twice blocked his effort to elevate Zeng Qinghong, his right-hand man, to full Politburo membership, in 2000 and 2001. Some may oppose Zeng because they object to his tough hand in anti-corruption and personnel cases (he is often viewed as Jiang's "hatchet man"). Others may worry that Jiang will use Zeng either to challenge Hu Jintao's succession as core leader or that Zeng will move up to the Standing Committee in 2002 as a Jiang stand-in. Zeng appears to represent to many an attempt by Jiang to assert his own power into the indefinite future in a way that violates institutional rules and norms. A vote against Zeng Qinghong was a vote not only against Jiang, but also against personalistic dictatorship and for institutionalization within the Party.

Jiang's efforts to have his notion of the "Three Representations" inserted into the Party Constitution, integrated into official Party ideology and inculcated by means of a mass nationwide campaign (including the dispatching of central work teams to localities) drew heated criticism in a broadside signed by prominent officials, many from the propaganda realm,[30] and at the Beidaihe meetings in summer 2001. Even those who welcomed the political legitimization of private businesspeople, which was the most important point of substance of the "Three Representations", objected to the manner in which Jiang unilaterally promoted his own ideas and tried to create his own cult of personality. Jiang was criticized for "placing himself above the Party" and violating the Party Constitution.[31] As

---

[29] Dittmer makes the interesting observation that under Jiang "institutionalization has … entailed a plugging of 'leaks' and a decline in transparency" (p. 220).

[30] "Deng Liqun, Others Criticize Jiang Zemin for Deciding to Admit Capitalists", *Renmin Bao Dispatch* <www.renminbao.com>, 28 July 2001.

[31] Ibid.

Joseph Fewsmith notes, officials understood the subtext of Jiang's actions: that is, to "reinforce his authority at the very time that he is presumably leaving the political stage" (p. 268). In the end, Jiang succeeded in obtaining Central Committee ratification of his initiative, but the body's vigorous pushback indicated real resistance to Jiang's efforts to engineer the succession to sustain his own influence.

One reason that Jiang, Li and Zhu will have difficulty sustaining their power beyond 2002 is that they lack the revolutionary prestige of the Long March generation of elders. The rationale for perpetuating their authority, therefore, is weaker. A military confrontation in the Taiwan Strait would strengthen the case for Jiang Zemin to keep the reins of power, and a collapse of the banking system or other economic crisis would raise calls for Zhu Rongji to remain in charge. In the absence of such emergencies, however, most senior Party officials are likely to prefer new leaders and regular, predictable opportunities to pursue their own ambitions. The Jiang-Li-Zhu regime has produced policies that have broad support (market reform, opening up to the world, stable relations with other countries including the United States, a firm stance on Taiwan) and most officials would like these to continue. But they expect that Hu Jintao will favour much the same policies. In addition, their ties of factional loyalty to Jiang, Li and Zhu are much weaker than the factional allegiances of previous generations that were forged in the hills of Yanan.

Another factor that may influence the thinking of some Party officials is China's international reputation. A "normal" premortem transition including the retirement of incumbent leaders will be interpreted internationally as "progress" in China, although there will be some anxiety about whether it might mean a change in domestic and foreign policy. US policymakers always look for "movement in the right direction" in China's domestic situation to validate the wisdom of their engagement policies. To the extent that the world perceives an orderly succession as progress in China, China gains the benefit of a supportive international environment. Deng Xiaoping, for one, was aware of the positive international response that would be evoked by the changes in Party practices he introduced in 1980–81.[32]

The publication of *The Tiananmen Papers* puts the issue of rule by elders squarely on the table during the succession process. The documents confirm what many already knew from rumour and the Hong Kong press, namely that the

---

[32] Deng anticipated a favourable international response from the changes he introduced in 1980–81: "For some time, people abroad have been saying that though the line and policies of the Chinese Communist Party and the People's Republic of China may be correct, their continuity and stability are in some doubt. The documents of this session and the series of political and organizational measures it has adopted provide a good answer to this sort of talk. ... Internationally, they will certainly help strengthen the confidence reposed in us by foreign comrades and friends and by others who co-operate with us in varying degrees". "Adhere to Party Line and Improve Work Methods", *Selected Works of Deng Xiaoping, 1975–1982*, p. 260.

"sitting committee" of elders was responsible for the massacre of the young protestors. The elders overruled the deadlocked Politburo Standing Committee. Informal personalistic power trumped formal institutional authority. Although the Jiang regime has sought to discredit *The Tiananmen Papers* by casting doubt on their authenticity and charging the as-yet-unidentified leakers of treason, the substance of the papers has become well known within the Chinese political elite.

The papers will play into the succession debate not just by casting positive or negative light on particular figures (Li Peng and Li Ruihuan are the only current leaders who were directly involved in the 1989 drama) or by casting doubt on the legitimacy of Jiang's 1989 selection as the core leader, but by linking the question of personalistic versus institutional rule with any possible future reassessment of Tiananmen. An official reassessment is probably some years in the future, but it is already in the minds of China's senior officials. Just as Mao's successors blamed the launching of the Cultural Revolution on "one-man rule", Deng's successors may assign responsibility for the Tiananmen tragedy to "informal oligarchic rule". Such an approach would have a broad appeal because it would be forward-looking and reformist, would exculpate the PLA and would place the blame on a type of rule instead of on particular individuals. Even Li Peng and his followers could support it.

The Founder Generation and China's Delayed Institutionalization

If Jiang Zemin, Li Peng and Zhu Rongji retire from all their positions during 2002–03, it will indicate that institutionalization in Chinese leadership politics has finally taken hold. Just as modernization theory and the experience of other Communist political systems would predict, political institutionalization will have been stimulated by economic development and social modernization. Such an outcome would lead to the conclusion that the crucial difference between China's delayed institutionalization and institutionalization in the Soviet Union and Eastern Europe is that the generation of revolutionary founders dominated the political landscape much longer than did their European counterparts. Mao Zedong, Deng Xiaoping and their Long March comrades, in their efforts to perpetuate and resist constraints on their own power, were responsible for impeding the institutionalization of the Chinese political system.

The fact that this group of Long March veterans managed to hold on to power for so long is something of a puzzle. Although bound together by their formative experiences during the revolutionary struggle, the leaders were in competition with one another. Each of them had an incentive, if he was losing out in the contest, to try to change the rules and mobilize additional support by expanding the decision-making arena to the Central Committee that holds formal sovereign power in the political system. Frequent informal consultation with members of the Central Committee to help anticipate their reactions to policymaking and personnel decisions made at the top was normal practice. And both Mao and Deng, finding their initiatives resisted by other senior leaders, sometimes mobilized mass support. Yet no one tried to reverse high-level decisions by formally appealing to the Central Committee. Nor, as far as we know, have any senior leaders advocated fixing the number of seats in the Central

Committee, Politburo or Standing Committee.

It is not surprising that the Central Committee, a body of approximately two hundred provincial and central government Party leaders and military officials, has not been able to overcome the collective action problem in order to assert its own authority. It has never organized an effective committee structure and its members have focused on obtaining particularistic benefits for their own localities and agencies. What is surprising, however, is that of the 20 to 30 most senior leaders from the founder generation, no one ever tried to play an institutional card by appealing to the Central Committee when he lost a policy or personnel decision of the Standing Committee, or later of the informal "sitting committee". Perhaps the collective norms (the informal "rules of the game") were enough to inhibit such bold action, as Teiwes suggests. The formal rules on necessary approvals to present a speech or talk to the press probably also helped. And perhaps the group was usually able to maintain a sharing of power and patronage among various factions so successfully, as Nathan and Tsai would suggest, that no one, even if he was on the losing end of a decision, had reason to risk changing the rules of the political game.[33]

If the 2002 succession proves that the political game finally is changing, the consequences for China and its future could be highly significant. What is at stake in the contest over the institutionalization of the Party leadership and its decision-making processes is not just the question of who holds power—retired oligarchs or younger formal leaders. The quality of policies will also be affected: officials who are directly engaged in running their agencies and communicating with subordinates on a day-to-day basis will have better, more systematic information about actual situations than elders who pick up only sporadic information, much of it in the form of personal complaints. At the same time, as the experience of other countries shows, there is no guarantee that reform within the ruling Party will serve as a catalyst for broader political reform instead of stabilizing authoritarian rule.

---

[33]   The ability of Jiang's generation of leaders to hang together despite their competition with one another is impressive and difficult to explain. In recent years they have engaged in internecine combat by launching investigations of corruption against one another (or one another's families), using anti-corruption campaigns much as ideological campaigns were used in the past. To prevent this competition from tearing the group apart, they reportedly have agreed that formal prosecutions of corruption of individuals at the levels of minister and above require the approval of the Politburo.

Selected Bibliography

Ahn, Byung-joon. *Chinese Politics and the Cultural Revolution: Dynamics of Policy Processes*. Seattle: University of Washington Press, 1976.

Bachman, David. *Chen Yun and the Chinese Political System*. Berkeley: Institute of East Asian Studies, 1985.

Bachman, David. *Bureaucracy, Economy, and Leadership in China: The Institutional Origins of the Great Leap Forward*. Cambridge: Cambridge University Press, 1991.

Bachman, David. "The Limits of Leadership in China". *Asian Survey*, Vol. 32, No. 11 (November 1992).

Bachman, David. "Li Zhisui, Mao Zedong, and Chinese Elite Politics". *The China Journal*, No. 35 (January 1996).

Bachman, David. "The Paradox of Analysing Elite Politics under Jiang". *The China Journal*, No. 45 (January 2001).

Barnett, A. Doak (ed.). *Chinese Communist Politics in Action*. Seattle: University of Washington Press, 1969.

Barnett, A. Doak, with a contribution by Ezra Vogel. *Cadres, Bureaucracy, and Political Power in Communist China*. New York: Columbia University Press, 1967.

Barnouin, Barbara, and Yu Changgen. *Ten Years of Turbulence: The Chinese Cultural Revolution*. London: Kegan Paul International, 1993.

Baum, Richard. *Prelude to Revolution: Mao, the Party, and the Peasant Question, 1962-1966*. New York: Columbia University Press, 1975.

Baum, Richard, (ed.). *Reform and Reaction in Post-Mao China: The Road to Tiananmen*. New York: Routledge, Chapman, and Hall, 1991.

Baum, Richard. *Burying Mao: Chinese Politics in the Age of Deng Xiaoping*. Princeton: Princeton University Press, 1994.

Baum, Richard, "Jiang Takes Command: The Fifteenth National Party Congress and Beyond". In *China under Jiang Zemin*, edited by Hung-mao Tien and Yun-han Chu. London: Lynne Rienner, 2000.

Baum, Richard, and Frederick C. Teiwes. "Liu Shao-ch'i and the Cadre Question". *Asian Survey*, April 1968.

Baum, Richard, and Frederick C. Teiwes. *Ssu-Ch'ing: The Socialist Education Movement of 1962-1966*. Berkeley: Center for Chinese Studies, 1968.

Chan, Alfred L. "Leaders, Coalition Politics, and Policy-Formulation in China: The Great Leap Forward Revisited". *The Journal of Contemporary China*, Winter-Spring 1995.

Chan, Alfred L. *Mao's Crusade: Politics and Policy Implementation in China's Great Leap Forward*. Oxford: Oxford University Press, 2001.

Chang, Parris. *Power and Policy in China*, 2nd edition. University Park: Pennsylvania State University Press, 1978.

Chang, Parris. "Changing of the Guard". *The China Journal*, No. 45 (January 2001).

Cheek, Timothy, and Tony Saich (eds). *New Perspectives on State Socialism in China*. Armonk: M. E. Sharpe, 1997.

Ch'i, Hsisheng. *Politics of Disillusionment: The Chinese Communist Communist Party under Deng Xiaoping*. Armonk: M. E. Sharpe, 1991.

Chung, Jae Ho. *Central Control and Local Discretion in China: Leadership and Implementation during Post-Mao Decollectivization*. Oxford: Oxford University Press, 2000.

Clapham, Christopher, (ed.). *Private Patronage and Public Power: Political Clientalism in the Modern State*. New York: St. Martin's Press, 1982.

Deng, Maomao. *My Father Deng Xiaoping,* New York: Basic Books, 1995.

Dickson, Bruce. "What Explains Chinese Political Behavior? The Debate over Structure and Culture". *Comparative Politics*, Vol. 25, No. 1 (October 1992).

Dittmer, Lowell. "Bases of Power in Chinese Politics: A Theory and an Analysis of the Fall of the Gang of Four". *World Politics*, Vol. 32, No. 1 (October 1978).

Dittmer, Lowell. *China's Continuous Revolution: The Post-Liberation Epoch 1949-1981*. Berkeley: University of California Press, 1987.

Dittmer, Lowell. "Patterns of Elite Strife and Succession in Chinese Politics". *The China Quarterly*, No. 123 (September 1990).

Dittmer, Lowell. "Patterns of Leadership in Reform China". In *State and Society in China: The Consequences of Reform*, edited by Arthur L. Rosenbaum. Boulder: Westview Press, 1992.

Dittmer, Lowell. *Liu Shaoqi and the Chinese Cultural Revolution*. Revised edition, Armonk: M. E. Sharpe, 1998.

Dittmer, Lowell, and Yu-shan Wu. "The Modernization of Factionalism in Chinese Politics". *World Politics*, Vol. 47 (July 1995).

Domenach, Jean-Luc. *The Origins of the Great Leap Forward: The Case of One Chinese Province*. Boulder: Westview Press, 1995.

Domes, Jurgen. *China after the Cultural Revolution: Politics between Two Party Congresses*. London: C. Hurst & Co., 1976.

Domes, Jurgen. "The Gang of Four and Hua Kuo-feng: Analysis of Political Events in 1975-76", *China Quarterly*, No. 71 (September 1977).

Domes, Jurgen. *Peng Te-huai: The Man and the Image*. London: C. Hurst & Company, 1985.

Domes, Jurgen. *The Government and Politics of the PRC: A Time of Transition*. Boulder: Westview Press, 1985.

Dorrill, William F. "Power, Policy, and Ideology in the Making of the Chinese Cultural Revolution". In *The Cultural Revolution in China*, edited by Thomas W. Robinson. Berkeley: University of California Press, 1971.

Fewsmith, Joseph. *Dilemmas of Reform in China: Political Conflict and Economic Debate*. Armonk: M. E. Sharpe, 1994.

Fewsmith, Joseph. "Reaction, Resurgence, and Succession: Chinese Politics since Tiananmen". In *The Politics of China, Second Edition: The Eras of Mao and Deng*, edited by Roderick MacFarquhar. New York: Cambridge University Press, 1997.

Fewsmith, Joseph. "Elite Politics". In *The Paradox of China's Post-Mao Reforms*, edited by Merle Goldman and Roderick MacFarquhar. Cambridge: Harvard University Press, 1999.

Fewsmith, Joseph. "Institution Building and Democratization in China". In *Democracy and Its Limits: Lessons from Asia, Latin America, and the Middle East*, edited by Howard Handelman and Mark Tessler. Notre Dame: University of Notre Dame Press, 1999.

Fewsmith, Joseph. "Historical Echoes and Chinese Politics: Can China Leave the Twentieth Century Behind?". In *China Briefing 2000: The Continuing Transformation*, edited by Tyrene White. Armonk: M. E. Sharpe, 2000.

Fewsmith, Joseph. *Elite Politics in Contemporary China*. Armonk: M. E. Sharpe, 2001.

Fewsmith, Joseph. *China Since Tiananmen: The Politics of Transition*. Cambridge: Cambridge University Press, 2001.

Forster, Keith. "Localism, Central Policy and the Provincial Purges of 1957-58: The Case of Zhejiang". In *New Perspectives on State Socialism in China*, edited by Timothy Cheek and Tony Saich. Armonk: M. E. Sharpe, 1997.

Friedman, Edward, and Barrett L. McCormick (eds). *What If China Doesn't Democratize? Implications for War and Peace*. Armonk: M. E. Sharpe, 2000.

Gardner, John. *Chinese Politics and the Succession to Mao*. London: Macmillan, 1982.

Gilley, Bruce. *Tiger on the Brink: Jiang Zemin and China's New Elite*. Berkeley: University of California Press, 1998.

Goldman, Merle, and Rocerick MacFarquhar (eds). *The Paradox of China's Post-Mao Reforms*. Cambridge: Harvard University Press, 1999.

Goldstein, Avery. *From Bandwagon to Balance-of-Power Politics*. Stanford: Stanford University Press, 1991.

Goodman, David S. G. *Centre and Province in the People's Republic of China: Sichuan and Guizhou, 1955-1965*. Cambridge: Cambridge University Press, 1986.

Goodman, David S. G. *Deng Xiaoping and the Chinese Revolution: A Political Biography*. London: Routledge, 1994.

Guo, Xuezhi. "Dimensions of *Guanxi* in Chinese Elite Politics". *The China Journal*, No. 46 (July 1996).

Hamrin, Carol Lee. *China and the Challenge of the Future: Changing Political Patterns*. Boulder: Westview Press, 1990.

Hamrin, Carol Lee. "Inching Toward Open Politics". *The China Journal*, No. 45 (January 2001).

Hamrin, Carol Lee, and Suisheng Zhao (eds). *Decision-Making in Deng's China: Perspectives from Insiders*. Armonk: M. E. Sharpe, 1995.

Harding, Harry. *China's Second Revolution: Reform after Mao*. Washington, D.C.: The Brookings Institution, 1987.

Harding, Harry. "Competing Models of the Chinese Communist Policy Process: Toward a Sorting and Evaluation". *Issues & Studies*, Vol. 20, No. 2 (1984).

Harding, Harry. "The Chinese State in Crisis". In *The Politics of China 1949-1989: The Eras of Mao and Deng*, edited by Roderick MacFarquhar. Cambridge: Cambridge University Press, 1997.

Harding, Harry, and Melvin Gurtov. *The Purge of Lo Jui-ch'ing: The Politics of Chinese Strategic Planning*. Santa Monica: RAND Report R-548-PR, February 1971.

Huang, Jing. *Factionalism in Chinese Communist Politics*. Cambridge: Cambridge University Press, 2000.

Joffe, Ellis. *Party and Army: Professionalism and Political Control in the Chinese Officer Corps, 1949-1964*. Cambridge, Mass.: Harvard East Asian Monographs, 1967.

Joffe, Ellis. *The Chinese Military after Mao*, Cambridge, Mass.: Harvard University Press, 1987.

Johnson, Chalmers (ed.). *Ideology and Politics in Contemporary China*. Seattle: University of Washington Press, 1973.

Joseph, William A. *The Critique of Ultra-Leftism in China, 1958-1981*. Stanford: Stanford University Press, 1984.

Joseph, William A, Christine P. W. Wong, and David Zweig (eds). *New Perspectives on the Cultural Revolution*. Cambridge: The Council on East Asian Studies/Harvard University, 1991.

Lam, Willy Wo-Lap. *The Era of Jiang Zemin*. Singapore: Simon and Schuster, 1999.

Lampton, David M. (ed.). *Policy Implementation in Post-Mao China*. Berkeley: University of California Press, 1987.

Lampton, David M., with the assistance of Yeung Sai-cheung. *Paths to Power: Elite Mobility in Contemporary China*. Ann Arbor: Michigan Monographs in Chinese Studies, 1986.

Lee, Hong Yung. *The Politics of the Chinese Cultural Revolution: A Case Study*. Berkeley: University of California Press, 1978.

Lee, Hong Yung. *From Revolutionary Cadres to Party Technocrats in Socialist China*. Berkeley: University of California Press, 1993.

Lee, Peter Nan-shong. "The Informal Politics of Leadership Succession in Post-Mao China". In *Informal Politics in East Asia*, edited by Lowell Dittmer, Haruhiro Fukui and Peter N. S. Lee. Cambridge: Cambridge University Press, 2000.

Lewis, John Wilson. *Leadership in Communist China*. Ithaca: Cornell University Press, 1963.

Lewis, John Wilson (ed.). *Party Leadership and Revolutionary Power in China*. Cambridge: Cambridge University Press, 1970.

Lewis, John Wilson, and Xue Litai. *China's Strategic Seapower: The Politics of Force Modernization in the Nuclear Age*. Stanford: Stanford University Press, 1994.

Li, Cheng. "University Networks and the Rise of Qinghua Graduates in China's Leadership". *The Australian Journal of Chinese Affairs*, No. 22 (July 1994).

Li, Cheng. *China's Leaders: The New Generation*. Lanham: Rowman and Littlefield, 2001.

Li, Linda Chelan. *Centre and Provinces, China 1978-1993: Power as Non-Zero Sum*. Oxford: Clarendon Press, 1998.

Li, Zhisui, with Anne Thurston. *The Private Life of Chairman Mao: The Inside Story of the Man Who Made Modern China*. London: Chatto & Windus; New York: Random House, 1994.

Lieberthal, Kenneth. *Governing China: From Revolution through Reform*. New York: W. W. Norton & Co., 1995.

Lieberthal, Kenneth, and Michel Oksenberg. *Policy Making in China: Leaders, Structures, and Processes*. Princeton: Princeton University Press, 1988.

Lieberthal, Kenneth, and David Lampton (eds). *Bureaucracy, Politics and Decision Making in Post-Mao China*. Berkeley: University of California Press, 1992.

Lieberthal, Kenneth, with the assistance of James Tong and Sai-cheung Yeung. *Central Documents and Politburo Politics in China*. Ann Arbor: Michigan Papers in Chinese Studies, No. 33, 1978.

Lindbeck, John M. H. (ed.). *China: Management of a Revolutionary Society*. Seattle: University of Washington Press, 1971.

MacFarquhar, Roderick (ed.). *China Under Mao: Politics Takes Command*. Cambridge, Mass.: MIT Press, 1966.

MacFarquhar, Roderick. *The Origins of the Cultural Revolution 1: Contradictions among the People 1956-1957*. New York: Columbia University Press, 1974.

MacFarquhar, Roderick. *The Origins of the Cultural Revolution 2: The Great Leap Forward 1958-1960*. New York: Columbia University Press, 1983.

MacFarquhar, Roderick. *The Origins of the Cultural Revolution 3: The Coming of the Cataclysm 1961-1966*. New York: Columbia University Press, 1997.

MacFarquhar, Roderick. "The Succession to Mao and the End of Maoism". In *The Politics of China 1949-1989: The Eras of Mao and Deng*, edited by Roderick MacFarquhar. Cambridge: Cambridge University Press, 1997.

McCormick, Barrett L. *Political Reform in Post-Mao China: Democracy and Bureaucracy in a Leninist State*. Berkeley: University of California Press, 1990.

Moody, Peter R. Jr. *Chinese Politics after Mao: Development and Liberalization, 1976 to 1983*. New York: Praeger, 1983.

Nathan, Andrew J. "A Factionalism Model for CCP Politics". *The China Quarterly*, No. 53 (January 1973).

Nathan, Andrew J. "Is Chinese Culture Distinctive?—A Review Article". *The Journal of Asian Studies*, Vol. 52, No. 4 (November 1993).

Nathan, Andrew J. *China's Crisis*. New York: Columbia University Press, 1990.

Nathan, Andrew J., and Tianjian Shi. "Left and Right with Chinese Characteristics: Issues and Alignments in Deng Xiaoping's China". *World Politics*, Vol. 48, No. 4 (July, 1996).

Nathan, Andrew J. *China's Transition*. New York: Columbia University Press, 1997.

Nathan, Andrew J., Zhaohui Hong, and Steven R. Smith (eds). *Dilemmas of Reform in Jiang Zemin's China*. Boulder: Lynne Reinner Publishers, 1999.

Nee, Victor, and David Mozingo (eds). *State and Society in Contemporary China*. Ithaca: Cornell University Press, 1983.

O'Brien, Kevin. *Reform without Liberalization: China's National People's Congress and the Politics of Institutional Change*. New York: Cambridge University Press, 1990.

Oksenberg, Michel. "Policy Making Under Mao, 1949-68: An Overview". In *China: Management of a Revolutionary Society*, edited by John M. H. Lindbeck. Seattle: University of Washington Press, 1971.

Oksenberg, Michel. "Political Changes and their Causes in China, 1949-1972". *The Political Quarterly*, Vol. 45, No. 1 (January 1974).

Oksenberg, Michel. "Mao's Policy Commitments, 1921-1976". *Problems of Communism*, Vol. 25, No. 6 (November 1976).

Oksenberg, Michel. "Exit Patterns in Chinese Politics". *The China Quarterly*, No. 67 (September 1976).

Oksenberg, Michel. "The Political Leader". In *Mao Tse-tung in the Scales of History*, edited by Dick Wilson. Cambridge: Cambridge University Press, 1977.

Oksenberg, Michel. "Economic Policy-Making in China: Summer 1981". *The China Quarterly*, No. 90 (June 1982).

Paltiel, Jeremy. "PLA Allegiance on Parade: Civil-Military Relations in Transition". *The China Quarterly*, No. 143 (September 1995).

Paltiel, Jeremy. "Jiang Talks Politics—Who Listens? Institutionalization and Its Limits in Market Leninism". *The China Journal*, No. 45 (January 2001).

Parrish, William L. "Factions in Chinese Military Politics". *China Quarterly*, No. 56 (October 1973).

Pye, Lucian W. "An Introductory Profile: Deng Xiaoping and China's Political Culture". *China Quarterly,* No. 135 (September 1993).

Pye, Lucian W. *The Dynamics of Chinese Politics.* Cambridge: Oelgeschlager, Gunn, and Hain, 1981.

Pye, Lucian W. *The Spirit of Chinese Politics.* Cambridge: Harvard University Press, 1992.

Pye, Lucian W. "Rethinking the Man in the Leader". *The China Journal,* No. 35 (January 1996).

Qiu, Jin. *The Culture of Power: The Lin Biao Incident in the Cultural Revolution.* Stanford: Stanford University Press, 1999.

Rice, Edward E. *Mao's Way.* Berkeley: University of California Press, 1972.

Robinson, Thomas W. "Chou En-lai and the Cultural Revolution in China". In *The Cultural Revolution in China,* edited by Thomas W. Robinson. Berkeley: University of California Press, 1971.

Ruan Ming. *Deng Xiaoping: Chronicle of an Empire.* Boulder: Westview Press, 1994.

Saich, Tony (ed.), with a contribution by Benjamin Yang. *The Rise to Power of the Chinese Communist Party: Documents and Analysis.* Armonk: M. E. Sharpe, 1996.

Saich, Tony, and Hans van de Ven (eds). *New Perspectives on the Chinese Revolution.* Armonk: M. E. Sharpe, 1994.

Schoenhals, Michael. "The 1978 Truth Criterion Controversy". *The China Quarterly,* No. 126 (1991).

Schoenhals, Michael. "The Central Case Examination Group, 1966-79". *The China Quarterly,* No. 145 (1996).

Schram, Stuart R. *Mao Tse-tung.* Harmondsworth: Penguin Books, 1967.

Schram, Stuart R. "Introduction: The Cultural Revolution in Historical Perspective". In *Authority, Participation and Cultural Change,* edited by Stuart R. Schram. London: Cambridge University Press, 1973.

Schram, Stuart R. (ed.). *Chairman Mao Talks to the People: Talks and Letters, 1956-1971.* New York: Pantheon Press, 1975. (Published in Great Britain as *Mao Tse-tung Unrehearsed*).

Schram, Stuart R. *Mao Zedong: A Preliminary Reassessment.* Hong Kong: Chinese University Press, 1983.

Schurmann, Franz. *Ideology and Organization in Communist China.* 2nd edition, Berkeley: University of California Press, 1968.

Shambaugh, David (ed.). *Deng Xiaoping: Portrait of a Chinese Statesman.* New York: Oxford University Press, 1995.

Shambaugh, David. "China's Commander-in-Chief: Jiang Zemin and the PLA". In *Chinese Military Modernization*, edited by C. Dennison Lane et al. London: Kegan Paul, 1996.

Shambaugh, David. "China's Post-Deng Military Leadership". In *China's Military Faces the Future*, edited by James Lilley and David Shambaugh. Armonk: M. E. Sharpe, 1999.

Shambaugh, David. "The Dynamics of Elite Politics During the Jiang Era". *The China Journal*, No. 45 (January 2001).

Shambaugh, David, and Richard H. Yang (eds). *China's Military in Transition.* Oxford: Clarendon Press, 1997.

Shirk, Susan L. "The Politics of Industrial Reform". In *The Political Economy of Reform in Post-Mao China*, edited by Elizabeth J. Perry and Christine Wong. Cambridge, Mass: Harvard University Press, 1985.

Shirk, Susan L. *The Political Logic of Economic Reform in China.* Berkeley: University of California Press, 1993.

Solinger, Dorothy J. *China's Transition from Socialism: Statist Legacies and Market Reforms.* Armonk: M. E. Sharpe, 1993, Chs. 1-3.

Solomon, Richard H. *Mao's Revolution and the Chinese Political Culture.* Berkeley: University of California Press, 1971.

Starr, John Bryan. *Ideology and Culture: An Introduction to the Dialectic of Contemporary Chinese Politics.* New York: Harper and Row, 1973.

Tanner, Murray Scot. *The Politics of Lawmaking in China: Institutions, Processes, and Democratic Prospects.* Oxford: Oxford University Press, 1999.

Teiwes, Frederick C. "The Purge of Provincial Leaders 1957-1958". *The China Quarterly*, No. 27 (July 1966).

Teiwes, Frederick C. *Provincial Party Personnel in Mainland China, 1956-1966*. New York: Occasional Papers of the East Asian Institute, Columbia University, 1967.

Teiwes, Frederick C. "The Evolution of Leadership Purges in Communist China". *The China Quarterly*, No. 41 (January 1970).

Teiwes, Frederick C. "'Provincial Politics in China: Themes and Variations". In *China: Management of a Revolutionary Society*, edited by John M. H. Lindbeck. Seattle: University of Washington Press, 1971.

Teiwes, Frederick C. "'Rules of the Game' in Chinese Politics". *Problems of Communism*, (September-December 1979).

Teiwes, Frederick C. *Leadership, Legitimacy, and Conflict in China: From A Charismatic Mao to the Politics of Succession*. Armonk: M. E. Sharpe, 1984.

Teiwes, Frederick C. "Mao and his Lieutenants". *The Australian Journal of Chinese Affairs*, No. 19-20 (January/July 1988).

Teiwes, Frederick C. "Peng Dehuai and Mao Zedong". *The Australian Journal of Chinese Affairs*, No. 16 (July 1986).

Teiwes, Frederick C. *Politics at Mao's Court: Gao Gang and Party Factionalism in the Early 1950s*. Armonk: M. E. Sharpe, 1990.

Teiwes, Frederick C. "Leaders, Institutions, and the Origins of the Great Leap Forward". *Pacific Affairs*, Vol. 66, No. 2 (Summer 1993).

Teiwes, Frederick C. *Politics and Purges in China: Rectification and the Decline of Party Norms, 1950-1965*. 2nd edition. Armonk: M. E. Sharpe, 1993.

Teiwes, Frederick C. "Seeking the Historical Mao". *The China Quarterly*, No. 145 (March 1996).

Teiwes, Frederick C. "The Establishment and Consolidation of the New Regime, 1949-57". In *The Politics of China 1949-1989: The Eras of Mao and Deng*, edited by Roderick MacFarquhar. Cambridge: Cambridge University Press, 1997.

Teiwes, Frederick C. "The Problematic Quest for Stability: Reflections on Succession, Institutionalization, Governability, and Legitimacy in Post-Deng China". In *China under Jiang Zemin*, edited by Hung-mao Tien and Yun-han Chu. Boulder: Lynne Rienner, 2000.

Teiwes, Frederick C. "The Chinese State During the Maoist Era". In *The Modern Chinese State*, edited by David Shambaugh. Cambridge: Cambridge University Press, 2000.

Teiwes, Frederick C. "Politics at the 'Core': The Political Circumstances of Mao Zedong, Deng Xiaoping and Jiang Zemin". *China Information*, Vol. 15, No. 1 (2001); also on the web as an Australian National University Morrison Lecture, at http://rspas.anu.edu.au/ccc/home.htm

Teiwes, Frederick C., and Warren Sun (eds). *The Politics of Agricultural Cooperativization in China: Mao, Deng Zihui, and the "High Tide" of 1955*. Armonk: M. E. Sharpe, 1993.

Teiwes, Frederick C., with Warren Sun. "From a Leninist to a Charismatic Party: The CCP's Changing Leadership, 1937-1945". In *New Perspectives on the Chinese Revolution*, edited by Tony Saich and Hans van de Ven. New York: M. E. Sharpe, 1994.

Teiwes, Frederick C., and Warren Sun. *The Tragedy of Lin Biao: Riding the Tiger during the Cultural Revolution, 1966-1971*. London: C. Hurst & Co., 1996.

Teiwes, Frederick C., with Warren Sun. *The Formation of the Maoist Leadership: From the Return of Wang Ming to the Seventh Party Congress*. London: Contemporary China Institute Research Notes and Studies, No. 10, 1994.

Teiwes, Frederick C., with Warren Sun. "The Politics of an 'Un-Maoist' Interlude: The Case of Opposing Rash Advance, 1956-57". In *New Perspectives on State Socialism in China*, edited by Timothy Cheek and Tony Saich. Armonk: M. E. Sharpe, 1997.

Teiwes, Frederick C., with Warren Sun. *China's Road to Disaster: Mao, Central Politicians, and Local Leaders in the Unfolding of the Great Leap Forward, 1955-1959*. Armonk: M. E. Sharpe, 1999.

Tien, Hung-mao, and Yun-han Chu (eds). *China Under Jiang Zemin*. Boulder: Lynn Riener, 2000.

Tsou, Tang. "Prolegomenon to the Study of Informal Groups in CCP Politics". *The China Quarterly*, No. 65 (March 1976).

Tsou, Tang (ed.), *The Cultural Revolution and Post-Mao Reforms: A Historical Perspective*. Chicago: University of Chicago Press, 1986.

Tsou, Tang. "The Tiananmen Tragedy: The State-Society Relationship, Choices, and Mechanisms in Historical Perspective". In *Contemporary Chinese Politics in Historical Perspective*, edited by Brantly Womack. Cambridge: Cambridge University Press, 1991.

Unger, Jonathan. *The Transformation of Rural China*. Armonk: M. E. Sharpe, 2002, Ch. 5.

Vogel, Ezra F. *Canton under Communism: Programs and Politics in a Provincial Capital, 1949-1968*. Cambridge: Harvard University Press, 1969.

Wilson, Dick (ed.). *Mao Tse-tung in the Scales of History*. Cambridge: Cambridge University Press, 1977.

White, Gordon. *Riding the Tiger: The Politics of Economic Reform in Post-Mao China*. Stanford: Stanford University Press, 1993.

White, Lynn. *Policies of Chaos: The Organizational Causes of Violence in China's Cultural Revolution*. Princeton: Princeton University Press, 1989.

Whitson, William W., with Chen-hsia Huang. *The Chinese High Command: A History of Communist Military Politics, 1927-71*. New York: Praeger Publishers, 1973.

Womack, Brantly. "Where Mao Went Wrong: Epistomology and Ideology in Mao's Leftist Politics". *The Australian Journal of Chinese Affairs*, No. 16 (July 1986).

Womack, Brantly (ed.). *Contemporary Chinese Politics in Historical Perspective*. Cambridge: Cambridge University Press, 1991.

Wu, Guoguang. "Legitimacy Crisis, Political Economy, and the Fifteenth Party Congress". In *Dilemmas of Reform in Jiang Zemin's China*, edited by Andrew J. Nathan, Zhaohui Hong and Steven R. Smith. London: Lynne Rienner Publishers, 1999.

Yang, Benjamin. *Deng: A Political Biography*. Armonk: M. E. Sharpe, 1998.

Yang, Dali L. *Calamity and Reform in China: State, Rural Society, and Institutional Change Since the Great Leap Famine*. Stanford: Stanford University Press, 1996.

Yang, Zhongmei. *Hu Yaobang: A Chinese Biography*. Armonk: M. E. Sharpe, 1988.

You Ji. "Jiang Zemin: In Quest of Post-Deng Supremacy". In *China Review 1996*, edited by Maurice Brosseau, Suzanne Pepper, and Tsang Shu-ki. Hong Kong: The Chinese University Press, 1996.

You Ji. "Zhao Ziyang and the Politics of Inflation". *The Australian Journal of Chinese Affairs*, No. 25 (July 1991).

You Ji. "Jiang Zemin's Formal and Informal Sources of Power and China's Elite Politics after June 4". *China Information*, Vol. 6, No. 2 (Autumn 1991).

You, Ji. *The Armed Forces of China*. Sydney: Allen & Unwin, 1999.

Zhang Liang, comp., Andrew J. Nathan and Perry Link (eds). *The Tiananmen Papers*. New York: Public Affairs, 2001.

Zhao, Suisheng. "The Feeble Political Capacity of a Strong One-Party Regime: An Institutional Approach toward the Formulation and Implementation of Economic Policy in Post-Mao Mainland China". *Issues and Studies*, Vol. 26, No. 1 (January 1990).

Zong Hairen. *Zhu Rongji in 1999*. English translation of *Zhu Rongji zai 1999*. Carle Place, NY: Mingjing Chubanshe, 2001, published in January-February and March-April 2002 issues of *Chinese Law and Government*.

INDEX

Yan Mingfu, 127
Yang Baibang, 224, 244, 275, 279
Yang Dezhi, 279
Yang family clique, 108, 221, 229,
    244-5, 283; *see also* Yang
    Baibang, Yang Shangkun
Yang Shangkun, 5, 67, 68, 74, 81,
    83, 84, 116, 141, 223, 224, 227,
    229, 236, 244, 245n, 275, 289
Yao Wenyuan, 5, 18, 26, 31, 125,
    136, 222
Yao Yilin, 18, 68, 79, 223, 249
Ye Guangyuan, 87
Ye Jianying, 6, 10, 14, 16, 71, 82,
    118, 141, 226, 289
Ye Qing, 151
Ye Qun, 106, **109**, 137
Ye Rongzhen, 141
You Ji, xv, 254, 304
"Youth League Faction", 18

Zeng Qinghong, 237, 250n, 272, 308
Zhang Chunqiao, 5, 16, 17, 18, 30,
    31, 120, 125, 136, 140
Zhang Guotao, 16, **109**, 110, 151
Zhang Wannian, 249n, 279-80, 285
Zhang Wentian, 110
Zhang Yufeng, 17n, 104
Zhang Zhen, 224, 226, 248, 276,
    279-80, 283
Zhao Yang, 141
Zhao Ziyang, 6, 13, 28, 29, 31, 34,
    78, 79, 82, 85, 88, 90, 91, 139,
    142, 179, 187, 203, 204, 218,
    221, 226-7, 229, 230, 231, 233,
    234, 237-8, 242-3, 247, 248,
    278, 303;
  and Deng Xiaoping, 13n, 31, 51,
    66, 67, 68, 69, 71, 79, 108, 127,
    139, 203, 204, 218, 226, 233;
  and Hu Yaobang, 7, 29, 37, 63n,
    91, 95, 158, 184, 223;

ouster of, 11, 21, 29, 31, 36, 73,
    88, 106, 127-8, 142, 155, 221,
    229
Zheng Yongnian, 262
Zhou Enlai, 6, 7, 11, 14, 22, 29, 31,
    70, 71n, 125, 127, 136, 137,
    144, 259;
  and Deng Xiaoping, 20
Zhu Rongji, 6, 11, 22, 127, 202, 214,
    224, 226, 227, 235, 251n, 256,
    262, 270, 288, 290, 295, 305,
    306, 307, 309-10
Zou Jiahua, 19